Disclaimer

The publisher of this book is by no way associated with the National Institute of Standards and Technology (NIST). The NIST did not publish this book. It was published by 50 page publications under the public domain license.

50 Page Publications.

Book Title: Committee Reports of the 91st National Conference on Weights and Measures, July 9 - 13, 2006, Chicago, IL (SP 1053)

Book Author: Linda D. Crown; L T. Sebring

Book Abstract: The 91st Annual Meeting of the National Conference on Weights and Measures was held in Chicago, IL, July 9 - 14, 2006. The theme of the conference was Back to Basics as Stepping Stones to our Future. The NCWM develops and recommends laws and regulations, technical codes for weighing and measuring devices used in commerce, tests, methods, enforcement procedures, and administrative guidelines for adoption by regulatory agencies in the interest of promoting uniformity of requirements and methods in state and local jurisdictions. The annual meeting brings together government officials and representatives of business, industry, trade associations, and consumer organizations for the purpose of hearing and discussing subjects that relate to the field of weights and measures technology.

Citation: NIST SP - 1053

Keyword: legal metrology;mass-flow meters;motor-fuel dispensers;scales;specifications & tolerances;weights and measures

Report Of The 91st National Conference On Weights And Measures

NIST
United States
Department of
Commerce

Technology
Administration

National
Institute of
Standards and
Technology

as adopted by
the 91st
National
Conference on
Weights and
Measures 2006

NIST
Special
Publication 1053

2006

The National Institute of Standards and Technology was established in 1988 by Congress to "assist industry in the development of technology ... needed to improve product quality, to modernize manufacturing processes, to ensure product reliability ... and to facilitate rapid commercialization ... of products based on new scientific discoveries."

NIST, originally founded as the National Bureau of Standards in 1901, works to strengthen U.S. industry's competitiveness; advance science and engineering; and improve public health, safety, and the environment. One of the agency's basic functions is to develop, maintain, and retain custody of the national standards of measurement, and provide the means and methods for comparing standards used in science, engineering, manufacturing, commerce, industry, and education with the standards adopted or recognized by the Federal Government.

As an agency of the U.S. Commerce Department's Technology Administration, NIST conducts basic and applied research in the physical sciences and engineering, and develops measurement techniques, test methods, standards, and related services. The Institute does generic and precompetitive work on new and advanced technologies. NIST's research facilities are located at Gaithersburg, MD 20899, and at Boulder, CO 80303. Major technical operating units and their principal activities are listed below. For more information visit the NIST Website at http://www.nist.gov, or contact the Public Inquiries Desk, 301-975-NIST.

Office of the Director
- National Quality Program
- International and Academic Affairs

Technology Services
- Standards Services
- Technology Partnerships
- Measurement Services
- Information Services
- Weights and Measures

Advanced Technology Program
- Economic Assessment
- Information Technology and Applications
- Chemistry and Life Sciences
- Electronics and Photonics Technology

Manufacturing Extension Partnership Program
- Regional Programs
- National Programs
- Program Development

Electronics and Electrical Engineering Laboratory
- Microelectronics
- Law Enforcement Standards
- Electricity
- Semiconductor Electronics
- Radio-Frequency Technology
- Electromagnetic Technology
- Optoelectronics
- Magnetic Technology

Materials Science and Engineering Laboratory
- Intelligent Processing of Materials
- Ceramics
- Materials Reliability
- Polymers
- Metallurgy
- NIST Center for Neutron Research

Chemical Science and Technology Laboratory
- Biotechnology
- Process Measurements
- Surface and Microanalysis Science
- Physical and Chemical Properties
- Analytical Chemistry

Physics Laboratory
- Electron and Optical Physics
- Atomic Physics
- Optical Technology
- Ionizing Radiation
- Time and Frequency
- Quantum Physics

Manufacturing Engineering Laboratory
- Precision Engineering
- Manufacturing Metrology
- Intelligent Systems
- Fabrication Technology
- Manufacturing Systems Integration

Building and Fire Research Laboratory
- Applied Economics
- Materials and Construction Research
- Building Environment
- Fire Research

Information Technology Laboratory
- Mathematical and Computational Sciences
- Advanced Network Technologies
- Computer Security
- Information Access
- Convergent Information Systems
- Information Services and Computing
- Software Diagnostics and Conformance Testing
- Statistical Engineering

---

[1] At Boulder, CO 80303
[2] Some elements at Boulder, CO

Report of the 91st National Conference on Weights and Measures

Chicago, Illinois – July 9 through 13, 2006
as adopted by the 91st National Conference on Weights and Measures 2006

Editors:
Kenneth Butcher
Linda Crown
Lynn Sebring
Technical Advisors to the Standing Committees

National Institute of Standards and Technology
Weights and Measures Division
Gaithersburg, MD 20899-2600

U.S. Department of Commerce
Carlos M. Gutierrez, Secretary

Technology Administration
Robert Cresanti, Under Secretary of Commerce for Technology

National Institute of Standards and Technology
William Jeffrey, Director

NIST Special Publication **1053**

November 2006

The National Conference on Weights and Measures is supported by the National Institute of Standards and Technology and is attended by officials from various states, counties, and cities, as well as representatives from the U.S. Government, other nations, industry, and consumer organizations.

Abstract

The 91st Annual Meeting of the National Conference on Weights and Measures (NCWM) was held July 9 - 13, 2006, at the Chicago Marriot in Chicago, Illinois. The theme of the meeting was "Back to Basics as the Stepping Stones to Our Future."

Reports by the NCWM Board of Directors, Standing Committees, and Special Purpose Committees constitute the major portion of this publication, along with the addresses delivered by Conference officials and other authorities from government and industry.

Special meetings included those of the Scale Manufacturers Association, Meter Manufacturers Association, Gasoline Pump Manufacturers Association, American Petroleum Institute, National Association of State Departments of Agriculture, the Industry Committee on Packaging and Labeling, and Associate Membership Committee.

Key words: laws and regulations; legal metrology; meters; scales; specifications and tolerances; training; type evaluation; uniform laws; weights and measures.

Library of Congress Catalog Card Number 26-27766.

Note: The policy of the National Institute of Standards and Technology is to use metric units of measurement in all of its publications. In this publication, however, recommendations received by the NCWM technical committees have been printed as they were submitted and, therefore, may contain references to inch-pound units where such units are commonly used in industry practice. Opinions expressed in non-NIST papers are those of the authors and not necessarily those of the National Institute of Standards and Technology. Non-NIST speakers are solely responsible for the content and quality of their material.

Natl. Inst. Stand. Technol. Spec. Pub. 1053, 264 Pages (November 2006) CODEN: NSPUE2

U. S. GOVERNMENT PRINTING OFFICE
WASHINGTON: 2006

For sale by the Superintendent of Documents, U. S. Government Printing Office
Internet: bookstore.gpo.gov – Phone: (202) 512-1800 – Fax: (202) 512-2104
Mail: Stop SSPO, Washington, DC 20402-0001

Table of Contents

	Page
Abstract	ii
Past Chairmen of the Conference	iv
Organization Chart	v

General Session

President's Address – Dr. William A. Jeffrey, National Institute of Standards and Technology	GS - 1
Chairman's Address – Don Onwiler, Nebraska Department of Agriculture/ Weights & Measures	GS - 5
New Chairman's Address – Michael Cleary, California Division of Measurement Standards	GS - 9
2006 Annual Meeting Honor Award Recipients	GS - 11

Standing Committee Reports

Report of the Board of Directors (BOD)	BOD - 1
Appendix A. Report on the Activities of the International Organization of Legal Metrology (OIML) and Regional Legal Metrology Organizations	BOD - A1
Appendix B. Associate Membership Committee Interim Report	BOD - B1
Report of the Committee on Laws and Regulations (L&R)	L&R - 1
Appendix A. Item 270-1: Developing Items – Handbook 130	L&R - A1
Appendix B. Item 270-1: Developing Items – Handbook 133	L&R - B1
Appendix C. Item 250-1: Basic Engine Fuels, Petroleum Products, and Lubricants Laboratory Guidelines	L&R - C1
Appendix D. NCWM Petroleum Subcommittee Report	L&R - D1
Report of the Committee on Specifications and Tolerances (S&T)	S&T - 1
Appendix A. Item 360-4: Developing Items	S&T - A1
Report of the Professional Development Committee (PDC)	PDC - 1
Appendix A. Strategic Direction for the Professional Development Committee	PDC - A1
Report of the National Type Evaluation Program (NTEP) Committee	NTEP - 1
Appendix A. NTETC Grain Analyzer Sector Meeting Summary	NTEP - A1
Appendix B. NTETC Measuring Sector Meeting Summary	NTEP - B1
Appendix C. NTETC Weighing Sector Meeting Summary	NTEP - C1
2006 Annual Meeting Attendees	ATTEND - 1

Past Chairmen of the Conference

Conference Year Chairman

Conference	Year	Chairman
43rd	1958	J. P. McBride, MA
44th	1959	C. M. Fuller, CA
45th	1960	H. E. Crawford, FL
46th	1961	R. E. Meek, IN
47th	1962	Robert Williams, NY
48th	1963	C. H. Stender, SC
49th	1964	D. M. Turnbull, WA
50th	1965	V. D. Campbell, OH
51st	1966	J. F. True, KS
52nd	1967	J. E. Bowen, MA
53rd	1968	C. C. Morgan, IN
54th	1969	S. H. Christie, NJ
55th	1970	R. W. Searles, OH
56th	1971	M. Jennings, TN
57th	1972	E. H. Black, CA
58th	1973	George L. Johnson, KY
59th	1974	John H. Lewis, WA
60th	1975	Sydney D. Andrews, FL
61st	1976	Richard L. Thompson, MD
62nd	1977	Earl Prideaux, CO
63rd	1978	James F. Lyles, VA
64th	1979	Kendrick J. Simila, OR
65th	1980	Charles H. Vincent, TX
66th	1981	Edward H. Stadolnik, MA
67th	1982	Edward C. Heffron, MI
68th	1983	Charles H. Greene, NM
69th	1984	Sam F. Hindsman, AR
70th	1985	Ezio F. Delfino, CA
71st	1986	George E. Mattimoe, HI
72nd	1987	Frank C. Nagele, MI
73rd	1988	Darrell A. Guensler, CA
74th	1989	John J. Bartfai, NY
75th	1990	Fred A. Gerk, NM
76th	1991	N. David Smith, NC
77th	1992	Sidney A. Colbrook, IL
78th	1993	Allan M. Nelson, CT
79th	1994	Thomas F. Geiler, MA
80th	1995	James C. Truex, OH
81st	1996	Charles A. Gardner, NY
82nd	1997	Barbara J. Bloch, CA
83rd	1998	Steven A. Malone, NE
84th	1999	Aves D. Thompson, AK
85th	2000	G. Wes Diggs, VA
86th	2001	L. Straub, MD
87th	2002	Ron Murdock, NC
88th	2003	Ross J. Andersen, NY
89th	2004	Dennis Ehrhart, AZ
90th	2005	G. Weston Diggs, VA

National Conference on Weights and Measures, Inc.
Organization Chart
2005/2006

Board of Directors		
Office Representation	**Name/Affiliation**	**Term Expires**
Chairman:	Don Onwiler, NE*	2006
Chairman-Elect:	Michael Cleary, CA	2006
NTEP Committee Chair:	James Truex, OH*	2006
Treasurer:	Thomas Geiler, MA	2006
Active Membership/Northeastern:	Charles Carroll, MA*	2009
Active Membership/Central:	Judy Cardin, WI	2010
Active Membership/Southern:	Stephen Pahl, TX*	2008
Active Membership/Western:	Joe Gomez, NM	2007
At-Large:	Christopher Guay, Procter & Gamble	2008
At-Large:	Russ Wyckoff, OR	2006
Associate Membership:	Darrell Flocken, Mettler-Toledo	2007
*National Type Evaluation Program (NTEP) Committee Member		
Honorary NCWM President:	Dr. William A. Jeffrey, NIST Director	
NCWM Executive Secretary:	Carol Hockert, Chief, NIST W&M Division	
NCWM Executive Director:	Beth Palys, CAE, NCWM Headquarters	
BOD Advisor:	Gilles Vinet, Measurement Canada	
NTEP Director:	Stephen Patoray, NCWM Headquarters	
NTEP Committee Technical Advisor:	Steven Cook, NIST W&M Division	

Laws & Regulations Committee		Specifications & Tolerances Committee	
Position	**Name/Affiliation (Term Expires)**	**Position**	**Name/Affiliation (Term Expires)**
Chair:	Joe Benavides, TX (2006)	Chair:	Clark Cooney, OR (2006)
Members:	James Cassidy, MA (2007)	Members:	Michael Sikula, NY (2007)
	Vickey Dempsey, OH (2008)		Carol Fulmer, SC (2008)
	Dennis Johannes, CA (2009)		Todd Lucas, OH (2009)
	Stephen Benjamin, NC (2010)		Brett Saum, CA (2010)
Associate Member Rep:	Vincent Orr, ConAgra Foods	Associate Member Rep:	TBD
Canadian Tech Advisors:	Doug Hutchinson Brian Lemon	Canadian Tech Advisor:	Ted Kingsbury
NIST Tech. Advisors:	Thomas Coleman Kathryn Dresser	NIST Tech. Advisors:	Richard Suiter Juana Williams

Professional Development Committee		Metrology Committee	
Position	**Name/Affiliation (Term Expires)**	**Position**	**Name/Affiliation (Term Expires)**
Chair:	Celeste Bennett, MI (2006)	Chair:	TBD
Members:	Kenneth Deitzler, PA (2007) Agatha Shields, OH (2008) Open (TBA) (2009) Richard Wotthlie, MD (2010)	Co-Chair: Members:	TBD
Safety Liaison:	Charles Gardner, NY		
Staff Liaison:	Linda Bernetich, NCWM		
Associate Member Rep:	Michael Sarachman, Kraft Foods Global, Inc.	NIST Tech Advisor:	Val Miller
Nominating Committee		**Legislative Liaison**	
Chair:	Dennis Ehrhart, AZ	Chair:	TBD
Members:	Ross Andersen, NY Maxwell Gray, FL Thomas Geiler, MA Steven Malone, NE Aves Thompson, AK James Truex, OH	Members:	TBD
Credentials Committee		**Appointed Officers**	
Chair:	Raymond Johnson, NM (2006)	Parliamentarian:	Aves Thompson, AK
Members:	William Cobb, WV (2007) Mark Buccelli, MT (2008)	Chaplain:	F. Michael Belue, Belue Associates
Coordinator:	Linda Bernetich, NCWM Staff	Sergeants-At-Arms:	Thomas Malesh, City of Chicago Javier Ortiz, City of Chicago
		Presiding Officers:	John Junkins, WV Steve Pedersen, IA Michael Timmons, MA Kristen Young, CO
Associate Membership Committee			
Chair:		Gary Lameris, Lameris Consulting (2006)	
Vice Chair:		Stephen Langford, Cardinal Scale (2007)	
Secretary/Treasurer:		Vincent Orr, ConAgra Foods (2008)	
Members:		Robert Murnane, Jr., Seraphin Test Measures (2006) William Sveum, Kraft Foods (2007) Darrell Flocken, Mettler-Toledo (2008) Cary Frye, International Dairy Foods Assoc. (2008) Paul Lewis, Rice Lake Weighing Systems (2009) Michael Gaspers, Farmland Foods, Inc. (2009)	

Regional Weights and Measures Contacts

Northeastern Weights and Measures Assn. (NEWMA):
Annual Meeting 2006: May 22 - 25
Trump Plaza – Atlantic City, NJ

Stephen Agostinelli
Town of Barnstable Weights & Measures
200 Main Street
(508) 862-4669
steve.agostinelli@town.barnstable.ma.us

Southern Weights and Measures Assn. (SWMA):
Annual Meeting 2006: October 22 - 25
Radisson Hotel Annapolis – Annapolis, MD

Richard (Will) Wotthlie
Maryland Department of Agriculture
(410) 841-5790
wotthlrw@mda.state.md.us

Central Weights and Measures Assn. (CWMA):
Annual Meeting 2006: April 30 - May 3
Holiday Inn – Dayton Mall, Miamisburg, OH

Vicky Dempsey
Montgomery County Weights & Measures
(937) 225-6309
DempseyV@mcohio.org

Western Weights and Measures Assn. (WWMA):
Annual Meeting 2006: September 10 - 14
Radisson Downtown – Salt Lake City, UT

Brett Gurney
Utah Department of Agriculture & Food
(801) 538-7158
bgurney@utah.gov

	Weighing Sector		**Measuring Sector**
Chair:	Darrell Flocken, Mettler-Toledo	Chair:	Michael Keilty, Endress & Hauser Flowtec AG
Technical Advisor:	Steven Cook, NIST/WMD	Technical Advisor:	Richard Suiter, NIST/WMD
Public Sector Members:	Cary Ainsworth, GIPSA Ross Andersen, NY William Bates, GIPSA Andrea Buie, MD Luciano Burtini, Measurement Canada Tina Butcher, NIST/WMD Charles Carter, OK Gary Castro, CA Terry Davis, KS Jack Kane, MT Don Onwiler, NE Ken Jones, CA James Truex, OH James Vanderwielen, GIPSA William West, OH Juana Williams, NIST/WMD Russ Wyckoff, OR	Public Sector Members:	Ross Andersen, NY Tina Butcher, NIST/WMD Jerry Butler, NC Gary Castro, CA Steve Hadder, FL Ted Kingsbury, Measurement Canada John Makin, Measurement Canada Steven Malone, NE Dan Reiswig, CA William West, OH Richard Wotthlie, MD
Private Sector Members:	Doug Biette, Sartorius North America John Elengo, Contractor Robert Feezor, Norfolk Southern Corp. David Hawkins, Thurman Scale Co. Scott Henry, NCR John Hughes, Avery Weigh-Tronix, Inc. Rafael Jimenez, Association of American Railroads Gary Lameris, Lameris Consulting Stephen Langford, Cardinal Scale Mfg. Paul Lewis, Rice Lake Weighing Systems Thomas Luna, Scales Unlimited, Inc. L. Edward Luthy, Brechbuhler Scales, Inc. Naresh Puri, NMB Technologies, Inc. David Quinn, Weighing Consultants, Inc. Louis Straub, Fairbanks Scales, Inc. Jerry Wang, A&D Engineering, Inc. Otto Warnlof, Consultant Walter Young, Emery Winslow Scale	Private Sector Members:	F. Michael Belue, Belue Associates Joseph Beyer, Liquid Controls Marc Buttler, Emerson Process Management - Micro Motion Joe Buxton, Daniel Measurement & Control Rodney Cooper, Actaris Neptune Maurice Forkert, Tuthill Transfer Systems Mike Gallo, Clean Fueling Technologies Paul Glowacki, Murray Equipment Melvin Hankel, MCH Engineering Assoc. David Hoffman, TopTech Systems Gordon Johnson, Gilbarco, Inc. Yefim Katselnik, Dresser Wayne, Inc. Douglas Long, RDM Industrial Electronics Wade Mattar, Invensys/Foxboro Richard Miller, FMC Measurement Solution Robert Murnane, Jr., Seraphin Test Measure Andre Noel, Neptune Technology Charlene Numrych, Liquid Controls Johnny Parrish, Brodie Meter Company, LLC David Rajala, Veeder-Root Company Otto Warnlof, Consultant

	Software Sector		**Grain Analyzer Sector**
Chair:	TBD	Chair:	Cassie Eigenmann, DICKEY-john Corp.
Technical Advisor:	Stephen Patoray, NCWM	Technical Advisors:	G. Diane. Lee, NIST/WMD John Barber, J. B. Associates
Public Sector Members:	Dennis Beattie, MC Andrea Buie, MD Bill Fishman, NY Mike Frailer, MD Norman Ingram, CA Todd Lucas, OH John Roach, CA Jim Truex, OH	Public Sector Members:	Randy Burns, AR Tina Butcher, NIST/WMD Don Onwiler, NE Richard Pierce, GIPSA Edward Szesnat, Jr., NY Cheryl Tew, NC Robert Wittenberger, MO
Private Sector Members:	Doug Bliss, Mettler-Toledo George Brazis, Avery Weigh-Tronix Andre' Elle, Endress & Hauser Flowtec AG Travis Gibson, Rice Lake Weighing Systems Torsten Hansen, FOSS Analytical A/S Keith Harper, Gencor Industries, Inc. Bryan Haynes, Liquid Controls Scott Henry, NCR Tony Herrin, Cardinal Scale Mfgr. Co. Robert Hoblit, IBM David Hoffman, Toptech Systems, Inc. Gordon Johnson, Gilbarco, Inc. Gary Lameris, Lameris Consulting Paul Lewis, Rice Lake Weighing Systems Achim Luedtke, Flow Measurements & Engineering GmbH Mike McGhee, Actaris US Liquid Measurement Richard Miller, FMC Measurement Solutions Tim Morrison, KJM Software Jim Pettinato, FMC Measurement Solutions Mike Roach, Verifone Robin Sax, CompuWeigh Corp. Jim Sexton, Rice Lake Weighing Systems Chris Scott, Gilbarco, Inc. Roland Wagner, Flow Measurements & Engineering GmbH David Vande Berg, Vande Berg Scales	Private Sector Members:	James Bair, NA Miller's Association Helmut Biermann, Bizerba GmbH & Co KG Martin Clements, The Steinlite Corp. Victor Gates, Shore Sales Company Andrew Gell, Foss North America Charles Hurburgh, Jr., Iowa State University David Krejci, Grain Elevator & Processing Society John Kennedy, Perten Instruments Thomas Runyon, Seedboro Equipment

Belt Conveyor Sector

Chair:	TBD
Technical Advisor:	Steven Cook, NIST/WMD
Public Sector Members:	Andrea Buie, MD
Private Sector Members:	R. Jimenez, Association of American Railroads
	L. Marmsater, Merrick Industries
	B. Ripka, Thermo Electron
	P. Sirrico, Thayer Scale - Hyer Industries, Inc.
	T. Vormittag, Sr, SGS Minerals Services
	O. Warnlof, Consultant

President's Address
National Conference on Weights and Measures
Chicago, Illinois
July 11, 2006

Dr. William A. Jeffrey
NIST Director

Determining the accurate weight or volume of an object is fundamental to ensuring fair commerce. We all know this; everyone in this room lives this every day. But with the rapidly changing technologies and globalization of the economy, the types of products we will be called on to accurately weigh or measure will soon push our current capabilities to the limits.

So hang on – the future promises to be an exciting and dynamic ride!

But before we jump into the future, let's take a step back and see where all this began. The earliest known uniform systems of weights and measures date back 5000 years – to the Bronze Age and the ancient peoples of Mesopotamia, Egypt, and the Indus Valley.

At that point, the world population was estimated to be between 7 to 14 million – about equal to the current population of the state of Illinois. And not surprising, this period of time also coincided with a period of human progress and enlightenment including the dawn of writing.

The critical importance to society in adopting a uniform set of weights and measures can be demonstrated in that it appears to be a common discovery in virtually all cultures. Further evidence of its importance can be derived from the prominence that fair measures are given in seminal documents such as the Torah, the Bible, the Koran, The Analects of Confucius, and the religious texts in early India.

Most early measurement systems used parts of the body and the natural surroundings. Length was first measured with the forearm, hand, or finger and time was measured by the periods of the sun, moon, and other heavenly bodies.

The cubit is perhaps the oldest and longest-lived example of a standard measurement unit. The oldest documented cubit is the Egyptian royal cubit – traced back to 2750 BC and used for about 3000 years.

And the Egyptians took their cubit seriously. In fact, it has been reported that: *"The death penalty faced those who forgot or neglected their duty to calibrate the standard unit of length at each full moon..."*[1]

To measure volume, people would fill containers with plant seeds which were then counted. When means for weighing were invented, seeds served as standards. For instance, the carat, still used as a unit for gems, was derived from the carob seed.

In China, some 3500 years ago, a system of standard instruments for measuring length, mass, and volume was created. A special organization, *perhaps* the predecessor to NCWM, was established with the responsibility for checking the accuracy of these instruments twice a year.

The Chinese may also have been the first to use an unvarying physical constant as a standard of measure. Similar to the way we now use the distance light travels in a second as a length standard, 2700 years ago the Chinese used the resonance tone of bamboo whistles to ascertain a length standard.

---

[1] "Metrology – in short" 2nd edition, December 2003; an EU publication

The good news is that every country, region, and city-state recognized the need for a uniform set of weights and measures. The bad news is that virtually every commercial center developed its own *unique* measurement system making commerce between trading centers cumbersome.

The problems and confusion caused by this measurement menagerie did not go unnoticed. The Magna Carta, for example, called for "*one measure for ale, one measure for wine, one measure for corn*."

But the problem continued to grow. France in 1788 had about 800 different names for measures and, taking into account their different values in different towns, resulted in around a quarter of a million different units.

From this chaos, the beginnings of the metric system emerged.

Everyone in this room is aware that the U. S. federal responsibility for uniform weights and measures, was written, first, into the Articles of Confederation and, then, into the Constitution. What you may not know was how much attention this topic received from our top leaders.

George Washington called for uniform measures in his first State of the Union Address. Other early proponents of a uniform measurement system in the United States included Thomas Jefferson, John Adams, James Madison, James Monroe, and Alexander Hamilton.

In 1821, future president and then Secretary of State John Quincy Adams issued a report that described measurements as one of "*the necessaries of modern life*." He likened the metric system to the invention of the printing press and predicted that it would save more human labor than the steam engine.

In 1836, Congress directed that standards be distributed to the states. Two years later Congress directed that the Treasury Department distribute balances to the states to use with those standards.

But serious progress toward uniform weights and measures did not begin until the turn of the century – first with the creation of the National Bureau of Standards (now NIST) and four years later with the first meeting of the National Conference on Weights and Measures.

The second meeting of the Conference, held one hundred years ago fundamentally changed the way this country ensures uniform weights and measures. In 1906, this new organization drafted the outline of a "Model State Weights and Measures Law," which was formalized the following year.

This organization jumped into the breach, addressing an unmet fundamental need that was undermining the performance of the national economy.

There are many stories from that period – each one a telling reminder of the incredibly valuable role that weights and measures operations play.

For example, the proceedings of the 1906 meeting pointed out that the entire salaries of clerks in New York groceries and butcher shops were paid with the money they cheated out of the public – by, in effect, keeping a thumb on the scales.

The inspector's righteous anger was well-founded. Around 1910, NBS staff tested more than 30,000 scales across the United States and found that almost 50 % were significantly off – and, not surprisingly, in favor of the storekeepers.

The annual loss at that time to the consumer in butter alone amounted to more than $8 million.

History repeated itself 90 years later. In 1997, NIST staff assisted a collaboration of 40 states, the USDA, the FDA, and the FTC in investigating school prepackaged milk. They found that 45 % of containers were short filled, at a cost to consumers of nearly $30 million.

The weights and measures system is a key component of the Nation's technical infrastructure. It is basic to the flow of commerce, to the functioning of our economy, and to realizing the Nation's ambitions to remain a leader in technological innovation.

Ken Alder, a history professor at Northwestern University, reasons that our measurement systems are, in fact, a defining characteristic of who we are as a nation. He makes the case eloquently in the prologue of his book, *The Measure of All Things*:

> "... the use a society makes of its measures expresses its sense of fair dealing. That is why the balance scale is a widespread symbol of justice... Our methods of measurement define who we are and what we value."

Put another way, measurements are about *trust, confidence,* and, in the antiseptic terminology of the economist, *transactional efficiency*.

Every commercial transaction has an element of trust. Trust cultivated over time breeds confidence. Reliable, accurate measurements are the vital ingredients of both, but especially in transactions that lack transparency, such as in the sale of fuel.

Thanks to what this organization and NIST have accomplished together, American consumers and businesses can be confident in the quantity of product being purchased – making transactions more reliable and cost effective.

Analyses done in the United States and in other developed economies demonstrate that weights and measures underpin transactions that account for over half of the GDP.

And continual verification of the accuracy is critical. In 1997, a Canadian case study reported that, on average, each weights and measures inspector discovered and corrected about $2 million worth of "measurement inequity."

Unfortunately, we don't have a comparable estimate for the United States. But we do know that in 2002, the median investment in state Weights and Measures operations was about $50,000 a year for each inspector.

If we assume similar levels of performance in the United States as in Canada – about $2 million in benefits per inspector – then a rough estimate of society's rate of return would be 40 to 1 – a phenomenal result.

Not all countries have the same rigor in checking and enforcing their weights and measures. In a 2002 survey, 93 % of U. S. gas meters fully complied with required standards. Compare that with Mexico. Mexico's consumer watchdog agency recently found that pumps at 90 % of the country's gas stations dispense less than indicated – on average, about 1 liter less for every 20 liters sold. This rigging of gas pump meters cheats the Mexican consumer out of about $1 billion per year [2].

With the advance of technology and the growth of the global economy and its increasing interdependencies, accurate weights and measures will become even more important. And like most components of the Nation's technical infrastructure, the system will be challenged to do better – and to do more.

Clearly we must keep up with the quickening pace of innovation. New technologies can transform the marketplace and consumer expectations. And as these new technologies arrive in the marketplace, we must be able to continue instilling the level of trust in the transaction that members of NCWM have been doing for the past century.

For example, anyone who owns a car or pays an electric bill understands why the government is aggressively pursuing new forms of energy. Biofuels are already established in some countries and will likely see increasing demand in the United States requiring new tests for purity and volume. Since many different processes can convert biomass into fuel, we need to have a variety of tests and procedures at the ready to meet the demand.

---

[2] Source: *Los Angeles Times,* June 13, 2006

Slightly longer term, the Nation is committed to exploiting hydrogen to fuel the economy. Almost every stage of hydrogen production, distribution, and sale will require new measurement tests and methodologies to establish confidence in the transaction. Today when we drive to a gasoline station, we don't worry because we know the fuel pump reads accurately to better than 0.1 %.

But what happens in the future when we drive to the service station to buy a tank of hydrogen? The infrastructure to measure hydrogen fuel accurately does not exist. Anecdotal evidence from current demonstration facilities indicates that we're at about 8 % accuracy. This is equivalent to over or undercharging about 20 to 25 cents per gallon of gasoline-equivalent.

NIST is committed to working with the Department of Energy and state and local officials to ensure that the required tests are established in a timely fashion so as not to impede the development of the hydrogen economy. In fact we are establishing a program at NIST as part of the American Competitiveness Initiative to accelerate efforts in hydrogen standards.

New technologies will require novel approaches to addressing measurements in the future. To get a feel for the evolving demands in the future, just look at the magnitude of current weights and measurement requirements in today's laboratories – which often foreshadow the requirements in the marketplace.

Researchers at NIST currently have requirements to measure force from picoNewtons to MegaNewtons (18 orders of magnitude). For example, NIST has a 4.4 MegaNewton deadweight machine that is used for testing the strength of bridge abutments. This is the largest such device in the world.

On the small end, we are measuring the force to pull apart a single DNA molecule – 65 picoNewtons – which is equivalent to the momentum imparted from the photons from 6 laser pointers.

And as nanotechnology quickly evolves into a potentially trillion dollar industry over the next decade, the requirements for measuring mass and size at the smallest scales will become critical. We are not yet ready for the amazing potential that nanotechnology offers, so NIST – again as part of the American Competitiveness Initiative – is also accelerating its efforts in the development of nanometrology.

NIST is committed to work with the Conference to ensure that the requisite weights and measures methodologies are developed before the consumer demands them. Supporting this mission is one of NIST's oldest – and remains one of our most important – functions.

In this year's State of the Union address, President Bush outlined the American Competitiveness Initiative, which is designed to enhance the Nation's capacity to innovate and remain globally competitive. As part of this initiative, NIST's core budget will be increased, while most of the federal Government's non-defense discretionary budget experiences a decrease. This is a tremendous recognition of the importance of the NIST mission and the recognition of the role that weights and measures plays in keeping the United States economically strong.

For over a century, NIST and the Conference have been strong partners. Going forward, we must build on our shared accomplishments. The world is smaller, trade is global, and technology is international. Weights and measures must keep up with the changes.

NCWM can benefit from NIST's technical expertise, its experience with standards development, and its position in the international measurement system.

NIST can benefit from NCWM's forum for bringing all stakeholders together, their ability to reach many jurisdictions simultaneously, and their ability to influence state and local programs.

While it's impossible to predict where the future will lead, it's likely that it will require the NCWM, NIST, and our weights and measures system to reach new heights, address new needs, and build new capabilities – including some that may even appear alien to our shared experience over the last century.

NIST looks forward to working with NCWM over the <u>next</u> century in making this all possible. Thank you.

Chairman's Address
National Conference on Weights and Measures
Chicago, Illinois
July 11, 2006

Don Onwiler
Nebraska Department of Agriculture/Weights & Measures

Thank you, Dr. Jeffrey, for your support of the important work of the National Conference on Weights and Measures and the NIST Weights and Measures Division, as exemplified by your presence here today and your comments. The pulse rate of volunteer organizations, government agencies, and private industries may weaken from time to time under the influence of economic constraints, but the necessity of the work we do does not waiver. It is in our mutual best interest to assist each other in strengthening our abilities to meet our respective charges that are so frequently for the benefit of common stakeholders.

Thank you, NCWM, for what has proven to be a journey beyond my expectations of serving as your Chairman. Never did I expect to receive so many offerings of assistance and support. It makes serving all the more an honor, knowing such fine professionals are at one's side to assure success.

Never did I expect the magnitude of professional growth offered by serving in this capacity. Had I known a year ago what I know now, there are a few things I would do differently, but there are no regrets.

Never did I expect to be so sorry, yet so grateful, to see it come to an end. It will be good to get back full time to my duties at home, but this has been a wonderful year and I am excited with the prospects for the future of NCWM.

Our theme this year has been *Back to Basics as Stepping Stones to our Future*. In all of our activities, I have done my best to ensure that we are implementing those basic elements that have proven successful in the past in helping us reach our objectives. It has not been my goal to make a mark or leave a legacy except that we would be on the right track in all of our endeavors.

One of those endeavors has been to continue revitalizing our working relationship between the NCWM and NIST. We faced a potential setback when, just prior to assuming my Chairmanship, we learned that Henry Oppermann was leaving his position as Chief of the NIST Weights and Measures Division. The selection of Carol Hockert as the new Chief put any of my anxieties to rest. Carol has demonstrated a commitment to continue working effectively with NCWM toward goals of mutual benefit. Carol's understanding of weights and measures in the United States is only surpassed by the level of energy she brings to everything she does. Carol, I congratulate you and wish you every success.

One of the difficulties faced by field officials and the NCWM has been in finding an effective and responsible method of addressing software in weighing and measuring systems. To address this problem, the NCWM has implemented the National Type Evaluation Technical Committee approach. Also known as "sectors," these groups have been most successful in the past in dealing with device-related issues. As we discussed yesterday, the Software Sector is up and running. Our thanks go to Jim Truex for his willingness to serve this sector as its Chair. As a side note, Jim and I were amused to have so many software engineers in one room, yet none of them had a definition for software. He mentioned at the CWMA meeting this spring that we defaulted to a definition from a 1970 dictionary sitting on a shelf back in Nebraska. Judy Cardin was quick to point out that in Nebraska software is defined as a no-starch cotton shirt with bib overalls.

Another focus has been to conduct our first NCWM marketplace survey, targeting inspection of random-weight meat and poultry packages wrapped and labeled for sale at retail. We started with joint planning between the Board of Directors and NIST Weights & Measures Division. Soon, we were carrying out our respective roles to ensure its success. Roger Macey of the California Division of Measurement Standards stepped up to manage this initial survey. Thank you, Roger, for your assistance and, Mike Cleary, for sharing the talents of your staff with us. This survey has been a fine example of the cooperative spirit within our system.

With the preparation and field inspections completed, we will proceed with data entry and begin analyzing that data. Our goals for this survey are simple. This marketplace snapshot should demonstrate a difference in levels of compliance between those jurisdictions with a regulatory presence and those jurisdictions without a regulatory presence in the discipline of package testing. The data may aid jurisdictions in securing adequate funding for these activities, especially where funding has been limited primarily to device inspections. We will also examine our ability to use this type of survey data to gain stronger public awareness and appreciation for weights and measures regulatory activities.

A basic element to the success of NCWM is a large and diverse membership base and strong participation at our meetings. We understand that two things must happen as we recover from the economic stresses of the past five years. First, we must provide real value in membership. Second, we must have a method of outreach to prospective members, the stakeholders whom we affect. As an organization becomes less effective, members find less benefit in participation. A downward spiral ensues to the point where the organization can no longer support its mission. Conversely, as an organization becomes stronger and provides increased benefit for membership, current and prospective members can see value in participation. Under this scenario, the organization increases its pool of experts and volunteers. It becomes easier for the organization to take on difficult issues with methodical proficiency.

This is the direction I believe our organization is moving. We must improve in providing meaningful benefits to membership while we increase efforts to market our organization to these prospective members. Success will be measured not only by numbers, but more importantly, by our agility in addressing the difficult issues that are brought to our table.

Most of you have had an opportunity to participate in a survey to help us fully understand where we can improve. Based on the responses to that survey, a team within the Board of Directors has developed marketing strategy options designed to promote membership and participation in NCWM. The Board was presented with these options this week. Some improvements you will soon see include on-line meeting registration and on-line membership renewal capabilities on our website.

There are many interesting dynamics in serving the NCWM as its Chairman. Ultimately, I would say effective communication is the key in everything we do. As an example of communication barriers, I'll share a story. During a break at the NEWMA meeting this spring, Mark Coyne of Brocton, Massachusetts, said to me, "All this increase in ethanol use must be really good for the con business in Nebraska." I said, "Excuse me?" I did __not__ appreciate Mark characterizing the ethanol business in Nebraska as some sort of scam. He said, "The con business must be really good in Nebraska right now with all the ethanol." At this point, I was beside myself, when Bob McGrath came to the rescue. Bob said, "The corn business, Don." Now, it's not that Bob speaks any differently than Mark. Bob's from Massachusetts, too. But Bob and I have served on the Board together and, as scary as it may be, I can actually understand the man.

Just the week before, I was attending the Milestones in Metrology Congress in The Netherlands. If I can have difficulty communicating with a guy I've known for years right here in my own country, imagine how difficult it can be communicating with people from various parts of the world whom I'm meeting for the first time. The words we use may be taken very differently than intended. We have to overcome this and communicate more effectively and more frequently. In the process, we will begin to know and understand each other.

It was suggested to me by one of the attendees at the Milestones meeting that because the United States is the largest economic power in the world, we have the attitude that it's our way or no way when it comes to weighing and measurement standards. I was surprised by this comment considering all the efforts and progress we've made toward harmonization over the past several decades. I simply smiled and told him many of my colleagues in the United States say the same thing about the European Union. We both found this amusing, realizing that the combination of attitudes and limited communication can go a long way in supporting barriers to progress.

Thank you, Pieter van Breugel, Director of NMi in The Netherlands for being here this week to learn more about the NCWM. It is another step toward gaining mutual understanding in the international community. Thank you also, Pieter, for the opportunity you gave me to speak, listen, and learn at the Milestones meeting. The primary purpose for NCWM presence was to help the rest of the world understand our system and our approach to the Mutual Acceptance Arrangements for OIML, but it also provided me a much greater understanding of the dynamics in play in the international community. It was a terrific exercise in communication.

Of course, the NCWM has long recognized the need to work together with outside interests toward harmonization and mutual recognition. NCWM and Measurement Canada have collaborated for many years. We have learned through this cooperative effort that it is not necessary for our standards to be identical, yet we can still allow for a single type evaluation to serve both countries' type approval needs. In 1994, the NCWM and Measurement Canada broke new ground by forming a Mutual Recognition Agreement that allowed sharing of type evaluation data for the purpose of administering our respective type approval programs. This early agreement was for scales up to 500 kilograms in capacity and for electronic indicators used for scales. In 2002, we initiated a pilot program, expanding the Mutual Recognition Agreement to include retail motor-fuel dispensers. These Mutual Recognition Agreements signify our desire to work together for the betterment of our organizations and our stakeholders in North America. It is my honor at this time to invite Alan Johnston, President of Measurement Canada, to join me in signing a renewal of the Mutual Recognition Agreement for retail motor-fuel dispensers, expanding it from a two-year term to a five-year term.

(Signing of the MRA)

For several decades, the NCWM has recognized the benefit to industry that international harmonization would provide. Our partners at NIST have been diligent in representing the United States at the international table so that harmonization can take place on both sides for better and more uniform standards for everyone. As we have learned from our experience with Canada, it is possible to collaborate in type evaluation even though our respective standards are not identical.

Now we find ourselves again breaking new ground in international recognition agreements in legal metrology by entering into the Mutual Acceptance Arrangement for OIML R 60, load cells. Under this arrangement, NCWM will accept type evaluation data from participating laboratories in other countries for the purpose of issuing NTEP certification. Chuck Ehrlich and Steve Cook of NIST and Steve Patoray, our NTEP Director, have been instrumental in helping NCWM reach this point. They have represented U. S. and NCWM interests in international meetings and provided great assistance to the NTEP Committee and Board of Directors as we formed our decisions.

Today, I will sign two more documents on behalf of NCWM. The first is the Acceptance Form indicating we accept all participants in the agreement. The second is the Document of Mutual Confidence, or DoMC. This is the formal document entering the NCWM and the United States into the Mutual Acceptance Arrangement for R 60 load cells. We have the added honor today of witnessing Alan Johnston sign the DoMC entering Canada into the MAA for R 76 and Pieter Van Breugle signing the DoMC entering The Netherlands into the MAA for R 60. So now, it is my privilege to invite Regine Gaucher, BIML, to present these documents for signature. Alan and Pieter, please join me as we celebrate in the signing of these documents. I also invite Chuck Ehrlich, Steve Cook, and Steve Patoray to join us in recognition of their dedicated efforts to make this event possible for the NCWM.

(Signing of the MAA)

The NCWM has continued to move forward through difficult challenges thanks to the hard work of many people and organizations, including our partners at NIST, our colleagues from across the ocean, our neighbors in Canada, the staff at Management Solutions, and of course, all of you within NCWM who volunteer your time, talent, and expertise. There is a reason why we present awards of recognition each year during our opening ceremony. In the course of the history of NCWM since 1905, volunteerism has been the key to our success. We celebrate you.

Thank you.

THIS PAGE LEFT INTENTIONALLY BLANK.

New Chairman's Address
National Conference on Weights and Measures
Chicago, Illinois
July 13, 2006

Michael Cleary
California Department of Agriculture/Weights & Measures

Thank you, Don, and hello to everyone. And thank you all for being here. I know you are all probably anxious to return home to your families. I promise I won't keep you too long. I am truly honored and privileged to stand here today as your Chairman.

I want to thank everyone for the many expressions of congratulations and offers of assistance that I have received – not only this past week but in the last year as I made my rounds as your Chair-Elect.

I would also like to express my thanks and appreciation to all those past officers, committee members, chairmen, and industry representatives who, through their diligence, commitment and long hours, have ensured the continuation and maintenance of our wonderful conference.

I consider our conference to be one of the best examples in the world of a time-tested consensus organization comprised of government, industry and consumer interests working together towards our collective common goals – consumer protection, equity in the marketplace which results in a level playing field for everyone to do business.

That having been said, I would like to tell you what my theme for this year is and why I have chosen the phrase, "United by common purpose we can and shall prevail in all that we do." First of all because it sounds cool, and I've always wanted to use the word 'prevail' in a sentence. But in all seriousness, more now than any other time it is imperative that we find ways to work closely with our partners to achieve success. Now more than ever we have to realize how, in the words of Thomas Freidman, "The World is flat and getting flatter by the day." The global marketplace is a reality, and we must face that challenge head on.

Considering our existing agreements with our partner nation Canada and our upcoming OIML agreement on R 60, we have started to face that challenge, but there is more work to be done. Whether it be in the USA, Asia, Europe or anywhere else in the world our many partnerships take us, our collective mission remains the same – equity, quality, fairness, and, when at all possible, uniformity.

This next year we will continue to work to enhance our partnership with NIST WMD, our closest and most-valued federal partner. I very much look forward to working with Dr. Jeffery, Belinda Collins and Carol Hockert as this long-time, mutually beneficial partnership continues to evolve and improve. I feel our collective success depends on our mutual reciprocity. And by partnership I do mean full partnerships with all those we work with. We, the NCWM, will not follow; we will not and cannot afford to wait to be led.

Our national marketplace survey is an example of how we must seize opportunities as they occur and lead when necessary. We have to be proactive and anticipate the changes that will most certainly occur in this modern global economy. Working together we can and will accomplish wonderful things and make investments in our future. One example of this is how our PDC committee is working in partnership with our regional associations in order to improve the competency of our membership through training and certification. Another is how our L&R and S&T committees, along with our sector groups, are working diligently and in the true spirit of due process and disclosure with all those concerned.

This professional effort has resulted in some of the most comprehensive and well thought-out proposals in the history of this conference. I will continue to support any and all recommendations on how to improve that process.

General Session 2006 Final Report

But know this, I have confidence and trust in the standing committees, and I am secure in the talent we have to do the work we need to do. I promise not to get in the way.

Will there be challenges? Of course! We will need to address issues within the conference itself such as the recruitment and mentoring of new talent for leadership in this organization. We also need to concentrate on the recruitment of new members in general, retain current membership and improve this conference in order to increase the overall value to our members.

We must also make sure to take every opportunity to get our message of value out to the public at large. This is a big challenge, I know, but I am confident that, working together, we shall and will prevail in all these areas of concern.

In closing I would again like to thank you all for this opportunity to serve, and for your trust in me and your Board of Directors. At this time I would like to make the following appointments to the standing committees:

To the BOD to fill the vacancy caused by Judy Cardin's advancement to Chair-Elect, I have recommended to the Board, and they have voted in the affirmative, Steve Malone from Nebraska.

To the L&R Committee, I have re-appointed Joe Benavides for another term.

To the S&T Committee, I have appointed Kristin Young from Colorado.

To the PDC, I have appointed Stacy Carlson, Marin County, California; John L. Sullivan, Mississippi; and Ross Andersen, New York.

Nominating committee:
Thomas Geiler
Ross Andersen
Steven Malone
Dennis Ehrhart
Maxwell Gray
Jim Truex

Chaplain:
Mike Belue

Parliamentarian:
Lou Straub

Credentials Committee:
Raymond Johnson

NCWM 2006 Annual Meeting Honor Award Recipients

Full Name	Organization	State	No. of Years
Steven Cook	NIST, Weights & Measures Division	MD	10
Clark Cooney	Oregon Department of Agriculture	OR	10
Rodney Cooper	Actaris Neptune	SC	10
Chuck Ehrlich	NIST, Weights & Measures Division	MD	10
Dennis Johannes	California Div. of Measurement Standards	CA	10
Vincent Orr	ConAgra Foods	NE	10
Cary Woodward	Hamilton County Weights & Measures	IN	10
Richard Suiter	NIST, Weights & Measures Division	MD	20
Aves D. Thompson	Alaska Div of Measurement Standards/CVE	AL	20
James Truex	Ohio Department of Agriculture	OH	25
Charles Carroll	Massachusetts Division of Standards	MA	25
Thomas Geiler	Town of Barnstable	MA	30

THIS PAGE LEFT INTENTIONALL BLANK.

Report of the Board of Directors
Don Onwiler
Nebraska Department of Agriculture/Weights & Measures

Introduction

The Board held its quarterly Board of Directors (BOD) meeting on Saturday, July 8, 2006, and continued that meeting during work sessions throughout the remainder of the Annual Meeting. The Board of Directors and the NTEP Committee invited members to dialogue with the BOD on the following issues: Conformity Assessment, NCWM Organizational Structure, the National Training Program, Voting Procedures, Public Relations campaign and participation internationally, i.e., OIML, CFTM, APLMF, and USNWG.

Table A
Table of Contents

Subject	Page
Introduction	1
1. Improving Standards Development	2
2. Marketplace Surveys	2
3. Meetings	3
4. Membership Marketing	3
5. NCWM Website – www.ncwm.net	4
6. Electronic Copies of NCWM Publication 14	4
7. Mutual Acceptance Arrangements	4
8. Participation in International Standard Setting	5
9. NCWM Registration Fees Refund Policy	5

Table B
Appendices

Appendix	Title	Page
A	Report on the Activities of the International Organization of Legal Metrology (OIML) and Regional Legal Metrology Organizations	A1
B	Report of the Associate Membership Committee (AMC)	B1

Details of all Items
(In order by Reference Key Number)

1. Improving Standards Development

Technical issues forwarded to the NCWM standing committees appear in various stages of development and degrees of technical complexity. Following are some concerns that have been raised regarding the NCWM's ability to develop properly such issues:

- The NCWM may need to draw in additional technical expertise on occasion.
- More outreach may be necessary to inform stakeholders.
- Development of issues needs to occur throughout the year, not just at Annual and Interim meetings.
- New proposals need proper development and supporting documentation prior to reaching standing committees.

The NCWM and NIST developed a plan to address these concerns in an effort to improve the NCWM standards development process. A review panel was formed to study all new items forwarded to the NCWM standing committees. The purpose of the panel was to assess the needs of each new item in order to gain proper development and consensus within the NCWM. For each new proposal, the panel will provide the standing committee with a recommendation for the proper course of action. Recommendations were to include utilizing a work group of experts, returning the item to the source for further development, development through the routine open hearings of the NCWM and regional associations, etc.

Don Onwiler and Henry Oppermann presented this plan at the 2005 NCWM Annual Meeting and at the 2005 Annual Meetings of each of the regional associations. The NCWM gave the plan a trial run in the fall of 2005. All new proposals forwarded to the NCWM standing committees for consideration at the 2006 Interim Meeting were assessed by the review panel and recommendations were provided to the standing committees. The recommendations were posted on the NCWM website and were made available to Interim Meeting attendees. They were included in NCWM Publication 16 and will become part of the NCWM Annual Report following the Annual Meeting.

At its spring meeting in 2006, the BOD held further discussions based on comments heard from members during the 2006 NCWM Interim Meeting. Many members have viewed the review panel as nothing more than an added layer of bureaucracy. The BOD is in consensus that the review panel was not meant to be a permanent fixture, but rather a tool to assist the organization in improving its process. In this respect, the panel has been a success. Weaknesses have been identified giving the Board a better understanding of ways to improve.

Therefore, the BOD has made the following decisions:

- Discontinue the review panel and allow standing committees to fulfill those duties as part of their normal process;
- Redevelop Form 15 and seek universal acceptance and use by all regional associations;
- Develop programs of team-building among NCWM leadership including BOD, standing committees, and technical advisors; and
- Use those programs to discuss and improve our respective roles in standards development.

The BOD expresses gratitude to officials, industry, and NIST WMD who assisted in the efforts of the panel.

2. Marketplace Surveys

The NCWM conducted a marketplace survey this year. Marketplace surveys benchmark levels of compliance and provide a tool to evaluate the effect of weights and measures presence in a given area of regulation. Surveys can be done on a specific device type, on net quantity verification of various commodities, scanner accuracies, tare on sales from bulk, and so forth. It is our hope that jurisdictions may be able to use this data to demonstrate the need for sufficient funding for a comprehensive weights and measures program.

The BOD is following NCWM protocol for national surveys. A team within the BOD set the direction for the first survey.

The goals of the survey are to:

1) Benchmark the variances in compliance between jurisdictions where inspections are conducted versus those where inspections do not take place;
2) Promote funding for this discipline of inspection in jurisdictions by demonstrating the effect of a regulatory presence in the marketplace; and
3) Generate public awareness of weights and measures activities.

This year the survey was on net quantity of random weight meat and poultry items wrapped and labeled at retail stores. It began with joint planning between NCWM and NIST WMD. NIST provided test reports, outlined test procedures, and provided training to participating jurisdictions. Roger Macey, California Division of Measurement Standards, served as project manager and coordinated the activities of 14 participating jurisdictions, which represented a good cross-section of jurisdictions in the United States. Half of the participating jurisdictions currently are active in package inspections. NIST will provide a spreadsheet to NCWM staff that will perform the data entry. Once that is completed, the data will be assessed.

There is no plan to hold press conferences to announce the results. Industry expressed concern about the protocol that was going to be used. Most of these concerns were addressed satisfactorily during the open hearings at the 2006 Interim Meeting.

The BOD determined that marketplace surveys would be conducted on an annual basis.

3. Meetings

Interim Meetings
January 21 - 24, 2007   Omni Jacksonville, Jacksonville, FL
January 27 - 30, 2008   Hyatt Regency Albuquerque, Albuquerque, NM

Annual Meetings
July 8 - 12, 2007   Snowbird Resort, Salt Lake City, UT
July 13 - 17, 2008   Sheraton Burlington Hotel & Conference Center, Burlington, VT

Staff was directed to continue to look for a warm location for the 2009 Interim Meeting. The 2009 Annual Meeting will be held in the Southern region. Members are encouraged to submit suggestions for meeting locations to the NCWM staff.

4. Membership Marketing

The BOD recognizes the need to address membership and meeting attendance. The management company, Management Solutions Plus (MSP), hired Judy Markoe to assist the various associations in gaining public recognition and membership. Judy met with the BOD at its 2005 fall meeting. Based on information shared in that meeting, Judy created a focused marketing concept tailored to the needs of NCWM, which was presented to the BOD at the 2006 Interim Meeting. The marketing plan is geared to increase public awareness of the NCWM and weights and measures activities. The BOD hopes that the regional associations will also realize some of the benefits reaped by the NCWM.

A task force consisting of Judy Cardin, Stephen Pahl, Chris Guay, and Darrell Flocken has been formed to work with Judy Markoe on this initiative. An online survey tool was used to gather information from both current and past NCWM members. The task force developed recommendations based on this survey and presented them to the NCWM BOD at the 2006 Annual Meeting. From those recommendations, the BOD has elected to:

- Update the NCWM website to enable on-line meeting registration;
- Update the NCWM website to enable on-line membership renewal; and
- Have the work group continue developing recommendations for further consideration at the fall 2006 BOD meeting.

5. NCWM Website – www.ncwm.net

Many positive comments have been received regarding recent improvements to the NCWM website. The site continues to evolve in order to better serve the members and gain the interest of first-time viewers. As always, the BOD accepts suggestions to further improve the website.

One suggestion was to include mailing addresses in the membership directory, which is available only through the "Members Only" portion of the website. Following feedback at the open hearings of the 2006 Interim Meeting, the BOD decided to include members' street addresses in the online directory. Each member has the choice to opt out of including his street address.

Additional future improvements to the website include on-line meeting registration and membership renewals.

6. Electronic Copies of NCWM Publication 14

At the request of our industry membership, the NCWM developed an electronic version of Publication 14 and made it available on CD. The CD contains Publication 14 Administrative Policy and all NTEP technical policies, checklists and test procedures. An order form is available on the NCWM website at http://www.ncwm.net.

The BOD received some comments at the 2006 Interim Meeting regarding the use and pricing of the electronic version of Publication 14. These recommendations will be addressed after more information is available on its use during 2006.

7. Mutual Acceptance Arrangements

The purpose of Mutual Acceptance Arrangements is to establish bilateral and multilateral agreements. Under such agreements and arrangements, manufacturers would be able to submit their equipment to any of the participating countries for testing to OIML-recommended requirements. The resulting test data would be accepted by other participants, as a basis for issuing each country's own type approval certificate.

NTEP Director, Stephen Patoray, attended an MAA Seminar for Assessors on September 5 - 6, 2005. During this seminar, Mr. Patoray provided the attendees an overview of the additional requirements in the United States for both OIML R 76 and R 60. He updated the attendees at the 2006 NCWM Interim Meeting regarding the current status of the MAA and other developments. The next scheduled meeting of the Committee on Participation Review (CPR) for R 76 and R 60 is now scheduled for March 7, 8 and 10 in Sydney, Australia.

The NTEP Committee discussed this item during the fall 2006 NTEP Committee meeting. Based on previous input from the NCWM membership and other discussion on this topic, the NTEP Committee believes the United States should be a Country A (issuing participant) with full laboratory capabilities for OIML R 76 "non-automatic weighing instruments" and should not participate in a Declaration of Mutual Confidence (DoMC) as a Country B (utilizing participant) for R 76. However, the NTEP Committee recognizes there are no identified resources available to move forward with a laboratory for R 76 at this time.

The NTEP Committee discussed the NIST Force Group's position not to participate as a testing laboratory for OIML R 60 "load cells." There are relatively few load cell evaluations requested on an annual basis, and it would be unreasonable to invest in such laboratory facilities, as the costs are not justified by the demand for services.

Based on these discussions, the NTEP Committee recommended the NCWM BOD sign the DoMC as a Country B for R 60 "load cells" only. The BOD approved this recommendation at the 2006 NCWM Interim Meeting.

This BOD decision allows NTEP to accept test data for load cells tested by foreign laboratories recognized by the DoMC. The United States will not have the ability to test to OIML requirements for international recognition.

The BOD maintains its commitment only to sign a DoMC for R 76 "non-automatic weighing instruments" if it can do so as a Country A with a viable lab.

During the opening ceremony of the 2006 NCWM Annual Meeting, Regine Gaucher, MAA Project Leader for BIML, presented NCWM Chair, Don Onwiler, with the DoMC for R 60 for his signature. Ms. Gaucher also presented the DoMC for R 76 to Alan Johnston (Measurement Canada) and the DoMC for R 60 to Pieter van Breugel, NMI Certin (The Netherlands) for their signatures at this same event.

Alan Johnston and Don Onwiler also took the opportunity at the 2006 Annual Meeting to renew the MRA between Canada and the United States for retail motor-fuel dispensers extending the term of the agreement from two years to five years.

8. Participation in International Standard Setting

As the international community continues to draw closer in legal metrology issues, the NCWM is receiving requests for participation at various meetings and conferences. The NTEP director is participating in international meetings of the Committee on Participation Review (CPR) for the Mutual Acceptance Arrangements for R 60 and R 76. The NCWM received an invitation to attend the Milestones Metrology Congress in May 2006 in The Netherlands to speak on the philosophy of the United States in the MAA process, explain the NCWM system, and provide a broad understanding of our legal metrology system.

The BOD discussed identifying appropriate individuals to represent the NCWM in the international arena based on the nature of the event and the type of input requested. Our participation is primarily requested for one of two reasons:

1) To provide technical input on standards alignment or mutual recognition of testing data, or
2) To provide insight into the legal metrology system of the United States.

It is the decision of the NCWM BOD that the NTEP Director will continue to represent U. S. interests in the international arena as it pertains to technical discussions. It will be the role of the NCWM Chair or the Chair's designated appointee to represent the United States in the international arena when the purpose is to represent the U. S. legal metrology system.

9. NCWM Registration Fees Refund Policy

The BOD has adopted the following policy regarding all NCWM scheduled conferences, non-conference meetings sanctioned by the NCWM, and activities such as, but not limited to, meetings associated with the functions of the National Type Evaluation Committee:

Cancellations received prior to any early registration deadline date are subject to a 15 % cancellation fee. No refunds will be given after that date except as follows:

1) In the case of a state-declared natural emergency that results in the member's inability to attend the conference, there will be a <u>full refund</u> of the member's registration fee.
2) In the case of personal medical emergency associated with the NCWM member, and in the case of fatal or life-threatening illness or injury of an immediate family member, <u>full or partial refunds</u> may be considered based on documentation of the specific medical emergency and BOD review and approval.

In any other instance of requests for refunds of conference registration fees, it shall be the policy of the BOD to deny such requests. However, the BOD recognizes the need to be flexible based on yet-to-be-determined circumstances out of the control of individual members.

National Conference on Weights and Measures, Inc.
Statement of Activities, Year Ended September 30, 2005

Revenue

Government Dues	$89,715
Associate Dues	$56,250
National Type Evaluation Program	$467,066
Interim Meeting Fees	$25,730
Annual Meeting Fees	$73,565
Publications $24,246	
Advertising $825	
Investment Return	$15,804
Miscellaneous 100	
Total Revenue	**$753,301**

Expenses

Programs

National Type Evaluation Program	$428,618
Annual Meeting	$94,012
Interim Meeting	$56,814
Publications $15,267	
Newsletter $14,602	
Membership $11,550	
Total Programs	**$620,863**

Management and General

Management Fees	$49,774
Website $32,178	
Board of Directors	$22,734
Bank Fees	$13,619
Legal and Accounting	$6,493
Office Supplies	$2,390
Insurance $1,989	
Committee Contingency Fund	$1,929
Printing and Duplicating	$1,317
Telephone $1,206	
Workgroup Travel	$426
Postage $63	
Miscellaneous $24	
Total Management and General	**$134,142**
Total Expenses	**$755,005**

Change in net assets	(1,704)
Net Assets, beginning of year	$606,632
Net Assets, end of year	$604,928

Assets

Current Assets

Cash and cash equivalents	$193,399
Certificates of Deposit	566,918
Accounts Receivable	299
Prepaid Expenses	3,785
Interest Receivable	1,751
Total Assets	$766,152

Liabilities and Net Assets

Current Liabilities

Accounts Payable $	4,629
Deferred Dues Revenue	151,170
Total Liabilities	155,799

Net Assets

Unrestricted	610.353
Total Liabilities and net Assets $766,152	

Don Onwiler, Nebraska, NCWM Chair
Michael Cleary, California, NCWM Chairman-Elect
Jim Truex, Ohio, NTEP Committee Chair
Judy Cardin, Wisconsin
Charles Carroll, Massachusetts
Tom Geiler, Town of Barnstable, Massachusetts
Joe Gomez, New Mexico
Stephen Pahl, Texas
Russell Wyckoff, Oregon
Christopher B. Guay, Procter & Gamble Co.
Darrell Flocken, Mettler-Toledo, Inc.
NCWM Staff: Beth Palys, CAE
NIST: Henry Oppermann

Board of Directors

BOD 2006 Final Report
Appendix A – Report on Activities of OIML

Appendix A

Report on the Activities of the
International Organization of Legal Metrology (OIML)
And Regional Legal Metrology Organizations

International Legal Metrology Group
Weights and Measures Division, NIST

The International Legal Metrology Group (ILMG) of the Weights and Measures Division (WMD) of the National Institute of Standards and Technology (NIST) is responsible for coordinating U. S. participation in OIML and other international legal metrology organizations. Learn more about OIML at the OIML website at http://www.oiml.org and the WMD website at http://www.nist.gov/owm on the Internet. Dr. Charles Ehrlich, Group Leader of the ILMG, can be contacted at charles.ehrlich@nist.gov or at (301) 975-4834 or by fax at (301) 975-8091.

Please note: OIML publications are now available without cost at http://www.oiml.org

Table A
Table of Contents

I. Report on the Activities of the OIML Technical Committees..A2
II. Mutual Acceptance Arrangement (MAA) on OIML Type Evaluations..A4
III. Future CIML Meetings..A5

Table B
Glossary of Acronyms*

BIML	Bureau of International Legal Metrology	IR	International Recommendation
CD Committee	Draft[1]	MAA	Mutual Acceptance Arrangement
CIML	International Committee of Legal Metrology	OIML	International Organization of Legal Metrology
CPR	Committee on Participation Review	PTB	Physikalisch-Technischen Bundsanstalt
DD Draft	Document[2]	R Recommendation	
DR Draft	Recommendation[2]	SC Subcommittee	
DV Draft	Vocabulary[2]	TC Technical	Committee
DoMC	Declarations of Mutual Confidence WD Working		Document[3]

[1] CD: a draft at the stage of development within a technical committee or subcommittee; in this document, successive drafts are numbered 1 CD, 2 CD, etc.

[2] DD, DR, DV: draft documents approved at the level of the technical committee or subcommittee concerned and sent to BIML for approval by CIML.

[3] WD: precedes the development of a CD; in this document, successive drafts are number 1 WD, 2 WD, etc.

* Explanation of acronyms provided by OIML.

BOD 2006 Final Report
Appendix A – Report on Activities of OIML

I. Report on the Activities of the OIML Technical Committees

This section reports on recent activities and the status of work in OIML Technical Committees (TCs) and Technical Subcommittees (SCs) of specific interest to members of the NCWM. Also included are schedules of future activities of the Secretariats, the U. S. National Work Groups (USNWGs), and the International Work Groups (IWGs) of the Committees and Subcommittees. The country named in parentheses after the title of the technical committee is the Secretariat of that committee.

TC 3/SC 1 "Pattern Approval and Evaluation" (United States)
The subcommittee approved the U. S. proposal for a combined revision of OIML D 19 "Pattern evaluation and pattern approval" and D 20 "Initial and subsequent verification of measuring instruments and processes" into a single document entitled "Principles of metrological control of measuring instruments: type approval and verification." Key elements of OIML D 3 "Legal Qualification of Measuring Instruments," R 34 "Accuracy Classes of Measuring Instruments," and R 42 "Metal Stamps for Verification Officers" will also be incorporated into the combined revision of OIML D 19 and D 20. The revised documents will incorporate recent developments such as the OIML certificate system, D 27 "Initial verification of measuring instruments utilizing the manufacturer's quality management system," and the "Framework for a mutual acceptance arrangement (MAA) on OIML type evaluations." Consideration will be given to the appropriate conformity assessment options developed by the ISO Council Committee on Conformity Assessment (ISO CASCO), including quality systems, product certification, and accreditation. Consideration needs to be given as well to information technology and statistical methods to increase or decrease verification intervals based upon proven instrument performance. For more information on this activity, contact Dr. Ambler Thompson at (301) 975-2333 or at ambler@nist.gov.

TC 5/SC 2 Software (Germany and France)
In 2004 all OIML TCs and SCs that were revising an OIML Recommendation were contacted to ensure that software aspects are considered in revised Recommendations. All OIML Documents and Recommendations published since 1990 were reviewed for terms and requirements related to software. A pre-draft of the document "Software in Legal Metrology" was circulated in October 2004 by the Secretariat. When complete, this document will serve as guidance for OIML technical committees addressing software requirements in Recommendations for software-controlled instruments. The ILMG submitted U. S. comments on a working draft of this document in June 2006. This document can be viewed on the WMD website at http://ts.nist.gov/ts/htdocs/230/235/TC5-SC2.htm. Please contact Wayne Stiefel at (301) 975-4011 or at stiefel@nist.gov if you would like to participate in this project.

TC 8/SC 1 "Static Volume and Mass Measurement" (Austria and Germany)
The Secretariat submitted 1 CD revisions in January 2005 for OIML R 71 "Fixed Storage Tanks," R 80 "Road and Rail Tankers," and R 85 "Automatic Level Gages for Measuring the Level of Liquid in Fixed Storage Tanks." U. S. comments, including those of the American Petroleum Institute, on all three of these documents were sent in April 2005. The Secretariat held a subcommittee meeting in April 2005 in Vienna, Austria. The United States provided a vote and comments on the 2 CD of all of these documents in April 2006, and a meeting of the subcommittee was held in Hamburg, Germany, in April 2006. Please contact Wayne Stiefel at (301) 975-4011 or at stiefel@nist.gov if you would like copies of the documents or to participate in these projects.

TC 8/SC 3 "Measuring Instruments for Liquids other than Water." (Germany) and TC 8/SC 4 "Dynamic Mass Measurements (Liquids other than Water)" (United States)
OIML R 117 "Measuring Instruments for Liquids other than Water" is undergoing an extensive revision, incorporating new instrument technologies and merging the document with OIML R 86 "Drum Meters" and R 105 "Mass Flowmeters." This is a high priority project for OIML. ILMG is working with the USNWG, Germany, and The Netherlands on this effort. Meetings of the USNWG on flowmeters were held during the NCWM Annual Meeting in July 2005 in Orlando, Florida, the NCWM Interim Meeting in January 2006 in Jacksonville, Florida, and the NCWM Annual Meeting in July 2006 in Chicago, Illinois. Measurement Canada has been a strong contributor to this effort. A 2 CD of R 117 was circulated to the two international subcommittees and received over 90 % international "yes" votes. OIML member nations will vote on the DR of R 117-1 by postal ballot with an objective of receiving full CIML approval on R 117 in early 2007. If you have questions or would like to become involved in this effort, please contact Ralph Richter (301) 975-3997 or at ralph.richter@nist.gov.

BOD 2006 Final Report
Appendix A – Report on Activities of OIML

TC 8/SC 7 "Gas Metering" (Belgium and France)
The Secretariat circulated a 3 CD of the Recommendation "Measuring Systems for Compressed Natural Gas (CNG) for Vehicles" and annexes covering performance tests for electronic devices and basic test procedures. In April 2003, the United States cast a negative ballot on the 3 CD because the testing requirements were considered to be unrealistic. A 4 CD is being prepared by the Secretariat.

A ballot was circulated on the 4 CD "Measuring Systems for Gaseous Fuel" and U. S. comments were returned in November 2005. This Recommendation is intended for large pipelines with large flowrates and high operating pressures, or systems not fitted with diaphragm gas meters. Different types of measuring systems are covered by the Recommendation: measuring systems providing indications of volume at base conditions or mass converted from a volume of gas determined at metering conditions, measuring systems providing directly the mass of gas, and measuring systems providing indication of energy corresponding to a volume at base conditions or a mass of gas. The United States voted "no" on the 4 CD of this document. Please contact Wayne Stiefel at (301) 975-4011 or at stiefel@nist.gov if you would like to obtain a copy of these documents or to participate in these projects.

TC 8/SC 8 "Gas Meters" (The Netherlands)
Based on a poll of TC 8/SC 8 members, R 6 "General provisions for gas volume meters," R 31 "Diaphragm Gas Meters," and R 32 "Rotary Piston Gas Meters and Turbine Gas Meters" were revised and combined into a single Recommendation. The Secretariat circulated a 2 CD of this document, and U. S. comments were returned in March 2005. A subcommittee meeting to discuss the document was held in June 2005 in The Netherlands. The United States voted "yes" with comments on the 3 CD of this document in January 2006. Please contact Wayne Stiefel at (301) 975-4011 or at stiefel@nist.gov if you would like to participate in this project.

TC 9 "Instruments for Measuring Mass" (United States)
The United States will begin the review cycle for R 60 "Load Cells" after the revision of R 76 "Non-automatic Weighing Instruments" is complete, probably late in 2006. If you would like to participate in the revision of R 60, please contact Steve Cook at (301) 975-4003 or steven.cook@nist.gov.

TC 9/SC 1 "Nonautomatic Weighing Instruments" (Germany and France)
The current review cycle of R 76 "Non-automatic Weighing Instruments" is of major importance to U. S. interests because the Recommendation serves as the foundation for a majority of the laws and regulations that govern weighing instruments around the world. This review is significant for U. S. weighing instrument manufacturers because international harmonization of requirements would eliminate technical barriers to trade and reduce the delays and the cost of getting new weighing instruments into the global marketplace. The United States returned comments on the 1 CD of the revised R 76 in April 2005. The revision included new language addressing metrological controls for type evaluations, conformity, and initial and subsequent inspections. The USNWG held a meeting in July 2005 and is being consulted concerning proposals to harmonize Handbook 44 and R 76. The United States voted "yes" on the 2 CD of R 76 in January 2006, voted "yes" on the 3 CD of R 76 in June 2006, and expects the DR to be approved by the CIML in October 2006. If you would like to participate in this effort, please contact Steve Cook at (301) 975-4003 or steven.cook@nist.gov.

TC 9/SC 2 "Automatic Weighing Instruments" (United Kingdom)
The Recommendation R 134-1 "Automatic Instruments for Weighing Road Vehicles in Motion – Total Load and Axle Weighing" is having its final comments incorporated and should be published in 2006. The test report format of this document, R 134-2, has been distributed in the United States and comments were submitted to the Secretariat in January 2006. Two other documents in this subcommittee are now being revised. The United States has returned comments on a WD of R 106 "Automatic Rail-weighbridges" and a 1 CD of R 107 "Discontinuous Totalizing Automatic Weighing Instruments (Totalizing Hopper Weighers)." If you would like to receive copies of any of these documents or work on these projects, please contact Richard Harshman at (301) 975-8107 or at harshman@nist.gov.

TC 17/SC 1 "Humidity" (China)
The Secretariat is working closely with the United States and a small international work group (IWG) to revise OIML R 59 "Moisture Meters for Cereal Grains and Oilseeds." All drafts have been distributed to the USNWG, which for the most part is a subset of the NTEP Grain Sector. In October 2003, China hosted a meeting of the TC 17/SC 1 subcommittee in Beijing to review and discuss this revised document. A 2 CD that incorporated U. S. comments was circulated in May 2004 by the Secretariat. A meeting of the IWG was held in Paris in September 2004 to resolve

BOD 2006 Final Report
Appendix A – Report on Activities of OIML

conflicts on the document. U. S. comments on the 3 CD of R 59 were returned to the Secretariat in August 2005 and are being incorporated into the next draft. Please contact Diane Lee at (301) 975-4405 or at diane.lee@nist.gov if you would like to participate in this work group.

TC 17/SC 8 "Quality Analysis of Agricultural Products" (Australia)
A new subcommittee has been formed to study the issues and write a WD document "Measuring Instruments for Protein Determination in Grains." Australia is the Secretariat for this new subcommittee. A work group meeting was held in May 2004 in Sydney. A 2 WD of this document was received in August 2004, and a 3 WD was received in May 2005. A work group meeting was held in June 2005 in Berlin to discuss the latest round of comments on the 3 WD. Please contact Diane Lee at (301) 975-4405 or at diane.lee@nist.gov if you would like to participate in this work group.

II. Mutual Acceptance Arrangement (MAA) on OIML Type Evaluations

The OIML MAA is now being implemented. The first "provisional" Committee on Participation Review (CPR) has been established for OIML R 60 (Load Cells) and R 76 (Non-automatic Weighing Instruments). The CPR is being called 'provisional' to reflect the fact that the participants are under no obligation to sign either of the Declarations of Mutual Confidence (DoMCs) that are expected to result.

The first meeting of the CPR was held June 15 - 16, 2005, in Lyon, France, in conjunction with the 40th CIML Meeting and the 50th Anniversary Celebration of OIML. Mr. Stephen Patoray represented the NCWM, Mr. Steve Cook represented the Secretariat of OIML TC 9 responsible for OIML R 60, and Dr. Charles Ehrlich represented the Secretariat for OIML TC 3/SC 5 responsible for the MAA. Twenty-one countries had representatives at the meeting, with eight of the countries indicating interest in participating as an "Issuing Participant" for at least one of the two DoMCs. (An "Issuing Participant" is one that performs tests and issues certificates under the DoMC.) The CPR reviewed the application files of the eight countries wishing to be Issuing Participants, and decided that two of the countries needed to have peer reviews conducted. (For reasons of confidentiality, no countries are being identified by name until the DoMC is signed.) A seminar (training course) for peer review assessors was held on September 5 - 6, 2005, in Paris, and the peer reviews were completed in January 2006.

Also at the first CPR meeting, a draft "Operating Rules" for CPRs was discussed, and it was agreed among CPR members that an 80 % voting rule would apply, with no more than one negative vote from an "Issuing Participant" allowed. The "Operating Rules," containing this and other proposals, was put forward to the CIML for postal vote. A draft implementation document on using ISO/IEC 17025 (requirements for testing laboratories), to be used for conducting the legal metrology audits, was also discussed. Another implementation document on ISO Guide 65 (requirements for issuing authorities) was circulated to the CPR for comment after the meeting. These implementation documents are being distributed as working drafts to OIML TC 3/SC 5 to be developed as OIML documents.

The NCWM Board of Directors (BOD) had indicated to the BIML its desire to participate on the CPR, primarily to help answer many of the NCWM's questions and concerns, and realized that many details regarding the implementation of the MAA will be developed through discussions of the CPR. The NCWM also indicated to the BIML that the NCWM anticipated it would sign a DoMC for R 76 only when it is prepared to do so as an OIML Issuing Authority that issues test data and OIML Certificates under the MAA (i.e., as an Issuing Participant). The BIML allowed the NCWM to participate on the CPR under this arrangement. In order not to pay the 1500 Euro fee for "examination of their candidacy" as an Issuing Participant, the United States has for now been considered as a country that will not issue OIML Certificates under the MAA, but rather will utilize those issued by other countries (a "Utilizing Participant"). This arrangement could change as negotiations continue and the CPR discussions advance.

At the January 2006 Interim Meeting in Jacksonville, Florida, the Board considered whether the NCWM should be a Utilizing Participant for R 60 since all of the necessary load cell testing capability to be an Issuing Participant is not available in the United States. The Board decided to sign the DoMC for R 60. After the second CPR meeting was held in March 2006 in Sydney, the signing of the DoMCs for R 60 and R 76 started. The NNCWM signed the DoMC (as a "Utilizing Participant") for R 60 during a ceremony at the July 2006 NCWM Annual Meeting in Chicago. Under this DoMC, the National Type Evaluation Program (NTEP), administered by NCWM, will accept test data on load cells that are tested according to the requirements in OIML R 60 (and "additional," agreed-upon requirements), from "Issuing Participants" under the DoMC, to use as the basis of issuing NTEP Certificates.

OIML TC 3/SC 5 will start revising both publication B 10-1 (MAA) and publication B 3 "OIML Certificate System for Measuring Instruments" after some additional experience with the MAA has been gained. Further implementation of the MAA may require that other detailed regulations be developed.

For further information on the MAA and its implementation, please contact Dr. Charles Ehrlich at charles.ehrlich@nist.gov or at (301) 975-4834 or by fax at (301) 975-8091.

III. Future CIML Meetings

The 41st CIML Meeting will be hosted by South Africa in Capetown in October 2006. The Committee noted that the People's Republic of China was considering inviting the CIML to hold its 42nd Meeting in China in October 2007. A decision on this will be made at the 41st CIML Meeting.

THIS PAGE LEFT INTENTIONALLY BLANK.

BOD 2006 Final Report
Appendix B – AMC Final Report

Appendix B

Report of the Associate Membership Committee (AMC)

Gary Lamaris, Hobart Corporation

July 10, 2006
Chicago, Illinois

The following individuals were in attendance:

Gary Lameris, Chairman	Lameris Consulting
Stephen Langford, Vice-Chair	Cardinal Scale
Vince Orr, Secretary-Treasurer	Conagra Foods
Janet Sheiner	Petco
Cary Frye	International Dairy Foods Association
Richard Davis	Georgia Pacific Corporation
Paul Lewis	Rice Lake Weighing Systems
Mike Sarachman	Kraft Foods
Chris Guay	Procter & Gamble
Bob Murnane	Seraphin Test Measures
Gale Prince	Kroger
Darrell Flocken	Mettler-Toledo
Louis Straub	Fairbanks Scales
Steve Steinborn	Hogan & Hartson
Pete O'Bryan	Foster Farms
Doug Biette	Sartorius
Leon Lammers	Avery Weigh-Tronix
Stephanie Siedschlag	Conagra Foods
Michelle Wright	ConAgra Foods
Keith Tsujimoto	Safeway Stores
Thomas Herrington	Nestle USA
Beth Palys	NCWM Headquarters

Chairman Lameris called the meeting to order at 12:05 p.m.

<u>Minutes</u>

The minutes of July 2005 and January 2006 meetings were approved.

<u>Financial Condition</u>

Chairman Lameris reported that as of June 30, 2006, the AMC fund balance was $15,322.29 before the cost of the outing. This compares to $18,810 at this time last year. Revenue this fiscal year from dues was $13,440, which would equate to 896 Associate members. To date, three of the five training requests have been partially funded. Maryland, Massachusetts, and Colorado have been reimbursed.

BOD 2006 Final Report
Appendix B – AMC Final Report

Board of Directors Report

Darrell Flocken, the AMC representative on the NCWM Board of Directors, gave a report on Board activities:

- NIST announced a work group meeting for August 8, 2006, (now postponed) on Handbook 133. Additional discussion occurred in the new business below.

- The NCWM is continuing to develop a marketing plan. When called, 43 % of those who did not renew their dues stated they "just forgot." The Board has planned to implement changes to the website to allow online registration and billing for meetings and dues to help increase the membership. They may ask the AMC for some funding. The cost estimate is $2250 for adding the membership feature and $5900 for adding meeting registration.

- NIST WMD has announced they are revamping their website to improve navigation.

- NIST is considering publishing Handbook 130 and 133 on an "as needed" basis.

- The NCWM Review Committee has been discontinued after some positive and negative outcomes during the first year. The Committee pointed to some changes needed in the process such as:

  - Form 15, the form required to submit an item to the committees, needs to be reworked and published in an easier-to-find location on the website. Currently, according to Beth Palys, the plan is to create an editable PDF form on the website so members can type directly on the form.

- The data collection phase of the marketplace survey has been completed. The product surveyed will be revealed this afternoon in the Board of Directors open hearing.

- There will be no increase in NTEP fees this year.

- Aves Thompson from Alaska is retiring effective the end of July.

Election of Committee Members and Officers

Thomas Herrington and Chris Guay have been elected to terms expiring in 2010
Paul Lewis, Sr., has been elected as the Secretary-Treasurer

Training Funds

- Maryland has completed their training session and only required $1443 of the $2500 grant.

- MWMA has been reimbursed $800 of the $1300 granted. They originally planned two sessions.

- Colorado Department of Agriculture has been reimbursed $1300.

- Schenectady County and Ohio have not yet submitted reimbursement receipts.

AMC Membership Report

AMC membership is again increasing after a couple of slow years. The recent totals are:

- 2006 – 844 members,

- 2005 – 828 members,

- 2004 – 837 members, and
- 2003 – 953 members

Old Business

Steve Steinborn of Hogan & Hartson stated the NIST memo dated January 1, 2006, concerning the packaged food industry has been withdrawn.

New Business

Much discussion occurred from the BOD report concerning a NIST work group on HB 133. After some discussion, it appears the major concern is with moisture loss, blister packs, and gel soakers. The AMC encourages the use of work groups and adopted the following resolution by unanimous consensus:

> *Any NIST Handbook 133 work group should be developed with a specific scope through guidance and coordination by the NCWM, Inc., Laws and Regulation Committee; any output of the work group shall go through the normal NCWM, Inc., process.*

Vince Orr, AMC representative on the L&R Committee, reported that an update on stored vehicle tare and other issues will be presented at the 2007 NCWM Interim Meeting.

Adjournment

The meeting was adjourned at 12:55 p.m.

Respectfully submitted,

Stephen Langford,
Vice Chairman

Gary Lameris
Chairman

THIS PAGE LEFT INTENTIONALLY BLANK.

Report of the Laws and Regulations Committee

Joe Benavides, Chairman
Texas Weights and Measures

Reference
Key Number

200 INTRODUCTION

This is the report of the Laws and Regulations (L&R) Committee (hereinafter referred to as "Committee") for the 91st Annual Meeting of the National Conference on Weights and Measures (NCWM). It is based on the Interim Report offered in the NCWM Publication 16, "Committee Reports," testimony at public hearings, comments received from the regional weights and measures associations and other parties, the addendum sheets issued at the Annual Meeting, and actions taken by the membership at the voting session of the Annual Meeting. The informational items presented below were adopted as presented when this report was approved.

Table A identifies the agenda items in the Report by Reference Key Number, title, and page number. The first three digits of the Reference Key Numbers of the items are assigned from the subject series listed below. Voting items are indicated with a "**V**" after the item number. Items marked with an "**I**" are informational. Items marked with a "**D**" are developing items. The developing designation indicates an item has merit; however, the item is returned to the submitter for further development before any further action is taken by the Committee. Items marked "**W**" have been withdrawn from consideration. Table B lists the appendices to the report, and Table C provides a summary of the results of the voting on the Committee's items and the report in entirety.

This report contains recommendations to amend National Institute of Standards and Technology (NIST) Handbook 130, 2006 Edition, "Uniform Laws and Regulations," or NIST Handbook 133, "Checking the Net Contents of Packaged Goods," Fourth Edition (January 2005). Proposed revisions to the handbook(s) are shown in **bold face print** by ~~striking out~~ information to be deleted and __underlining__ information to be added. New items proposed for the handbooks are designated as such and shown in **bold face print**. Text presented for information only is shown in *italic* print. When used in this report, the term "weight" means "mass."

Subject Series

Introduction ....200 Series
NIST Handbook 130 – General..210 Series
   Uniform Laws..220 Series
   Weights and Measures Law (WML)..221 Series
   Weighmaster Law (WL)..222 Series
      Engine Fuels, Petroleum Products, and Automotive Lubricants Inspection Law (EFL)...........223 Series

   Uniform Regulations...230 Series
   Packaging and Labeling Regulation (PLR)...231 Series
      Method of Sale Regulation (MSR)..232 Series
      Unit Pricing Regulation (UPR)..233 Series
   Voluntary Registration Regulation (VRR)..234 Series
      Open Dating Regulation (ODR)..235 Series
      Uniform National Type Evaluation Regulation (UNTER)..236 Series
      Engine Fuels, Petroleum Products, and Automotive Lubricants Regulation (EFR)..................237 Series
   Examination Procedure for Price Verification..240 Series
   Interpretations and Guidelines...250 Series

NIST Handbook 133 ....260 Series
Other Items ....270 Series

Table A
Index to Reference Key Items

Reference Key Number	Title of Item	Page

200 INTRODUCTION 1

232 METHOD OF SALE REGULATION 3
    232-1   I   Temperature Compensation for Petroleum Products..3
    232-2   I   Biodiesel and Fuel Ethanol Labeling..6

250 INTERPRETATIONS AND GUIDELINES..8
    250-1   V   Basic Engine Fuels, Petroleum Products, and Lubricants Laboratory...............................8

270 OTHER ITEMS..8
    270-1   D   Developing Items..8

Table B
Appendices

Appendix Title Page

A   **Item 270-1: Developing Items – Handbook 130**
    Part 1: Premium Diesel Lubricity..A1
    Part 2: Guidelines for the Method of Sale of Fresh Fruits and Vegetables...A2

B   **Item 270-1: Developing Items – Handbook 133**
    Part 1: Moisture Loss..B1

C   **Item 250-1: Basic Engine Fuels, Petroleum Products, and Lubricants Laboratory Guidelines**.........C1

D   **NCWM Petroleum Subcommittee Report**..D1

Table C
Voting Results

Reference Key Number	House of State Representatives		House of Delegates		Results
	Yeas	Nays	Yeas	Nays	
250-1	37	0	45	0	Adopted

L&R Committee 2006 Final Report

Details of all Items
(In order by Reference Key Number)

232   METHOD OF SALE REGULATION

232-1   I   Temperature Compensation for Petroleum Products

Source: Southern Weights and Measures Association (SWMA). (See Item 232-4 in the Report of the 89th NCWM Annual Meeting held in 2004.)

Recommendation: Amend the Method of Sale Regulation in Handbook 130 by adding the following:

> **2.XX.   Refined Petroleum Products**
>
> > **2.XX.A.** – Where not in conflict with other statutes or regulations, refined petroleum products delivered through: (1) vehicle tank meters, (2) stationary meters with flow rates of 115 L (30 gal) or more per minute, and (3) loading rack meters, ~~may~~ be sold with the volume adjusted to compensate for temperature. When petroleum products are sold temperature compensated:
> >
> > (a)   All sales shall be in terms of liters or U. S. gallons at 15 °C (60 °F);
> >
> > (b)   The temperature compensation shall be accomplished through automatic means;
> >
> > (c)   The primary indicating elements, recording elements, and all recorded representations (receipts, invoices, bills of lading, etc.) shall be clearly and conspicuously marked to show that the volume delivered has been adjusted to the volume at 15 °C (60 °F);
> >
> > (d)   For vehicle tank meters, all sales by the same person or company for the same metering application within the same state shall be sold temperature compensated in 12-month increments. For example, a company may not choose to operate some vehicle tank meters with automatic temperature compensators and others without. Nor may a company choose to engage the automatic temperature compensator on a device only during certain times of the year.
> >
> > (e)   For stationary meters with flow rates of 115 L (30 gal) or more per minute, all sales by the same person or company for the same metering application at the same location shall be sold temperature compensated in 12-month increments. For example, a company may not choose to operate some stationary meters with automatic temperature compensators and others without. Nor may a company choose to engage the automatic temperature compensator on a device only during certain times of the year.
> >
> > (f)   For loading rack meters, except for contract sales, all sales by the same person or company for the same metering application at the same location shall be sold temperature compensated in 12-month increments. Contract sales may have the method of sale specified within the terms of the contract, but whichever method of sale is selected shall be implemented in 12-month increments. For example, a company may not choose to engage the automatic temperature compensator on a device only during certain times of the year.

> **2.XX.B.** – Where not in conflict with other statutes or regulations, petroleum products delivered through meters other than those specified in section 2.XX.A. shall be sold ~~without~~ the volume adjusted to compensate for temperature.
>
> ~~**Note 1:** As defined in the Handbook 130 Engine Fuels, Petroleum Products, and Automotive Lubricants Inspection Law, refined petroleum products are products obtained from distilling and processing of petroleum (crude oil), unfinished oils, recycled oils, natural gas liquids, refinery blend stocks, and other miscellaneous hydrocarbon compounds.~~
>
> ~~**Note 2:** Paragraphs 2.XX.A.(d) and (e) shall only be effective as long as temperature-compensated sales remain permissive in at least some relevant applications. If temperature compensation becomes mandatory for all relevant applications, then these paragraphs shall be removed.~~

Discussion: Selling fuel adjusted to the volume at 15 °C (60 °F) throughout the distribution system is the most equitable way fuel can be sold without the buyer or seller gaining a competitive advantage.

This item is considered in conjunction with a temperature compensation item that is before the Specifications and Tolerances (S&T) Committee, Item 331-3, although the S&T Committee's item is limited to vehicle-tank meters.

A similar proposal was made by the Northeast Weights and Measures Association (NEWMA) in 2000. NEWMA noted that Pennsylvania, New Hampshire, Maine, and Canada permit temperature compensation in sales of products like home heating fuel and retail gasoline. In 2001 the Committee withdrew this item after hearing testimony from several jurisdictions that opposed it.

The Committee has heard numerous comments in support of, and a few comments in opposition to, temperature-compensated sales of petroleum fuels. While most comments were generally supportive of the idea of temperature-compensated sales, the Committee received comments from a couple of jurisdictions that were concerned about the additional inspection time and resources that would be needed to test devices equipped with temperature compensators.

Among the comments received in support of temperature-compensated sales, there was a fair amount of disagreement about how this should be accomplished. Most of the discussion fell into one of three broad categories: (1) If temperature-compensated sales are allowed, what should they look like? (2) In which metering applications should temperature-compensated sales be allowed? (3) Should temperature-compensated sales be permissive or mandatory?

<u>What should temperature-compensated sales look like?</u>
The Committee heard from the Western Weights and Measures Association (WWMA), the Central Weights and Measures Association (CWMA), and the Southern Weights and Measures Association (SWMA) that temperature-compensated sales needed to have certain parameters established so that all sales conducted in this manner are comparable. All three regions agreed that (1) temperature-compensated sales should be adjusted to the volume at 15 °C (60 °F), (2) temperature compensation should be accomplished through automatic means, (3) indicating and recording elements and all written representations should indicate that the volume delivered is temperature compensated, and (4) all sales by the same person/company for the same metering application within the same jurisdiction must be sold either compensated or uncompensated for full calendar years.

The Committee adopted these criteria into its recommendation.

<u>In which metering applications should temperature-compensated sales be allowed?</u>
The Committee heard from the WWMA and the SWMA that temperature-compensated sales should be allowed in all metering applications through meters with flow rates of 20 gal or more per minute. The flow rate of 20 gal per minute was selected because it was believed this would effectively allow temperature-compensated sales in all

applications except for standard retail motor-fuel devices. Both regions thought that temperature-compensated sales should be prohibited through standard retail motor-fuel devices.

The Committee heard from the CWMA that temperature-compensated sales should be limited to sales through vehicle tank meters, loading rack meters, and retail motor-fuel devices used exclusively for fueling trucks in sales of 100 gallons or more. The CWMA was concerned that allowing temperature-compensated sales in all metering applications except standard retail motor-fuel devices was overly broad. The CWMA was more comfortable with listing specific applications where temperature-compensated sales would be allowed and wanted it made clear that temperature-compensated sales would be prohibited through standard retail motor-fuel devices. The CWMA submitted the following language for the Committee's consideration:

> 2.X.X. – Wholesale refined petroleum product sales, sales of diesel fuel for truck refueling, and bulk sales of refined petroleum products of 100 gal or more may be dispensed through a meter that automatically compensates for the temperature to represent a gallon as 231 cubic inches at 60 °F.
>
> > 2.XX.1. – Implementation: Wholesalers and retailers that implement temperature compensation for wholesale sales, devices used exclusively for diesel fuel for truck refueling, or bulk sales of refined petroleum products of 100 gal or more shall implement this practice for all meters or dispensers at such location.
> >
> > 2.XX.2. – Temperature compensation disclosure: All meters or dispensers which employ temperature compensation shall be labeled on the meter or dispenser, and the printed representation must state that the volume represented has been corrected to 60 °F.
>
> Note 1. Refined petroleum products are derived from crude oils through processes such as catalytic cracking and fractional distillation.
>
> Note 2. Diesel fuel means a refined middle distillant suitable for use as a fuel in a compression-ignition (diesel) internal combustion engine.

The Committee's recommendation constitutes a compromise. The Committee agreed with the CWMA that the most prudent approach to temperature-compensated sales was to limit them to specific metering applications where almost everyone would be comfortable with its use. The Committee preferred the approach of the WWMA and the SWMA when defining retail motor-fuel devices used exclusively for fueling trucks and opted to define these devices based upon the meter flow rate rather than the delivery quantity. The Committee selected a flow rate of 115 L (30 gal) per minute to be consistent with the thresholds in the LMD code in Handbook 44. Section S.4.4. and Table T.2. of the LMD code specify the minimum flow rate of large-capacity metering devices as 115 L (30 gal) per minute. Finally, the Committee included language in the recommendation that makes it clear that, where not expressly permitted, temperature-compensated sales are prohibited.

Should temperature-compensated sales be permissive or mandatory?

The Committee heard from the WWMA and the SWMA that temperature-compensated sales should be implemented on a permissive basis, but that future mandatory dates should be established. Those who support a mandatory requirement believe that in the long run a permissive requirement will cause confusion within the marketplace and hinder the consumer's ability to make value comparisons between companies that sell products compensated and those that don't. Particularly with regard to home heating fuel sales, jurisdictions are concerned customers will not be told whether the price per gallon they are being quoted prior to the sale is compensated or uncompensated (even if it is disclosed on the invoice they receive after the delivery). In addition, even if consumers are informed that a product quote is for a temperature-compensated delivery, consumers won't know what it means and won't be able to make a meaningful comparison between quotes for compensated and uncompensated products. The WWMA and SWMA recommended that future mandatory dates be established based on a reasonable timetable for each type of metering application that takes into consideration equipment replacement costs and existing device life-expectancy. NIST suggested, as an alternative, that mandatory dates for each type of metering application be established initially for new installations and that later dates could be established for existing devices.

The Committee heard from the CWMA that temperature-compensated sales should be implemented on a purely permissive basis. The CWMA opposes the inclusion of any future mandatory dates at this time. The CWMA believes that temperature-compensated sales should be market-driven and that suppliers will make sales on a temperature-compensated basis when consumers demand it and should not be required to do so before then. Many jurisdictions believe that the imposition of a mandatory requirement is too burdensome on the industry, requiring upgrades and possibly the replacement of many meters without adequate justification.

The Committee agreed that the inclusion of mandatory dates during the initial implementation of this item was too controversial and would elicit too much opposition. The Committee felt it was important to get some form of regulation regarding temperature-compensated sales of petroleum adopted into Handbook 130 and thought that as many barriers as possible should be removed in order to achieve this goal. Although the Committee's recommendation reflects a purely permissive requirement for temperature-compensated sales, the Committee may be willing to consider establishing future mandatory dates if a need is demonstrated after this permissive regulation is implemented.

Finally, the Committee heard requests from the American Petroleum Institute (API) to: (1) recognize and permit different methods of sale at loading-rack meters when such sales are under contract, and (2) prohibit temperature compensated sales through stationary meters with flow rates of 115 L (30 gal) or more per minute. The Committee agreed with API's first request regarding contract sales, and included language in the loading-rack meter paragraph (2.XX.A (f)) to permit the method of sale to be determined by contract when an active and valid contract is present. The Committee carefully considered and then decided against API's request to prohibit temperature-compensated sales through high-flow stationary meters. The Committee rejected this request because the idea behind implementing a permissive temperature compensation standard is to allow the marketplace to drive the implementation of such a standard. The Committee has heard strong support for temperature-compensated sales through high-flow stationary meters from the market segment that uses these meters. The Committee believes that with the support of a well-educated and well-defined end user, it is inconsistent with the idea of marketplace-driven implementation for the Committee to create a barrier to temperature-compensated sales in this limited, well-defined application. The Committee notes that since this is a permissive requirement, the decision of whether or not to sell petroleum products with the volume adjusted to compensate for temperature remains with the seller, and that the seller will not incur any additional expense or be required to upgrade his equipment unless he makes the decision to change his current method of sale practices.

232-2   I   Biodiesel and Fuel Ethanol Labeling

Source: Central Weights and Measures Association (CWMA)

Recommendation: Add the biodiesel and fuel ethanol labeling requirements that currently appear in Handbook 130 Engine Fuels, Petroleum Products, and Automotive Lubricants Regulation to the Method of Sale Regulation.

Add the following text to the Method of Sale Regulation in Handbook 130:

> **2.XX. Biodiesel.**
>
> > **2.XX.1. Identification of Product.** – Biodiesel and biodiesel blends shall be identified by the capital letter B followed by the numerical value representing the volume percentage of biodiesel fuel. (Examples: B10, B20, B100)
> >
> > **2.XX.2. Labeling of Retail Dispensers Containing Between 5 % and 20 % Biodiesel.** Each retail dispenser of biodiesel blend containing more than 5 % and up to and including 20 % biodiesel shall be labeled with either:
> >
> > > **2.XX.2.1.** The capital letter B followed by the numerical value representing the volume percentage of biodiesel fuel and ending with "biodiesel blend." (Examples: B10 biodiesel blend, B20 biodiesel blend), or;

2.XX.2.2. The phrase "biodiesel blend between 5 % and 20 %" or similar words.

2.XX.3. Labeling of Retail Dispensers Containing More Than 20 % Biodiesel. – Each retail dispenser of biodiesel or biodiesel blend containing more than 20 % biodiesel shall be labeled with the capital letter B followed by the numerical value representing the volume percentage of biodiesel fuel and ending with either "biodiesel" or "biodiesel blend." (Examples: B100 Biodiesel, B60 Biodiesel Blend)

2.XX.4. Documentation for Dispenser Labeling Purposes. – The retailer shall be provided, at the time of delivery of the fuel, with a declaration of the volume percent biodiesel on an invoice, bill of lading, shipping paper, or other document. This documentation is for dispenser labeling purposes only; it is the responsibility of any potential blender to determine the amount of biodiesel in the diesel fuel prior to blending.

2.XX.5. Exemption. – Biodiesel blends containing 5 % or less biodiesel by volume are exempted from requirements 2.XX.1 through 2.XX.4.

2.YY. Fuel Ethanol.

2.YY.1. How to Identify Fuel Ethanol. – Fuel ethanol shall be identified by the capital letter E followed by the numerical value volume percentage. (Example: E85)

2.YY.2. Retail Dispenser Labeling. – Each retail dispenser of fuel ethanol shall be labeled with the capital letter E followed by the numerical value volume percent denatured ethanol and ending with the word "ethanol." (Example: E85 Ethanol)

2.YY.3. Additional Labeling Requirements. – Fuel ethanol shall be labeled with its automotive fuel rating in accordance with 16 CFR Part 306.

Discussion: This proposal does not impose any new requirements. These requirements have already been adopted and are published in the Engine Fuels, Petroleum Products, and Automotive Lubricants Regulation in Handbook 130. This proposal would place duplicate requirements into the Method of Sale Regulation.

Section 2.20. of the Method of Sale Regulation in Handbook 130 currently contains requirements for the disclosure of oxygenates in gasoline blends. Including requirements for the disclosure of biodiesel, biodiesel blends, and fuel ethanol is consistent with this practice and should be required in order to ensure consumers are fully informed when making purchasing decisions.

The Committee has received numerous comments in support of this item and has heard from the National Biodiesel Board that, in general, they support this item. However, the National Biodiesel Board has requested that the Committee keep this item on its agenda as an informational item until ASTM finalizes its recommendations for biodiesel specifications. Waiting for the ASTM biodiesel specifications before moving this item forward for a vote will ensure there are no conflicts resulting from language discrepancies between the ASTM biodiesel specifications and the wording of this item.

The Committee has heard some concerns about perceived discrepancies between this item's ethanol labeling requirements and the Federal Trade Commission's (FTC's) regulation regarding ethanol labeling. These concerns were also raised during the placement of this language in the Engine Fuels, Petroleum Products, and Automotive Lubricants Regulation. The Committee has previously evaluated this with the assistance of the FTC and believes there is no conflict.

L&R Committee 2006 Final Report

250 INTERPRETATIONS AND GUIDELINES

250-1   V   Basic Engine Fuels, Petroleum Products, and Lubricants Laboratory

Source: Western Weights and Measures Association (WWMA)

Recommendation: Remove the Basic Engine Fuels, Petroleum Products, and Lubricants Laboratory Guidelines from Handbook 130 and instead post an updated version (see Appendix C) at http://www.nist.gov/owm.

Amend Handbook 130 Interpretations and Guidelines Section 2.6.6. by striking all of the current text and replacing it with the following:

> **2.6.6. Basic Engine Fuels, Petroleum Products, and Lubricants Laboratory**
> **(Developed by the Petroleum Subcommittee)**
>
> <u>The petroleum fuels and lubricant laboratory is an integral element of an inspection program and is generally developed to satisfy the testing requirements as described in the laws and rules of the regulating agency. Guidelines have been developed to assist states in evaluating their options of employing a private lab or building or expanding their own lab. This information is available at http://www.nist.gov/owm.</u>

Discussion: Handbook 130 Interpretations and Guidelines Section 2.6.6., Basic Engine Fuels, Petroleum Products, and Lubricants Laboratory, was adopted in 1994. Since that time it has not been updated despite the fact that laboratory equipment and costs change continually. It is believed that posting these guidelines on the Internet will allow them to be updated in a more expedient manner than what is permitted by the NCWM process. Eliminating the NCWM process from the updating of these guidelines is not believed to be detrimental because the guidelines are informative, not regulatory.

The Committee has received no comments opposing this item. The Committee has also assigned the Petroleum Subcommittee the task of reviewing and updating these guidelines on a bi-annual basis and providing the Committee with recommendations for updates.

The Committee has expressed its support for the request from NIST that it not publish a new edition of Handbook 130 this year since the removal of this guideline is the only change being made. Upon its adoption, NIST will publish the new guidelines on its website and will update the web version of Handbook 130 to reflect the changes set forth by this item. In addition, NIST will issue a letter and addendum sheet to NCWM members informing them:

- That the current, 2006, version of Handbook 130 will remain valid through 2007,
- Of the change that has been made to the handbook, and
- The location of the updated laboratory guidelines on the web.

270 OTHER   ITEMS

270-1 D Developing   Items

The NCWM established a mechanism to disseminate information about emerging items which have merit and are of national interest. Developing items have not received sufficient review by all parties affected by the proposals or may be insufficiently developed to warrant review by the NCWM L&R Committee. The developing items listed are currently under review by at least one regional association, subcommittee, or work group.

The developing items are listed in the following appendices according to the specific NIST handbook into which they fall:

Appendix A – Handbook 130
Appendix B – Handbook 133

The Committee encourages interested parties to examine the proposals included in the appendices and to send their comments to the contact listed in each part.

The Committee asks that the regional weights and measures associations, subcommittees, and work groups continue their work to fully develop each proposal. Should an association, subcommittee, or work group decide to discontinue work on a developing item, the Committee asks that it be notified. When the status of an item changes because the submitter withdraws the item, the item will be listed in a table below. For more details on items that are moved from the Developing Items list to the Committee's main agenda, refer to the new reference number in the main agenda.

Joe Benavides, Texas, Chairperson
James Cassidy, Cambridge, Massachusetts
Vicky Dempsey, Montgomery County, Ohio
Dennis Johannes, California
Stephen Benjamin, North Carolina

Vince Orr, ConAgra Foods, Associate Membership Committee Representative
Doug Hutchinson, Canada, Technical Advisor
Brian Lemon, Canada, Technical Advisor
Kathryn Dresser, NIST, Technical Advisor
Tom Coleman, NIST, Technical Advisor

Laws and Regulations Committee

THIS PAGE LEFT INTENTIONALLY BLANK.

Appendix A

Item 270-1: Developing Items – Handbook 130

Part 1   D   Premium Diesel Lubricity

Source: Southern Weights and Measures Association (SWMA)

Proposal: Amend Section 2.2.1. in Handbook 130 Uniform Engine Fuels, Petroleum Products, and Automotive Lubricants Regulation as follows:

2.2.1. Premium Diesel Fuel – All diesel fuels identified on retail dispensers, bills of lading, invoices, shipping papers, or other documentation with terms such a premium, super, supreme, plus, or premier must conform to the following requirements:

> (a) Cetane Number – A minimum cetane number of 47.0 as determined by ASTM Standard Test Method D 613.
>
> (b) Low Temperature Operability – A cold flow performance measurement which meets the ASTM D 975 tenth percentile minimum ambient air temperature charts and maps by either ASTM Standard Test Method D 2500 (Cloud Point) or ASTM Standard Test Method D 4539 (Low Temperature Flow Test, LTFT). Low temperature operability is only applicable October 1 - March 31 of each year.
>
> (c) Thermal Stability – A minimum reflectance measurement of 80 % as determined by ASTM Standard Test Method D 6468 (180 min, 150 °C).
>
> (d) Lubricity – A maximum wear scar diameter of 520 μm as determined by ASTM D 6079. ~~If an enforcement jurisdiction's single test of more than 560 μm is determined, a second test shall be conducted. If the average of the two tests is more than 560 μm, the sample does not conform to the requirements of this part.~~

Discussion: A member of the petroleum industry believes that the test and associated tolerances for lubricity on premium diesel specified in Section 2.2.1.(d) are inconsistent with that for regular diesel. Effective January 1, 2005, the test tolerance for regular diesel lubricity will be the ASTM D 6079 reproducibility of 136 μm (see ASTM D 975-04b). NCWM has chosen to accept the ASTM reproducibility limits for all diesel (D 975) and gasoline (D 4814) properties (see Section 7.2.2., Reproducibility), but has chosen a different reproducibility limit for premium diesel lubricity without providing any explanation as to why the ASTM reproducibility limit is insufficient. If the NCWM intends to impose a stricter lubricity requirement for premium diesel, it should designate a tighter specification for this property instead of a different test tolerance (e.g., for regular and premium gasoline, premium has a different octane specification than regular but the test tolerance is the same). ASTM reproducibility limits are, by definition, based on establishing a 95 % probability that product that should pass, will pass. Applying an average test as specified in Section 2.2.1.(d) reduces this probability to only 80 %.

The Committee received comments from several members of the Premium Diesel Work Group (Work Group) who do not support the item as presented by the petroleum industry member. Work Group members believed the process that led to the current definition was very thorough and complete and the premium diesel lubricity requirements were established with a full understanding of their implications. The Work Group members felt that knowledgeable individuals provided input to the process, which lead to the consensus position contained in the current regulation. The work being done by the Work Group was reported at meetings of ASTM Subcommittee E-2 every six months. The current regulation has been endorsed by the American Petroleum Institute, the Engine Manufacturer's Association, and the NCWM.

Prior to this requirement being adopted, the ASTM Lubricity Task Force conducted a great deal of research on this topic. Based on their research, the ASTM Lubricity Task Force had concluded that a limit of 520 μm would meet the requirements of equipment in the field. Since the passage of this model regulation, ASTM included a lubricity requirement for No. 1 and No. 2 diesel fuel effective January 1, 2005. The ASTM requirement is also 520 μm.

Work Group members reported that when this regulation was being written, fuels with adequate lubricity provided a functional benefit to the end user. The Work Group agreed with the ASTM Lubricity Task Force that 520 μm was the correct limit to set for premium diesel. However, the Work Group's review process also indicated increased pump wear for fuels with High-Frequency Reciprocating Rig (HFRR) values greater than 560 μm. The current reproducibility value of the HFRR test method would have placed enforcement well beyond the 560 μm level, essentially allowing fuels with little lubricity protection to be sold as premium. The Work Group believed they could not recommend a premium fuel standard that would permit excessive pump wear. Using the statistical tools provided in ASTM D 3244, the Work Group evaluated an enforcement limit of 560 μm. The statistical tools indicated that a single laboratory reporting the assigned test value would have an enforcement limit of approximately 80 % probability of acceptance, while the average of two separate laboratories reporting the assigned test value would have an enforcement limit of approximately 90 % probability of acceptance. It was agreed that for a premium fuel the average of two test results was the best approach given the current test methods and precision available. Therefore, if a test exceeds 560 μm, then a second test must be run. The average of the two tests must exceed 560 μm before a violation would occur. At this time, the Work Group members believe this remains the best approach.

The Committee has forwarded this proposal to the Petroleum Subcommittee for review and has requested that the Subcommittee provide the Committee with its recommendation. The Subcommittee has requested that this item remain on the Committee's agenda as a developing item until the Subcommittee can make a recommendation.

Contact: NCWM Petroleum Subcommittee, Ron Hayes, Chair, (573) 751-2922, ron.hayes@mda.mo.gov.

Part 2   D   Guidelines for the Method of Sale of Fresh Fruits and Vegetables

Source: Northeast Weights and Measures Association (NEWMA)

Proposal: Amend Handbook 130 Interpretations and Guidelines Section 2.3.2. to recognize and support innovation in modern retail food marketing approaches at all forms of outlets from typical grocery stores to the age-old farm markets.

Discussion: The method of sale guidelines for the sale of fresh fruits and vegetables that currently appear in Handbook 130 are outdated and in need of revision. The present guidelines do not recognize current retailing practices and are not expansive enough to cover many exotic and unusual fruits and vegetables that are becoming more common in the marketplace. Additionally, the present guidelines do not take into consideration the necessary limitations experienced by retailers at roadside stands and farmers markets.

The original proposal for this item reflected input from only a single jurisdiction. The Committee was informed that several industry associations have requested an opportunity to review and respond to this proposal. The Committee believes there are several factual errors within the classifications of produce provided, and there are several types of produce still not covered by the proposal provided. The Committee has made this item developmental so it may receive input from jurisdictions throughout the country and from affected industry associations and businesses.

Contact: Ross Andersen, NY Bureau of Weights and Measures, (518) 457-3146, ross.andersen@agmkt.state.ny.us.

Appendix B

Item 270-1: Developing Items – Handbook 133

Part 1   D   Moisture Loss

Source: Northeast Weights and Measures Association (NEWMA)

Proposal: Amend Handbook 133 Section 2.3, Moisture Allowances (pages 17 through 19 of the handbook) to provide clearer guidance.

Discussion: The issue of moisture loss is complex. NIST Handbook 133 currently provides specific guidance on the determination and application of moisture allowances for only a limited number of commodities. Concerns have been raised that this guidance is confusing and difficult to understand, particularly with regard to when moisture loss is applied (i.e., at the time of inspection or subsequent to the inspection). Requests have been received to reword this section to make it easier to understand and apply.

In addition, NIST Handbook 133 provides little guidance on the determination and application of moisture allowances for commodities other than those specifically listed. Weights and measures jurisdictions across the country have been struggling with how to properly handle moisture loss during packaging inspections and need more definite guidance on this issue.

The Committee does not believe it has the time or expertise to properly address the issue of moisture loss within the structure of the NCWM. The Committee has decided to activate a NIST Moisture Loss Work Group to establish more effective and extensive guidance to the NCWM regarding the proper determination and application of moisture loss. The Committee decided to submit a funding request to the NCWM Board of Directors to fund one individual from each regional association, selected by the regional association, to participate in the work group.

Contact: NIST Moisture Loss Work Group – Tom Coleman, Technical Advisor, (301) 975-4868, t.coleman@nist.gov.

THIS PAGE LEFT INTENTIONALLY BLANK.

Appendix C

Item 250-1: Basic Engine Fuels, Petroleum Products, and Lubricants Laboratory Guidelines

Introduction

The petroleum fuels and lubricant laboratory is an integral element of an inspection program and is generally developed to satisfy the testing requirements as described in the laws and rules of the regulating agency. This document outlines the basic facets of such a laboratory and can be used as a model to initiate or upgrade a program. Since a testing program is of little value unless recognized standards and methods are utilized, this description of a model laboratory has been developed under the assumption that recognized ASTM International and SAE International standards and test methods have been incorporated into the laws, rules, and policies of the regulating agency.

This document provides sufficient information to investigate cost associated with the development of a fuels and lubricant laboratory. Information pertaining to facility needs, recommended ASTM test procedures, test equipment, and the number of personnel required for staffing has been included. Hidden costs associated with the unique working environment of laboratories are often overlooked during initial evaluations; therefore sections have also been included dealing with quality assurance, safety, and hazardous materials.

Laboratories may be required to perform additional analysis outside the purview of consumer regulations, e.g., analyses pertaining to environmental regulations or tax fraud investigations. This document will not address those areas specifically; however, information presented here may assist in the determination of general costs and requirements.

State-Operated or Contract

The decision to operate a state testing laboratory, to enter into a contractual agreement with a private testing laboratory, or to have a hybrid of the two depends on a variety of factors: the scope of the program, funding sources, political climate, etc. The question is often asked: "Is there a point at which it is cheaper for a state to operate its own fuels laboratory?" The Motor Fuel Task Force assembled in 1984 concluded that a program testing 6000 samples per year (500 samples per month) is the minimum level to justify building and equipping a fuel laboratory.

Consideration must be given to the time required for the laboratory to complete the analyses. The value of any inspection program is diminished if laboratory turnaround time is so great that the product is consumed before the results of an analysis are known. If a contract laboratory is chosen, analysis time should be given consideration during negotiations to ensure an effective program. Because of the hazardous nature of fuels, transportation can be difficult and costly and should be factored into the decision. A state-owned laboratory should be assured the proper resources, e.g., a full staff and well-maintained instruments, to be able to meet satisfactory turnaround time.

Laboratory Facility

A testing laboratory requires a unique building designed to accommodate laboratory instruments ranging from a delicate gas chromatograph to octane engines capable of producing severe vibrations. In addition, extremely flammable liquids will be stored and tested throughout the facility. Obviously, the facility design must minimize the chances for explosion and fire and also be capable of withstanding the forces of an explosion. National Fire Protection Association (NFPA) 45, "Standard on Fire Protection for Laboratories Using Chemicals," should be reviewed with contractors to ensure minimum standards are met.

The actual design of the laboratory is dependant upon the products which will be tested. For example, if the octane or cetane number is to be determined, special considerations must be made for foundation and utilities.

Special considerations should be given to the following:

1. Sufficient ventilation to ensure workers are not unduly exposed to gasoline fumes and other toxic vapors.

2. Fume hoods and exhaust systems in laboratory areas.

3. Drain lines resistant to acid and petroleum products.

4. Traps to prevent petroleum products from entering the sewer system.

5. Special foundations for ASTM/Cooperative Fuel Research Committee (CFR) engines. It is recommended that sufficient foundations for future expansion be installed during initial construction.

6. Necessary safety equipment, such as fire blankets, fire extinguishers, eyewash stations, etc.

7. Automatic fire extinguishing system for laboratory areas. The extinguishing system's design should include considerations regarding the susceptibility of laboratory instruments to damage when exposed to water or dry chemicals.

8. An adequate heating, ventilation, and air conditioning (HVAC) system to handle excess heat generated by distillation instruments and octane engines.

9. A properly designed and sized electrical system.

10. The laboratory's design to ensure all fuel testing can be performed in accordance with ASTM requirements. Volume 05.04 of the Annual Book of ASTM Standards contains valuable information regarding the design of a knock-testing laboratory.

11. Automatic hydrocarbon monitors to warn of critical accumulation of explosive vapors.

Several fixed equipment items are necessary for the laboratory's operation, including:

1. Air compressor, vacuum pump and piping of sufficient size to supply the entire laboratory's needs.

2. Gas and water piped to all areas of the laboratory.

3. Storage area for retained evidence, reference fuel and excess fuel and lubricant after analysis. Depending on the number of samples, this may consist of a properly ventilated storage area with locking storage cabinets and 208 L (55 gal) drums, to a flammable storage room and several 1892 L (500 gal) storage tanks. (Larger tanks may be needed if they are to supplement the program's vehicle's needs.)

The size of the laboratory will depend upon the products tested and the estimated sample flow. The following space listing is for a small laboratory capable of testing approximately 6000 fuel samples per year. Some space requirements, such as those for octane testing, may seem large, but it is strongly recommended that two additional engine foundations be installed during initial construction.

1. Office, bathroom facilities, conference room, etc. (as required). No space requirements are listed as this must be determined by the user based on program needs and local building codes.

2. Octane laboratory – designed for four engines (75 m^2 [750 ft^2]).

3. General laboratory (70 m^2 [750 ft^2]).

4. Distillation laboratory (37 m^2 [400 ft^2]).

5. Shipping and receiving (includes preparation area for empty sample containers) (37 m^2 [400 ft^2]).

6. Flash point laboratory (19 m^2 [200 ft^2]).

7. Shop area (23 m^2 [225 ft^2]).

8. Storage for supplies (23 m^2 [225 ft^2]).

9. Secured, cooled, and ventilated sample and flammable storage area (23 m^2 [225 ft^2]). (Insulation and a dedicated ventilation and cooling system should be considered for this room.)

Total square footage (exclusive of item 1) – 30 m^2 (322 ft^2) including offices, bathroom facilities, hallways, etc., the total building size may exceed 372 m^2 (4000 ft^2). It is not necessary to isolate each testing operation into separate laboratories. However, because of the noise generated, it is recommended that the test engines (octane and cetane) be placed in a separate room.

If lubricant testing is to be performed, the size of the general laboratory will need to be increased. The amount of increase is dependant upon the tests which will be performed. However, if work is limited to viscosity measurement, an additional 37 m^2 (400 ft^2) should be sufficient.

Tests and ASTM Test Procedures

Careful consideration should be given to the selection of laboratory test procedures since these selections will affect instrument costs, number of personnel, timeliness of samples, and confidence in results. As previously mentioned, ASTM and SAE specifications and test methods are universally recognized standards for fuels and lubricants and should be the primary choice for test procedures. The ASTM Subcommittee D 02 on Petroleum Products and Lubricants is responsible for developing specifications and test procedures and is generally comprised of representatives from the petroleum industry, automotive manufacturers, and regulating agencies. This representation ensures that test procedures have been reviewed by each segment of the testing community and laboratory results obtained utilizing these procedures will be widely accepted.

New instrumental methods are often introduced to facilitate testing. Chemical methods have been devised to replace or screen physical methods which may enhance efficiency by reducing staff or analysis time necessary to perform physical methods. These methods are normally devised for a controlled environment, such as a processing plant, where physical parameters may be drawn with confidence. A new laboratory is cautioned to refrain from investing in this instrumentation and the laboratory expertise necessary to perform the test procedures until they are approved by ASTM. Screening methods have been employed by state laboratories to maintain or increase sample coverage. Screening procedures are a deviation of accepted ASTM procedures; certain sections of a procedure may be excluded or modified, such as chilling a sample to the appropriate temperature or accurately timing a distillation analysis. When a screen sample exceeds a predetermined parameter, the sample is analyzed using the proper ASTM procedure. Screening should be discouraged as a means to increase sample coverage. Strategies, such as selective sampling and testing, should be employed as a means for effective regulation.

Following are references to ASTM and SAE specifications and testing procedures which form an effective nucleus for a testing laboratory with regulatory responsibilities. ASTM test methods listed here do not necessarily exclude other ASTM procedures that are designed for the purpose and that give comparable results. The significance of each of these analyses is included in the ASTM specifications. Some of the test procedures listed make provisions to allow the use of automated equipment. Such equipment is usually more expensive. However, the increased cost can be recovered in a high production lab by reduced labor costs. The asterisks after test methods indicate a preferred method due to cost or ease of implementation.

L&R Committee 2006 Final Report
Appendix C – Item 250-1

Spark Ignition Engine Fuel Specifications – D 4814

1. Distillation   D 86

2. Octane (Antiknock Index)
   Research   D 2699
   Motor   D 2700

3. Vapor Pressure
   Dry Method   D 4953
   Automatic Method   D 5190*
   Mini Method   D 5191*
   Mini Method - Atmospheric   D 5482*

4. Oxygenate Content
   GC with TC or FID   D 4815
   GC with OFID   D 5599
   Infrared Spectroscopy   D 5845

5. Sulfur Content (Due to environmental law and regulations, the sulfur limits shown in D 4814 may be significantly higher than specified. The detection limit and precision of each method should be considered when selecting a test method.)

   X-Ray Spectrometry   D 2622
   Microcoulometry   D 3120
   Ultraviolet Fluorescence   D 5453

6. Water Tolerance   D 6422

7. Workmanship   D 4814

Diesel Fuel Specifications – D 975

1. Flash Point   D 93

2. Distillation   D 86

3. Sulfur Content (The appropriate test method is dependent upon the grade. The forthcoming reduction in sulfur content by EPA starting in June, 2006, will require equipment with lower detection limits and better precision.)

   X-Ray Spectrometry   D 2622
   Microcoulometry   D 3120
   X-Ray Fluorescence   D 4294

4. Cloud Point
   Manual Method   D 2500
   Stepped Cooling (Automatic)   D 5771
   Linear Cooling Rate (Automatic)   D 5772
   Constant Cooling Rate (Automatic)   D 5773

5. Water and Sediment   D 2709

6. Cetane   D 613

    7. Lubricity   D 6079

Kerosene Specifications – D 3699

    1. Flash Point   D 56

    2. Distillation   D 86

    3. Sulfur Content
        X-Ray Spectrometry   D 2622
        X-Ray Fluorescence   D 4294*
        Ultraviolet Fluorescence   D 5453

    4. Color   D 156

    5. Water and Sediment   D 1796

Aviation Turbine Fuel - D 1655

    1. Flash Point   D 56

    2. Distillation   D 86

    3. Water Reaction   D 1094

    4. Freeze Point   D 2386

Motor Oil – SAE J300

    1. Kinematic Viscosity   D 445

    2. Cold Cranking Simulator   D 5293

Gear Oil – SAE J306

    1. Kinematic Viscosity   D 445

    2. Brookfield Viscosity   D 2983

Automatic Transmission Fluid

    1. Kinematic Viscosity   D 445

    2. Brookfield Viscosity   D 2983

Laboratory Equipment and Supplies

Scientific instrumentation is typically more expensive than initially anticipated even when one has experience purchasing equipment. ASTM has approved methods utilizing automated instruments which may prove to be a better long-term investment when the cost of operating personnel is included. The costs of equipment and supplies change, therefore providing estimates in this document would be of little value. Because of the relatively small demand for laboratory equipment, it is common to have only one source. However, when possible, obtaining competitive bids can reduce costs. Purchasing used equipment from other labs or vendors can provide a source of equipment at reduced costs.

Information Management System

No recommendations are made for an information management system. However, it should be noted that an information management system is an effective tool to manage data and statistical information when devising sampling strategies and when measuring the general effectiveness of a program.

Minimum requirements for an information management system include a database server and database adequate to handle sample biographical and analyses information. A means to network technicians and staff to the information is necessary to facilitate transfer of information. Considerations for software security and equipment security (limited access to the database server) should be given to ensure the integrity of the data.

Many departments have established information management centers which are consulted for this information. Generally, these departments have a particular protocol for developing information management systems.

Office Equipment and Supplies

No listing is given since needs are determined by the program's scope. However, the costs of items such as desks, filing cabinets, computers, forms, and miscellaneous office supplies must be considered when planning an initial budget.

Quality Assurance/Quality Control

The previous sections have addressed structural aspects of an engine fuels testing laboratory: building requirements, testing procedures, and analytical instruments. The management system for a laboratory is as unique as the structural requirements. Quality assurance/quality control programs were originally devised to give statistical verification of analytical results; however, they are now evolving to become the standard management model for laboratories. Chain of custody procedures, sample retention procedures, sample distribution procedures, and documentation of each step have been integrated into the quality assurance program.

ASTM has developed two documents which provide quality assurance guidelines for a petroleum laboratory. They are ASTM D 6792, Quality System in Petroleum Products and Lubricants Testing Laboratories and ASTM D 6299, Applying Statistical Quality Assurance Techniques to Evaluate Analytical Measurement System Performance. The first document, D 6792, provides a guide to the essential aspects of a quality assurance program. It includes such issues as sample management, record management, accurate test data, proficiency testing, corrective actions, and training. The second document, D 6299, describes in great detail methods to assure test precision and accuracy.

Another source of information in establishing a quality assurance program is the International Organization for Standardization (ISO) model quality assurance program, ISO 9000. There is no accreditation program specifically for state testing laboratories, and ISO 9000 accreditation is currently quite expensive; however, the ISO 9000 is an excellent model to use in developing a management system.

One excellent method to evaluate the performance of a laboratory is to compare the results obtained with other laboratories. ASTM has developed an Interlaboratory Crosscheck Program to achieve this goal. Samples are periodically sent to participating labs for analysis. The results are submitted to the summarizer and statically compared to other participating laboratories. The summarized results are then compared to the published precision statements. Coded summary reports (to maintain confidentiality) are sent to each participant. The program includes automatic transmission fluid, aviation turbine fuel, engine oil, gear oil, gasoline and diesel fuel as well as other products.

ASTM operates a National Exchange Group (NEG) to distribute fuels among participating laboratories and provides a statistical report of the results. There are three subgroups of the NEG: the Motor Fuel Exchange Group, the Diesel Fuel Exchange Group, and the Aviation Gasoline Exchange Group. Of the three types of participation, only two will concern a state laboratory: a member laboratory receives monthly samples and agrees to participate in special method research; and a "quarterly participant" receives two sets of samples every three months but is not bound to run special tests. The NEG will provide a means for assessment of quality at the national level. There are also regional groups which provide similar quality assessment exchange programs: Appalachian, Atlantic, Great

Lakes, Mid-Continent, Northwest, Pacific Coast, Rocky Mountain, Texas Regional and Louisiana Gulf Coast, Sabine, and Texas City-Houston Subgroups.

Safety Program

A laboratory can be an extremely hazardous work environment, so safety must be integrated into all operations of a laboratory. The Occupational Safety and Health Administration (OSHA) established a requirement effective January 1, 1991, for laboratories to develop a Chemical Hygiene Plan (29 CRF 1910.1450). The guidelines for the Chemical Hygiene Plan were intentionally left general so that an organization's plan could be customized for unique situations in individual laboratories. The Chemical Hygiene Plan details an organization's responsibilities for safety training, supply and maintenance of safety equipment and personal protective equipment, monitoring employees' exposure level to hazardous chemicals, medical consultation and examination, and availability of documents addressing safety procedures and emergency response. The Chemical Hygiene Plan is required to be reviewed annually which provides a format to plan and track improvements.

Reference documents are an essential part of an effective safety program. Safety procedures should accompany and complement testing procedures to ensure an employee is performing functions in an acceptable manner. Emergency response manuals address hazardous or potentially hazardous situations. Proper procedures for handling large spills, evacuation of work areas, and employees who have been overexposed to hazardous materials are typically found in the emergency response manual. Material Safety Data Sheets (MSDS) contain pertinent information regarding the hazards of chemicals and the necessary precautions. These documents should be distributed to employees or located in an easily accessible location.

Coordination with local fire and hazmat (hazardous material) departments is essential to ensure rapid emergency response. A chemical inventory and a diagram of the laboratory space are often requested by these departments to expedite their response. Periodic review of the chemical inventory will ensure unnecessary chemicals will be disposed of in a timely manner.

The most effective safety tool is thorough training of employees. Each new employee should be trained with the Chemical Hygiene Plan, safety procedures, emergency response manual, and MSDS's. Subsequent review sessions should be scheduled to ensure familiarity of individual responsibilities and actions. Educational videos are available specifically addressing laboratory safety which can assist in the training process. Hands-on training should be utilized to demonstrate the proper use of fire extinguishers, fire blankets, and other safety equipment in the laboratory. An effective safety program will produce aware employees who can suggest enhancements to the safety of the laboratory.

Personal safety equipment should be provided to all laboratory personnel. Eye protection, lab coats/aprons, and gloves will provide minimum protections. If the use of a fume hood is not practical and an employee is exposed to petroleum or chemical fumes, organic respirators should be provided to minimize exposure. Determination of which equipment is necessary for handling particular chemicals can be found in the MSDS accompanying the chemicals.

General laboratory safety equipment should be considered during the design or selection of a building. In addition to a good ventilation system, fume hoods should be provided where practical to isolate fumes from the laboratory. Due to the explosive nature of gasoline, even safety equipment needs to be evaluated for safety; for example, explosion-proof motors should be installed to evacuate fumes from a hood. Eyewash stations, fire extinguishers, emergency showers, and fire blankets should all be placed strategically for maximum protection.

In the event of a spill, several safety items will prove useful. Activated charcoal, sold under a variety of names, is effective for absorbing small petroleum spills with the added benefit of quickly reducing vaporization. Other companies offer pads to quickly absorb spills. Similar products are offered to neutralize and absorb acids and bases. Safety signs should be posted at the entrance of each laboratory room listing possible hazards and restricted activities (e.g., No Smoking, Flammables, Eye Protection Required, etc.). These signs assist visitors and emergency response personnel to identify hazards quickly.

L&R Committee 2006 Final Report
Appendix C – Item 250-1

Hazardous Waste

Testing laboratories generate quantities of hazardous waste. Waste chemicals from various analyses and residual samples must be stored and disposed of in an appropriate manner. The majority of regulations for storage, disposal, and documentation of hazardous materials may be found in EPA's SARA Title III, 40 CFR 1500. Additional regulations and permits may be required by state, county or municipal agencies. Familiarity with the regulations will be advantageous when considering the design of the laboratory. Specific expenses related to hazardous waste disposal will often be determined by local regulations and the availability of hazardous waste handlers. Some companies provide disposal services which recycle products. This type of service is usually less expensive and provides protection from future "cradle to grave" liabilities. Therefore, waste materials should be segregated to take advantage of recycling services.

Personnel

The staffing requirements for a testing laboratory will be dependent on the number of samples, the number of tests performed on the samples, and the testing instruments chosen. The staff recommended here will be suitable for a fuels testing laboratory with moderate automation (auto-sampler for the gas chromatograph, automated RVP instrument, etc.) running approximately 6000 to 8000 samples per year.

1 Laboratory Administrator

2 Chemists

2 CFR Engine Operators

2 Laboratory Technicians

1 Clerk

The laboratory administrator should have strong management skills and familiarity with laboratory operations and chemical techniques. The administrator's responsibilities include the development and implementation of the quality assurance program, safety program, and hazardous waste program, as well as providing guidance for the daily operation of the laboratory.

The chemists should have a strong chemistry background and familiarity with instrumental techniques. In addition to normal analytical responsibilities, chemists should assist with the review of analytical results by technicians. Chemists also can assist in the development and implementation of the quality assurance, safety, and hazardous waste programs.

The engine operators are the most difficult positions to fill. The ideal operator will have petrochemical experience with a mechanic's background since the majority of the engine maintenance will be performed by the operators. The petroleum industry estimates approximately five years of engine operation is necessary to develop an expertise. To expedite this process, engine operators should periodically attend training workshops and regional exchange group meetings. Laboratory technicians should have laboratory experience and a familiarity with scientific methods. Cross training of these individuals is an effective means of maintaining an even workflow through the laboratory.

Concluding Note

There is no better way to understand the complexities of testing than to visit a state with an active program. Several states, such as Arkansas, California, Florida, Georgia, Maryland, North Carolina, Missouri, Michigan, Washington and Tennessee (a contractual laboratory) have active programs and are willing to host tours of their facilities. Interested parties are encouraged to make such a visit.

References

John E. Nunemaker, "Planning Laboratories: A Step by Step Process" *American Laboratory,* March 1987, 19 (4), 104 - 112.

Jerry Koenigsberg, "Building a Safe Laboratory Environment" *American Laboratory,* June 1987, 19 (9), 96 - 106.

THIS PAGE LEFT INTENTIONALLY BLANK.

Appendix D

NCWM Petroleum Subcommittee Report

The Premium Diesel Work Group and NCWM Petroleum Subcommittee met from 4:00 to 6:00 p.m. on December 6, 2005, in Norfolk, Virginia. This meeting was during the ASTM D2 meeting on Petroleum Products with twenty-five members and guests present. The main purpose of this meeting was to discuss the NCWM lubricity requirement for premium diesel. This item now appears on the L&R Committee agenda in Appendix A as Item 270-1 Part 1. (Page L&R-10)

Several options were discussed including:
- Removal of the 560 μm enforcement tolerance;
- Removal of the 560 μm enforcement tolerance and lower the 520 μm requirement;
- Elimination of the lubricity requirement from the premium diesel definition.

Discussion:
- Particularly for the term "premium" a higher assurance of protection from equipment damage is essential.
- Once a level of protection has been met, lowering the requirement to a more restrictive value provides no additional benefit.
- Do not lower the 520μm without supportive data.
- The committee discussed activities underway at ASTM:
  > An HFRR workshop will be meeting in the first quarter of 2006 to discuss ways to improve this test method, hoping to reduce the lab-to-lab variability.
  > A CRC test program will begin in the near future on new equipment used in light duty passenger vehicles with high pressure common rail injection systems. A specification change may result from data generated from this program.

Summary: The Subcommittee decided not to make a change at this time without supportive data. The Subcommittee encouraged the equipment manufacturers to provide any new data that would support a specification change. Otherwise, the Subcommittee will wait to see the outcome of the CRC program and the HFRR test method task force recommendations.

The Subcommittee also discussed the need to do a complete review of the motor fuel regulation because some ASTM standards have changed since the last revision.

One possible future date and location discussed was to meet immediately following the NCWM 2007 Interim Meeting in Jacksonville, Florida.

Submitted by:
Ronald G. Hayes
Chairman NCWM Petroleum Subcommittee

THIS PAGE LEFT INTENTIONALLY BLANK.

Report of the
Specifications and Tolerances Committee

Clark Cooney, Chairman
Assistant Administrator
Measurement Standards Division
Oregon Department of Agriculture

300 INTRODUCTION

This is the final report of the Committee on Specifications and Tolerances (S&T) (hereinafter referred to as "Committee") for the 91st Annual Meeting of the National Conference on Weights and Measures (NCWM). The report is based on the Interim Report offered in the NCWM Publication 16, "Committee Reports," testimony at public hearings, comments received from the regional weights and measures associations and other parties, the addendum sheets issued at the Annual Meeting, and actions taken by the membership at the voting session of the Annual Meeting.

Table A identifies the agenda items in the report by Reference Key Number, Item Title, and Page Number. The item numbers are those assigned in the Interim Meeting Agenda. Voting items are indicated with a " **V**," or if the item was part of the voting consent calendar by the suffix " **VC**" after the item number. Items marked with an " **I**" after the reference key number are information items. Items marked with a " **D**" after the key numbers are developing items. The developing designation indicates that an item, while it has merit, may not be adequately developed for action at the national level. Items marked "**W**" have been withdrawn from consideration. Items marked with a " **W**" will generally be referred to the regional weights and measures associations because they either need additional development, analysis, and input or did not have sufficient Committee support to bring them before NCWM. Table B lists the appendices to the report, Table C identifies the acronyms for organizations and technical terms used throughout the report, and Table D provides a summary of the results of the voting on the Committee's items and the report in entirety.

This report contains recommendations to amend National Institute of Standards and Technology (NIST) Handbook 44, 2006 Edition, "Specifications, Tolerances, and Other Technical Requirements for Weighing and Measuring Devices." Proposed revisions to the handbook are shown in **bold face print** by ~~striking out~~ information to be deleted and <u>underlining</u> information to be added. New items proposed for the handbook are designated as such and shown in **bold face print**.

Note: The policy of NIST is to use metric units of measurement in all of its publications; however, recommendations received by the NCWM technical committees have been printed in this publication as they were submitted and may, therefore, contain references to inch-pound units.

Table A
Index to Reference Key Items

Reference Key Number		Title of Item	Page
300		**INTRODUCTION**	1
310		**GENERAL CODE**	6
310-1	V	G-S.1.(d) Identification; Software for Not-Built-for-Purpose Devices	6
310-2	V	G-S.1.1. Location of Marking Information for Not-Built-for-Purpose Software-Based Devices	7
310-3	I	G-S.8.1. Multiple Weighing or Measuring Elements with a Single Provision for Sealing	8
310-4	W	G-T.1. (e) Acceptance Tolerances	9
320		**SCALES**	10
320-1	I	S.1.1. (c) Zero Indication; Requirements for Markings or Indications for Other than Digital Zero Indications	10
320-2	I	S.1.4.6. Height and Definition of Minimum Reading Distance, UR.2.10. Primary Indicating Elements Provided by the User, UR.2.11. Minimum Reading Distance, and Definitions of Minimum Reading Distance and Primary Indications	12
320-3	V	N.1.3.1. Bench or Counter Scales, N.1.3.8. All Other Scales Except Crane Scales, Hanging Scales, Hopper Scales, Wheel–Load Weighers, and Portable Axle-Load Weighers, and Appendix D; Definitions of Bench Scale and Counter Scale	15
320-4	I	Table 4. Minimum Test Weights and Test Loads	19
320-5	W	Table 6. Maintenance Tolerances	20
320-6	VC	T.N.4.5.1. Time Dependence; Class II, III, and IIII Non-automatic Weighing Instruments	21
320-7	VC	T.N.4.6.(b) Apportionment Factors, Table T.N.4.6. Maximum Permissible Error (mpe)* for Load Cells During Type Evaluation, T.N.4.7. Creep Recovery for Load Cells During Type Evaluation, and Appendix D; Definitions of D_{min} and E_{min}	23
320-8	W	UR.1.6. Computing Scale Interfaced to a Cash Register	25
320-9	VC	UR.2.6.1. Vehicle Scales; Approaches	26
320-10	VC	UR.3.7. Minimum Load on a Vehicle Scale	27
320-11	VC	List of International Symbols Noted as Acceptable	29
321		**BELT-CONVEYOR SCALE SYSTEMS**	32
321-1	V	N.1.1. Official Test, N.4. As-found Inspection and Tests, and UR.4.1. As-found Inspection and Tests	32
330		**LIQUID-MEASURING DEVICES**	34
330-1	VC	S.1.2. Units	34
330-2	I	S.1.2.3. Value of the Smallest Unit	34
330-3	VC	Table S.2.2. Categories of Device and Methods of Sealing	35
330-4	V	S.3.1. Diversion of Measured Liquid	37
330-5	VC	Table T.2. Accuracy Classes for Liquid Measuring Devices Covered in NIST Handbook 44 Section 3.30	38
331		**VEHICLE-TANK METERS**	40
331-1	V	S.1.1.3. Value of Smallest Unit	40
331-2	VC	S.2.2. Provision for Sealing and Table S.2.2. Categories of Device and Methods of Sealing	41
331-3	I	Temperature Compensation	43
332		**LIQUEFIED PETROLEUM GAS AND ANHYDROUS AMMONIA LIQUID-MEASURING DEVICES**	45
332-1	VC	S.2.2. Provision for Sealing and Table S.2.2. Categories of Device and Methods of Sealing	45
332-2	VC	S.4.3. Location of Marking Information; Retail Motor-Fuel Dispensers	47
334		**CRYOGENIC LIQUID-MEASURING DEVICES**	48
334-1	VC	S.2.5. Provision for Sealing and Table S.2.5. Categories of Device and Methods of Sealing	48

335	**MILK METERS**..**50**		
	335-1	VC S.2.3. Provision for Sealing and Table S.2.3. Categories of Device and Methods of Sealing...............50	
336	**WATER METERS**...**52**		
	336-1	W Table N.4.2. Flow Rate and Draft Size for Water Meters Special Tests...52	
337	**MASS FLOW METERS**...**53**		
	337-1	VC S.3.5. Provision for Sealing and Table S.3.5. Categories of Devices and Methods of Sealing.............53	
	337-2	VC S.4.1. Diversion of Measured Product...55	
	337-3	VC S.5.1. Location of Marking Information; Retail Motor-Fuel Dispensers...56	
338	**CARBON DIOXIDE LIQUID-MEASURING DEVICES**...**56**		
	338-1	VC S.2.5. Provision for Sealing and Table S.2.5. Categories of Device and Methods of Sealing..............56	
360	**OTHER ITEMS**..**59**		
	360-1	I International Organization of Legal Metrology (OIML) Report...59	
	360-2	W Appendix A – Fundamental Considerations Section 11 Health and Safety Considerations....................61	
	360-3	W Add International Terms that are Synonymous to NIST Handbook 44 Terms in Appendix D; Definitions..61	
	360-4	Developing Items...62	

Table B
Appendices

Appendix	Title	Page
A	Item 360-4: Developing Items **A1**	
	Part 1, Item 1, General Code: G-UR.4.1.1. Proper Operating Conditions for Retail Motor-Fuel Devices................ A1	
	Part 2, Item 1, Scales: S.2.1.7. Tare Rounding on a Multiple Range Scale... A2	
	Part 3, Item 1, Belt-Conveyor Scale Systems: UR.3.2.(c) Maintenance; Zero Load Tests.. A2	
	Part 3, Item 2, Belt-Conveyor Scale Systems: UR.2.2.(n) Belt Alignment.. A4	
	Part 4, Item 1, Automatic Weighing Systems: Temperature Limits.. A4	

Table C
Glossary of Acronyms

CC	Certificate of Conformance	NIST	National Institute of Standards and Technology
CWMA	Central Weights and Measures Association	NTEP	National Type Evaluation Program
EPO	Examination Procedure Outline	NTETC	National Type Evaluation Technical Committee
GPMA	Gasoline Pump Manufacturers Association	RMFD	Retail Motor-Fuel Dispenser
H44	NIST Handbook 44	SMA	Scale Manufacturers Association
H130	NIST Handbook 130	SWMA	Southern Weights and Measures Association
LMD	Liquid-Measuring Device	VTM	Vehicle-Tank Meter
LPG	Liquefied Petroleum Gas	WMD	Weights and Measures Division
MMA	Meter Manufacturers Association	WWMA	Western Weights and Measures Association
MFM	Mass Flow Meter	USNWG	NIST/OIML U. S. National Working Group
NCWM	National Conference on Weights and Measures		
NEWMA	Northeastern Weights and Measures Association, Inc.		

"Handbook 44" means the 2006 Edition of NIST Handbook 44 "Specifications, Tolerances, and Other Technical Requirements for Weighing and Measuring Devices."

"Handbook 130" means the 2006 Edition of NIST Handbook 130 "Uniform Laws and Regulations in the Areas of Legal Metrology and Fuel Quality."

Note: NIST does not imply that these acronyms are used solely to identify these organizations or technical topics.

Table D
Voting Results

Reference Key Number	House of State Representatives		House of Delegates		Results
	Yeas	Nays	Yeas	Nays	
300 (Consent Calendar)	37	0	45	0	Passed
310-1 35 2			43	0	Passed
310-2 35 2			39	1	Passed
320-3	21	16	28	15	Returned to Committee
321-1 37 1			41	0	Passed
330-4	20	19	21	19	Returned to Committee
331-1 38 0			44	1	Passed
300 (Report in its Entirety Voice Vote)	All Yeas	No Nays	All Yeas	No Nays	Passed

Details of All Items
(In Order by Reference Key Number)

310 GENERAL CODE

310-1 V G-S.1.(d) Identification; Software for Not-Built-for-Purpose Devices

(This item was adopted.)

Source: Western Weights and Measures Association (WWMA)

Recommendation: Modify Paragraph G-S.1.(d) as follows:

G-S.1. Identification. – All equipment, except weights and separate parts necessary to the measurement process but not having any metrological effect, shall be clearly and permanently marked for the purposes of identification with the following information:

(a) the name, initials, or trademark of the manufacturer or distributor;

(b) a model ~~designation~~ **identifier** that positively identifies the pattern or design of the device;

*(1) The model ~~designation~~ **identifier** shall be prefaced by the word "Model," "Type," or "Pattern." These terms may be followed by the word "Number" or an abbreviation of that word. The abbreviation for the word "Number" shall, as a minimum, begin with the letter "N" (e.g., No or No.). The abbreviation for the word "Model" shall be "Mod" or "Mod." Prefix lettering may be initial capitals, all capitals or all lower case.*
[Nonretroactive as of January 1, 2003]
(Added 2000) (Amended 2001)

(c) a nonrepetitive serial number, except for equipment with no moving or electronic component parts and not-built-for-purpose, software-based devices;
[Nonretroactive as of January 1, 1968]
(Amended 2003)

(1) The serial number shall be prefaced by words, an abbreviation, or a symbol, that clearly identifies the number as the required serial number.
[Nonretroactive as of January 1, 1986]

(2) Abbreviations for the word "Serial" shall, as a minimum, begin with the letter "S," and abbreviations for the word "Number" shall, as a minimum, begin with the letter "N" (e.g., S/N, SN, Ser. No., and S. No.).
[Nonretroactive as of January 1, 2001]

(d) the current software version **or revision** ~~designation~~ **identifier** for not-built-for-purpose, software-based devices;
[Nonretroactive as of January 1, 2004]
(Added 2003)

(1) The version or revision identifier shall be prefaced by words, an abbreviation, or a symbol, that clearly identifies the number as the required version or revision.
[Nonretroactive as of January 1, 2007]
(Added 2006)

(2) ~~Abbreviations for the word "Version" shall, as a minimum, begin with the letter "V" and may be followed by the word "Number." Abbreviations for the word "Revision" shall, as a minimum, begin with the letter "R" and may be followed by the word "Number." The abbreviation for the word "Number" shall, as a minimum, begin with the letter "N" (e.g., No or No.).~~
~~[Nonretroactives of January 1, 2007]~~
~~(Added 2006)~~

(e) an NTEP Certificate of Conformance (CC) number or a corresponding CC Addendum Number for devices that have a CC. The CC Number or a corresponding CC Addendum Number shall be prefaced by the terms "NTEP CC," "CC," or "Approval." These terms may be followed by the word "Number" or an abbreviation of that word. The abbreviation for the word "Number" shall, as a minimum, begin with the letter "N" (e.g., No or No.).
[Nonretroactive as of January 1, 2003]

The required information shall be so located that it is readily observable without the necessity of the disassembly of a part requiring the use of any means separate from the device.
(Amended 1985, 1991, 1999, 2000, 2001, ~~and~~ 2003, and 2006)

Discussion: At its fall 2005 Annual Meeting, WWMA reviewed a proposal to add to Paragraph G-S.1. requirements for identifying the software version designation for not-built-for-purpose devices using acceptable words, abbreviations, or symbols. This is consistent with the current requirements for identifying other markings such as the serial number and model designation. WWMA agreed to forward the proposal shown above to the Committee for consideration.

At its 2005 fall meeting, CWMA agreed with the intent of the WWMA proposal, but suggested that the word "designation" for software be changed to "identification." NEWMA supported the WWMA proposal as a developing item. SWMA recommended the proposal be a voting item on the Committee's 2006 agenda.

At the 2006 NCWM Interim Meeting, SMA supported this item with the comment that the word "designation" is redundant as used in both parts (b) and (c) and that the word "revision" should be an acceptable alternative to the word "version." The Committee agreed with SMA that "designation" as an identifier is redundant and that "revision" is a commonly used term for software. One manufacturer commented that, on devices using a seven-segment display, the letter "V" cannot be displayed. The Committee commented that the letters "N" or "M", which are already recognized, also cannot be shown on a seven-segment display. The Committee modified Item 310-1 as shown above and agreed to present the item for a vote at the 2006 NCWM Annual Meeting since the intent of the proposal is to gain uniformity in the identifier prefix for marking information already required in G.S.1.

At the 2006 NCWM Annual Meeting, SMA supported this item, but indicated that it continued to believe "built-for-purpose" devices and "not-built-for-purpose" devices should be held to the same standard for marking requirements.

310-2   V   G-S.1.1. Location of Marking Information for Not-Built-for-Purpose Software-Based Devices

(This item was adopted.)

Source: Western Weights and Measures Association (WWMA)

Recommendation: Modify Paragraph G-S.1.1. as follows:

G-S.1.1. Location of Marking Information for Not-Built-For-Purpose, Software-Based Devices. – *For not-built-for-purpose, software-based devices, the* ~~following shall apply.~~ required information in G.S.1 Identification (a), (b), (d), and (e) shall:

(a) ~~the manufacturer or distributor and the model designation~~ *be continuously displayed* ~~or marked on the device (see note below)~~, *or*

(b) the Certificate of Conformance (CC) Number shall be continuously displayed or ~~permanently~~ marked on the device (see note below), or

(c) ~~all required information in G-S.1. Identification. (a), (b), (d), and (h) shall be continuously displayed. Alternatively, a clearly identified "view only" System Identification, G-S.1. Identification, or Weights and Measures Identification shall be accessible through the "Help" menu. Required information includes that information necessary to identify that the software in the device is the same type that was evaluated.~~ *shall* be accessible through ~~the "Help"~~ **an easily recognized** menu**, and if necessary a submenu;** **or**

~~(d)~~**(c)** have the G-S.1 identification permanently marked on the device.

Note: Examples of menu and submenu identification include, but are not limited to, "Help," "System Identification," "G-S.1. Identification," or "Weights and Measures Identification."

Note: *Clear instructions for accessing the remaining required G-S.1. information shall be listed on the CC. Required information includes that information necessary to identify that the software in the device is the same type that was evaluated.*

[Nonretroactive as of January 1, 2004]
(Added 2003) **(Amended 2006)**

Discussion: At its fall 2005 Annual Meeting, WWMA reviewed a proposal to modify Paragraph G-S.1.1. to clarify what information must be marked, displayed, or accessible through the help menu on not-built-for-purpose software-based devices. WWMA agreed to forward the proposal to the Committee for consideration.

In fall 2005, CWMA supported the concept of the WWMA proposal, but suggested the proposal remain a developing item pending input from the new NTETC Software Sector scheduled to begin activities in the spring of 2006. SWMA supported the WWMA proposal, but questioned if the word "Help" is the only word that can be used to identify the function that accesses the weights and measures menu.

At the 2006 NCWM Interim Meeting, SMA supported this item, but recommended that Paragraph G-S.1.1.(b) be eliminated as it is already contained in Paragraph G-S.1.1.(c). The Committee heard additional input that access identification should not be limited to the term "Help" as currently listed in Paragraph G-S.1.1. The Committee modified the proposal to address the stated concerns and agreed to present the item for a vote at the 2006 NCWM Annual Meeting.

At the 2006 NCWM Annual Meeting, SMA supported this item, but indicated it continued to believe that "built-for-purpose" devices and "not-built-for-purpose" devices should be held to the same standard for marking requirements. The Committee received a comment that if a manufacturer chooses to physically mark the CC number on the device, then that marking should be permanent. The Committee agreed and modified Paragraph (b) accordingly.

310-3   I   G-S.8.1. Multiple Weighing or Measuring Elements with a Single Provision for Sealing

Source: Western Weights and Measures Association (WWMA)

Discussion: The Committee considered a proposal to add a new Paragraph G-S.8.1. as follows:

G.S.8.1. Multiple Weighing or Measuring Elements with a Single Provision for Sealing. – A change to the metrological parameters (calibration or configuration) of any weighing or measuring element shall be individually identified.

Note: Examples of acceptable identification of a change to the metrological parameters of a weighing or measuring element include, but are not limited to:

> (1) ~~a broken, missing, or replaced physical seal on an individual weighing, measuring, or indicating element or active junction box;~~
> (2) ~~a change in a calibration factor or configuration setting for each weighing or measuring element;~~
> (3) ~~a display of the date of or the number of days since the last calibration or configuration event for each weighing or measuring element; or~~
> (4) ~~counters indicating the number of calibration or configuration events per weighing or measuring element.~~
>
> ~~[Nonretroactive as of January 1, 200X]~~
> (Added   200X)

At its September 2005 Annual Meeting, WWMA reviewed a proposal to add to all the liquid-measuring device codes requirements for identifying when an adjustment is made to any ___ measuring element in a device that has multiple measuring elements but is only equipped with a single provision for sealing the adjustment mechanism. The proposed requirement is similar to the requirements in Section 3.30. Paragraph S.2.2.1. Multiple Measuring Elements with a Single Provision for Sealing. The submitter of the proposal suggested an alternative approach in which the requirement would be added to the General Code to address all weighing and measuring devices. WWMA favored the alternate proposal to modify the General Code and received no opposition from either the weighing industry or the measuring industry representatives present at the meeting. Therefore, WWMA agreed to forward the proposal to the Committee for consideration.

At their 2005 fall meetings, CWMA and SWMA both supported and recommended the proposal be added to the Committee's 2006 agenda.

At the 2006 NCWM Interim Meeting, the Committee heard that SMA opposed this item because it is not appropriate for all devices. The Committee also heard that the list of examples should include an acceptable means for securing systems where access to adjustments is controlled by a physical seal on the indicator. The Committee believes when systems have multiple weighing or measuring elements with a single provision for sealing ___, a General Code requirement for identification of adjustments to individual weighing or measuring elements are appropriate regardless of device type. The Committee modified Item 310-3 to include indicators and active junction boxes. The Committee believes it is important to be sure no specific Handbook 44 codes are adversely affected by placing the requirements in the General Code; therefore, the Committee agreed to make Item 310-3 an information item to provide the opportunity for the National Type Evaluation Technical Committee Sectors and the regional weights and measures associations to evaluate the item further, especially for any adverse impact on a particular device type(s).

At the 2006 NCWM Annual Meeting, the Committee received a comment that if Item 310-3 is proposed as a voting item and passes, next year the proposal should be modified to recommend that LMD Code Paragraph S.2.2.1. be deleted.

310-4 W G-T.1. (e) Acceptance Tolerances

(This item was withdrawn.)

Source: Carryover Item 310-2. (This item originated from the National Type Evaluation Technical Committee (NTETC) Measuring Sector and first appeared on the Committee's 2005 agenda.)

Discussion/Background: The Committee considered a proposal to modify Paragraph G-T.1.(e) as follows:

> **G-T.1. Acceptance Tolerances. – Acceptance tolerances shall apply to:**
>
> (a) equipment to be put into commercial use for the first time;
>
> (b) equipment that has been placed in commercial service within the preceding 30 days and is being officially tested for the first time;
>
> (c) equipment that has been returned to commercial service following official rejection for failure to conform to performance requirements and is being officially tested for the first time within 30 days after corrective service;

(d) equipment that is being officially tested for the first time within 30 days after major reconditioning or overhaul; and

(e) equipment undergoing type evaluation **(special test tolerances are not applicable)**.
(Amended 1989 **and 200X**)

At its October 2004 meeting, the NTETC Measuring Sector noted that the intent of Paragraph G-T.1.(e) was to specify that acceptance tolerances apply to all equipment undergoing type evaluation; however, the language is not clear regarding what tolerance would apply during "special tests."

Special test tolerances are intended to recognize that a larger tolerance for test drafts conducted under certain conditions, such as at a slow rate of flow, is appropriate. Normal wear of the measuring elements frequently produces larger performance errors at a slow flow rate, compared to performance errors at full flow rate. The Sector agreed that devices submitted for NTEP evaluation should be held to a higher standard than devices in normal service and special test tolerances should not be applicable during an NTEP evaluation.

At the 2005 NCWM Annual Meeting, MMA indicated they had not understood that the proposal submitted to the Committee from the Measuring Sector would apply to all types of liquid-measuring devices submitted for NTEP evaluation. MMA thought the proposed requirement would apply only to retail motor-fuel dispensers. MMA stated that without special test tolerances, most meters, especially those installed in vehicle-mounted applications, would not meet tolerances for tests conducted at lower flow rates during both field and NTEP evaluations. The Committee agreed to make the proposal an information item to allow MMA and the Measuring Sector additional time to develop an alternate proposal.

At its October 2005 meeting, the NTETC Measuring Sector agreed with MMA that some devices should have a larger tolerance for special tests conducted during type evaluation and forwarded a recommendation to the Committee that it withdraw this item and instead amend Section 3.30. as shown in Item 330-5.

At the 2006 NCWM Interim Meeting, the Committee agreed to withdraw Item 310-4 from the S&T Committee agenda as requested by the NTETC Measuring Sector.

320 SCALES

320-1 I S.1.1. (c) Zero Indication; Requirements for Markings or Indications for Other than Digital Zero Indications

Source: Carryover Item 320-1. (This item originated from the Committee and first appeared on its 2004 agenda.)

Discussion: The Committee considered a proposal to amend Paragraph S.1.1.(c) as follows:

S.1.1. Zero Indication.

(a) On a scale equipped with indicating or recording elements, provision shall be made to either indicate or record a zero-balance condition.

(b) On an automatic-indicating scale or balance indicator, provision shall be made to indicate or record an out-of-balance condition on both sides of zero.

(c) A zero-balance condition may be indicated by other than a continuous digital zero indication, provided that an effective automatic means is provided to inhibit a weighing operation or to return to a continuous digital indication when the scale is in an out-of-balance condition **and is marked or includes supplemental indications prominently visible to the customer to indicate that the "other than continuous digital zero indication" represents a no-load condition of the scale.**
(Added 1987) (Amended 1993 **and 2006**)

Note: The markings or supplemental indications in S.1.1.(c) are not required if, prior to the start of a transaction: (1) operator intervention is required to verify the zero-balance condition with a digital zero indication, or (2) no weight value is indicated when an item is placed on the load-receiving element.
(Added 200X)
(Amended 1987)

Past inconsistencies and ongoing disagreements about the interpretation of Paragraph S.1.1.(c) warranted an effort to clarify the intent of the requirement. The proposed changes to the requirement specify that all primary indicators on scales that use anything other than a digital zero indication (e.g., scrolling messages, dashes, etc.) to indicate zero require additional markings or indications to inform customers that the scales are at a zero-balance condition. No markings are necessary on these devices when operator intervention is required to return the indication to a digital zero before conducting a transaction.

The Committee agreed that General Code Paragraphs G-S.6. Marking Operational Controls, Indications, and Features and S.1.1. require weighing devices to be marked or provide an indication that states the zero-balance is represented by other than a digital zero indication. Historically, this position is supported by the 1993 amendment to Paragraph S.1.1.(c) as well as type evaluation requirements and other requirements adopted to ensure that customers have sufficient information about displays and recorded transaction information to make an informed decision during a direct sale transaction.

At the July 2005 NCWM Annual Meeting, the Committee changed the status of the item from "voting" to "information" to allow additional time to determine: (1) if the proposed markings could be displayed as part of the indication rather than being physically marked on the device and (2) if self-service systems provide information on the zero-load condition of the scale prior to each weighment.

In the fall of 2005, several regional associations and the NTETC Weighing Sector reconsidered the proposal. After hearing opposition to the proposal from SMA, WWMA indicated that the proposal should remain an information item pending a review by the Weighing Sector. CWMA restated its earlier position that the proposal should be withdrawn because appropriate protections and labeling criteria are applied during type evaluation. At the September 2005 meeting of the Weighing Sector, a majority of the Sector's membership voted against the proposal because they did not believe labeling is necessary if a scale has an automatic means to inhibit a transaction when it is out of balance or returns to a continuous digital indication when in an out-of-balance condition. The Weighing Sector agreed that additional markings would not be required during type evaluation on devices that have an effective automatic means to inhibit a weighing operation or return the device to a continuous digital indication when the scale is in an out-of-balance condition.

SMA opposed the proposal because it believes the current language in Paragraph S.1.1.(c) provides sufficient guidance to prevent use of this feature to facilitate fraud. SMA supported the analysis of the item made by the Weighing Sector.

At the 2006 NCWM Interim Meeting, the Committee continued its support for a requirement that requires additional markings to clarify when zero is indicated by other than a continuous digital zero indication based on General Code Paragraph G-S.6. Marking Operational Controls, Indications, and Features and the 1993 interpretation made by the S&T Committee. The Committee noted that the proposed language is not in conflict with current practices or recently modified language in Publication 14 that NTEP laboratories use to address this situation. The Committee also believes that the changes are needed to provide definitive guidelines to the field official and in support of corresponding language in NCWM Publication 14. The Committee believes there is sufficient language in the proposal to address instances where the original equipment manufacturer elects to display rather than mark the information. Additionally, the Committee slightly modified the note, which it added to the proposal in 2005, and believes that it addresses some of the Weighing Sector's concern about unnecessarily requiring labeling when weighing operations are inhibited on a device in an out-of-balance condition. The proposed changes are meant to be applied retroactively and, therefore, apply to all equipment including self-service applications that have undergone type evaluation.

During the 2006 NCWM Annual Meeting, the Committee agreed that provisions should be in place for all devices to clearly indicate a zero-balance condition either with a digital zero, annunciator, or using some other accepted means. The Committee is concerned there are no definitive guidelines available for the field official to verify a zero-balance condition on software-based devices that are modified after type evaluation. The Committee continues to believe the proposal has some merit, but modified the language in response to concerns about markings and indications. The Committee made changes to S.1.1.(c) to: (1) specify that markings and indications must be visible to the customer, and (2) clarify one instance where markings and indications are not required.

The Committee heard mixed reviews of the proposal from public and private sector members; however, a majority still believe the wording in Paragraph S.1.1.(c) is adequate to prevent fraud. One jurisdiction in support of the proposal noted that an indication other than zero would not be acceptable for devices such as retail motor-fuel dispensers and questioned the impact of software changes made after type evaluation on zero indications. In fact, that jurisdiction noted it has found scales operating with no indication of zero. Consequently, the Committee changed the status of the proposal from a voting item to an information item. The Committee asks that the regional weights and measures associations consider the reworked proposal during their fall 2006 sessions.

For additional background information, refer to the 2004 and 2005 S&T Final Reports.

320-2 I S.1.4.6. Height and Definition of Minimum Reading Distance, UR.2.10. Primary Indicating Elements Provided by the User, UR.2.11. Minimum Reading Distance, and Definitions of Minimum Reading Distance and Primary Indications

Source: National Type Evaluation Technical Committee Weighing Sector

Discussion: The Committee considered the Weighing Sector's first attempt at a proposal that adds new Paragraphs S.1.4.6., UR.2.10., and UR.2.11. to the Scales Code and adds new definitions of "minimum reading distance" and "primary indications" to Appendix D as follows:

S.1.4. Indicators.

> **S.1.4.6. Height.** – All primary indications shall be indicated clearly and simultaneously.
>
> > (a) On digital devices that display primary indications during direct sales to the customer, the numerical figures displayed to the customer shall be at least 9.5 mm (0.4 in) high.
> >
> > (b) The units of mass and other descriptive markings or indications, such as lb, kg, gross, tare, net, etc., shall be clearly and easily read and shall be at least 2 mm (0.08 in) high.
>
> [Nonretroactive as of January 1, 2007]
> (Added 200X)

UR.2. Installation Requirements

UR.2.10. Primary Indicating Elements Provided by the User. – Primary indicating elements that are not the same as the primary indicating elements provided by the original equipment manufacturer (e.g., video display monitors) shall comply with the following:

> (a) On digital devices that display primary indications during direct sales to the customer, the numerical figures displayed to the customer shall be at least 9.5 mm (0.4 in) high.
>
> (b) The units of mass and other descriptive information, such as gross, tare, net, etc., shall be displayed or marked on the device and shall be at least 2 mm (0.08 in) high.

(Added 200X)

UR.2.11. Minimum Reading Distance – On digital devices that display primary indications, the height of the numbers expressed in millimeters should be not less than three times the minimum reading distance expressed in meters, without being less than 2 mm (0.08 in). (Example: If the height of the primary indications is 10 mm, then the minimum reading distance should not be greater than 30 m).

(Added   200X)

minimum reading distance. The shortest distance that an observer is freely able to approach the indicating device to take a reading under normal conditions of use. This approach is considered to be free for the observer if there is a clear space of at least 0.8 m in front of the indicating device. However, if the minimum reading distance "S" in Figure X is less than 0.8 m, then the minimum reading distance is "L" in Figure X. [2.20]
(Added 200X)

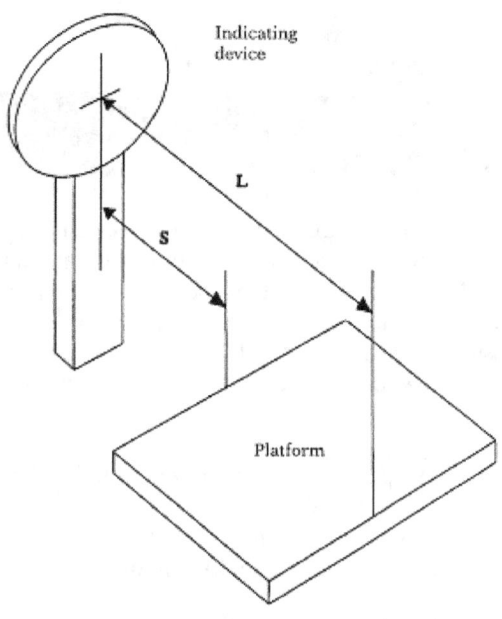

Figure X

primary indications. Weight or other units of measurement values that are displayed by a primary indicating element. The primary indications are used as the determining factor in arriving at the sale representation when the device is used commercially. (Examples of primary indications include the measurement value, unit price or count, and total price on instruments capable of price computing. Primary indications do not include indications from auxiliary indicating devices such as totalizing registers and pre-determined stop mechanisms.) [1.10], [2.20]
(Added 200X)

This proposal was developed to address a growing problem with the readability of weight indications and the values that define transaction information. Field and laboratory officials indicate that both are becoming increasingly smaller, as demonstrated in the following example of a weight display where the actual size of the weight values are 23 mm in height, but the unit of measurement (g) is 4 mm in height.

Field and laboratory officials need more specific requirements in order to consistently determine if indications are suitable for the environment in which the device is used. Currently only the Taximeters, Grain Moisture Meters, and Near-Infrared Grain Analyzers Codes include requirements that specify the minimum height of figures, words, and symbols. The size requirements for all three device technologies were developed primarily because of concerns about the visibility of indications from the customer's position. NIST Handbook 44 and NCWM Publication 14 include no uniform size requirements or guidelines on how to evaluate display information for clarity and readability for other than these three device types.

The Weighing Sector developed and voted on a proposal which provides guidelines for determining whether or not indications are appropriate in a particular installation. The Weighing Sector's proposal was aligned with OIML R 76 requirements for visibility of indications to the customer in direct sale applications, minimum height of lettering for identification information, and the minimum height of numbers for analog indicating devices.

In 1999 a similar proposal to amend General Code Paragraph G-S.5.2.3. Size and Character to include minimum height requirements was considered but later withdrawn. GPMA expressed strong opposition to the 1999 proposal because many of the measuring devices were equipped with quantity displays that would not meet the proposed 9.5 mm size requirement. The Committee agreed at the time that officials need uniform guidelines that are not ambiguous as to which transaction information must meet size requirements. However, the Committee also believed that any future proposals should address a specific device technology since it is difficult to address all device configurations and the environmental conditions that exist at each installation site.

After its September 2005 meeting, the Weighing Sector agreed to further develop the proposal for a requirement that specifies the height of the weight results and its corresponding unit of measurement indications to ensure information is adequately visible to the customer in direct sale applications. The Weighing Sector agreed that any proposed language should be aligned with OIML R 76 height requirements to the extent possible. After submitting the proposed language to the Committee, the Weighing Sector balloted its members with expectations of only minor changes to the proposal. The Weighing Sector supported the proposed new definition of "primary indications" and alternate wording for a proposed new Paragraph S.1.4.6. as follows:

> **S.1.4.6. Height. – All primary indications shall be indicated clearly.**
>
> (a) **On digital devices that display primary indications during direct sales to the customer, the numerical figures displayed to the customer shall be at least 9.5 mm high.**
>
> (b) **The units of mass and other descriptive information such as gross, tare, net, etc., shall be displayed or marked on the device and shall be at least 2 mm high.**
> **[Nonretroactive as of January 1, 2007]**
> **(Added 200X)**

Receiving feedback that the definition and illustration of a minimum reading distance were confusing, the Weighing Sector learned that it did not have a consensus on the proposal or the language for corresponding user requirements for a primary indicating element that is provided by the user. SMA also opposed the proposal because it believed a reading distance requirement is unenforceable.

In November 2005, the Committee received comments from a consultant that the proposal is unnecessary. General Code Paragraph G S.5.1. Indicating and Recording Elements can be applied in type approval, eliminating the need to borrow any corresponding language from R 76 or add any language to Handbook 44. Comments suggested that the United States should stick to performance-based requirements, noting that the proposal does not adhere to that principal.

During the 2006 NCWM Interim Meeting, the Committee agreed that although the clarity and readability of indications is a growing issue, the proposal has only limited support from the public and private sectors. The Committee recognized the proposal requires a significant amount of work before the language is clear, technically correct, and deemed applicable to the different types of installations and technologies in use. The Committee agreed to make the proposal an information item since the Weighing Sector has a group actively working on the language.

The Committee has concerns about whether or not the proposed 2 mm height requirements for units of measurement and other markings are adequate. The Committee also questioned the clarity of the proposed user requirements for the minimum reading distance. Therefore, the Committee asks the Weighing Sector to continue its work to fully develop the proposal and possibly consider two separate proposals—a design specification and a user requirement—since the specification for the primary indication height is nearer to completion. The Committee agreed that the proposal should remain an information item to allow the Weighing Sector sufficient time to work on the language. No updates to the proposal were received during the 2006 NCWM Annual Meeting.

320-3 V **N.1.3.1. Bench or Counter Scales, N.1.3.8. All Other Scales Except Crane Scales, Hanging Scales, Hopper Scales, Wheel–Load Weighers, and Portable Axle-Load Weighers, and Appendix D; Definitions of Bench Scale and Counter Scale**

(This item did not pass or fail; therefore, it returns to the Committee.)

Source: Carryover Item 320-6. (This item originated from the National Type Evaluation Technical Committee (NTETC) Weighing Sector and first appeared on the Committee's 2005 agenda.)

Discussion: The Committee considered the Weighing Sector's proposal to delete Paragraph N.1.3.1. and renumber subsequent paragraphs as follows:

N.1.3. Shift Test.

~~N.1.3.1. Bench or Counter Scales. A shift test shall be conducted with a half-capacity test load centered successively at four points equidistant between the center and the front, left, back, and right edges of the load-receiving element.~~

Renumber and amend Paragraph N.1.3.8. All Other Scales Except Crane Scales, Hanging Scales, Hopper Scales, Wheel-Load Weighers, and Portable Axle-Load Weighers as follows:

N.1.3.~~8~~7. All Other Scales Except Crane Scales, Hanging Scales, Hopper Scales, Wheel-Load Weighers, and Portable Axle-Load Weighers. A shift test shall be conducted using the following prescribed test loads and test patterns. __A single field standard weight used as the prescribed test load shall be applied centrally in the prescribed test pattern. When multiple field standard weights are used as the prescribed test load, the load shall be applied in a consistent pattern in the shift test positions throughout the test and applied in a manner that does not concentrate the load in a test pattern that is less than when that same load is a single field standard weight on the load-receiving element.__

(a) ~~A one-quarter nominal capacity test load centered as nearly as possible, successively over each main load support as shown in the diagram below; or~~

(b) ~~A one-half nominal capacity test load centered as nearly as possible, successively at the center of each quarter of the load-receiving element as shown in the diagram below.~~

(a) For scales with a nominal capacity greater than 500 kg (1 000 lb), a shift test may be conducted by either using a one-third nominal capacity test load (defined as test weights in amounts of at least 30 % of scale capacity, but not to exceed 35 % of scale capacity) centered as nearly as possible at the center of each quadrant of the load-receiving element using the prescribed test pattern as shown in Figure 1 below, or by using a one-quarter nominal capacity test load centered as nearly as possible, successively, over each corner of the load-receiving element using the prescribed test pattern as shown in Figure 2 below.

(b) For scales with a nominal capacity of 500 kg (1 000 lb) or less, a shift test shall be conducted using a one-third nominal capacity test load (defined as test weights in amounts of at least 30 % of scale capacity, but not to exceed 35 % of scale capacity) centered as nearly as possible at the center of each quadrant of the load-receiving element using the prescribed test pattern as shown in Figure 1 below.

(c) For livestock scales, ~~the~~ shift test ~~load~~ shall be conducted using a test load of one-half nominal capacity provided that the test load does not exceed one-half the rated section capacity or one-half the rated concentrated load capacity, whichever is applicable. ~~A shift test shall be conducted using either:~~ The test load shall be centered as nearly as possible at the center of each quadrant of the load-receiving element using the prescribed test pattern as shown in Figure 1 below, or one-quarter the rated section capacity or one-quarter the rated concentrated load capacity load centered as nearly as possible, successively over each corner of the load-receiving element using the prescribed test pattern as shown in Figure 2 below.

(Amended 1987~~;~~ ~~and~~ 2003, and 200X)

Delete the two diagrams that correspond to existing Paragraphs N.1.3.8. (a) and (b) and add new Figures 1 and 2 to correspond with proposed revisions to N.1.3.8. as follows:

Figure 1

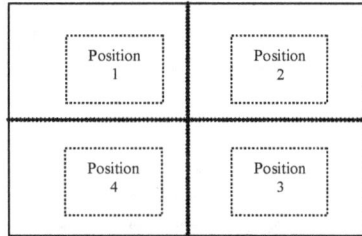

Figure 2

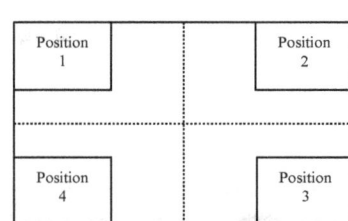

(Added 2003) **(Amended 200X)**

Delete Appendix D definitions for "bench scale" and "counter scale" as follows:

~~bench scale. See "counter scale." [2.20]~~

~~counter scale. One that, by reason of its size, arrangement of parts, and moderate nominal capacity, is adapted for use on a counter or bench. Sometimes called "bench scale." [2.20]~~

The proposal is intended to clarify the appropriate shift test pattern and test loads for bench/counter scales and other platform-type scales. Currently, bench and counter scale shift tests are conducted with a one-half capacity test load centered successively at four points equidistant between the center and the front, left, back, and right edges of the load-receiving element. Other platform scale shift tests are conducted with a one-half capacity test load centered, as nearly as possible, successively at the center of each quadrant or one-quarter capacity test load over each main load support. The proposal eliminates references to bench and counter scales and instead prescribes that the shift test load and test pattern used for those and all scales other than livestock scales be based on the scale's nominal capacity. For livestock scales the proposal further clarifies, but does not change, the existing requirements for shift tests.

At the 2005 NCWM Interim Meeting, the proposal was kept on the agenda as an information item in response to comments indicating that data should be collected on shift tests to verify that the proposed test loads and positions are equivalent to existing test patterns.

WWMA and CWMA encouraged the Committee to keep the proposal an information item until more data could be collected and reviewed by the Weighing Sector, NIST, and the NTEP laboratories. The Committee also reviewed an alternate proposal recommended in 2005 by CWMA to modify Paragraph N.1.3.8. CWMA proposal differed from the Weighing Sector's proposal because the test pattern in Figure 2 was referenced in the test procedure for scales with a nominal capacity less than 300 lb, illustrated the load bearing points in Figure 2, and used other terminology for the term "quadrant."

During the 2006 NCWM Interim Meeting, the Committee received the results of data for shift tests conducted using current shift test requirements and shift tests conducted using the proposed test requirements on the same scales. Comments were also received from the public and private sectors in support of the proposal. SMA supported the proposal. The NIST technical advisor to the Weighing Sector provided a summary of data gathered by multiple jurisdictions on 207 scales. The summary verified the proposed procedures (i.e., shift test loading pattern and the amount of test weights) based on scale capacity are adequate to demonstrate an instrument with load points of any design configuration can meet performance tolerances during off-center loading. There is no demonstrated difference in scale performance based on the location of the scale; thus the terms "bench" and "counter" should be eliminated.

NIST WMD supported the intent of the proposal with two changes to clarify what is meant by one-third nominal capacity and the proper placement of test weights to avoid overloading load-bearing points. WMD recommended language that specifies the test load at one-third capacity shall not be less than 30 % or greater than 35 % of scale capacity. WMD also noted inconsistencies in the manner in which weights are distributed within the test pattern during shift tests; therefore, it also recommended including language in renumbered Paragraph N.1.3.7. that specifies "when multiple test weights are used, the load shall not be concentrated in a test pattern smaller than that which a single test weight of equivalent mass would occupy."

Consequently, the Committee modified the entire proposal, parts (a) through (c), to include language that is technically correct and consistent in its description of how to conduct a shift test on all types of scales. The Committee modified the language to: (1) clarify what defines "acceptable" weight values for a test load that is one-third of the scale's nominal capacity, (2) ensure uniform procedures are followed when applying test weights on the load-receiving element, and (3) eliminate instances where test weights are concentrated in a pattern that overloads the load-bearing points as illustrated in the example below. The Committee agreed that the scale nominal capacity that determines the appropriate test pattern and maximum amount of test weights used in the shift test should be changed from 150 kg (300 lb) to 500 kg (1000 lb). This modification aligns the proposed one-third capacity shift test load requirement with existing minimum test weight requirements for the greater of 25 % device capacity or 300 lb for devices with 1000 lb capacity already specified in Table 4. Minimum Test Weights and Test Loads.

Consider the example of a livestock scale with a section capacity of 1000 lb. A shift test is performed as shown in Figure 1 (see the following page), using a test load of 500 lb.

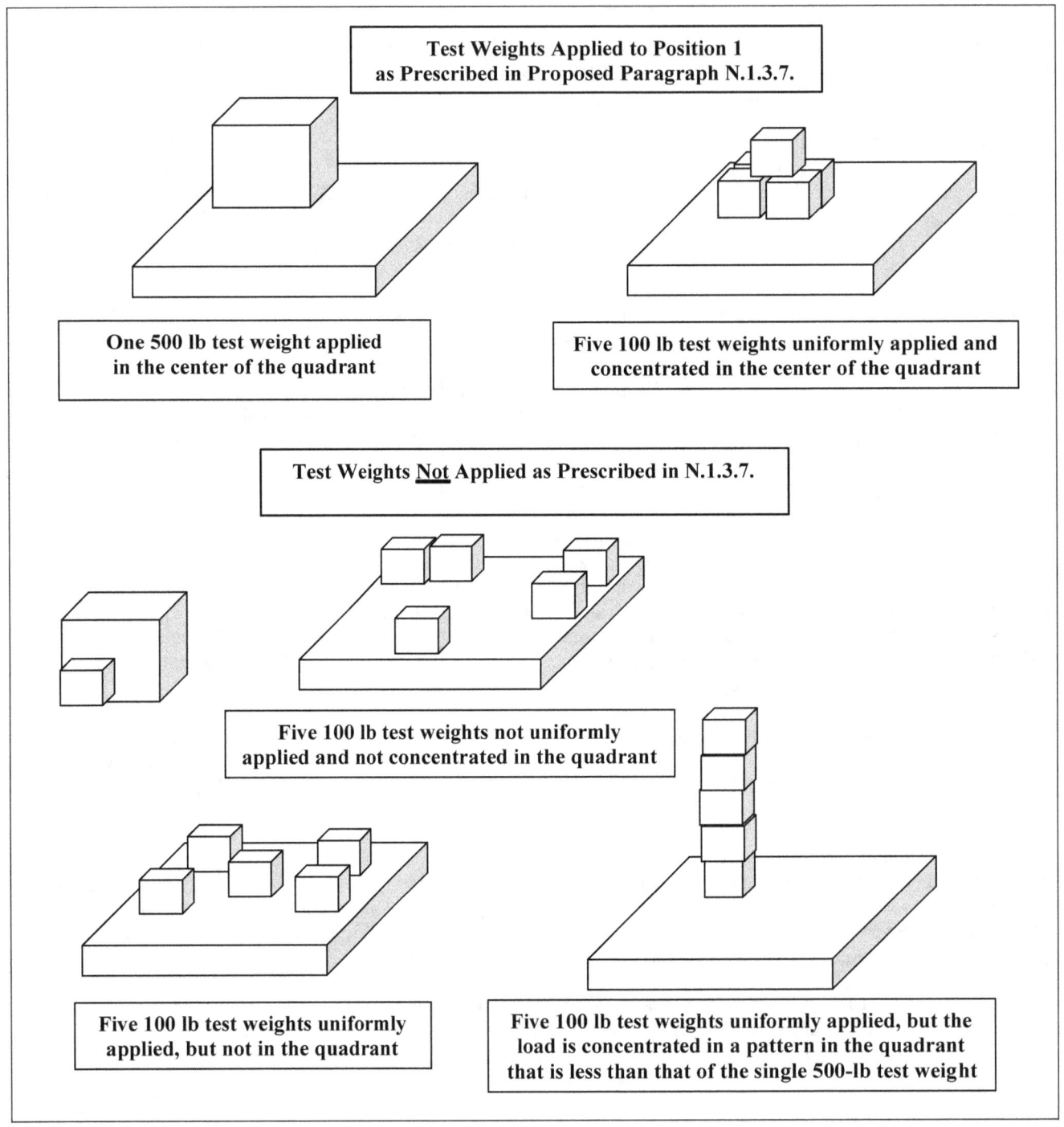

The Committee agreed there was sufficient data to present the proposal for a vote at the July 2006 NCWM Annual Meeting. However, if the Committee were to receive any data indicating there was a problem with the proposed shift test procedures, then it planned to downgrade the proposal in status from a voting item to an information item.

At the 2006 NCWM Annual Meeting, the Committee addressed concerns about the lack of a guideline for a minimum test load and the extensive nature of modifications to livestock scale requirements. The Committee pointed out that it had only reorganized the livestock scale requirements. The Committee further modified proposed new Paragraph (c) to specify a minimum shift test load of one-half nominal capacity to ensure sufficient test weights are used during the test. Industry acknowledged that although the shift test loads for other scale types were reduced from one-half to one-third, the rated nominal capacity specified in the newly proposed test load patterns for the lighter test load can sometimes create a more stringent test of the scale's performance.

The Committee heard further concerns that substantive changes were made to livestock scale requirements and that it should revisit a simpler, earlier proposal. Some members suggested that perhaps the United States should push for OIML to adopt existing U. S. requirements, viewed by some as a more stringent test. The vote on the item did not receive sufficient votes to pass or fail, consequently the item was returned to the Committee.

For more background information, refer to the Committee's 2005 Final Report.

320-4 I Table 4. Minimum Test Weights and Test Loads

Source: Northeastern Weights and Measures Association (NEWMA)

Discussion: The Committee considered a proposal to modify Table 4. Minimum Test Weights and Test Loads as follows:

Table 4. Minimum Test Weights and Test Loads [1]			
Device Capacity	**Minimums (in terms of device capacity)**		**(where practicable)**
	Test Weights (greater of)	**Test Loads [2]**	
0 to 150 kg (0 to 300 lb)	100 %		
151 to 1 500 kg (301 to 3 000 lb)	25 % or 150 kg (300 lb)	75 %	Test weights to dial face capacity, 1 000 d, or test load to used capacity, if greater than minimums specified During initial verification, a scale should be tested to capacity.
1 501 to 20 000 kg (3 001 to 40 000 lb)	12.5 % or 500 kg (1000 lb)	50 %	
20 001 kg~~+~~ **to 250 000 kg** (40 001 lb~~+~~ **to 500 000 lb**)	12.5 % or 5 000 kg (10 000 lb)	25 % [3]	
250 001 kg+ (500 001 lb+)	12.5 % or 30 000 kg (62 500 lb)	**25 %** [3]	

[1] If the amount of test weight in Table 4 combined with the load on the scale would result in an unsafe condition, then the appropriate load will be determined by the official with statutory authority.

[2] The term "test load" means the sum of the combination of field standard test weights and any other applied load used in the conduct of a test using substitution test methods. Not more than three substitutions shall be used during substitution testing, after which the tolerances for strain load tests shall be applied to each set of test loads

[3] The scale shall be tested from zero to at least 12.5 % of scale capacity using known test weights, and then to at least 25 % of scale capacity using either a substitution or strain load test that utilizes known test weights of at least 12.5 % of scale capacity. Whenever practical, a strain load test should be conducted to the used capacity of the scale. When a strain load test is conducted, the tolerances apply only to the test weights or substitution test loads.
(Amended 1988, 1989, 1994, and 2003)

[**Note:** GIPSA requires devices subject to their inspection to be tested to at least "used capacity," which is calculated based on the platform area of the scale and a weight factor assigned to the species of animal weighed on the scale. "Used capacity" is calculated using the formula:

Used Scale Capacity = Scale Platform Area x Species Weight Factor

Where species weight factor = 540 kg/m^2 (110 lb/ft^2) for cattle, 340 kg/m^2 (70 lb/ft^2) for calves and hogs, and 240 kg/m^2 (50 lb/ ft^2) for sheep and lambs]

(Amended 2006)

Some jurisdictions encounter scales with nominal capacities of 1 000 000 lb or more and must determine the minimum test loads needed to conduct an acceptable test. NEWMA believes that NIST Handbook 44 is flexible, but does not provide any definitive guidelines on test loads for scales with capacities at the high end of that range. NEWMA modified its original proposal by reducing the scale maximum capacity from 1 000 000 lb to 500 000 lb and removing a footnote that permitted officials to establish the minimum test load. Industry and other regional associations have developed alternate proposals to address concerns that the original proposal did not address the minimum test weights and test load requirements for a scale with a nominal capacity greater than 500 000 lb.

This item was part of the Developing Items agenda. However, in the fall of 2005, NEWMA, the original submitter of the proposal, agreed the proposal was ready for national consideration and should be presented to the Committee for consideration on its 2006 agenda. WWMA recommended the proposal remain a developing item. CWMA recommended withdrawing the proposal since the current table already addresses most installations.

SMA recommended that for scale capacities above 250 000 lb, the greater of either 62 500 lb of test weights or 12.5 % of scale capacity be used to test the scale to at least 25 % of scale capacity using either "substitution" or "strain load" test methods. For other scale capacities, SMA agreed that it was not necessary to specify use of the "greater" amount of weight standards. Additionally, SMA recommended a strain load test should be conducted up to the scale's nominal capacity whenever possible.

The Committee agreed to SMA proposal; however, to ensure that a sufficient test load is selected to test the performance of larger capacity scales, it kept the requirement for testing with the "greater of" a percentage of scale capacity or a specified amount of test weights as applicable to scales with capacities greater than 300 lb.

The Committee noted that the proposal as written did not change the current requirement for the minimum amount of test weights or test load for scales with more than a 40 001 lb nominal capacity. The Committee believes officials might have difficulty placing the recommended minimum 25 % test load on the load-receiving element because of the limited size of the platform. Consequently, the Committee agreed that until the submitter develops alternate language and justification that warrants a change to existing Handbook 44 requirements, the proposal should be an information item.

320-5   W   Table 6. Maintenance Tolerances

(This item was withdrawn.)

Source: Carryover Item 320-7. (This item originated from the NIST Weights and Measures Division (WMD) and first appeared on the Committee's 2005 agenda.)

Discussion: The original intent of the step tolerances was to provide a relationship between scale accuracy and scale resolution. The Committee considered a proposal to modify Table 6. as follows to meet that objective.

Table 6. ~~Maintenance~~ Tolerances (All values in this table are in <u>verification</u> scale divisions <u>e</u>)					
Tolerance in <u>verification</u> scale divisions <u>e</u>					
1 2 3 5					–
Class Test			Load		
I	0 - 50 000	50 001 - 200 000	200 001 +		
II	0 - 5 000	5 001 - 20 000	20 001 +		
III	0 - 500	501 - 2 000	2 001 -	~~4 000~~	~~4 001 +~~
IIII	0 - 50	51 - 200	201 -	~~400~~	~~401 +~~
IIIL	0 - 500	501 - 1 000	(Add 1 ~~d~~<u>e</u> for each additional 500 ~~d~~<u>e</u> or fraction thereof)		

(Amended 200X)

The USNWG on R 76 "Non-automatic Weighing Instruments" agreed that NIST Handbook 44 Class III and Class IIII tolerances should be aligned with OIML R 76. Manufacturers indicated that they build identically performing instruments and load cells for both U. S. and international markets. However, some industry representatives are concerned about eliminating the 5 d tolerance step because of questions about the ability of many scales and load cells with an n_{max} greater than 5 000 e to comply with the temperature effect at zero in U. S. and OIML requirements.

The current Class III L tolerance structure in NIST Handbook 44 deviates most from the original intent of the step tolerances. A scale with a higher resolution is not an indication of a higher level of accuracy for devices set to meet Table 6. tolerances. For example, if a Class III L scale has an e = 20 lb, then at 80 000 lb the maintenance tolerance would be ± 8 e (160 lb), whereas a Class III scale with an e = 50 lb would have a ± 2 e (100 lb) maintenance tolerance at 80 000 lb. The accuracy of weighments on the Class III L scale are less reliable if uncertainties in the weighing process are factored into reading indications for a scale with a 20 lb e. The Class III scale (where e = 50 lb and there is a 100 lb (2 e) allowable error) results in a more appropriate relationship than that of the Class III L scale (where e = 20 lb and there is a 160 lb (8 e) allowable error). It should be noted that the tolerance values, zero-tracking limit, and motion detection requirements in NIST Handbook 44 are roughly equivalent to an R 76 instrument when e = 50 lb.

During the 2005 NCWM Interim Meeting, the Committee agreed the proposal has merit. However, the Committee made the proposal an information item in response to requests from jurisdictions for more time to examine data from test results using the proposed tolerances and to determine if there are devices that cannot comply without the additional 5 d tolerance presently in Table 6.

At present, only NEWMA recommended the proposal move forward for a vote. WWMA and CWMA recommended the proposal remain an information item until more data is gathered to determine whether or not it creates any problems regarding field equipment or how field officials apply the requirement.

During the 2006 NCWM Interim Meeting, SMA opposed the proposal based on one member's data that demonstrated devices it manufactured with 6 000 e do not meet the proposed tolerances unless they are given the extra step in tolerance.

The Committee acknowledged this proposal is meant to harmonize U. S. and OIML requirements, yet there is not sufficient feedback on the impact of changing tolerances on existing scales and new equipment. The Committee also considered the concerns of industry and those expressed earlier by field officials indicating a need for the additional tolerance in the fifth step for scales to comply with acceptance tolerance. Consequently, the Committee withdrew the proposal from its agenda.

For more background information, refer to the Committee's 2005 Final Report.

320-6 VC T.N.4.5.1. Time Dependence; Class II, III, and IIII Non-automatic Weighing Instruments

(This item was adopted.)

Source: Southern Weights and Measures Association (SWMA)

Recommendation: Modify Paragraph T.N.4.5.1. Time Dependence as follows:

T.N.4.5.1. Time Dependence; Class II, III, and IIII Non-automatic Weighing Instruments. – A non-automatic weighing instrument of classes II, III, and IIII shall meet the following requirements at constant test conditions. **During type evaluation, this test shall be conducted at 20 °C ± 2 °C (68 °F ± 4 °F):**

(a) When any load is kept on an instrument, the difference between the indication obtained immediately after placing the load and the indication observed during the following 30 min shall not exceed 0.5 e. ~~(b)~~ However, the difference between the indication obtained at 15 min and that at 30 min shall not exceed 0.2 e.

(b) If the conditions in (a) are not met, the difference between the indication obtained immediately after placing the load on the instrument and the indication observed during the following 4 hr shall not exceed the absolute value of the maximum permissible error at the load applied.

(c) The deviation on returning to zero as soon as the indication has stabilized, after the removal of any load which has remained on the instrument for 30 min, shall not exceed 0.5 e.

For a multi-interval instrument, the deviation shall not exceed 0.5 e_1 (where e_1 is the interval of the first partial weighing range or segment of the scale).

On a multiple range instrument, the deviation on returning to zero from Max_i (load in the applicable weighing range) shall not exceed 0.5 e_i (interval of the weighing segment). Furthermore, after returning to zero from any load greater than Max_1 (capacity of the first weighing range) and immediately after switching to the lowest weighing range, the indication near zero shall not vary by more than e_1 (interval of the first weighing range) during the following 5 min.
(Added 2005) **(Amended 2006)**

Discussion: The proposal is intended to further harmonize the test conditions in U. S. requirements for time dependence tests with procedures included in OIML requirements. OIML requires that factors such as temperature, which might contribute to errors in test results, be kept constant. Consequently, SWMA proposed to modify Paragraph T.N.4.5.1. to specify that a constant temperature of 20 °C must be maintained during laboratory test conditions for type evaluation.

The Committee considered a further modification of Paragraph T.N.4.5.1. to include a range of temperatures representative of a typical laboratory environment that is less restrictive than the current proposal. However, the industry proposed alternate language that specified a constant temperature of "only" 20 °C during type evaluation test conditions. Given the comparison of the new and old tolerances applied to Class III instruments as illustrated in the graph below, it is apparent that sources for error and uncertainty must be controlled or eliminated under the new, more stringent tolerances.

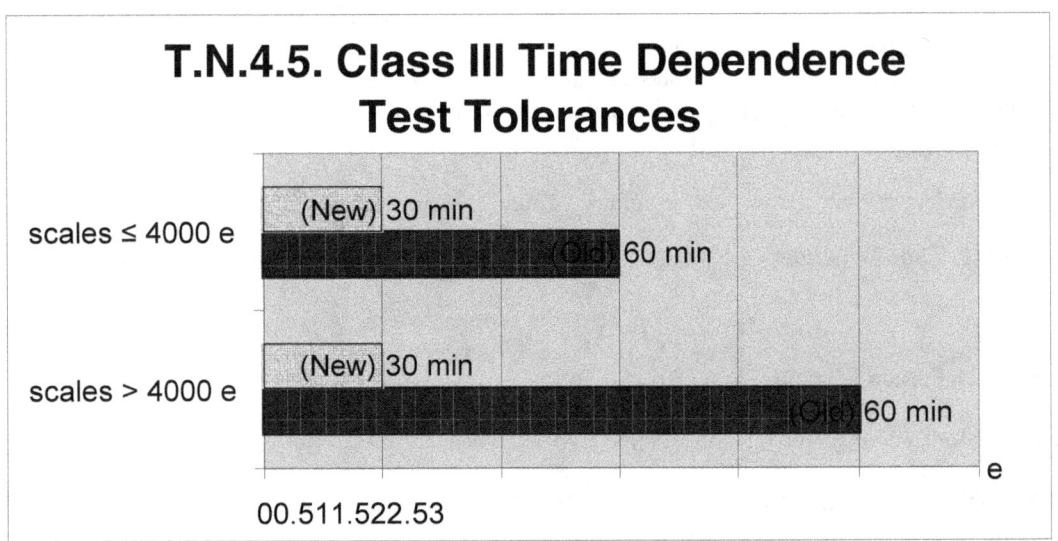

Although the time period required for the test has decreased by half from 60 min to 30 min, the new 0.5 e tolerance (see Paragraph T.N.4.5.1.(a)) for the change in the indication while the scale is under load is three to five times more stringent for the 30 min test than it was for the previous 60 min test.

The time dependence test requirements adopted in 2005 included two additional tolerances the instrument must meet. First, the instrument must comply with the 0.2 e tolerance (see Paragraph T.N.4.5.1.(b)) that applies to the change of the indication during the last 15 min of the time dependence test or the device faces a lengthier test period. There was no such tolerance prior to 2006. For example, if the scale indication shifted 0.2 e in the first 15 min and shifted another

0.3 e in the last 15 min, the time dependence test would be extended to a 4 hr test even though the total shift in indications is 0.5 e. Secondly, the instrument must also meet a zero return tolerance of 0.5 e for any load that remains on the scale for 30 min.

The Committee recognized that it is not appropriate for type evaluation tests to be performed where fluctuating temperatures contribute uncertainty to test results. Initially, the Committee recommended time dependence tests for Class I, II, III, and IIII non-automatic weighing instruments undergoing type evaluation be conducted at only 20 °C. The Committee modified the proposal accordingly as recommended by industry. The Committee did so in keeping with the original intent of the OIML requirement, which is to eliminate the effects of influence factors on the instrument's performance during the time dependence test.

During the 2006 NCWM Annual Meeting, the Committee reconsidered the language that specifies time dependence tests should be conducted at "only" 20 °C since some interpret that to be an absolute for the temperature conditions during the tests. The Committee modified the proposed temperature limits while recognizing good laboratory practices in Publication 14, OIML R 76, and the Canadian Laboratory Manual to include an acceptable temperature variation in the laboratory environment of ± 2 °C. The Committee also included the corresponding Fahrenheit equivalent in the proposed language. The Committee agreed that the modified proposal is consistent with the temperature requirement for a constant reference temperature in OIML R 76 Section A.5.3.1. Static Temperatures.

320-7 VC T.N.4.6.(b) Apportionment Factors, Table T.N.4.6. Maximum Permissible Error (mpe)* for Load Cells During Type Evaluation, T.N.4.7. Creep Recovery for Load Cells During Type Evaluation, and Appendix D; Definitions of D_{min} and E_{min}

(This item was adopted.)

Source: National Type Evaluation Technical Committee (NTETC) Weighing Sector

Recommendation: Modify Paragraph T.N.4.6.(b) and Table T.N.4.6. as follows:

> **T.N.4.6. Time Dependence (Creep) for Load Cells During Type Evaluation.** – A load cell (force transducer) marked with an accuracy Class shall meet the following requirements at constant test conditions:
>
> **(a) Permissible Variations of Readings** . – With a constant maximum load for the measuring range (D_{max}) between 90 % and 100 % of maximum capacity (E_{max}), applied to the load cell, the difference between the initial reading and any reading obtained during the next 30 min shall not exceed the absolute value of the maximum permissible error (mpe) for the applied load (see Table T.N.4.6.). The difference between the reading obtained at 20 min and the reading obtained at 30 min shall not exceed 0.15 times the absolute value of the mpe (see Table T.N.4.6.).
>
> **(b) Apportionment Factors** . – The mpe for creep shall be determined from Table T.N.4.6. Maximum Permissible Error (mpe) * for Load Cells During Type Evaluation using the following apportionment factors (p_{LC}):
>
> > p_{LC} = 0.7 for load cells marked with S (single load cell applications), ~~and~~
> > p_{LC} = 1.0 for load cells marked with M (multiple load cell applications)**, and**
> > **p_{LC} = 0.5 for Class III L load cells marked with S or M**.
> > **(Amended 2006)**
>
> (Added 2005)

Table T.N.4.6. Maximum Permissible Error (mpe) * for Load Cells During Type Evaluation			
mpe in Load Cell Verifications Divisions (v) = p_{LC} x Basic Tolerance in v			
Class	p_{LC} x 0.5 v	p_{LC} x 1.0 v	p_{LC} x 1.5 v
I	0 - 50 000 v	50 001 v - 200 000 v	200 001 v +
II	0 - 5 000 v	5 001 v - 20 000 v	20 001 v +
III	0 - 500 v	501 v - 2 000 v	2 001 v +
IIII	0 - 50 v	51 v - 200 v	201 v +
III L	0 - 500 v	501 v - 1 000 v	(Add 0.5 v to the basic tolerance for each additional 500 v or fraction thereof up to a maximum load of 10 000 v)
v represents the load cell verification interval p_{LC} represents the apportionment factors applied to the basic tolerance p_{LC} = 0.7 for load cells marked with S (single load cell applications) p_{LC} = 1.0 for load cells marked with M (multiple load cell applications) **p_{LC} = 0.5 for Class III L load cells marked with S or M** * mpe = p_{LC} x Basic Tolerance in load cell verifications divisions (v)			

(Table Added 2005) **(Amended 2006)**

Add new Paragraph T.N.4.7. as follows:

T.N.4.7. Creep Recovery for Load Cells During Type Evaluation. – The difference between the initial reading of the minimum load of the measuring range (D_{min}) and the reading after returning to minimum load subsequent to the maximum load (D_{max}) having been applied for 30 min shall not exceed:

(a) 0.5 times the value of the load cell verification interval (0.5 v) for Class I, II, III, and IIII load cells, or

(b) 1.5 times the value of the load cell verification interval (1.5 v) for Class III L load cells.
(Added 2006)

Add new definitions of D_{min} and E_{min} to Appendix D as follows:

D_{min} (minimum load of the measuring range). Smallest value of a quantity (mass) which is applied to a load cell during test or use. This value shall not be less than E_{min}. [2.20]
(Added 2006)

E_{min} (minimum dead load). Smallest value of a quantity (mass) which may be applied to a load cell during test or use without exceeding the mpe. [2.20]
(Added 2006)

Discussion: In 2005 the NIST Handbook 44 Scales Code was modified to include requirements for time dependence tests and to align U. S. requirements and OIML test procedures. Creep recovery test procedures and the appropriate apportionment factor for Class III L load cells were inadvertently omitted from the proposal to modify NIST Handbook 44. This current proposal modifies the test notes to include the necessary procedures and to add corresponding terminology that defines the limits for error permitted during the creep recovery test.

After making several suggested changes to the definitions of D_{min} and E_{min} to correctly set minimum limits for each value and hearing no negative input during the 2006 Interim Meeting, the Committee made the proposal a voting item.

During the discussion of this item at the 2006 NCWM Annual Meeting, the Committee was questioned on whether or not it was necessary to include additional language in the requirements to specify that the temperature testing remain consistent with current temperature testing requirements and procedures in NIST Handbook 44. Based on comments from NIST WMD and the NTEP director, the Committee acknowledged the proposal should be revisited to include language to clarify that the allowable temperature limits and temperature ranges by class in Paragraphs T.N.8.1.1. and T.N.8.1.2 apply to the creep test for load cells. In the interest of providing due process and because most parties involved in NTEP who apply these requirements on a regular basis are familiar with how to interpret these tolerances, the Committee did not want to include such substantive changes to the proposal at this time.

320-8 W UR.1.6. Computing Scale Interfaced to a Cash Register

(This item was withdrawn.)

Source: Carryover Item 320-3. (This item originated from SWMA and first appeared on the Committee's 2005 agenda.)

Discussion: The Committee considered a proposal to add a new Paragraph UR.1.6. to the Scales Code as follows:

UR.1.6. Computing Scale Interfaced to a Cash Register. – A computing scale may interface with a cash register provided all displayed and recorded indications agree.
(Added 200X)

Discussion: This item proposed the creation of a new requirement in the Scales Code to address the proper interface of computing scales with electronic cash registers (ECRs). Simultaneously, work continues in SWMA to develop additional language to clarify for the field official how each component must display transaction information, function in taking tare, and operate with Price-Look-Up (PLU) capability. Currently, General Code provisions specifying that weighing and measuring equipment and associated devices shall not facilitate fraud may not be sufficient to clarify how a computing scale interfaced with an ECR should operate.

The proposal was developed in response to reports of computing scales interfaced with ECRs where the ECR accepts weighing results from the computing scale and uses the ECR's PLU feature to retrieve tare and unit price information and calculate the total price. In this instance a different unit price, tare, and total price were already manually entered and displayed on the computing scale. What customers viewed on the computing scale as the net weight, unit price, and total price was not what was actually used by the ECR to calculate the customer's charge. In this example, the devices in commercial use were also found out of compliance because the interface was not listed on their NTEP CC as an approved application.

The proposal began as a new specification (rather than a user requirement) with the exact wording as shown above. It was thought that the language should clarify the acceptability of the ECR and computing scale to communicate the total price, but not to the point where the input process involves the ECR calculating the total price. The Committee recommended that jurisdictions, if they have not already done so, establish clear examination procedures (e.g., enter a new price per pound at the ECR) so that officials also have field examination procedures to verify that an ECR and computing scale interface are in compliance.

The Committee heard numerous comments that the proposed specification would be too restrictive to new technology. Industry believed the proposal written as a specification might limit future technology to interface equipment. Subsequently, industry developed an alternate proposal that stated the ECR and POS indications must agree as shown above in the recommendation. Industry did so because it believes the proposed subparagraphs were too restrictive when a POS system reads UPC codes and recomputes prices for frequent shopper discounted prices. The Committee decided to consider an alternate proposal that only specifies "all indications must agree" since type evaluation already verifies the requirements proposed in the new paragraph. The Committee believes that if ECR input is part of the criteria for determining that an interface complies, then the language should be expanded to provide more detail to the field official as to how the interface works. The Committee concluded that a requirement is needed to ensure the user properly interfaces the equipment as approved by NTEP and as intended by the manufacturer's design once it is in commercial use. Consequently, the Committee modified the proposal making it a user requirement with the recommendation that it be adopted by NCWM.

S&T Committee 2006 Final Report

During the 2005 NCWM Annual Meeting, the Committee heard more details as to how a computing scale may be inappropriately interfaced with an ECR to create a POS system contrary to the intended device application covered on the device's CC. The Committee found that neither the earlier design specification nor the currently proposed user requirement addressed computing scales with multiple sales accumulation capability. The current definition of a POS was thought to require some modification to clarify the specific type of weighing element permitted as part of the POS assembly. After hearing this information, the Committee questioned whether or not this item should include both a design specification and a user requirement. The Committee changed the item status from "voting" to "information" and recommended SWMA rework the proposal to (1) provide more detail to the field official about how the cash register must function, (2) include a corresponding specification in NIST Handbook 44 to assist device manufacturers who are considering design modifications to a computing scale or cash register, and (3) ensure there are no conflicts with requirements in corresponding paragraphs such as Scales Code Paragraph S.1.8.4. Recorded Representations, Point-of-Sale Systems.

During the 2006 NCWM Interim Meeting, the Committee considered input from the 2005 fall regional weights and measures association meetings. WWMA recommended withdrawing the item since it believed there is sufficient language in General Code Paragraphs G-S.2. Graduations, Indications, and Recorded Representation, G-S.5.2.2. Digital Indication and Representation, and G-UR.1.1. Suitability of Equipment to address the proper interface of a POS with an ECR. NEWMA indicated the item should be withdrawn because it needed further development. SWMA received limited comments on the proposal and decided to take no position on the item. The Committee believes there is a need to alert POS operators about indiscriminately interfacing a POS and ECR. However, until such time as more work can be put into creating more explicit language that is not restrictive to technology and is self-explanatory to the field official, the Committee agreed with industry's alternate proposal for a simply stated user requirement that specifies the POS and ECR transaction information must agree.

At the 2006 NCWM Annual Meeting, the Committee concluded that the proposal as written is too general to clarify to the operator or field official what must occur in the interface of a computing scale and cash register. Consequently the Committee agreed to withdraw the item from its agenda. The Committee believes that jurisdictions either already or will take enforcement action when computing scales and cash registers are improperly interfaced based on existing General Code requirements. In the meantime, the Committee continues to encourage jurisdictions and NIST to include examination procedures as part of the field test and classroom instruction to address the issue of equipment interface. The Committee will consider revisiting the issue when the proposed language is more fully developed and can offer specific information on the proper interface of equipment.

For more background information, refer to the Committee's 2005 Final Report of the 90th NCWM Annual Report.

320-9 VC UR.2.6.1. Vehicle Scales; Approaches

(This item was adopted.)

Source: Central Weights and Measures Association (CWMA)

Recommendation: Modify Paragraph UR.2.6.1. as follows:

> **UR.2.6.1. Vehicle Scales.** – *On the entrance and exit end(s) of a vehicle scale installed in any one location for a period of 6 months or more, there shall be a straight approach as follows:*
>
> *(a) the width at least the width of the platform,*
>
> *(b) the length at least one-half the length of the platform but not required to be more than 12 m (40 ft), and*

(c) not less than 3 m (10 ft) of any approach adjacent to the platform shall be constructed of concrete or similar durable material to ensure that this portion remains smooth and level and in the same plane as the platform. However, grating of sufficient strength to withstand all loads equal to the concentrated load capacity of the scale may be installed in this portion. Any slope in the remaining portion of the approach shall ensure (1) ease of vehicle access, (2) ease for testing purposes, and (3) drainage away from the scale.
[Nonretroactive as of 1976]
(Amended 1977, 1983, ~~and~~ 1993 **and 2006**)

Discussion: The CWMA proposal was developed to clarify that Paragraph U.R.2.6.1. permits installations that have a combination entrance and exit because of space limitations at the installation site. NEWMA did not support the proposal because it believed the current language can already be interpreted to permit such installations.

NIST WMD cautions that improper exiting may cause excessive wear on the scale that can lead to inaccuracy and increased maintenance. In 1993 Paragraph UR.2.6.1. was modified to ensure a good exit path on scales, thus reducing unnecessary wear and tear on the device. The modification to Paragraph UR.2.6.1. was not intended to prohibit a scale with a single end used for both entry and exit of the scale, and the S&T Committee specifically noted this at the time. The text which originally read "the approach end or ends of a vehicle scale" was modified to read "the entrance and exit ends of a vehicle scale." This change promoted a good exit path that met specific requirements for width, length, and durability in construction. Prior to any modification of Paragraph UR.2.6.1., the single end of those scales being used for an entrance and exit were already being held to approach requirements.

During the 2006 NCWM Interim Meeting, the Committee agreed that the proposal as worded provided no new information about the requirement and this item was previously addressed when the requirement was modified in 1993. However, the Committee acknowledged that in the thirteen years since Paragraph UR.2.6.1. was last modified, some jurisdictions have prohibited scales from operating because the requirement was misinterpreted. Consequently, the Committee recommended adding a new note to Paragraph UR.2.6.1. to clarify that the requirement does not prohibit use of a single end of the vehicle scale that is properly designed for entering and exiting the scale.

At the 2006 NCWM Annual Meeting, the Committee agreed that previous modifications to Paragraph UR.2.6.1. already clarify that a single entrance and exit are permissible. The Committee did not want to add extensive language to this or other paragraphs on points covered in training or already documented in the Handbook and NCWM S&T Final Reports. Therefore, the Committee modified only one term by pluralizing the word "end" to become "end(s)" to clarify that both a separate entrance and exit or a single end serving dual duty as an entrance and an exit are recognized for a vehicle scale.

320-10 VC UR.3.7. Minimum Load on a Vehicle Scale

(This item was adopted.)

Source: Southern Weights and Measures Association (SWMA)

Recommendation: Modify Paragraph UR.3.7.(a) Minimum Load on a Vehicle Scale as follows:

UR.3.7. Minimum Load on a Vehicle Scale. – A vehicle scale shall not be used to weigh net loads smaller than:

(a) 10 d when weighing scrap material for recycling **or weighing refuse materials at landfills and transfer stations**;

(b) 50 d for all other weighing.

As used in this paragraph, scrap materials for recycling shall be limited to ferrous metals, paper (including cardboard), textiles, plastic, and glass.
(Amended 1988 ~~and~~ 1992 **and 2006**)

Background/Discussion: SWMA believes the same 10 d minimum load requirement granted in 1992 for the weighing of certain scrap materials and recyclables should apply to refuse hauled to landfills. Both types of material are redeemed or disposed of in small quantities and are awkward and sometimes unsafe to handle (e.g., they have long, sharp, protruding edges). Thus they fall under the earlier rationale that allowed the 10 d minimum load for recyclable materials. Due to the low value of refuse material, SWMA believes it is not profitable for centers to accept those materials nor feasible for them to purchase a suitable scale. SWMA noted that many municipal landfills accept refuse materials in quantities that are in violation of Paragraph UR.3.7., but do so to prevent citizens from improperly disposing of materials. SWMA believes that expanding the 10 d minimum load requirement is sensible and environmentally responsible.

The current minimum load requirement for vehicle scales evolved over a period of seventy years as the weights and measures community began to examine the uncertainties and errors that can occur when weighing small loads on vehicle scales. The history of the requirement is excerpted from the 1987, 1992, and 1995 S&T Final Reports of their respective NCWM Annual Reports. In 1937 a 1 000 lb minimum gross load requirement was adopted for vehicle scales. The focus of the 1937 discussions was the relationship of the minimum tolerance to the gross load with no consideration given to errors that occur as a result of rounding indications to the nearest division.

In 1980 the scale industry discussed proposals for OIML scale requirements that included a minimum load requirement for each accuracy class based on both the applicable scale tolerance and rounding error. In 1984 a recommended minimum load requirement was adopted for scales marked with an accuracy class since weighing of light loads was likely to result in relatively large errors.

In 1987 a minimum net load requirement was addressed. The load weighed on a scale should be sufficiently large so that the resolution of the scale (rounded to the nearest scale division) does not result in an excessively large error as a percentage of the weighed load. This principle is more important since net weight is determined by two weighings where the results are rounded to the nearest division at each weighing, thus the potential error becomes $\pm$ 1 d. In 1988 a minimum net load requirement of 50 d was adopted for vehicle scales.

In 1992 an exemption was granted from the 50 d minimum net load requirement to allow a 10 d minimum net load requirement for scrap material to promote recycling and conservation. Examples of scrap material for recycling for the purpose of the exemption were specifically defined as: ferrous metals, paper (including cardboard), textiles, plastic, and glass typically with low redemption value and difficult to handle thus requiring more labor to offload, further reducing the material's value. The Committee encouraged weights and measures officials and the recycling industry to work together to ensure good business practices were followed to include education and weighing all materials on a suitable scale.

In 1994 the Committee considered a proposal to modify Paragraph UR.3.7. to return to a 50 d minimum gross load requirement for all vehicle scales. At that time adequate justification was not heard for returning to a less stringent minimum load requirement. The Committee also heard an alternative proposal to permit a 10 d minimum net load on a vehicle scale for solid wastes disposed of in landfills. The Committee found it self-defeating to adopt a requirement and then continually revisit the requirement further adding to a laundry list of exemptions.

At its October 2005 Interim Meeting, NEWMA supported an alternative proposal which would require a 20 d minimum load for all commodities weighed on a vehicle scale. NEWMA reported that some jurisdictions do not enforce the 50 d minimum load requirement at municipal landfills and other sites because of the low cost of the commodity. NEWMA suggested several points for consideration when there is a 10 d minimum load requirement. First, the price of the commodity should be a factor in deciding the minimum load limit. Additionally, it is also inappropriate to have a 10 d minimum load requirement especially for large-capacity scales where rounding errors may contribute to uncertainties in the measurement.

The Committee was asked to consider that the proposal is not meant to limit the application to "landfills" and should also include materials transported to "refuse transfer stations." These facilities are in use because local landfills have reached capacity. Transfer stations accept materials typically not picked up at curbside by municipal waste trucks. Materials are transported from transfer stations to a regional facility. Transfer stations charge town residents a fee based on the vehicle's inbound and outbound weight; however, the net load is frequently less than 1000 lb and in violation of Paragraph UR.3.7. Conditions similar to those found at recycling centers exist at refuse transfer stations where the environment is dirty and unsafe. Unloading small loads from truck beds and car trunks requires more time and human intervention since equipment such as skip loaders are not practical. Consequently, any fees associated with handling refuse material are higher to recoup even though weighment occurs on a more suitable 1000 lb capacity scale. The unfortunate consequence of following a practice that is more labor intensive and involving higher fees is that jurisdictions see an increase in illegal dumping of materials by town residents.

During the 2006 NCWM Interim Meeting, the Committee considered the NCWM review panel's recommendations and heard numerous comments on the proposal during the open hearing session. The review panel indicated the proposal was not ready for consideration by the Committee since no data was provided to demonstrate the impact of weighing errors occurring nationally at landfills that accept refuse materials. During the open hearing, multiple jurisdictions reported that although officials are aware that landfills are not complying with the minimum load requirements, they have difficulties enforcing the requirement especially on weekends when residents are most likely to use landfills. Some jurisdictions were in favor of a flat rate for loads less than 50 d, but noted that centers use the same scale prohibited for use in weighing light loads to determine when a customer's load should be assessed at the flat rate. One jurisdiction noted that even though a customer is assessed a flat rate, there are environmental regulations that require weighing of that same customer's load so that there is some record of the amount of materials going into landfills. NIST WMD recommended use of a suitable scale to ensure (1) there is sufficient scale resolution to reduce the potential error introduced when rounding weight indications to the nearest division and (2) the tolerance that applies to the device under test does not represent a significant portion of the smallest net load. The Committee was cautioned about where to set the minimum load limit since wind can affect readings for loads even at 20 d. One question that could not be answered was whether there is any effort to educate business operators about scale errors and other good weighing practices.

The Committee considered the lengthy history of the requirement as well as comments made during the 2006 NCWM Interim Meeting to reach a recommendation on the proposal. The Committee acknowledged past changes to the requirement to address the relationship of tolerances and rounding of indications to light loads and exemptions granted to promote recycling and conservation. The Committee also recognized the reluctance of past committees to further add to a laundry list of exemptions. The Committee believes there is national concern about the difficulties in handling refuse materials and wants to discourage roadside dumping of refuse materials. The proposal does not clarify what materials fall into the category of "refuse" nor does it address instances where some jurisdictions may prohibit disposal of certain materials such as tires. The original language of the proposal exempted the less valuable recyclable materials. The Committee asked for input to determine if a similar distinction should be made based on value of refuse materials. This may not be an appropriate approach since some jurisdictions indicate that the cost of disposing of some refuse material makes these items more valuable than recyclable materials. The Committee heard that for many officials the higher priority was to ensure proper disposal of refuse material. The Committee agreed that proper disposal should be recognized at transfer station installations; therefore, they modified the proposal to include refuse transfer stations and made the proposal a voting item.

During the 2006 NCWM Annual Meeting, the Committee made minor modifications to the proposed text to clarify that the 10 d minimum net load exclusion applies to weighing of recyclable scrap material *or* when weighing refuse at sites considered landfills or transfer stations.

320-11 VC List of International Symbols Noted as Acceptable

(This item was adopted.)

Source: Carryover Item 320-9. (This item originated from the Southern Weights and Measures Association (SWMA) and first appeared on the Committee's 2005 agenda.)

Recommendation: Add a new list of acceptable abbreviations and symbols to NIST Handbook 112, Examination Procedure Outlines for Commercial Weighing and Measuring Devices as follows:

S&T Committee 2006 Final Report

Appendix to NIST Handbook 112

List of Acceptable Abbreviations/Symbols

Device Application	Term/Function	Acceptable Abbreviations/Symbols	Not Acceptable
The following symbols are intended for operator controls, indications, and features. When they are also intended for the customer (including customer-operated devices), they cannot be used without additional descriptions, directions, or marks displayed or marked on the device.			
Operational Controls, Indications, Features:	Zero Key or Center of Zero Indicator	■	"z" alone is not acceptable unless term is defined on device
	Off (Power)	■	
	On (Power)	|	
	On/Off (Power)	ⓘ	
	Print	■	
	Weighing	⚖	
	Scale n (n = 1, 2, ...)	⚖n	
	Range n (n = 1, 2, ...)	→|n|←	
	High Resolution	△HR	
	Enter Key	↵	
Operational Controls, Indications, Features:	Tare Enter Key	←◇T	
	Tare Clear Key	T◇→	
	Tare Enter/Tare Clear	↔◇T	←→T (hexagon)
	Verify Tare	←◇T	
	Not For Direct Sales to the Public	👤⊘	
	Combined Zero/Tare – See S.2.1.6. For Additional Information	→0/T←	
	Taring	→T←	
	Mass/Weight	⚖	

S&T - 30

Device Application	Term/Function	Acceptable Abbreviations/Symbols	Not Acceptable
	The following symbols are intended for operator controls, indications, and features. When they are also intended for the customer (including customer-operated devices), they cannot be used without additional descriptions, directions, or marks displayed or marked on the device.		
	Money	(symbol)	
	Price Per Weight Unit	(symbol)	
	Piece Count	(symbol)	
	Counter	1 2 3	
	Read Counter	↑ 1 2 3	
	Print Certificate	(symbol)	
	Information	(symbol)	
	This list does not standardize the abbreviations/symbols that must be used. Rather, it identifies abbreviations/symbols that are routinely acceptable. This list is not limiting or all-inclusive; other abbreviations/symbols may be acceptable.		

(Table Added 2006)

Discussion: The list of symbols in the proposal introduces the U. S. weights and measures official to a set of international symbols for use in marking operator controls, indications, and device features. Recognition and use of these symbols are consistent with efforts to harmonize U. S. and international device requirements.

Currently, the list of symbols in the proposal is part of NCWM Publication 14 "Technical Policy, Checklists, and Test Procedures" for weighing devices. NTEP uses international symbols whenever possible. Style differences, such as variations in the shape of arrows, are acceptable.

The Committee heard various recommendations for making the symbols readily accessible. The recommendations ranged from posting the list on a weights and measures website to placing the list in NIST Handbook 44 as an appendix.

The Committee agreed with the need to familiarize U. S. officials with international symbols and considered a recommendation for making the list of acceptable new symbols a new Appendix E in NIST Handbook 44. During the 2005 NCWM Annual Meeting, the Committee agreed that unless the table references a specific code, then the table applies to all types of devices. The Committee believed that if the table is to be used as an enforcement tool, then only symbols in the proposed list would be considered acceptable. The Committee preferred an all-inclusive list of acceptable symbols if the list is to appear as part of Handbook 44. If the table is intended to be all-inclusive, other acceptable symbols currently in use for all device types, such as the dollar sign ($) on retail motor-fuel dispensers and taxi meters, must be added to the list. The Committee changed the status of the item from voting to information to allow time to determine how the table could be linked to specific codes and to fully assess whether or not the table should be all-inclusive.

At their fall 2005 meetings, the regional weights and measures associations differed in their positions. WWMA recommended withdrawing the proposal since the owner's manual or NCWM Publication 14 can be referenced for symbols and other markings and any device that holds a CC must have approved markings. CWMA recommended listing the symbols in NIST Handbook 44. NEWMA suggested an alternate title "List of Acceptable Commonly Used Abbreviations/Symbols."

SMA supported the proposal with the following recommendations: (1) change the table's title to read, "List of Common International Symbols, (2) make the symbols consistent in size and font, (3) completely eliminate the "Device Application" and "Not Acceptable" columns, one and four respectively, (4) remove the heading "Term" in column two and replace it with the word "Function" and remove the heading "Acceptable" in column three and replace it with the word "Symbol," and (5) add a note stating there are other approved symbols that are not included in the table.

During the 2006 Interim Meeting, the Committee agreed that the list with several modifications to column headings should be a voting item at the 2006 NCWM Annual Meeting. The Committee changed the column headings to ensure they correctly identify all subject matter listed in a specific section. Consequently, the heading in column two specifies term and function and the heading in column three identifies that section as abbreviations and symbols that are acceptable. The Committee also agreed the list should be made available as an appendix to the EPOs. The list should also be routinely updated to delete more commonly accepted and recognized symbols. The EPOs are used by field officials during test and inspection of devices to determine the appropriate procedure and code references and are accessible on the NIST WMD website at www.nist.gov/owm. The Committee recommended examining up-to-date lists of international symbols such as those published by DIN (Deutsches Institut fur Normung e.V.), the German Institute for Standardization, as a source for adding new acceptable symbols to the table.

At the 2006 NCWM Annual Meeting, the Committee agreed to several modifications to the table to provide uniformity in the format of the text case and to explain how the table of abbreviations and symbols are meant to apply. The Committee kept the list of "Not Acceptable" symbols because it is important to specify abbreviations, terms, and symbols, etc., for officials responsible for inspection of devices. Additionally, the list recognizes the work done by technical committees and other such bodies to identify specific designations that are not appropriate, and it helps to avoid unnecessary disputes or investment in characters deemed not suitable for use in commercial device applications. The Committee included a new footnote to clarify how the abbreviations and symbols are used that is consistent with the policy for markings and indications approved for devices that undergo type evaluation. The Committee agreed that timely maintenance of the table is critical to the value of the information to weights and measures officials, but did not elaborate on a plan for this process at this time.

For more background information, refer to the Committee's 2005 Final Report of the 90th NCWM Annual Report.

321 BELT-CONVEYOR SCALE SYSTEMS

321-1 V N.1.1. Official Test, N.4. As-found Inspection and Tests, and UR.4.1. As-found Inspection and Tests

(This item was adopted.)

Source: Western Weights and Measures Association (WWMA)

Recommendation: Modify Paragraph N.1.1. as follows:

N.1.1. Official Test. – An official test of a belt-conveyor scale system shall be a include tests specified in N.3.1. Zero Load Tests, N.3.2. mMaterials tTests, and, if applicable, N.3.3. Simulated Load Tests. (Amended 2006)

Discussion: Most commercial weighing and measuring devices are subject to unannounced inspections by weights and measures officials. However, the nature of the inspection and test described in Paragraph N.1.1. usually requires advance scheduling to arrange the logistics for testing the reference scale(s) and, if necessary, procurement of vehicles or railcars to transport the pre-weighed or post-weighed material. This practice provided many owner/users of belt-conveyor scales with an opportunity to inspect, clean, and prepare the systems in advance of the test. The owner/user of the scale is required to notify the official with statutory authority that the scale is ready for test in accordance with Paragraph UR.4. Compliance. As a result, the official cannot verify compliance with NIST Handbook 44 General Code Paragraph G-UR.4.1. Maintenance of Equipment since the as-found condition and performance of the scale do not represent its as-used condition and performance.

The proposal encourages officials to perform as-found inspections and zero-load and simulated load tests to assess compliance with G-UR.4.1. Maintenance of Equipment rather than relying solely on the inspection conducted during the official material tests. The proposal further encourages scale owners and users to perform and document routine inspections and maintenance of the belt-conveyor scale system if they know they are subject to unannounced inspections. WWMA modified the proposal before recommending it for consideration by the Committee. SWMA asked for additional input from parties affected by the proposal before it took a position.

The Committee also considered some additional wording regarding tests conducted during the as-found inspection for proposed new Paragraph N.4. from the belt-scale service industry. The alternate language was recommended due to concerns about liability issues that might arise because the current wording in Paragraph N.4. implies it is the official who must run the test. However, the Committee did not agree with the recommendation because officials must and do use discretion in their abilities to perform tests based on the design, safety, etc., of systems at each installation.

The Committee acknowledged that officials have the authority to conduct as-found inspections based on General Code Paragraph G-UR.2.3. Accessibility for Inspection, Testing, and Sealing Purposes. However, previous committees have gone to great lengths to ensure that adequate provisions are in place to address the proper operation and maintenance of belt-conveyor scale systems. The Committee made one editorial change to Paragraph N.4. to include the word "certifies" to clarify the official does not have to wait for the owner of or agent for the system to certify the scale is ready for inspection. The Committee agreed the proposal provides necessary guidelines about when to test devices that have a significant impact on commerce and yet the timing, logistics, etc., required to conduct an official inspection can become a deterrent to performing official duties. Consequently, the Committee made the proposal a voting item.

The Committee made editorial changes to proposed new Paragraph N.4. to include text that clarifies the inspection frequency is based on the business's compliance history. The Committee further modified Paragraph N.4. and Paragraph N.1.1. in response to concerns that the language as written implied the statutory authority must perform the test when the official typically witnesses the test. The Committee moved forward with wording for an additional new test note and corresponding user requirement granting officials greater flexibility to make unannounced inspections as follows:

> N.4. As-found Inspection and Test. – The official with statutory authority may inspect the belt-conveyor scale system as found in normal operation without prior written notification from the owner or his agent that certifies the system is in compliance and ready for material testing as required in UR.4. Compliance. During the as-found inspection, the official may conduct zero-load and simulated load tests. The official with statutory authority will require that an official material test be conducted within a timeframe established by the official [1]. (Added 2006)
>
> [1] The official material test may be scheduled sooner than the normal frequency of testing based upon areas of non-compliance and the condition of the installation during the as-found inspection and tests.
>
> UR.4.1. As-found Inspection and Tests. – As a result of the tests and inspections performed according to Paragraph N.4. As-found Inspection and Tests, the scale owner and/or his agent shall correct any deficiencies identified by the official prior to the official material test. They may also continue performing scheduled or routine maintenance (e.g., cleaning and checking alignment, pulleys, idlers, etc.) prior to the official material tests provided these activities are documented as part of the operational procedures for the installation. The scale owner and/or his agent shall notify the official with statutory authority when the areas of non-compliance have been corrected and if repairs or adjustments are required or performed due to conveyor or scale equipment damage or failure.

(Added 200X)

The intent of the proposal is to provide the inspector with the option of requiring or not requiring a material test during an as-found inspection and test. The Committee acknowledged the importance of this language in spelling out the conditions for unannounced inspections not only for the field official, but also for the contractual customer who is not always familiar with NIST Handbook 44 requirements.

During the 2006 NCWM Annual Meeting voting session, the wording of proposed new Paragraphs N.4. and UR.4.1. were opposed because they set a precedence for specific device code language where powers for inspection were already granted. Consequently, Paragraphs N.4. and UR.4.1. were deleted from the proposal and Paragraph N.1.1. was left to clarify that the official test may consist of either the Zero Load, Materials, or Simulated Load Tests.

S&T Committee 2006 Final Report

330 LIQUID-MEASURING DEVICES

330-1 VC S.1.2. Units

(This item was adopted.)

Source: National Type Evaluation Technical Committee (NTETC) Measuring Sector

Recommendation: Modify Paragraph S.1.2. Units as follows:

> **S.1.2. Units.** – A liquid-measuring device shall indicate, and record if the device is equipped to record, its deliveries in liters, gallons, quarts, pints, **fluid ounces,** or binary-submultiples or decimal subdivisions of the liter or gallon. (Amended 1987, 1994**, and 2006**)

Background/Discussion: Some years ago NTEP issued a CC for a liquid-measuring device that displays its deliveries in fluid ounces. The device currently in use always makes a delivery of 4 fluid ounces. A jurisdiction would not approve the use of the device stating that those units of measurement are not recognized in Paragraph S.1.2. in the LMD code. Noting, however, that because Paragraph S.1.2. allows binary submultiples of the liter or gallon, an indication of $^{1}/_{32}$ gal would be acceptable.

At the spring 2005 NTEP Laboratory Meeting, the laboratories agreed that consumers would understand and accept a 4 fl oz unit better than a $^{1}/_{32}$ gal unit and asked the Measuring Sector to review the proposal shown above.

At their October 2005 meetings, the NTETC Measuring Sector and SWMA agreed to forward the proposal to the Committee for consideration.

At the 2006 NCWM Interim Meeting, the Committee heard no opposition to Item 330-1 and agreed to present the item for a vote at the 2006 NCWM Annual Meeting.

At the 2006 NCWM Annual Meeting, there was no opposition to this item.

330-2 I S.1.2.3. Value of the Smallest Unit

Source: National Type Evaluation Technical Committee (NTETC) Measuring Sector

Discussion: The Committee considered a proposal to modify NIST Handbook 44, Paragraph S.1.2.3. as follows:

> **S.1.2.3. Value of Smallest Unit.** – The value of the smallest unit of indicated delivery, and recorded delivery if the device is equipped to record, shall not exceed the equivalent of:
>
> (a) 0.5 L (~~1 pt~~ **0.1 gal**) on ~~retail~~ devices **with a maximum rated flow rate of 750 L/min (200 gal/min) or less.**
>
> (b) 5 L (1 gal) on ~~wholesale~~ devices **with a maximum rated flow of more than 750 L/min (200 gal/min)**
>
> This requirement does not apply to manually operated devices equipped with stops or stroke-limiting means. (Amended 1983**,** ~~and~~ 1986**, and 200X**)

In 2004 the definition of a "retail device" in NIST Handbook 44 was modified to include all devices used to measure product for the purpose of sale to the end user. At that time the Committee believed all affected parties were aware of the proposal and there was no opposition to the change. The Committee had not considered applications where very large deliveries are made to the end user, typically at high flow rates. After the 2005 edition of the handbook was published and distributed, WMD received a comment from a weights and measures jurisdiction that routinely tests large meters used to deliver fuel to fishing fleets and other large ocean-going boats. The jurisdiction stated that the average delivery is approximately 300 000 gal and may be as much as 1 000 000 gal. Prior to the revision of the definition of "retail," the value of the smallest unit of the indicated delivery for these devices was permitted to be 1 gal. Most of these devices have mechanical registers which make it impractical to have a smallest unit of 0.1 gal at the high flow rates used for such large deliveries. Because the fuel is being delivered to the end user, the jurisdiction believes this is a retail delivery. However, with the revisions to the definition of retail device, NIST Handbook 44 now requires a smallest unit of delivery of not more than 0.5 L (1 pt or 0.125 gal) for these devices.

At its October 2005 meeting, the NTETC Measuring Sector developed the proposal above and agreed to forward the proposal to the Committee for consideration. The Measuring Sector believed that, because the maximum flow rate for many applications has increased, 200 gal/min is an appropriate "break point" for determining what the smallest unit of measurement should be. At its October 2005 meeting, SWMA agreed with the Measuring Sector's proposal and recommended that the item move forward to the Committee.

At the 2006 NCWM Interim Meeting, it was suggested that the Committee should revisit the discussion on suitability of liquid-measuring devices that was discussed by NCWM in 1991 through 1993. In these earlier discussions, NCWM was unable to reach a consensus on any changes to NIST Handbook 44, and the item was withdrawn from the Committee agenda. The Committee was informed that there was interest expressed at the 2005 NTETC Measuring Sector Meeting in developing new criteria addressing suitability as it relates to flow rate, minimum measured quantity (MMQ), and the smallest unit of measure for applications using liquid-measuring devices. The Committee encourages the NTETC Measuring Sector to pursue development of suitability requirements for submission to the Committee for consideration. In the meantime, the Committee heard no opposition to Item 330-2 and agreed to present the item for a vote at the 2006 NCWM Annual Meeting.

At the 2006 NCWM Annual Meeting, the Committee received input from several manufacturers of aircraft refueling equipment that there is a safety concern with stationary refueling systems capable of delivering jet fuel through two different size hoses at different flow rates using two different meters. In this scenario, the operators of the refueling facility want both meters to have the same unit of indication; that is, 5 L or 1 gal. The Committee understood the concern, but was reluctant to modify the recommendation based on the limited information available at the meeting. The Committee believed that the aircraft refueling industry should propose a change during the next Conference cycle through the NTETC Measuring Sector and the regional associations. However, the Committee recognized that a legitimate problem may exist with existing jet aircraft refueling equipment and encouraged weights and measures jurisdictions to consider safety implications before taking official action on existing jet aircraft refueling devices that may not meet the requirements of Paragraph S.1.2.3. During the voting session there appeared to be concern that if this item was adopted weights and measures officials could be perceived as ignoring safety issues for aircraft refueling. There was an evident lack of support for the item without an exemption for jet aircraft refueling; therefore, the Committee changed the status of Item 330-2 to an information item to provide sufficient time for development of appropriate language to address the safety concerns with jet aircraft refueling equipment.

330-3   VC Table S.2.2. Categories of Device and Methods of Sealing

(This item was adopted.)

Source: National Type Evaluation Technical Committee (NTETC) Measuring Sector

Recommendation: Modify Paragraph S.2.2 and Table S.2.2. as follows:

S.2.2. Provision for Sealing. – Adequate provision shall be made for an approved means of security (e.g., data change audit trail) or for physically applying a security seal in such a manner that requires the security seal to be broken before an adjustment can be made of:

(a) any measur **ingement or indicating** element, or

(b) any adjustable element for controlling delivery rate when such rate tends to affect the accuracy of deliveries~~.~~; and

(c) any metrological parameter that will affect the metrological integrity of the device or system.

When applicable, the adjusting mechanism shall be readily accessible for purposes of affixing a security seal.

Audit trails shall use the format set forth in Table S.2.2.
[Nonretroactive and enforceable as of January 1, 1995]
(Amended 1991, 1993, ~~and~~ 1995, and 2006)

Table S.2.2. Categories of Device and Methods of Sealing	
Category of Device	**Method of Sealing**
Category 1: No remote configuration capability.	*Seal by physical seal or two event counters: one for calibration parameters and one for configuration parameters.*
~~[Category 2 applies only to devices manufactured prior to January 1, 2005. Devices with remote configuration capability manufactured after that date must meet the sealing requirements outlined in Category 3. Devices without remote configuration capability manufactured after that date must meet the minimum criteria outlined in Category 1.]~~ *Category 2: Remote configuration capability, but access is controlled by physical hardware.* *The device shall clearly indicate that it is in the remote configuration mode and record such message if capable of printing in this mode or shall not operate while in this mode.*	*[The hardware enabling access for remote communication must be on-site. The hardware must be sealed using a physical seal or an event counter for calibration parameters and an event counter for configuration parameters. The event counters may be located either at the individual measuring device or at the system controller; however, an adequate number of counters must be provided to monitor the calibration and configuration parameters of the individual devices at a location. If the counters are located in the system controller rather than at the individual device, means must be provided to generate a hard copy of the information through an on-site device.]** *[*Nonretroactive as of January 1, 1996]*
Category 3: Remote configuration capability access may be unlimited or controlled through a software switch (e.g., password). *[Nonretroactive as of January 1, 1995]* *The device shall clearly indicate that it is in the remote configuration mode and record such message if capable of printing in this mode or shall not operate while in this mode.* *[Nonretroactive as of January 1, 2001]* ~~Nonretroactive as of January 1, 2005, all devices with remote configuration capability must comply with the sealing requirements of Category 3.~~	*An event logger is required in the device; it must include an event counter (000 to 999), the parameter ID, the date and time of the change, and the new value of the parameter. A printed copy of the information must be available through the device or through another on-site device. The event logger shall have a capacity to retain records equal to 10 times the number of sealable parameters in the device, but not more than 1000 records are required.* (**Note**: *Does not require 1000 changes to be stored for each parameter.*)

[Nonretroactive as of January 1, 1995]
(Table Added 1993) (Amended 1995, 1998, ~~and~~ 1999**, and 2006**)

Background/Discussion: At its 1998 Annual Meeting, NCWM adopted a proposal to eliminate "Category 2" as an option for devices that fall under the sealing requirements for Liquid-Measuring Devices Code and the Mass Flow Meters Code. In 1992, the Committee agreed to add "Category 2" to the acceptable forms of audit trail because an event counter requires significant memory and many device manufacturers wanted to provide remote configuration capability for at least some of the sealable parameters. Because many devices in use at the time had limited memory, a "hybrid" form of audit trail was established. The restricted access to the hardware that inhibits and activates the remote configuration capability eliminated the need for the complete form of the event logger for this category. This hybrid form was intended to allow these devices to continue to be used until larger amounts of memory were more readily available. In 1998, a "sunset" date of January 1, 2005, was established for the Category 2 method of sealing, after which time it was expected that larger amounts of memory would be more common in these applications. Thus it was that, effective January 1, 2005, all devices falling under these two codes must be designed as a Category 1 device or, if equipped with remote configuration capability, must be a Category 3 device.

At its October 2005 meeting, the NTETC Measuring Sector discussed the elimination of "Category 2" from the LMD Code and also discussed the addition of electronic sealing criteria to other NIST Handbook 44 measuring codes, such as the Vehicle-Tank Meters Code or the LPG and Anhydrous Ammonia Liquid-Measuring Devices, for liquid-measuring devices that do not have specific provisions for electronic security (i.e., audit trails). At the meeting, manufacturers of these devices stated that they have designed metering systems with electronic security with remote configuration capability. They are currently seeking an NTEP CC for these systems. Currently, the specific NIST Handbook 44 code for these devices does not address electronic sealing; however, electronic sealing is recognized in the General Code and under the provisions of G-A.3. Special and Unclassified Equipment. The specific audit trail criteria in the LMD Code can be applied where appropriate. The manufacturers would prefer that each code include specific language similar to that in the LMD Code. During the discussion, the Sector concluded that some of these new applications and other applications currently in use would have been classified as the former "Category 2" devices. Some NTEP CCs have been issued stating that the device evaluated was a Category 1 device; however, because the mechanism for accessing sealable configuration parameters is not a permanent part of the device and can be removed without affecting normal operation, the device actually meets the definition of remote configuration capability. The manufacturers of these devices believe that no problems have been reported due to their current method of sealing and that it is inappropriate to require them to change the method of sealing to comply with Category 3. The Sector agreed that the industry would not have supported the decision to remove "Category 2" from the LMD Code and the Mass-Flow Meters Code had they had a clear understanding of "remote configuration capability" and that the decision should be reversed. The Committee also agreed that provisions for electronic sealing should be added to all appropriate liquid-measuring device codes as proposed in Items 330-3, 331-2, 332-1, 334-1, 335-1, 337-1, and 338-1. The Sector agreed to forward that proposal to the Committee for consideration.

At the 2006 NCWM Interim Meeting, two jurisdictions suggested that the requirements for audit trails provided in Table S.2.2. could be placed in the General Code. Several meter manufacturers stated concerns that if moving the table to the General Code would delay the proposal to recognize "Category 2" devices for liquid-measuring devices they would prefer to have Item 330-3 move forward as presented. The Committee was concerned that moving the requirements, as shown above, to the General Code could cause a conflict with other device-specific codes, such as the Belt-Conveyor Scale Systems Code, that do not recognize "Category 2" devices. The Committee also heard that Paragraph S.2.2. should be modified to require security for all changes to metrologically significant parameters. The Committee agreed to modify Paragraph S.2.2. as shown above and to present Item 330-3 for a vote at the 2006 NCWM Annual Meeting.

At the 2006 NCWM Annual Meeting, there was no opposition to this item.

330-4　V　S.3.1. Diversion of Measured Liquid

(This item did not pass or fail; therefore, it returns to the Committee.)

Source: Central Weights and Measures Association (CWMA)

Recommendation: Amend Paragraph S.3.1. as follows:

S.3. Discharge Lines and Valves.

S.3.1. Diversion of Measured Liquid. – No means shall be provided by which any measured liquid can be diverted from the measuring chamber of the meter or its discharge line. Two or more delivery outlets may be installed only if automatic means are provided to ensure that:

(a) liquid can flow from only one outlet at a time, and

(b) the direction of flow for which the mechanism may be set at any time is clearly and conspicuously indicated.

A**n** ~~manually-controlled~~ outlet that may be opened for purging or draining the measuring system or for recirculating**, if recirculation is required in order to maintain the** product in **a deliverable state,** ~~suspension~~ shall be permitted ~~only when the system is measuring food products or agri-chemicals.~~ Effective **automatic** means shall be provided to prevent passage of liquid through any such outlet during normal operation of the measuring system and to inhibit meter indications (or advancement of indications) and recorded representations while the outlet is in operation.
(Amended 1991, 1995, ~~and~~ 1996 **and 2006**)

Background/Discussion: CWMA noted that the requirements in Paragraph S.3.1. of Section 3.30 Liquid Measuring Devices and Paragraph S.4.1. Diversion of Measured Product of Section 3.37. Mass Flow Meters of NIST Handbook 44 (2005 edition) are not consistent with each other. Paragraph S.3.1. bans manual valves for recirculating product or purging or draining the measuring system except for foods and agri-chemicals. Paragraph S.4.1. allows manual valves but appears to ban automatic valves by omission, and it makes no distinction for types of products measured as long as the system meets the specified requirements.

Cold weather and physical characteristics make recirculation necessary for a number of products not currently recognized in Paragraph S.3.1. of Section 3.30., for example, #6 Fuel Oil and B100 Biodiesel. Although liquid-measuring devices exist which have NTEP CCs for these high viscosity products, the current wording of Handbook 44 restricts vendors of these products to using mass flow technology if they wish to recirculate their product in order to keep it in a deliverable state. This appears to be the unintended result of the fact that the two codes were written at different times with different input from industry lobbies. CWMA recommended that retailers of these products not be restricted to using only mass flow meters for commercial measurements if other suitable technologies are available. Likewise, both manual and automatic valves are suitable for recirculating products in discharge lines of these devices, and the use of either type should be allowed.

At the CWMA 2005 Interim Meeting, it was noted that adopting this proposal would create a logical and consistent standard of enforcement for mass flow meters and liquid-measuring devices, which are used for identical applications and products, thus ending an unintentional bias in favor of one technology over the other.

By stating uniform operation guidelines for when it is acceptable to allow purge lines and recirculation lines (i.e., the necessity for such lines to keep the product in a deliverable state), this proposal would eliminate the need for industry to petition NCWM for each product which requires such special handling. CWMA agreed to forward the proposal with the recommendation that it be a voting item on the Committee's 2006 agenda.

At the 2006 NCWM Interim Meeting, the Committee heard no opposition to Item 330-4 and agreed to present the item for a vote at the 2006 NCWM Annual Meeting. (See also corresponding Item 337-2.)

At the 2006 NCWM Annual Meeting, the Committee decided that the means to prevent passage of liquid through any such outlet during normal operation of the measuring system and to inhibit meter indications should be automatic and modified the proposal accordingly as shown in the recommendation above. During the voting session a member expressed concern that the proposal as submitted and modified would allow diversion of flow for any application. Item 330-4 received insufficient votes to pass or fail; therefore, the item returns to the Committee.

330-5 VC Table T.2. Accuracy Classes for Liquid Measuring Devices Covered in NIST Handbook 44 Section 3.30

(This item was adopted.)

Source: National Type Evaluation Technical Committee (NTETC) Measuring Sector

Recommendation: Modify Table T.2. as follows:

Table T.2. Accuracy Classes for Liquid Measuring Devices Covered in NIST Handbook 44 Section 3.30				
Accuracy Class	Application	Acceptance Tolerance	Maintenance Tolerance	Special Test Tolerance[1]
0.3	Petroleum products delivered from large capacity (flow rates over 115 L/min (30 gal/min))** devices including motor fuel devices, heated products at or greater than 50° C asphalt at or below temperatures 50° C, all other liquids not shown where the typical delivery is over 200 L (50 gal)	0.2 %	0.3 %	0.5 %
0.3A	Asphalt at temperatures greater than 50° C	0.3 %	0.3 %	0.5 %
0.5*	Petroleum products delivered from small capacity (at 4 L/min (1 gal/min) through 115 L/min (30 gal/min))** motor-fuel devices, agri-chemical liquids, and all other applications not shown where the typical delivery is ≤ 200 L (50 gal)	0.3 %	0.5 %	0.5 %
1.1	Petroleum products and other normal liquids from devices with flow rates** less than 1 gal/min and devices designed to deliver less than 1 gal	0.75 %	1.0 %	1.25 %

*For ~~5-gallon and 10-gallon~~ test **drafts ≤ 40 liters or 10 gallons,** the tolerances specified for Accuracy Class 0.5 in the table above do not apply. For these test drafts**, the following applies:**

(a) ~~the m~~**M**aintenance tolerances on normal and special tests ~~for 5-gallon and 10-gallon test drafts shall~~ **be 20 ml plus 4 ml per indicated liter or 1 in^3 plus 1 in^3 per indicated gal**~~are 6 cubic inches and 11 cubic inches, respectively~~.

(b) Acceptance tolerances on normal and special tests ~~are 3 cubic inches and 5.5 cubic inches~~ **shall be one-half the maintenance tolerance values.**

[1] Special test tolerances are not applicable to retail motor-fuel dispensers.

** Flow rate refers to designed or marked maximum flow rate.

(Added 2002) **(Amended 2006)**

Background/Discussion: Prior to the 2002 addition of Table T.2. "Accuracy Classes for Liquid-Measuring Devices Covered in NIST Handbook 44 Section 3.30." to the LMD Code of NIST Handbook 44, the applicable tolerances in T.2.1. Tolerance Values for "retail devices" of any flow rate, including RMFDs, were the same for normal and special tests. Special test tolerances were only applicable to "wholesale devices" measuring liquids other than agri-chemicals and asphalt.

At its October 2005 meeting, the NTETC Measuring Sector reviewed a proposal that would remove the special test tolerance for RMFDs and wholesale meters measuring agri-chemicals and asphalt. The Sector agreed that because of the extremely harsh environment and condition of use, some devices measuring agri-chemicals and asphalt should have a special test tolerance. The current definition of "retail" in Handbook 44 now applies to devices that, prior to 2004 when the definition of "retail" was changed, would have met the definition for a wholesale device with regard to flow rate. When the devices measuring agri-chemicals and asphalt were classified as "wholesale," they were permitted to have a special test tolerance during type evaluation. Those same devices may now be classified as "retail" because the product is being sold to an end user; however, they should still be allowed to have a special test tolerance because of the accuracy limitations of the devices at different flow rates for these specialized products. The Sector agreed to limit the proposal for eliminating special test tolerances to only RMFDs and to forward the proposal to the Committee for consideration. At its October 2005 Annual Meeting, SWMA agreed with the Measuring Sector that special test tolerances should not be applicable to RMFDs of any flow rate.

At the 2006 NCWM Interim Meeting, the Committee heard that repeating the exemption for RMFDs in the two parenthetical statements in footnote (designated with an "*"), as presented in the 2006 edition of Publication 15, conflicts with the intent of the language. The original intent of this footnote was to specify tolerances for 5 gal and 10 gal test drafts that were different from those listed in the table for accuracy Class 0.5 devices because of the uncertainty limitations on the test methods and standards used in these tests. The Committee also heard that footnote "*" should be modified to include other test draft sizes between 1 gal and 10 gal. Some jurisdictions are making undercover test purchases at other than 5 gal and 10 gal test draft sizes. The Committee agreed with both comments and modified Table T.2. as shown above. The Committee agreed to present Item 330-5 for a vote at the 2006 NCWM Annual Meeting.

At the 2006 NCWM Annual Meeting, the Committee heard support for this item.

331 VEHICLE-TANK METERS

331-1   V   S.1.1.3. Value of Smallest Unit

(This item was adopted.)

Source: National Type Evaluation Technical Committee (NTETC) Measuring Sector

Recommendation: Modify Paragraph S.1.1.3. as follows:

> **S.1.1.3. Value of Smallest Unit.** – The value of the smallest unit of indicated delivery, and recorded delivery if the meter is equipped to record, shall not exceed the equivalent of:
>
> (a) 0.5 L (0.1 gal) or 0.5 kg (1 lb) on milk-metering systems.
>
> (b) 0.5 L (0.1 gal) on meters with a rated maximum flow rate of ~~500~~750 L/min (~~100~~200 gal/min) or less used for ~~retail~~deliveries of liquid ~~fuel~~**commodities**, or
> (**Amended 2006)**
>
> **(c) 5 L or (1 gal) on meters with a rated maximum flow of 375 L/min (100 gal/min) or more used for jet fuel aviation refueling systems.**
> **(Added 2006)**
>
> (~~c~~**d**) 5 L (1 gal) on other meters.
> (Amended 1989, ~~and~~1994**, and 2006**)

Discussion/Background: Paragraph S.1.1.3. in the VTM Code requires the smallest unit of indicated delivery to be not greater than 0.5 L (0.1 gal) for deliveries on meters with a rated maximum flow rate of 500 L/min (100 gal/min) or less used for retail deliveries of liquid fuel and 5 L (1 gal) for all other meters (except milk-metering systems). VTMs with rated maximum flow rates up to approximately 150 gal/min are being introduced into the marketplace for use in making deliveries of approximately the same amount as those previously made with devices that had maximum flow rates of 100 gal/min or less. The amount of the increase in flow rate and the amount of product being delivered do not warrant a tenfold increase in the permitted value of the smallest unit of measurement.

At its 2005 meeting, the NTETC Measuring Sector reviewed a proposal to increase the rated maximum flow rate criteria in Paragraph S.1.1.3. from 100 gal/min to 200 gal/min. Some manufacturers of aviation refueling systems suggested that these systems need a separate criterion due to the unique nature of their application. The Sector agreed with the aviation refueler manufacturers and agreed to forward the proposal to the Committee for consideration. At its October 2005 meeting, SWMA supported the Measuring Sector's proposal and recommended the item move forward to the Committee.

After hearing comments at the 2006 NCWM Interim Meeting, the Committee agreed that Paragraph S.1.1.3.(b) should be applicable to commodities other than fuel, such as oil or dry cleaning solvents, that are delivered through a vehicle-tank meter. The Committee agreed to modify Paragraph S.1.1.3.(b) to address all liquid commodities and to present Item 331-1 for a vote at the 2006 NCWM Annual Meeting.

At the 2006 NCWM Annual Meeting, the Committee received input from several manufacturers of aircraft refueling equipment stating that there was a safety concern with vehicle-tank meter refueling systems capable of delivering jet fuel through two different size hoses at different flow rates using two different meters. One of the meters may have a rated flow that is less than 575 L/min (150 gal/min) which would require the smallest unit to be not greater than 0.5 L (0.1 gal) and allow the larger meter to have indications of 5 L (1 gal). In this scenario the operators of the refueling facility want both meters to have the same unit of indication, that is, 5 L (1 gal). The Committee met with members of the Meter Manufacturers Association to develop language that would resolve their concerns. The Committee agreed to change the rated maximum flow rate in Paragraph "c" from "575 L/min (150 gal/min) or more" to "375 L/min (100 gal/min) or more."

331-2 VC S.2.2. Provision for Sealing and Table S.2.2. Categories of Device and Methods of Sealing

(This item was adopted.)

Source: National Type Evaluation Technical Committee (NTETC) Measuring Sector

Recommendation: Modify Paragraph S.2.2., delete Paragraph S.2.2.1., and add a new Table S.2.2. Categories of Device and Methods of Sealing as follows:

> S.2.2. Provision for Sealing. – ~~Except on devices for metering milk,~~ ~~a~~Adequate provision shall be made for ~~applying security seals in such a manner that no~~ **an approved means of security (e.g., data change audit trail) or for physically applying a security seal in such a manner that requires the security seal to be broken before a change or an** adjustment may be made of:
>
> (a) any measur**ing**~~ement~~ or **indicating** element**, or**~~and~~
>
> (b) any adjustable element for controlling delivery rate, when such rate tends to affect the accuracy of deliveries~~.~~**, and**
>
> **(c) any metrological parameter that will affect the metrological integrity of the device or system.**
>
> ~~S.2.2.1. Milk Metering Systems. – Adequate provision shall be made for applying security seals to the adjustment mechanism and the register. The adjusting mechanism shall be readily accessible for purposes of affixing a security seal.~~
>
> **When applicable, the adjusting mechanism shall be readily accessible for purposes of affixing a security seal.**
>
> [Audit trails shall use the format set forth in Table S.2.2.]*
> [*Nonretroactive as of January 1, 1995]
> **(Amended 2006)**

Table S.2.2. Categories of Device and Methods of Sealing

Category of Device	Method of Sealing
Category 1: No remote configuration capability.	Seal by physical seal or two event counters: one for calibration parameters and one for configuration parameters.
Category 2: Remote configuration capability, but access is controlled by physical hardware. The device shall clearly indicate that it is in the remote configuration mode and record such message if capable of printing in this mode or shall not operate while in this mode.	The hardware enabling access for remote communication must be on-site. The hardware must be sealed using a physical seal or an event counter for calibration parameters and an event counter for configuration parameters. The event counters may be located either at the individual measuring device or at the system controller; however, an adequate number of counters must be provided to monitor the calibration and configuration parameters of the individual devices at a location. If the counters are located in the system controller rather than at the individual device, means must be provided to generate a hard copy of the information through an on-site device.
Category 3: Remote configuration capability access may be unlimited or controlled through a software switch (e.g., password). The device shall clearly indicate that it is in the remote configuration mode and record such message if capable of printing in this mode or shall not operate while in this mode.	An event logger is required in the device; it must include an event counter (000 to 999), the parameter ID, the date and time of the change, and the new value of the parameter. A printed copy of the information must be available through the device or through another on-site device. The event logger shall have a capacity to retain records equal to 10 times the number of sealable parameters in the device, but not more than 1000 records are required. (Note: Does not require 1000 changes to be stored for each parameter.)

[Nonretroactive as of January 1, 1995]
(Table Added 2006)

Background/Discussion: At its October 2005 meeting, the NTETC Measuring Sector discussed the elimination of "Category 2" from the LMD Code and also discussed the addition of electronic sealing criteria to other NIST Handbook 44 measuring codes, such as the Vehicle-Tank Meters Code or the LPG and Anhydrous Ammonia Liquid-Measuring Devices, for liquid-measuring devices that do not have specific provisions for electronic security (i.e., audit trails). At the meeting, manufacturers of these devices stated that they have designed metering systems with electronic security with remote configuration capability. They are currently seeking an NTEP CC for these systems. Currently, the specific NIST Handbook 44 code for these devices does not address electronic sealing; however, electronic sealing is recognized in the General Code and under the provisions of G-A.3. Special and Unclassified Equipment. The specific audit trail criteria in the LMD Code can be applied where appropriate. The manufacturers would prefer that each code include specific language similar to that in the LMD Code. During the discussion, the Sector concluded that some of these new applications and other applications currently in use would have been classified as the former "Category 2" devices. Some NTEP CCs have been issued stating that the device evaluated was a Category 1 device; however, because the mechanism for accessing sealable configuration parameters is not a permanent part of the device and can be removed without affecting normal operation, the device actually meets the definition of remote configuration capability. The manufacturers of these devices believe that no problems have been reported due to their current method of sealing and that it is inappropriate to require them to change the method of sealing to comply with Category 3. The Sector agreed that the industry would not have supported the decision to remove "Category 2" from the LMD Code and the Mass-Flow Meters Code had they had a clear understanding of "remote configuration capability" and that the decision should be reversed. The Committee also agreed that provisions for electronic sealing should be added to all appropriate liquid-measuring device codes as proposed in Items 330-3, 331-2, 332-1, 334-1, 335-1, 337-1, and 338-1. The Sector agreed to forward that proposal to the Committee for consideration.

At the 2006 NCWM Interim Meeting, the Committee agreed that a non-retroactive date of 1995, which is the same as the non-retroactive date in the LMD Code, is appropriate for Vehicle-Tank Meters because that date would have been applied to any devices NTEP evaluated using the criteria in G-A.3. Special and Unclassified Equipment. The Committee agreed to present Item 331-2 as shown above for a vote at the 2006 NCWM Annual Meeting. For additional discussion on this item see Item 330-3.

At the 2006 NCWM Annual Meeting, the Committee heard support for this item.

331-3 I Temperature Compensation

Source: Carryover Item 331-1 (This item originated from WWMA and first appeared on the Committee's 2000 agenda.)

Discussion/Background: The Committee considered a proposal to modify Section 3.31. VTM Code by adding the following new paragraphs to recognize temperature compensation as follows:

S.2.4. Automatic Temperature Compensation for Refined Petroleum Products.

S.2.4.1. Automatic Temperature Compensation for Refined Petroleum Products. – A device may be equipped with an automatic means for adjusting the indication and registration of the measured volume of product to the volume at 15 °C (60 °F), where not prohibited by state law.

S.2.4.2. Provision for Deactivating. – On a device equipped with an automatic temperature-compensating mechanism that will indicate or record only in terms of liters (gallons) compensated to 15 °C (60 °F), provision shall be made for deactivating the automatic temperature-compensating mechanism so that the meter can indicate and record, if it is equipped to record, in terms of the uncompensated volume.

S.2.4.3. Gross and Net Indications. – A device equipped with automatic temperature compensation shall indicate and record, if equipped to record, both the gross (uncompensated) and net (compensated) volume for testing purposes. If both values cannot be displayed or recorded for the same test draft, means shall be provided to select either the gross or net indication for each test draft.

S.2.4.4. Provision for Sealing Automatic Temperature-Compensating Systems. – Adequate provision shall be made for an approved means of security (e.g., data change audit trail) or physically applying security seals in such a manner that an automatic temperature-compensating system cannot be disconnected and that no adjustment may be made to the system.

S.2.4.5. Temperature Determination with Automatic Temperature Compensation. – For test purposes, means shall be provided (e.g., thermometer well) to determine the temperature of the liquid either:

(a) in the liquid chamber of the meter, or

(b) immediately adjacent to the meter in the meter inlet or discharge line.
(Added 200X)

S.5.6. Temperature Compensation for Refined Petroleum Products. – If a device is equipped with an automatic temperature compensator, the primary indicating elements, recording elements, and recording representation shall be clearly and conspicuously marked to show that the volume delivered has been adjusted to the volume at 15 °C (60 °F).
(Added 200X)

N.4.1.3. Automatic Temperature-Compensating Systems for Refined Petroleum Products. – On devices equipped with automatic temperature-compensating systems, normal tests shall be conducted:

(a) **by comparing the compensated volume indicated or recorded to the actual delivered volume corrected to 15 °C (60 °F); and**

(b) **with the temperature-compensating system deactivated, comparing the uncompensated volume indicated or recorded to the actual delivered volume.**

The first test shall be performed with the automatic temperature-compensating system operating in the "as-found" condition. On devices that indicate or record both the compensated and uncompensated volume for each delivery, the tests in (a) and (b) may be performed as a single test.
(Added 200X)

N.5. Temperature Correction for Refined Petroleum Products. – Corrections shall be made for any changes in volume resulting from the differences in liquid temperatures between the time of passage through the meter and time of volumetric determination in the prover. When adjustments are necessary, appropriate petroleum measurement tables should be used.
(Added 200X)

T.2.1. Automatic Temperature-Compensating Systems. – The difference between the meter error (expressed as a percentage) for results determined with and without the automatic temperature-compensating system activated shall not exceed:

(a) **0.4 % for mechanical automatic temperature-compensating systems; and**

(b) **0.2 % for electronic automatic temperature-compensating systems.**

The delivered quantities for each test shall be approximately the same size. The results of each test shall be within the applicable acceptance or maintenance tolerance.
(Added 200X)

UR.2.5. Temperature Compensation for Refined Petroleum Products.

UR.2.5.1. Automatic.

UR.2.5.1.1. When to be Used. – In a state that does not prohibit, by law or regulation, the sale of temperature-compensated product, a device equipped with an operable automatic temperature compensator shall be connected, operable, and in use at all times. An electronic or mechanical automatic temperature-compensating system may not be removed, nor may a compensated device be replaced with an uncompensated device, without the written approval of the responsible weights and measures jurisdiction.

[Note: This requirement does not specify the method of sale for products measured through a meter.]

UR.2.5.1.2. Invoices. – An invoice based on a reading of a device that is equipped with an automatic temperature compensator shall show that the volume delivered has been adjusted to the volume at 15 °C (60 °F).
(Added 200X)

When this item was originally submitted, several officials reportedly were confused about the specific applications of a meter covered by an NTEP CC that included the temperature-compensation feature. WWMA acknowledged some jurisdictions permit temperature-compensated deliveries in applications that are not addressed by NIST Handbook 44. Some states do not allow the use of automatic temperature compensation for the delivery of products using a VTM. At the 2002, 2003, and 2004 NCWM Annual Meetings, this proposal did not achieve a majority vote to pass or fail and was, therefore, returned to the Committee for further consideration.

At the 2005 NCWM Interim Meeting, the Committee participated in a combined open hearing with the NCWM L&R Committee for discussion of this item, which is a device requirement, and L&R Item 232-1 Temperature Compensation for Petroleum Products, which is a separate proposal for a corresponding method of sale regulation. A special forum was also held on the first day of the Interim Meeting to discuss temperature compensation items. However, the Committee was informed that the L&R Committee kept its Item 232-1 as a developing item. At one point, the L&R Committee considered splitting Item 232-1 to address separately the method of sale for meter types other than VTMs. However, the L&R Committee decided not to split the item and instead modified Item 232-1 to allow temperature compensation for the sale of petroleum products, other than LPG and petroleum products sold through retail motor-fuel devices, and changed the status of the item to "Developing." At the forum and the open hearings, the Committee received little or no new information on this item and considered withdrawing it from its agenda. However, because the L&R Committee continues to have a related item on its agenda, the Committee agreed to leave Item 331-3 on its agenda as an information item.

During the 2005 NCWM Annual Meeting, a manufacturer stated that the number of requests for retail motor-fuel dispensers with temperature compensation capability is increasing. The Committee agreed to maintain this item on its agenda until L&R Item 232-1 is further developed.

At its September 2005 Interim Meeting, CWMA agreed on the technical merit of the proposal and agreed that requirements are needed in NIST Handbook 44; however, CWMA agreed this is also a "method of sale" item and the proposal should be retained as an information item until an accompanying method of sale requirement is added to NIST Handbook 130.

At its September 2005 meeting, WWMA reaffirmed its strong support of this proposal and recommended this item go forward for adoption by NCWM.

At its October 2005 meeting, NEWMA recommended withdrawing this item. NEWMA feels there is not enough support for this item and that, if it went for a vote again in July, it would still not pass.

At the 2006 NCWM Interim Meeting, the Committee agreed to leave Item 331-3 on its agenda as an information item because the L&R Committee is close to fully developing a corresponding method of sale requirement on its agenda that is acceptable to most jurisdictions. The Committee encourages the weights and measures community to review the newly modified L&R Item 232-1 based on work at the 2005 fall meetings of the regional weights and measures associations.

At the 2006 NCWM Annual Meeting, weights and measures officials voiced a concern that recognizing temperature compensation for additional applications; (e.g., vehicle-tank meters and retail motor-fuel dispensers) would double the time required to test the devices used in these applications. Another official voiced support for the item because it is technically correct and indicated that the individual states could decide whether or not to allow temperature-compensated devices in additional applications in their own jurisdiction. The Meter Manufacturers Association supported this item.

For additional background on this item, see the Committee's 2000 through 2005 Final Reports.

332 LIQUEFIED PETROLEUM GAS AND ANHYDROUS AMMONIA LIQUID-MEASURING DEVICES

332-1 VC S.2.2. Provision for Sealing and Table S.2.2. Categories of Device and Methods of Sealing

(This item was adopted.)

Source: National Type Evaluation Technical Committee (NTEC) Measuring Sector.

Recommendation: Modify Paragraph S.2.2. and add a new Table S.2.2. as follows:

S.2.2. Provision for Sealing. – Adequate provision shall be made for ~~applying security seals in such a manner that no~~ **an approved means of security (e.g., data change audit trail) or for physically applying a security seal in such a manner that requires the security seal to be broken before an** adjustment may be made of:

(a) any measur**ing** ~~ement~~ **or indicating** element, ~~and~~**or**

(b) any adjustable element for controlling delivery rate, when such rate tends to affect the accuracy of deliveries~~.~~**, and**

(c) any metrological parameter that will affect the metrological integrity of the device or system.

When applicable, ~~T~~**t**he adjusting mechanism shall be readily accessible for purposes of affixing a security seal.

[Audit trails shall use the format set forth in Table S.2.2.]*
[*Nonretroactive as of January 1, 1995]
(Amended 2006)

Table S.2.2. Categories of Device and Methods of Sealing	
Category of Device	**Method of Sealing**
Category 1: No remote configuration capability.	**Seal by physical seal or two event counters: one for calibration parameters and one for configuration parameters.**
Category 2: Remote configuration capability, but access is controlled by physical hardware. **The device shall clearly indicate that it is in the remote configuration mode and record such message if capable of printing in this mode or shall not operate while in this mode.**	**The hardware enabling access for remote communication must be on-site. The hardware must be sealed using a physical seal or an event counter for calibration parameters and an event counter for configuration parameters. The event counters may be located either at the individual measuring device or at the system controller; however, an adequate number of counters must be provided to monitor the calibration and configuration parameters of the individual devices at a location. If the counters are located in the system controller rather than at the individual device, means must be provided to generate a hard copy of the information through an on-site device.**
Category 3: Remote configuration capability access may be unlimited or controlled through a software switch (e.g., password). **The device shall clearly indicate that it is in the remote configuration mode and record such message if capable of printing in this mode or shall not operate while in this mode.**	**An event logger is required in the device; it must include an event counter (000 to 999), the parameter ID, the date and time of the change, and the new value of the parameter. A printed copy of the information must be available through the device or through another on-site device. The event logger shall have a capacity to retain records equal to 10 times the number of sealable parameters in the device, but not more than 1000 records are required. (Note: Does not require 1000 changes to be stored for each parameter.)**

[Nonretroactive as of January 1, 1995]
(Table Added 2006)

Background/Discussion: At its October 2005 meeting, the NTETC Measuring Sector discussed the elimination of "Category 2" from the LMD Code and also discussed the addition of electronic sealing criteria to other NIST Handbook 44 measuring codes, such as the Vehicle-Tank Meters Code or the LPG and Anhydrous Ammonia Liquid-Measuring Devices, for liquid-measuring devices that do not have specific provisions for electronic security (i.e., audit trails). At the meeting, manufacturers of these devices stated that they have designed metering systems with electronic security with remote configuration capability. They are currently seeking an NTEP CC for these systems. Currently, the specific NIST Handbook 44 code for these devices does not address electronic sealing; however, electronic sealing is recognized in the General Code and under the provisions of G-A.3. Special and Unclassified Equipment. The specific audit trail criteria in the LMD Code can be applied, where appropriate. The manufacturers would prefer that each code include specific language similar to that in the LMD Code. During the discussion, the Sector concluded that some of these new applications and other applications currently in use would have been classified as the former "Category 2" devices. Some NTEP CCs have been issued stating that the device evaluated was a Category 1 device; however, because the mechanism for accessing sealable configuration parameters is not a permanent part of the device and can be removed without affecting normal operation, the device actually meets the definition of remote configuration capability. The manufacturers of these devices believe that no problems have been reported due to their current method of sealing and that it is inappropriate to require them to change the method of sealing to comply with Category 3. The Sector agreed that the industry would not have supported the decision to remove "Category 2" from the LMD Code and the Mass-Flow Meters Code had they had a clear understanding of "remote configuration capability" and that the decision should be reversed. The Committee also agreed that provisions for electronic sealing should be added to all appropriate liquid-measuring device codes as proposed in Items 330-3, 331-2, 332-1, 334-1, 335-1, 337-1, and 338-1. The Sector agreed to forward that proposal to the Committee for consideration.

At the 2006 NCWM Interim Meeting, the Committee agreed that a non-retroactive date of 1995, which is the same as the non-retroactive date in the LMD Code, is appropriate for LPG and Anhydrous Ammonia Meters because that date would have been applied to any devices NTEP evaluated using the criteria in G-A.3. Special and Unclassified Equipment. The Committee agreed to present Item 332-1 as shown above for a vote at the 2006 NCWM Annual Meeting. For additional discussion on this item see Item 330-3.

At the 2006 NCWM Annual Meeting, the Committee heard support for this item.

332-2 VC S.4.3. Location of Marking Information; Retail Motor-Fuel Dispensers

(This item was adopted.)

Source: National Type Evaluation Technical Committee (NTETC) Measuring Sector

Recommendation: Add a new Paragraph S.4.3. and renumber subsequent paragraphs as follows:

S.4.3. Location of Marking Information; Retail Motor-Fuel Dispensers. – The marking information required in the General Code, Paragraph G-S.1. Identification shall appear as follows:

(a) within 60 cm (24 in) to 150 cm (60 in) from the base of the dispenser;

(b) either internally and/or externally provided the information is permanent and easily read; and

(c) on a portion of the device that cannot be readily removed or interchanged (i.e., not on a service access panel).

Note: The use of a dispenser key or tool to access internal marking information is permitted for retail liquid-measuring devices.
[Nonretroactive as of January 1, 2003]
(Added 2006)

S.4.~~3~~4. **Temperature Compensation.** – If a device is equipped with an automatic temperature compensator, the primary indicating elements, recording elements, and recorded representation shall be clearly and conspicuously marked to show that the volume delivered has been adjusted to the volume at 15 °C (60 °F).

Background/Discussion: At the spring 2005 NTEP laboratory meeting it was recommended that the location of markings requirement from the LMD Code be added to Sections 3.32. LPG and Anhydrous Ammonia Liquid-Measuring Devices and 3.37. Mass Flow Meters. Both codes have other requirements for retail motor-fuel dispensers similar to those in the LMD Code. The laboratories agreed to forward its proposal to the NTETC Measuring Sector for consideration.

At their October 2005 meetings, the NTETC Measuring Sector and SWMA reviewed the proposal and both agreed to forward the proposal to the Committee for consideration.

At the 2006 NCWM Interim Meeting the Committee heard no comments on Item 332-2 and agreed to present it for a vote at the 2006 NCWM Annual Meeting.

At the 2006 NCWM Annual Meeting, the Committee heard support for this item.

334 CRYOGENIC LIQUID-MEASURING DEVICES

334-1 VC S.2.5. Provision for Sealing and Table S.2.5. Categories of Device and Methods of Sealing

(This item was adopted.)

Source: National Type Evaluation Technical Committee (NTETC) Measuring Sector

Recommendation: Modify Paragraph S.2.5. and add a new Table S.2.5. as follows:

S.2.5. Provision for Sealing. – Adequate provision shall be made for ~~applying security seals in such a manner that no~~ **an approved means of security (e.g., data change audit trail) or for physically applying a security seal in such a manner that requires the security seal to be broken before an** adjustment or interchange may be made of:

(a) any measur~~ingement~~ element **or indicating element,**

(b) any adjustable element for controlling delivery rate when such rate tends to affect the accuracy of deliveries, ~~and~~

(c) any automatic temperature or density compensating system~~,~~ **and**

(d) any metrological parameter that will affect the metrological integrity of the device or system.

When applicable ~~A~~**a**ny adjusting mechanism shall be readily accessible for purposes of affixing a security seal.

~~[Audit trails shall use the format set forth in Table S.2.5.]*~~
~~[*Nonretroactive as of January 1, 1995]~~
(Amended 2006)

Table S.2.5. Categories of Device and Methods of Sealing	
~~Category of Device~~	~~Method of Sealing~~
~~Category 1: No remote configuration capability.~~	~~Seal by physical seal or two event counters: one for calibration parameters and one for configuration parameters.~~
~~Category 2: Remote configuration capability, but access is controlled by physical hardware.~~ ~~The device shall clearly indicate that it is in the remote configuration mode and record such message if capable of printing in this mode or shall not operate while in this mode.~~	~~The hardware enabling access for remote communication must be on-site. The hardware must be sealed using a physical seal or an event counter for calibration parameters and an event counter for configuration parameters. The event counters may be located either at the individual measuring device or at the system controller; however, an adequate number of counters must be provided to monitor the calibration and configuration parameters of the individual devices at a location. If the counters are located in the system controller rather than at the individual device, means must be provided to generate a hard copy of the information through an on-site device.~~
~~Category 3: Remote configuration capability access may be unlimited or controlled through a software switch (e.g., password)~~ ~~The device shall clearly indicate that it is in the remote configuration mode and record such message if capable of printing in this mode or shall not operate while in this mode.~~	~~An event logger is required in the device; it must include an event counter (000 to 999), the parameter ID, the date and time of the change, and the new value of the parameter. A printed copy of the information must be available through the device or through another on-site device. The event logger shall have a capacity to retain records equal to 10 times the number of sealable parameters in the device, but not more than 1000 records are required. (Note: Does not require 1000 changes to be stored for each parameter.)~~

~~[Nonretroactive as of January 1, 1995]~~
(Table Added 2006)

Background/Discussion: At its October 2005 meeting, the NTETC Measuring Sector discussed the elimination of "Category 2" from the LMD Code and also discussed the addition of electronic sealing criteria to other NIST Handbook 44 measuring codes, such as the Vehicle-Tank Meters Code or the LPG and Anhydrous Ammonia Liquid-Measuring Devices, for liquid-measuring devices that do not have specific provisions for electronic security (i.e., audit trails). At the meeting, manufacturers of these devices stated that they have designed metering systems with electronic security with remote configuration capability. They are currently seeking an NTEP CC for these systems. Currently, the specific NIST Handbook 44 code for these devices does not address electronic sealing; however, electronic sealing is recognized in the General Code and under the provisions of G-A.3. Special and Unclassified Equipment. The specific audit trail criteria in the LMD Code can be applied, where appropriate. The manufacturers would prefer that each code include specific language similar to that in the LMD Code. During the discussion, the Sector concluded that some of these new applications and other applications currently in use would have been classified as the former "Category 2" devices. Some NTEP CCs have been issued stating that the device evaluated was a Category 1 device; however, because the mechanism for accessing sealable configuration parameters is not a permanent part of the device and can be removed without affecting normal operation, the device actually meets the definition of remote configuration capability. The manufacturers of these devices believe that no problems have been reported due to their current method of sealing and that it is inappropriate to require them to change the method of sealing to comply with Category 3. The Sector agreed that the industry would not have supported the decision to remove "Category 2" from the LMD Code and the Mass-Flow Meters Code had they had a clear understanding of "remote configuration capability" and that the decision should be reversed. The Committee also agreed that provisions for electronic sealing should be added to all appropriate liquid-measuring device codes as proposed in Items 330-3, 331-2, 332-1, 334-1, 335-1, 337-1, and 338-1. The Sector agreed to forward that proposal to the Committee for consideration.

At the 2006 NCWM Interim Meeting, the Committee agreed that a non-retroactive date of 1995, which is the same as the non-retroactive date in the LMD Code, is appropriate for Cryogenic Meters because that date would have been applied to any devices NTEP evaluated using the criteria in G-A.3. Special and Unclassified Equipment. The Committee agreed to present Item 334-1 as shown above for a vote at the 2006 NCWM Annual Meeting. For additional discussion on this item see Item 330-3.

At the 2006 NCWM Annual Meeting, the Committee heard support for this item.

335 MILK METERS

335-1 VC S.2.3. Provision for Sealing and Table S.2.3. Categories of Device and Methods of Sealing

(This item was adopted.)

Source: National Type Evaluation Technical Committee (NTETC) Measuring Sector

Recommendation: Modify S.2.3. and add new Table S.2.3. as follows:

S.2.3. Provision for Sealing. – Adequate provision shall be made for ~~applying security seals to the adjustment mechanism and the register.~~ **an approved means of security (e.g., data change audit trail) or for physically applying a security seal in such a manner that requires the security seal to be broken before an adjustment or interchange may be made of:**

(a) any measuring element or indicating element,

(b) any adjustable element for controlling delivery rate, when such rate tends to affect the accuracy of deliveries, and

(c) any metrological parameter that will affect the metrological integrity of the device or system.

When applicable the adjusting mechanism shall be readily accessible for purposes of affixing a security seal.

[Audit trails shall use the format set forth in Table S.2.3.]*
[*Nonretroactive as of January 1, 1995]
(Amended 2006)

Table S.2.3. Categories of Device and Methods of Sealing	
Category of Device	**Method of Sealing**
Category 1: No remote configuration capability.	Seal by physical seal or two event counters: one for calibration parameters and one for configuration parameters.
Category 2: Remote configuration capability, but access is controlled by physical hardware. The device shall clearly indicate that it is in the remote configuration mode and record such message if capable of printing in this mode or shall not operate while in this mode.	The hardware enabling access for remote communication must be on-site. The hardware must be sealed using a physical seal or an event counter for calibration parameters and an event counter for configuration parameters. The event counters may be located either at the individual measuring device or at the system controller; however, an adequate number of counters must be provided to monitor the calibration and configuration parameters of the individual devices at a location. If the counters are located in the system controller rather than at the individual device, means must be provided to generate a hard copy of the information through an on-site device.
Category 3: Remote configuration capability access may be unlimited or controlled through a software switch (e.g., password). The device shall clearly indicate that it is in the remote configuration mode and record such message if capable of printing in this mode or shall not operate while in this mode.	An event logger is required in the device; it must include an event counter (000 to 999), the parameter ID, the date and time of the change, and the new value of the parameter. A printed copy of the information must be available through the device or through another on-site device. The event logger shall have a capacity to retain records equal to 10 times the number of sealable parameters in the device, but not more than 1000 records are required. (Note: Does not require 1000 changes to be stored for each parameter.)

[Nonretroactive as of January 1, 1995]
(Table Added 2006)

Background/Discussion: At its October 2005 meeting, the NTETC Measuring Sector discussed the elimination of "Category 2" from the LMD Code and also discussed the addition of electronic sealing criteria to other NIST Handbook 44 measuring codes, such as the Vehicle-Tank Meters Code or the LPG and Anhydrous Ammonia Liquid-Measuring Devices, for liquid-measuring devices that do not have specific provisions for electronic security (i.e., audit trails). At the meeting, manufacturers of these devices stated that they have designed metering systems with electronic security with remote configuration capability. They are currently seeking an NTEP CC for these systems. Currently, the specific NIST Handbook 44 code for these devices does not address electronic sealing; however, electronic sealing is recognized in the General Code and under the provisions of G-A.3. Special and Unclassified Equipment. The specific audit trail criteria in the LMD Code can be applied, where appropriate. The manufacturers would prefer that each code include specific language similar to that in the LMD Code. During the discussion, the Sector concluded that some of these new applications and other applications currently in use would have been classified as the former "Category 2" devices. Some NTEP CCs have been issued stating that the device evaluated was a Category 1 device; however, because the mechanism for accessing sealable configuration parameters is not a permanent part of the device and can be removed without affecting normal operation, the device actually meets the definition of remote configuration capability. The manufacturers of these devices believe that no problems have been reported due to their current method of sealing and that it is inappropriate to require them to change the method of sealing to comply with Category 3. The Sector agreed that the industry would not have supported the decision to remove "Category 2" from the LMD Code and the Mass-Flow Meters Code had they had a clear understanding of "remote configuration capability" and that the decision should be reversed. The Committee also agreed that provisions for electronic sealing should be added to all appropriate liquid-measuring device codes as proposed in Items 330-3, 331-2, 332-1, 334-1, 335-1, 337-1, and 338-1. The Sector agreed to forward that proposal to the Committee for consideration.

At the 2006 NCWM Interim Meeting, the Committee agreed that a non-retroactive date of 1995, which is the same as the non-retroactive date in the LMD Code, is appropriate for Milk Meters because that date would have been applied to any devices NTEP evaluated using the criteria in G-A.3. Special and Unclassified Equipment. The Committee agreed to present Item 331-2 as shown above for a vote at the 2006 NCWM Annual Meeting. For additional discussion on this item see Item 330-3.

At the 2006 NCWM Annual Meeting, the Committee heard support for this item.

336 WATER METERS

336-1 W Table N.4.2. Flow Rate and Draft Size for Water Meters Special Tests

(This item was withdrawn.)

Source: Carryover Item 336-1. (This item originated from the Northeastern Weights and Measures Association (NEWMA) and first appeared on the Committee's 2005 agenda.)

Discussion/Background: The Committee considered a proposal to amend Table N.4.2. as follows:

Table N.4.2. Flow Rate and Draft Size for Water Meters Special Tests							
Meter size (inches)	Intermediate Rate			Minimum Rate		
	Rate of Flow (gal/min)	Meter Indication/Test Draft		Rate of Flow (gal/min)	Meter Indication/Test Draft	
		gal	ft³		Gal	ft³
Less than or equal to ⅝	2	10	1¼		~~5~~ **10**	1
¾	3	10	1½		~~5~~ **10**	1
1	4	10	1¾		~~5~~ **10**	1
1½	8	50	5	1½	10	1
2	15	50	5	2	10	1
3	20	50	5	4	10	1
4	40	100		10	7	~~50~~ **100**	5
6	60	100		10	12	~~50~~ **100**	5

(Table Added 2003) **(Amended 200X)**

At the fall 2004 NEWMA meeting, a manufacturer stated that a test draft of 5 gal is not large enough to provide repeatability for dial-indicating water meters sized 1   in and smaller. The dial indicator for these devices has 100 graduations of $\frac{1}{10}$ gal, which means one complete revolution equals 10 gal. The effect of parallax on the reading and gear backlash both contribute to the lack of repeatability of indications when using a 5 gal test draft. The manufacturer recommended that any test of the device include, at a minimum, at least one complete revolution of the dial indicator and submitted proposed changes to Table N.4.2. None of the jurisdictions represented at the NEWMA meeting routinely test water meters; therefore, they could not provide any input on the technical merits of the proposal. However, NEWMA agreed to forward the proposal to the Committee for consideration.

At the 2005 NCWM Interim Meeting, the only concern the Committee heard was that the time required for some tests would increase significantly if the current test draft size were doubled. The manufacturer that submitted the proposal to NEWMA was not at the Interim Meeting. The Committee agreed to make the proposal an information item to provide the opportunity for review and comment from the regional associations, especially jurisdictions routinely conducting water meter tests. If additional support and comments were not received, the Committee decided to consider withdrawing this item.

At the 2005 NCWM Annual Meeting, there was no discussion on this item.

At its September 2005 Annual Meeting, WWMA heard comments opposing the proposal. Officials indicated that the current minimum test draft size is adequate to determine a meter's performance. Since no data or comments were presented to support the proposal, WWMA recommended this item be withdrawn.

At its October 2005 meeting, NEWMA continued to support this proposal. The submitter indicated to NEWMA that, for water meters sized ⅝ in, ¾ in and 1 in indicating in U. S. gallons, a test draft of only 5 gal cannot give proper resolution and is inconsistent with good metering practice that reads that test drafts should be selected to yield nominally whole revolutions of the test dial. Only 50 dial divisions (only half of the entire dial revolution) are passed utilizing this test draft size. Normal reading parallax and gear backlash would yield resolution of + _ 1.5 % under the best conditions. Handbook 44 and good testing practice suggest that a resolution of one-third of the normal tolerance band is needed.

Prior to the 2006 NCWM Interim Meeting, the original submitter provided a limited amount of test data in an attempt to demonstrate what he sees as a problem with the current test criteria. However, because there is only a small sampling of data and the data is from only one model of the submitter's own meter design, the data is not sufficient to show that there is an industry-wide problem that supports a change to the current requirements in NIST Handbook 44.

At the 2006 NCWM Interim Meeting, the Committee agreed to make Item 336-1 an information item to provide the original submitter additional time to submit additional data to the Committee to support the increase in the size of test drafts for ⅝ in, ¾ in and 1 in meters. Typically, the Committee would expect to receive extensive data from several manufacturers on a larger number of meters to provide a compelling argument for making the requested change to requirements. The Committee and WMD are willing to provide assistance to the submitter in determining the appropriate number of manufacturers needing to submit data, the number of meters from each manufacturer to be tested, and the numbers and types of tests for each meter in order to provide sufficient justification for making the requested change to the requirements. If supporting data are not received prior to the 2006 NCWM Annual Meeting, Item 336-1 will be withdrawn from the Committee's agenda.

At the 2006 Annual meeting, the Committee heard opposition to the proposal from a jurisdiction that routinely tests water meters and from two regional associations. No data to support the change had been presented to the Committee as requested at the 2006 Interim Meeting; therefore the Committee withdrew the item from its agenda.

337 MASS FLOW METERS

337-1 VC S.3.5. Provision for Sealing and Table S.3.5. Categories of Devices and Methods of Sealing

(This item was adopted.)

Source: National Type Evaluation Technical Committee (NTETC) Measuring Sector

Recommendation: Modify Paragraph S.3.5. and Table S.3.5. as follows:

S.3.5. Provision for Sealing. – Adequate provision shall be made for an approved means of security (e.g., data change audit trail) or physically applying security seals in such a manner that no adjustment may be made of:

(a) any measur **ingement or indicating** element~~,~~ **or**

(b) any adjustable element for controlling delivery rate when such rate tends to affect the accuracy of deliveries~~, or~~**.**

(c) the zero adjustment mechanism~~.~~**, and**

(d) any metrological parameter that will affect the metrological integrity of the device or system.

When applicable, the adjusting mechanism shall be readily accessible for purposes of affixing a security seal.

[Audit trails shall use the format set forth in Table S.3.5.]*
[*Nonretroactive as of January 1, 1995]
(Amended 1992, and 1995 **and 2006**)

Table S.3.5. Categories of Device and Methods of Sealing	
Category of Device	**Method of Sealing**
Category 1: No remote configuration capability.	Seal by physical seal or two event counters: one for calibration parameters and one for configuration parameters.
[Category 2 applies to only devices manufactured prior to January 1, 2005. Devices with remote configuration capability manufactured after that date must meet the sealing requirements outlined in Category 3. Devices without remote configuration capability manufactured after that date must meet the minimum criteria outlined in Category 1]. Category 2: Remote configuration capability, but access is controlled by physical hardware. The device shall clearly indicate that it is in the remote configuration mode and record such message if capable of printing in this mode or shall not operate while in this mode.	[The hardware enabling access for remote communication must be on-site. The hardware must be sealed using a physical seal or an event counter for calibration parameters and an event counter for configuration parameters. The event counters may be located either at the individual measuring device or at the system controller; however, an adequate number of counters must be provided to monitor the calibration and configuration parameters of the individual devices at a location. If the counters are located in the system controller rather than at the individual device, means must be provided to generate a hard copy of the information through an on-site device.]* [*Nonretroactive as of January 1, 1996]
Category 3: Remote configuration capability access may be unlimited or controlled through a software switch (e.g., password). [Nonretroactive as of January 1, 1995] The device shall clearly indicate that it is in the remote configuration mode and record such message if capable of printing in this mode or shall not operate while in this mode. [Nonretroactive as of January 1, 2001] Nonretroactive as of January 1, 2005, all devices with remote configuration capability must comply with the sealing requirements of Category 3.	An event logger is required in the device; it must include an event counter (000 to 999), the parameter ID, the date and time of the change, and the new value of the parameter. A printed copy of the information must be available through the device or through another on-site device. The event logger shall have a capacity to retain records equal to 10 times the number of sealable parameters in the device, but not more than 1000 records are required. (Note: Does not require 1000 changes to be stored for each parameter.)

Nonretroactive as of January 1, 1995]
(Table Added 1995) (Amended 1995, 1998, and 1999**, and 2006**)

Background/Discussion: At its October 2005 meeting, the NTETC Measuring Sector discussed the elimination of "Category 2" from the LMD Code and also discussed the addition of electronic sealing criteria to other NIST Handbook 44 measuring codes, such as the Vehicle-Tank Meters Code or the LPG and Anhydrous Ammonia Liquid-Measuring Devices, for liquid-measuring devices that do not have specific provisions for electronic security (i.e., audit trails). At the meeting, manufacturers of these devices stated that they have designed metering systems with electronic security with remote configuration capability. They are currently seeking an NTEP CC for these systems. Currently, the specific NIST Handbook 44 code for these devices does not address electronic sealing; however, electronic sealing is recognized in the General Code and under the provisions of G-A.3. Special and Unclassified Equipment. The specific audit trail criteria in the LMD Code can be applied, where appropriate. The manufacturers would prefer that each code include specific language similar to that in the LMD Code. During the discussion, the Sector concluded that some of these new applications and other applications currently in use would have been classified as the former "Category 2" devices. Some NTEP CCs have been issued stating that the device evaluated was a Category 1 device; however, because the mechanism for accessing sealable configuration parameters is not a permanent part of the device and can be removed without affecting normal operation, the device actually meets the definition of remote configuration capability. The manufacturers of these devices believe that no problems have been reported due to their current method of sealing and that it is inappropriate to require them to change the method of sealing to comply with Category 3. The Sector agreed that the industry would not have supported the decision to remove "Category 2" from the LMD Code and the Mass-Flow Meters Code had they had a clear understanding of "remote configuration capability" and that the decision should be reversed. The Committee also agreed that provisions for electronic sealing should be added to all appropriate liquid-measuring device codes as proposed in Items 330-3, 331-2, 332-1, 334-1, 335-1, 337-1, and 338-1. The Sector agreed to forward that proposal to the Committee for consideration.

At the 2006 NCWM Interim Meeting, the Committee agreed to present Item 337-1 as shown above for a vote at the 2006 NCWM Annual Meeting. For additional discussion on this item see Item 330-3.

At the 2006 NCWM Annual Meeting, the Committee heard support for this item.

337-2   VC S.4.1. Diversion of Measured Product

(This item was adopted.)

Source: Central Weights and Measures Association (CWMA)

Recommendation: Modify Paragraph S.4.1. as follows:

S.4. Discharge Lines and Valves.

S.4.1. Diversion of Measured Product. – No means shall be provided by which any measured product can be diverted from the measuring instrument. However, two or more delivery outlets may be permanently installed and operated simultaneously, provided that any diversion of flow to other than the intended receiving receptacle cannot be readily accomplished or is readily apparent. Such means include physical barriers, visible valves or indications that make it clear which outlets are in operation, and explanatory signs if deemed necessary.

~~A manually-controlled~~ **An** outlet that may be opened for purging or draining the measuring system, or for recirculating product if recirculation is required in order to maintain the product in a deliverable state ~~,~~ shall be permitted. Effective **automatic** means shall be provided to prevent the passage of liquid through any such outlet during normal operation of the measuring system and to inhibit meter indications (or advancement of indications) and recorded representations while the outlet is in operation.
(Amended 2002 **and 2006**)

Background/Discussion: CWMA noted that the corresponding requirements in Paragraph S.3.1. of Section 3.30. Liquid-Measuring Devices and Paragraph S.4.1. Diversion of Measured Product of Section 3.37. Mass Flow Meters in NIST Handbook 44 (2006 edition) are not consistent. Paragraph S.3.1. prohibits manual valves for recirculating product or purging or draining the measuring system except for foods and agri-chemicals. On the other hand, Paragraph S.4.1. permits manual valves but appears to ban automatic valves by omission, and it makes no distinction for types of products measured as long as the system meets the specified requirements.

Cold weather and physical characteristics make recirculation necessary for a number of products not currently recognized in Paragraph S.3.1. of Section 3.30., for example, #6 Fuel Oil and B100 Biodiesel. Although liquid-measuring devices exist which have NTEP CCs for these high viscosity products, the current wording of Handbook 44 restricts vendors of these products to using mass flow technology if they wish to recirculate their product in order to keep it in a deliverable state. This appears to be the unintended result of the fact that the two codes were written at different times with different input from industry lobbies. CWMA recommended that retailers of these products not be restricted to using only mass flow meters for commercial measurements if other suitable technologies are available. Likewise, both manual and automatic valves are suitable for recirculating products in discharge lines of these devices, and the use of either type should be allowed.

At the CWMA 2005 Interim Meeting, it was noted that adopting this proposal will create a logical and consistent standard of enforcement for mass flow meters and liquid-measuring devices, which are used for identical applications and products, thus ending an unintentional bias in favor of one technology over the other.

By stating the uniform operation guidelines for when it is acceptable to allow purge lines and recirculation lines (i.e., the necessity for such lines is to keep the product in a deliverable state), this proposal would eliminate the need for industry to petition NCWM for each product which requires such special handling. CWMA agreed to forward the proposal with the recommendation that it be a voting item on the Committee's 2006 agenda.

At the 2006 NCWM Interim Meeting, the Committee heard no opposition to this item and agreed to present it for a vote at the 2006 NCWM Annual Meeting. (See also corresponding Item 330-4.)

At the 2006 NCWM Annual Meeting, the Committee heard support for this item.

337-3 VC S.5.1. Location of Marking Information; Retail Motor-Fuel Dispensers

(This item was adopted.)

Source: National Type Evaluation Technical Committee (NTETC) Measuring Sector

Recommendation: Add a new Paragraph S.5.1. as follows and renumber subsequent paragraphs:

S.5.1. Location of Marking Information; Retail Motor-Fuel Dispensers. – The required marking information in the General Code, Paragraph G-S.1. Identification shall appear as follows:

(a) within 60 cm (24 in) to 150 cm (60 in) from the base of the dispenser;

(b) either internally and/or externally provided the information is permanent and easily read; and

(c) on a portion of the device that cannot be readily removed or interchanged (i.e., not on a service access panel).

Note: The use of a dispenser key or tool to access internal marking information is permitted for retail liquid-measuring devices.
[Nonretroactive as of January 1, 2003]
(Added 2006)

Background/Discussion: At the spring 2005 meeting of the NTEP laboratories it was recommended that the location of markings requirement from the LMD Code be added to Sections 3.32. LPG and Anhydrous Ammonia Liquid-Measuring Devices and 3.37. Mass Flow Meters. Both codes have other requirements for retail motor-fuel dispensers similar to those in the LMD Code. The laboratories agreed to forward its proposal to the NTETC Measuring Sector for consideration.

At their October 2005 meetings, the NTETC Measuring Sector and SWMA reviewed the proposal and both agreed to forward it to the Committee for consideration.

At the 2006 NCWM Interim Meeting the Committee heard no comments on Item 337-3 and agreed to present it for a vote at the 2006 NCWM Annual Meeting.

At the 2006 NCWM Annual Meeting, the Committee heard support for this item.

338 CARBON DIOXIDE LIQUID-MEASURING DEVICES

338-1 VC S.2.5. Provision for Sealing and Table S.2.5. Categories of Device and Methods of Sealing

Source: National Type Evaluation Technical Committee (NTETC) Measuring Sector

(This item was adopted.)

Recommendation: Modify Paragraph S.2.5. and add new Table S.2.5. Categories of Device and Methods of Sealing as follows:

S.2.5. Provision for Sealing. – Adequate provision shall be made for ~~applying security seals in such a manner that no~~ **an approved means of security (e.g., data change audit trail) or for physically applying a security seal in such a manner that requires the security seal to be broken before an** adjustment or interchange may be made of:

(a) any measur ~~ingement~~ element **or indicating element,**

(b) any adjustable element for controlling delivery rate when such rate tends to affect the accuracy of deliveries, ~~and~~

(c) any automatic temperature or density compensating system ~~,~~ **and**

(d) any metrological parameter that will affect the metrological integrity of the device or system.

When applicable, A~~a~~ny adjusting mechanism shall be readily accessible for purposes of affixing a security seal.

[Audit trails shall use the format set forth in Table S.2.5.]*
[*Nonretroactive as of January 1, 1995]
(Amended 2006)

Table S.2.5. Categories of Device and Methods of Sealing	
Category of Device	Method of Sealing
Category 1: No remote configuration capability.	Seal by physical seal or two event counters: one for calibration parameters and one for configuration parameters.
Category 2: Remote configuration capability, but access is controlled by physical hardware. The device shall clearly indicate that it is in the remote configuration mode and record such message if capable of printing in this mode or shall not operate while in this mode.	The hardware enabling access for remote communication must be on-site. The hardware must be sealed using a physical seal or an event counter for calibration parameters and an event counter for configuration parameters. The event counters may be located either at the individual measuring device or at the system controller; however, an adequate number of counters must be provided to monitor the calibration and configuration parameters of the individual devices at a location. If the counters are located in the system controller rather than at the individual device, means must be provided to generate a hard copy of the information through an on-site device.
Category 3: Remote configuration capability access may be unlimited or controlled through a software switch (e.g., password). The device shall clearly indicate that it is in the remote configuration mode and record such message if capable of printing in this mode or shall not operate while in this mode.	An event logger is required in the device; it must include an event counter (000 to 999), the parameter ID, the date and time of the change, and the new value of the parameter. A printed copy of the information must be available through the device or through another on-site device. The event logger shall have a capacity to retain records equal to 10 times the number of sealable parameters in the device, but not more than 1000 records are required. (Note: Does not require 1000 changes to be stored for each parameter.)

[Nonretroactive as of January 1, 1995]
(Table Added 2006)

Background/Discussion: At its October 2005 meeting, the NTETC Measuring Sector discussed the elimination of "Category 2" from the LMD Code and also discussed the addition of electronic sealing criteria to other NIST Handbook 44 measuring codes, such as the Vehicle-Tank Meters Code or the LPG and Anhydrous Ammonia Liquid-Measuring Devices, for liquid-measuring devices that do not have specific provisions for electronic security (i.e., audit trails). At the meeting, manufacturers of these devices stated that they have designed metering systems with electronic security with remote configuration capability. They are currently seeking an NTEP CC for these systems. Currently, the specific NIST Handbook 44 code for these devices does not address electronic sealing; however, electronic sealing is recognized in the General Code and under the provisions of G-A.3. Special and Unclassified Equipment. The specific audit trail criteria in the LMD Code can be applied, where appropriate. The manufacturers would prefer that each code include specific language similar to that in the LMD Code. During the discussion, the Sector concluded that some of these new applications and other applications currently in use would have been classified as the former "Category 2" devices. Some NTEP CCs have been issued stating that the device evaluated was a Category 1 device; however, because the mechanism for accessing sealable configuration parameters is not a permanent part of the device and can be removed without affecting normal operation, the device actually meets the definition of remote configuration capability. The manufacturers of these devices believe that no problems have been reported due to their current method of sealing and that it is inappropriate to require them to change the method of sealing to comply with Category 3. The Sector agreed that the industry would not have supported the decision to remove "Category 2" from the LMD Code and the Mass-Flow Meters Code had they had a clear understanding of "remote configuration capability" and that the decision should be reversed. The Committee also agreed that provisions for electronic sealing should be added to all appropriate liquid-measuring device codes as proposed in Items 330-3, 331-2, 332-1, 334-1, 335-1, 337-1, and 338-1. The Sector agreed to forward that proposal to the Committee for consideration.

At the 2006 NCWM Interim Meeting, the Committee agreed that a non-retroactive date of 1995, which is the same as the non-retroactive date in the LMD Code, is appropriate for Carbon Dioxide Liquid Measuring Devices because that date would have been applied to any devices NTEP evaluated using the criteria in G-A.3. Special and Unclassified Equipment. The Committee agreed to present Item 338-1 as shown above for a vote at the 2006 NCWM Annual Meeting. For additional discussion on this item, see Item 330-3.

At the 2006 NCWM Annual Meeting, the Committee heard support for this item.

360 OTHER ITEMS

360-1 I International Organization of Legal Metrology (OIML) Report

Many items before the OIML, the Asian-Pacific Legal Metrology Forum (APLMF), and other international groups are within the purview of the Committee. Additional information on OIML activities appear in the 2006 Board of Directors Interim Report and on the OIML website at http://www.oiml.org. WMD staff provided updates on OIML activities during the open hearing sessions at the 2006 NCWM Interim and Annual Meeting. For more information on specific OIML-related device activities, contact the WMD staff listed in the table below. The OIML projects listed below represent only currently active projects. For additional information on other OIML device activities that involve WMD staff, please contact WMD using the information listed below:

\multicolumn{5}{c}{NIST Weights and Measures Division (WMD) Contact List}				
Staff	Telephone	Email	Responsibilities	Postal Mail or Fax
Mr. Steven Cook (LMDG)	(301) 975-4003	steven.cook@nist.gov	•R 60 "Metrological Regulations for Load Cells" •R 76 "Non-automatic Weighing Instruments"	NIST WMD 100 Bureau Drive MS 2600 Gaithersburg, MD 20899-2600 Tel: (301) 975-4004 Fax: (301) 975-8091
Dr. Charles Ehrlich (ILMG)	(301) 975-4834	charles.ehrlich@nist.gov	•B 10 "Framework for a Mutual Acceptance Arrangement (MAA) on OIML Type Evaluations" •TC 3/SC 5 "Expression of Uncertainty in Measurement in Legal Metrology Applications," "Guidelines for the Application of ISO/IEC 17025 to the Assessment of Laboratories Performing Type Evaluation Tests," & "OIML Procedures for Review of Laboratories to Enable Mutual Acceptance of Test Results and OIML Certificates of Conformity"	
Mr. Richard Harshman (LMDG)	(301) 975-8107	richard.harshman@nist.gov	•R 106 "Automatic Rail-weighbridges" •R 107 "Discontinuous Totalizing Automatic Weighing Instruments" (totalizing hopper weighers) •R 134 "Automatic Instruments for Weighing Road Vehicles In-Motion"	
Ms. Diane Lee McGowan (LMDG)	(301) 975-4405	diane.lee@nist.gov	•R 59 "Moisture Meters for Cereal Grains and Oilseeds" •TC 17/SC 8 "Measuring Instruments for Protein Determination in Grains"	

NIST Weights and Measures Division (WMD) Contact List

Staff	Telephone	Email	Responsibilities	Postal Mail or Fax
Mr. Ralph Richter (ILMG)	(301) 975-3997	ralph.richter@nist.gov	•R 35 "Material Measures of Length for General Use" •R 105 & R 117 "Measuring Systems for Liquids Other Than Water" (includes Direct Mass) •R 118 "Testing Procedures and Test Report Format for Pattern Examination of Fuel Dispensers for Motor Vehicles" •TC 3/SC 4 "Verification Period of Utility Meters Using Sampling Inspections"	
Mr. Wayne Stiefel (ILMG)	(301) 975-4011	s.stiefel@nist.gov	•TC 8/SC 8 "Gas Meters" (Diaphragm, Rotary Piston, & Turbine Gas Meters) •R 49 "Water Meters" (Cold Potable Water & Hot Water Meters) •R 71 "Fixed Storage Tanks" •R 80 "Road and Rail Tankers" •R 85 "Automatic Level Gauges for Measuring the Level of Liquid in Fixed Storage Tanks" •TC 5/SC 2 "General Requirements for Software Controlled Measuring Instruments" •TC 8/SC 7 P1 "Measuring Systems for Gaseous Fuel" (i.e., large pipelines) •TC 8/SC 7 P2 "Compressed Gaseous Fuels Measuring Systems for Vehicles"	
Dr. Ambler Thompson ILMG	(301) 975-2333	ambler@nist.gov	•D 16 "Principles of Assurance of Metrological Control" •D 19 "Pattern Evaluation and Pattern Approval" •D 20 "Initial and Subsequent Verification of Measuring Instruments and Processes" •D 27 Initial Verification of Measuring Instruments Using the Manufacturer's Quality Management System" •R 34 "Accuracy Classes of Measuring Instruments" •R 46 "Active Electrical Energy Meters for Direct Connection of Class 2"	
Ms. Juana Williams (LMDG)	(301) 975-3989	juana.williams@nist.gov	•R 21 "Taximeters"	

LIST OF ACRONYMS

ILMG – International Legal Metrology Group	LMDG – Legal Metrology Devices Group	B – Basic Publication D – Document P – Project	R – Recommendation SC – Subcommittee TC – Technical Committee

360-2 W Appendix A – Fundamental Considerations Section 11 Health and Safety Considerations

(This item was withdrawn.)

Source: Western Weights and Measures Association (WWMA)

Recommendation: The Committee considered a proposal to add a new Section 11. Health and Safety Considerations to NIST Handbook 44 Appendix A as follows:

<u>**11. Health and Safety Considerations**</u>

<u>**11.1. Health and Safety. –** This handbook cannot address all of the health and safety issues associated with device inspections. During the inspection and testing of weighing and measuring equipment safety is a major consideration in conducting inspections. If the inspection cannot be conducted in a safe manner, the inspector will terminate the inspection.</u>

<u>The inspector is responsible for determining appropriate safety and health hazards before beginning an inspection. The inspector should make himself/herself familiar with all warnings associated with the equipment and facility prior to conducting any inspection and must comply with federal, state, local and agency laws, regulations and policies in effect at the time of the inspection. Inspectors will bring hazards or deficiencies to the attention of the business owner/operator and to the appropriate Weights and Measures supervisor. It is only through good judgment and conscientious adherence to safety regulations and procedures on a regular basis that the inspector can decrease the likelihood of personal injury and damage to property and equipment.</u>
<u>**(Added 200X)**</u>

Discussion: At its September 2005 Annual Meeting, WWMA reviewed a proposal to add safety considerations to the General Code section of NIST Handbook 44. While WWMA supported the concept, it believed that Appendix A, Fundamental Consideration was a more appropriate place to add the proposed language. Therefore, WWMA submitted the proposal to the Committee for consideration.

At their 2005 fall meetings, the remaining regional associations reviewed the WWMA proposal. CWMA did not believe that safety is a NIST Handbook 44 issue. NEWMA supported the proposal as a developing item and recommended the NCWM L&R Committee consider a similar proposal for inclusion in NIST Handbook 130 "Uniform Laws and Regulations in the areas of legal metrology and engine fuel quality." SWMA recommended the item be withdrawn because safety considerations are already adequately addressed in the EPOs.

At the 2006 NCWM Interim Meeting, the Committee acknowledged that safety is a primary concern. However, the Committee agreed with CWMA and SWMA that safety is already adequately addressed in the EPOs and, consequently, withdrew Item 360-2 from its agenda.

360-3 W Add International Terms that are Synonymous to NIST Handbook 44 Terms in Appendix D; Definitions

Source: Carryover Item 360-4. (This item originated from the Northeastern Weights and Measures Association (NEWMA) and first appeared on the Committee's 2002 agenda.)

Discussion: Many NIST and OIML technical concepts and procedures are in harmony, yet there are significant differences in terminology used by the two organizations. The harmonization of language is not necessary to obtain uniform legal requirements provided the intent of the requirements are essentially equivalent; however, improvements should be considered to revise language that is confusing or has the potential for misinterpretation. This item was intended to familiarize the public and private sectors with a proposed approach to modify Appendix D. The USNWG was to identify terms or definitions that are equivalent to international vocabulary by placing the corresponding OIML term in parentheses adjacent to the NIST Handbook 44 term.

Later stages of the project would involve amending Appendix D to clarify terminology for international participants in the proposed Mutual Acceptance Arrangement (MAA), where it remains imperative that all affected parties are aware of and understand each other's requirements. Terms can have an entirely different meaning in NIST Handbook 44 than they do in R 76 and other OIML Recommendations. NIST Handbook 44 is also inconsistent in the use of many terms such as "division," "increment," and "interval." One additional goal was to eliminate any confusion about other frequently used terms such as "device," "element," "mechanism," "scale," "weigher," and "balance."

NEWMA supported this initiative. WWMA requested the proposal remain an information item. CWMA believes this is not a field issue and indicated that the item is covered in NCWM Publication 14; therefore, it recommended that the proposal be withdrawn from the Committee's agenda.

The USNWG on R 76 "Non-automatic Weighing Instruments" was unable to dedicate resources to work on a proposal to amend NIST Handbook 44 Appendix D, Definitions to include international terminology that is synonymous with Handbook 44 definitions. Therefore, during the 2006 NCWM Interim Meeting, the Committee agreed to withdraw the item from its agenda until sufficient resources can be devoted to fully developing this item. The Committee noted that as changes are considered to existing definitions and new definitions are considered for addition to Appendix D, the terminology should be thoroughly examined for consistency and to avoid any conflicts with related vocabulary.

360-4 Developing Items

NCWM established a category of items called "Developing Items" as a mechanism to share information about emerging items which have merit and are of national interest, but that have not received sufficient review by all parties affected by the proposal or that may be insufficiently developed to warrant review by the Committee. The developing items are currently under review by at least one regional association or technical committee.

Developing Items are listed in Appendix A according to the specific NIST Handbook 44 code section under which they fall. Periodically, proposals will be removed from the developing item agenda without further action because the submitter recommends that it be withdrawn. Any remaining proposals will be renumbered accordingly.

The Committee encourages interested parties to examine the proposals included in Appendix A and send comments to the contact listed in each item. The Committee asks that the regional associations and NTETC Sectors continue to develop fully each proposal. Should an association or Sector decide to discontinue work on an item, the Committee asks that it be notified.

Clark Cooney, Oregon, Chairman (1)
Carol P. Fulmer, South Carolina (3)
Todd R. Lucas, Ohio (4)
Brett Saum, San Luis Obispo County, California (5)
Michael J. Sikula, New York (2)

Ted Kingsbury, Canada, Technical Advisor
Richard Suiter, NIST, Technical Advisor
Juana Williams, NIST, Technical Advisor

Specifications and Tolerances Committee

Appendix A

Item 360-4: Developing Items

Part 1, Item 1, General Code: G-UR.4.1.1. Proper Operating Conditions for Retail Motor-Fuel Devices

Source: Central Weights and Measures Association (CWMA)

Recommendation: Add a new Paragraph G-UR.4.1.1. as follows:

> **G-UR.4.1.1. Proper Operating Condition for Retail Motor-Fuel Devices. – The equipment will not be considered maintained in proper operating condition when one or more of the following conditions are met:**
>
> **(a) Multiple (four or more) devices, defined as grades or types of fuel, in service at a single place of business shall not be considered in proper operating condition under any of the following:**
>
> **(1) The calculated average error of all devices is in favor of the device owner/user by more than one-third the maintenance tolerance.**
> **(2) The calculated average error for any particular grade or type of fuel averages in favor of the device owner/user by more than one-third the maintenance tolerance.**
>
> **Note: Special tests should not be included in calculations unless the special test alone is in favor of the device owner/user by more than one-third the maintenance tolerance.**

(Added 200X)

At its 2005 CWMA Interim Meeting the association membership reviewed a proposal to add a new Paragraph G-UR.4.1.1. Proper Operating Condition to aid field officials in determining if retail motor-fuel dispensers are being maintained in accordance with G-UR.4.1. Maintenance of Equipment.

In 1991 this issue was brought before NCWM as an information item. The intent of the proposal at that time was to provide guidance for states in the interpretation of General Code Paragraph G-UR.4.1. Maintenance of Equipment. In 1993, the State of Wisconsin adopted a policy that defined "predominance" as shown in the proposal. That policy was similar to the one proposed to NCWM in 1991 except that Wisconsin felt that one-third acceptance tolerance was too stringent as there was a need to take into account normal variability in testing procedures, equipment, and environmental conditions found in the field. Wisconsin, therefore, adopted a greater than one-third of maintenance tolerance guideline. In 2003 the Wisconsin policy was further refined by deleting the language "all devices are found to be in error in a direction favorable to the device user." The new guideline for permissible errors was "sixty percent or more of the devices are found to be in error in favor of the device owner/user by more than one-third of the maintenance tolerance." Both of these criteria were seldom used in the field because they made the policy confusing.

Recently NIST conducted a national survey of RMFD testing and the results point to a need to gain more uniformity in the application of tolerances. There is a wide variation in how different states handle the "predominance" question. Strides should be continually made to gain uniformity. It is felt that the adoption of the proposed requirement G-UR.4.1.1. would be one step toward gaining greater uniformity. With more than five years of history using the proposed criteria, Wisconsin sees a relatively low number of devices rejected on the basis of "predominance" and most station owners and all service companies have a working understanding of predominance.

CWMA agreed to submit the modified proposal to the NCWM S&T Committee with a recommendation that it be placed on the Committee's agenda as a "Developing Item."

S&T Committee 2006 Finall Report
Appendix A – Item 360-4: Developing Items

Part 2, Item 1, Scales: S.2.1.7. Tare Rounding on a Multiple Range Scale

Source: Southern Weights and Measures Association (SWMA)

Recommendation: Add a new Paragraph S.2.1.7. as follows:

S.2.1.7. Tare Rounding on a Multiple Range Scale. – A multiple range scale with tare capability must indicate and record values that satisfy the equation:

net = gross - tare

**and round the tare value up to the larger division size when entering the larger division.
(Added 200X)**

Discussion: Currently, there may be a conflict between NIST Handbook 44 requirements and NCWM Publication 14 policy for rounding tare values on multiple range scales. NIST Handbook 44 General Code Paragraph G-S.5.2.2.(c) Digital Indication and Representation requires that digital values round off to the nearest minimum unit that can be indicated or recorded. Also in question is a possible conflict with NIST Handbook 130 guidelines which specify that in no case shall rounded values result in overstating the net quantity. NTEP policy permits the operation of tare on multiple range scales to round down, thus overstating the quantity. The proposal was developed to eliminate any conflict in the operation of the tare function on multiple range scales. NTEP is also revising its tare criteria to ensure no further conflict with NIST Handbook 44. SWMA recognizes that OIML permits rounding tare down, but believes that customers are not able to make adjustments in unit prices to compensate for losses when tare is rounded down whereas businesses can adjust the price to compensate for overhead expenses and losses that occur if tare is rounded up.

The NTETC Weighing Sector established a Tare Work Group chaired by Scott Davidson (Mettler-Toledo, Inc.) to fully develop this proposal. To comment on this proposal contact Scott Davidson by email at scott.davison@mt.com, by telephone at (614) 438-4387 or by fax at (614) 438-4355.

Part 3, Item 1, Belt-Conveyor Scale Systems: UR.3.2.(c) Maintenance; Zero Load Tests

Source: Western Weights and Measures Association (WWMA) and NIST Weights and Measures Division (WMD)

Recommendation: Modify UR.3.2.(c) as follows:

UR.3.2. Maintenance. – Belt-conveyor scales and idlers shall be maintained and serviced in accordance with manufacturer's instructions and the following:

.
.
.

(c) **Zero-load tests, S**simulated load tests**,** or material tests, ~~and zero load tests~~ shall be conducted at periodic intervals between official tests in order to provide reasonable assurance that the device is performing correctly.
(Amended 200X)

**The action to be taken as a result of the zero-load tests is as follows:
(Added 2000X)**

- **if the change in the zero-load reference is greater than ± 0.25 %, inspect the conveyor and weighing area to be sure it conforms to UR.2. Installation Requirements and correct any deficiencies;
(Added 200X)**

- **if the change in the zero-load reference is greater than 0.5 % in a 24-hour period, inspect the conveyor and weighing area to be sure it conforms to UR.2. Installation Requirements, correct any deficiencies, and repeat the zero-load test.**
  (Added 200X)

The action to be taken as a result of the material tests or simulated load tests is as follows:
~~(Amended 2002)~~

- if the error is less than 0.25 %, no adjustment is to be made;

- if the error is at least 0.25 % but not more than 0.6 %, **inspect the conveyor and weighing area to be sure it conforms to UR.2. Installation Requirements, correct any deficiencies, and repeat the simulated or materials test.**
  (Amended 1991 **and 200X**)

  An adjustment **to the span calibration** may be made if **no deficiencies were identified during the above inspection and any correction to the installation did not result in errors less than or equal to ± 0.25 %. T**~~he~~ official with statutory authority is notified **if an adjustment is made to the span calibration**;
  (Amended 1991 **and 200X**)

- if the error is greater than 0.6 % but does not exceed 0.75 %, **inspect the conveyor and weighing area to be sure it conforms to UR.2. Installation Requirements, correct any deficiencies, and repeat the simulated or materials test**;

  A~~d~~justments **to the span calibration** shall be made only by a competent service person and the official with statutory authority shall be notified **if no deficiencies were identified during the above inspection and any correction to the installation did not result in errors less than or equal to ± 0.25 %.** After such an adjustment **to the span calibration,** ~~if the results of a subsequent test require adjustment in the same direction~~, **the official with statutory authority shall be notified and** an official test shall be conducted;
  (Amended 1991 **and 200X**)

- if the error is greater than 0.75 %, an official test is required.
  (Amended 1987 and 200X)

Discussion: NIST Handbook 44 gives limited guidance on what to do with zero-load test results. Belt loss is not the only factor which may require the scale operator to make physical adjustments to the belt-conveyor system to correct for deficiencies. For example, a dirty scale structure or a worn belt scraper will increase the zero reference number and the test results may exceed tolerances.

The scale user/owner has to protect his interest between weighing transactions. At present, some belt-conveyor systems may have error greater than 0.5 % in zero reference over a 24-hour period. The belt is part of tare (net load) on any empty running system and the system must be maintained within tolerance at all times.

WWMA indicated that, based on comments heard in September 2005, only part of the proposal has merit. Consequently, WWMA recommended the proposal become a developing item. NIST WMD indicated that it wanted to work with WWMA on the development of this item through its staff member, Steven Cook.

To comment on this proposal, contact Steven Cook, NIST WMD, at steven.cook@nist.gov, by telephone at (301) 975-4003, by fax at (301) 975-8091 or at NIST WMD, 100 Bureau Drive, MS 2600, Gaithersburg, MD 20899-2600.

S&T Committee 2006 Finall Report
Appendix A – Item 360-4: Developing Items

Part 3, Item 2, Belt-Conveyor Scale Systems: UR.2.2.(n) Belt Alignment

Source: Western Weights and Measures Association (WWMA) and NIST Weights and Measures Division (WMD)

Recommendation: Modify Paragraph UR.2.2.(n) as follows:

UR.2.2. Conveyor Installation

(n) Belt Alignment. – **The belt shall be centered on the idlers in the weighing area and shall track in practically the same position whether empty or loaded.** The belt shall not extend beyond the edge of the idler roller in any area of the conveyor.

(Amended 1998 **and 200X**)

Discussion: WWMA considered proposed changes to Paragraph UR.2.2. to provide needed guidance on belt tracking before, during, or after a materials test. Ideally, the belt should be in the same location at full load and empty conditions. If the belt location or belt tension is not constant, scale accuracy is affected. Consequently, WWMA agreed to develop a proposal to modify Paragraph UR.2.2. to make the scale user/owner aware that the belt position must be monitored and maintained.

CWMA supported the proposal, but recommended removing any ambiguity by deleting the word "practically" from the proposed text. SWMA supported the proposal being a voting item on the Committee's 2006 agenda.

The Committee considered the NCWM review panel's recommendations and heard comments from industry. The review panel indicated the proposal should have included national data that demonstrated a need for modifying Paragraph UR.2.2. The review panel agreed with the original submitter of the proposal, WWMA, that the item should be a developing item. One representative from the belt-conveyor scale service industry indicated there are too many factors that influence belt tracking to ensure a belt is centered at all times. The service representative recommended that the belt should not extend beyond the edge of the idler roller in any area of the conveyor on the carrying side or touch holding brackets on the return side to reduce any detrimental effects on accuracy. Industry representatives indicated the design of idlers and scales are such that the belt is not intended to stay in the exact center position. Industry also indicated there is no mechanism available to monitor the belt's tracking 24 hours a day, seven days a week. Industry requested either specifications for what constitutes "center" or an acceptable "range of center" for belt tracking. Originally, the proposal was placed on the Committee's agenda because SWMA reported the proposal was ready for national consideration. After some consideration, the Committee agreed that it is more appropriate to make the proposal a developing item until there is some clear indication that belt alignment can be tracked for maintenance and accuracy purposes. NIST WMD indicated that it wanted to work with WWMA on the development of this item through its staff member, Steven Cook.

To comment on this proposal, contact Steven Cook, NIST WMD, at steven.cook@nist.gov, by telephone at (301) 975-4003, by fax at (301) 975-8091 or at NIST WMD, 100 Bureau Drive, MS 2600, Gaithersburg, MD 20899-2600.

Part 4, Item 1, Automatic Weighing Systems: Temperature Limits

Source: National Type Evaluation Technical Committee (NTETC) Weighing Sector

Recommendation: The Weighing Sector asked for the Committee's interpretation of how to apply marking requirements for temperature limits based on the thermal conditions developed during type evaluation laboratory testing and those conditions that exist in real-world environments. The Sector also questioned why requirements that address instances where equipment operates in temperatures that are outside of the -10 °C to 40 °C temperature range such as Scales Code Paragraph T.N.2.3. Subsequent Examination Verification are not included in all weighing device codes. The Sector also noted there are inconsistencies in the language that specifies temperature requirements throughout the weighing device codes. The Weighing Sector agreed this is an important issue, yet recognizes the Committee may require time to research the codes and policies established on this topic. Consequently, the Weighing Sector recommended this issue as a developing item.

S&T Committee 2006 Final Report
Appendix A – Item 360-4: Developing Items

The Weighing Sector agreed that no evaluation would be conducted for temperature ranges outside of laboratory capabilities, which are -10 °C to 40 °C while it awaits input from the Committee. The Weighing Sector's *ad hoc* policy is contrary to an earlier NTEP policy where NTEP agreed to require testing to demonstrate compliance with the manufacturer's specified temperature range, including accepting data from recognized and approved laboratories for tests performed at temperature ranges that exceeded the -10 °C to 40 °C temperature range.

The Committee agreed the interpretation will require time to develop because work must be done to review existing language in Handbook 44 to determine if changes are necessary to ensure the identical language needs to be included in all weighing devices codes and is ultimately consistent with the Committee's final interpretation. The Committee acknowledged that the Weighing Sector has a work group consisting of NIST WMD staff, led by Steven Cook along with Juana Williams, and Darryl Flocken (Mettler-Toledo, Inc.) who are working with the Sector to fully develop all aspects of this item.

To comment on this proposal, contact Steven Cook, NIST Technical Advisor to the NTETC Weighing Sector, at steven.cook@nist.gov, by telephone at (301) 975-4003, by fax at (301) 975-8091, or at NIST WMD, 100 Bureau Drive, MS 2600, Gaithersburg, MD 20899-2600.

THIS PAGE LEFT INTENTIONALLY BLANK.

Professional Development Committee (PDC)[1]
Annual Report

Celeste Bennett, Chairman
Michigan Department of Agriculture
Williamston, Michigan

Reference
Key Number

400 INTRODUCTION

This is the report of the Professional Development Committee (hereinafter referred to as "Committee" or PDC) for the 91st Annual Meeting of the National Conference on Weights & Measures (NCWM). This report is based on the Interim Report offered in NCWM Publication 16, testimony heard at public hearings, comments received from the Regional Weights and Measures Associations and other parties, the Addendum Sheets issued at the Annual Meeting, and actions taken by the membership at the Voting Session of the Annual Meeting. The informational items presented below were adopted as presented when the Committee's report was approved.

Table A identifies the agenda items in the Report by Reference Key Number, Item Title, and Page Number. An item numbers are those assigned in the Interim Meeting Agenda. A voting item is indicated with a "V" after the item number. An item marked with an "I" after the reference key number is an information item. An item marked with "D" after the reference key number is a developing item. The developing designation indicates an item has merit; however, the item was returned to the submitter for further development before any action can be taken at the national level. Table B lists the Appendix to the Agenda.

Table A
Index to Reference Key Items

Reference Key Number		Title of Item	Page
400		**INTRODUCTION**	1
401		**EDUCATION**	2
401-1	I	National Training Program (NTP)	2
401-2	I	Create a Curriculum Plan (Carryover Item 401-4)	3
401-3	D	Instructor Improvement (Carryover Item 401-7)	4
401-4	D	Certification (Carryover Item 401-8)	5
401-5	D	Recommended Topics for Conference Training (Carryover Item 401-10)	7
402		**PROGRAM MANAGEMENT**	8
402-1	I	Safety Awareness (Carryover Item 402-3)	8
402-2	I	Standard Categories of Weighing and Measuring Devices (Carryover Item 402-4)	8
402-3	D	PDC Publication	10

Table B
Appendix

Appendix	Title	Page
A.	Strategic Direction for the Professional Development Committee	A1

---

[1] Note: Report content is published as received with the exception of minor editorial and format changes.

Details of All Items
(In Order by Reference Key Number)

401 EDUCATION

401-1   I   National Training Program (NTP)

Source: The Committee (2003)

Background: The Board of Directors established the Committee at the 2003 NCWM Annual Meeting. The first critical charge given to the Committee was to develop a national weights and measures professional development program in cooperation with its partners including:

- State and local weights and measures departments;
- Private industry; and
- Technical advisors from NIST Weights and Measures Division and Measurement Canada

NTP will address the following tasks in order of priority:

1. The education and professional development of weights and measures officials and the promotion of uniformity and consistency in the application of weights and measures laws and regulations;
2. The education of industry personnel with regard to weights and measures laws and regulations, including all areas from device manufacturer to service technician;
3. Quality standards for weights and measures activities and programs;
4. Safety awareness for weights and measures-related activities; and
5. Development of a firm partnership with the state and local weights and measures jurisdictions, private industry, and NCWM. It is critical that NIST Weights and Measures Division (NIST WMD) partner with the Committee and, where appropriate, provide technical advice. Measurement Canada is also encouraged to participate in Committee activities.

The Committee began developing the concept of a National Certification Program for weights and measures officials during the 2004 NCWM Annual Meeting. In December 2004 several Committee members met in Harrisburg, Pennsylvania, to further develop the Committee's overall strategic direction of a National Certification Program. The participants agreed NTP should take the following directions:

- The training responsibility remains with the state and local jurisdictions.
- Administrator training must be added to the curriculum.
- Training and structure used by agencies outside NCWM should be explored and used as models.
- The Central Weights and Measures Association (CWMA) offered to assist the Committee in determining what knowledge and prerequisites are required for beginning and advanced inspectors.
- The Western Weights and Measures Association (WWMA) recommended course outlines for shorter training courses.

The strategic direction is summarized in Appendix A.

Discussion: WWMA: Individual regional associations are encouraged to take it upon themselves to dedicate a portion of their Annual Meeting towards NTP. This time should be spent developing at least one of the weights and measures core competencies defined by the NCWM PDC. The resulting document should be forwarded to the NCWM PDC in order to complete the overall project. To this end the WWMA PDC committed to the development of the retail motor-fuel dispensers curriculum.

CWMA: State associations reported receiving comments from industry sectors that they would find it valuable to have the training expanded to include the addition of industry personnel. Focus should remain on establishing a training program for regulatory personnel, but inclusion of industry in training has merit since many jurisdictions report improved overall compliance when industry receives education and training.

The Committee will forward a training model to the regional weights and measures associations. The Committee appreciates the continued interest and support.

Action: No comments were received in open hearings.

401-2　I　Create a Curriculum Plan (Carryover Item 401-4)

Source: The Committee (2003)

Background: The Committee agreed the following steps must be addressed for NTP to be viable:

(a) Develop and maintain a curriculum plan in cooperation with our partners that establishes uniform and consistent training objectives for weights and measures professionals in all fields and at all levels.

(b) Develop objectives of the curriculum plan representative of a consensus of our partners and organize those objectives by scope, sequence, and level of complexity to assist those developing the curriculum materials.

The development of a training program should follow the steps below:

1. Study training programs of outside agencies and state and local jurisdictions.

2. Establish knowledge goals for weights and measures officials and administrators.

3. Develop curriculum based upon the findings and results of the steps 1 - 2 above.

    (a) Coordinate the development of curriculum materials to be used in the delivery of training (i.e., lesson plans, digital presentations, slide shows, testing guides, etc.) using a variety of formats (e.g., self-study, traditional instruction).

    (b) Consider creating a network of interested parties to establish priorities, share training resources, foster cooperation to reduce redundancy, and promote uniformity and consistency.

4. Develop examinations, quizzes or tests based on the content of the materials developed under Item 3.

5. Gather and share information from trainers on highly effective techniques, visual aids and other materials that have been used to facilitate learning. Use as many of these resources as available.

The Committee reviewed the notes from the NIST-sponsored administrators' workshops held in Denver, Colorado, and Baltimore, Maryland, and plans to explore many of these ideas.

During the 2004 Annual Meeting, the Committee discussed the idea of using work groups to develop courses that could be used for self-study or for traditional classroom settings. The Committee agreed the initial priority should be high profile devices (e.g., motor-fuel dispensers and retail computing scales). The Committee studied the survey results to focus on the membership's needs and desires.

There were several recommendations submitted by the regional associations. CWMA commented that the Committee should draw upon other sources, both external and internal, for establishment of curricula. WWMA recommended the Committee review current training courses on the NIST website at http://www.nist.gov/owm to establish and identify various levels of training. They also suggested the Committee review and update all existing NIST training courses and post them on the NIST website. The Northeast Weights and Measures Association (NEWMA) recommended the Committee set standards for education that include provisions for field tests.

During the 2005 Interim Meeting, recommendations were made to develop course curriculum with specific learning objectives and development of tests to determine mastery of the learning objectives. Training responsibility to meet the objectives would rest with the jurisdictions. Recommendations were made for the Committee to oversee development of the tests to be administered for each course. Upon successful testing, certificates would be issued. Protocol for preserving the integrity of the tests and the testing system would need to be developed.

Discussion: The regional associations have begun work on their designated curriculum plans.

NEWMA: The State of New York provided PDC with a final draft curriculum for small scales. The draft will be circulated for comment. New York also provided a proposed training outcome hierarchy. The State of New York presented the California Core Competency Model as a guideline to be considered by the Committee.

CWMA: PDC members working on a framework for the package-checking curriculum hope to have a draft for soliciting comments at the Interim Meeting. The draft will contain the training guidelines and curriculum framework detailing the responsibilities of the state conducting the training.

WWMA: Developing a curriculum plan is one of the most important components of an NTP. Individual regional associations should be encouraged to dedicate a portion of their Annual Meeting to this work. The time should be spent developing at least one of the weights and measures core competencies defined by the NCWM PDC. The resulting document should be forwarded to the NCWM PDC in order to complete the overall project. The WWMA PDC is working on a retail motor-fuel dispenser curriculum for comments at the NCWM Interim Meeting.

SWMA: The SWMA continues to support the work of the NCWM PDC in this important task. The SWMA PDC committed to developing the curriculum for motor vehicle scales by its next Annual Meeting.

Action: To assist the work groups, PDC will forward a small-scale example format developed by the prior Administration and Public Affairs Committee (A&P) and the documents provided by New York as example formats. The regional committee responsible for developing the curriculum segment is reminded to focus on a level of competency expected of the entry-level inspector. As the regions develop the curriculum, they should also begin development of the written certification questions needed to verify the curriculum goals have been met.

The Committee will request posting to the NCWM website: a Core Competency Model received from New York, the three curriculum segments developed by New York, and a short guidance memo on how to use the curriculum.

401-3　D　Instructor Improvement (Carryover Item 401-7)

Source: The Committee (2003)

Background: One Committee goal is to work with all interested parties to improve the competence of instructors and the uniformity of delivery of the curriculum.

The Committee concluded there are two parts of an instructor improvement strategy. The first part is educating trainers in effective methods of instruction. A variety of courses and training methods are available from state, federal, and private sources to develop instructional skills and techniques. Jurisdictions are encouraged to seek out and send selected staff to participate in this type of training.

The second area of instructor improvement is to provide trainers with the knowledge of the technical aspects of all types of devices. The Committee believes NIST WMD's continued leadership and participation is a valuable asset in this area and recommends that WMD continue to provide the technical training for instructors. The Committee invites and looks forward to working with WMD as a resource to consult with trainers and to work with the Committee to keep the curricula current as changes to the handbooks occur, new technologies are deployed, and emerging issues develop. While this is not an urgent issue, the item will be retained as a developing item.

Industry has continued to support and sponsor training on their new technology for weighing and measuring devices. NIST has assured the committee that they will continue their work towards providing technical training for the trainers.

Discussion: WWMA: The NCWM PDC should also consider the NTEP laboratories and their personnel as a valuable instructional resource.

Action: While important, this topic is on hold until progress is made in other areas.

401-4 D   Certification (Carryover Item 401-8)

Source: The Committee (2003)

Background: The Committee believes that an NCWM certification program should be developed based on the curriculum plan with measurable levels of competency.

The Committee agrees that weights and measures officials must pass written examinations to receive certification. Certificates could be presented at the NCWM Annual Meetings to administrators and weights and measures officials who complete training classes and pass the course examination. In 2004 then-Chairman Dennis Ehrhart indicated the Board of Directors would consider requests to fund training. The Committee is exploring certification of weights and measures officials as a means to demonstrate competency. WWMA and CWMA submitted extensive comments and recommendations regarding this item prior to the 2004 NCWM Annual Meeting. The Committee has designated this a developing item.

The 2005 Annual Meeting proposal on state-issued certification was redrafted to reflect the NCWM role in issuance of the certificates.

Discussion: CWMA: Certification is necessary for uniformity and professional development. The certification program should be for individuals. Accreditation of jurisdictions is a separate program that could be addressed at a later time. Certification testing could be administered by the state. NCWM issuance of certificates would carry a higher level of credibility with more prestigious recognition if given in conjunction with NCWM meetings. The development of both the training program and certification program could be effectively developed concurrently. The CWMA submitted the following State Certification Coordinators (SCCs) names.

State	First Name	Last Name	Contact
Alaska	Mike	Campbell	mike_Campbell@dot.state.ak.us
Arizona	Shawn	Marquez	smarquez@azdwm.gov
California	Ron	Flores	rflores@cdfa.ca.gov
Colorado	Jonathan	Handy	Jonathan.handy@ag.state.co.us
Hawaii	William	Pierpont	william.e.Pierpont@hawaii.gov
Idaho	Tom	Schafer	tschafer@agri.idaho.gov
Montana	Al	Page	(406) 841-2240
Nevada	Dave	Walch	(702) 486-4690
New Mexico	Raymond	Johnson	rjohnson@nmda.nmsu.edu
Oregon	Clark	Cooney	ccooney@odo.state.or.us
Utah	Brett	Gurney	bgurney@utah.gov
Washington	Bruce	Fagen	wsdabruce@earthlink.net
Wyoming	Albie	Mickelson	amicke@state.wy.us

WWMA: WWMA supports having the states meet the requirements established by NCWM. After demonstrating competency, NCWM would be the appropriate entity to issue the certificate. By exposing weights and measures inspectors to standardized training methodology, this certification process will lead to uniformity. Per the implementation plan, WWMA has identified the SCCs listed above. WWMA PDC recommends other regional associations assist NCWM PDC by offering such lists.

The Committee recommends a written test and is considering that a field test component be added sometime in the future. Curriculum developers will need to create questions for certification as the training material is developed. Upon successful completion of the certification test, NCWM will be the issuing authority for the certificate.

To maintain testing integrity, the testing protocol may need to include provisions for independent third party testing. Not to be restrictive to states without the ability to have third party testing, consideration should also be given to allow the states to determine how to conduct testing internally and meet the same integrity goals.

PDC 2006 Final Report

Other concerns were expressed that development of certification should be secondary to curriculum development. The Committee is seeking input as to whether NCWM members would like certificates for certification be issued based on individual device type or covering a broad-range device category.

Action: States that have not provided the name of their state certification coordinator (SCC) to PDC will receive a letter of request after this conference. The state director will be deemed the default SCC in the absence of a designated contact.

The Certification Proposal was redrafted to reflect the NCWM role in issuance of the certificates as follows:

NCWM-Issued Certification Proposal

Background: PDC strategic direction has established a plan for a certification program for individuals and programs. The Professional Development Committee has been charged with developing an NCWM certification program based on the curriculum plan with measurable levels of competency.

PDC will develop NCWM certification tests and testing protocol. Participating states would administer the tests as a measure of inspector competency. NCWM will issue the certificates. This certification program has been developed to use minimal NCWM resources, build upon each state's existing responsibilities for competency and training of their inspectors, and provide national merit and recognition for successful completion. This plan has been developed with the understanding that the states will train to ensure inspectors are able to meet the competency goals for certification.

Implementation:

Step One: Each State Director will identify a State Certification Coordinator (SCC) for its state, to work with PDC and NCWM. The SCC would be the main state contact and collection point for materials and information related to certification. The SCC would be responsible for:

1. Assisting PDC in developing:
    a. Test questions (or work group members would develop),
    b. Test protocol,
    c. Certification criteria, and
    d. Certification templates.
2. Implementing certification testing in their state,
3. Maintaining confidentiality of testing and test materials,
4. Scoring certification tests,
5. Submission of test scores to NCWM for the issuance of the certificate,
6. Reviewing their state's submitted questions annually for adherence to the handbook changes, and
7. Maintaining state certification files.

Step Two: PDC will establish work groups to identify core competencies and knowledge requirements for basic (beginning) and advanced (journey level) inspectors for a general W&M inspector, for specific devices, and W&M disciplines as identified in the training outline already developed by PDC. PDC and the SCC can work together to assist in establishing work groups for specialty areas to ensure the correct level of expertise.

Step Three: The work groups will develop certification tests and field competency verification methods to test the core competencies and knowledge requirements as established in Step Two. Get permission from the NCWM BOD to allow members of the work groups to utilize a secure area of the NCWM website to conduct their work without having costly meetings or conference calls. Each work group would submit questions to be used in the development of the test that would demonstrate the core competencies and knowledge requirements. This will establish a pool of potential questions for PDC and the SCC to use in development of certification tests. Use the ISWM 900-Question model and others for "developing," "recycling" and "updating" test questions as needed. SCCs or the work group members should review the questions they developed annually and update if necessary. This will ensure that as handbook requirements change, all questions will remain current and in agreement with the conference documents. Reviewing only a few questions should not be overly burdensome on any one jurisdiction or organization. Development of the tests must also include the testing minimums for certification of every test for each device and discipline for certification (i.e., must pass 75 % of the questions to be certified).

PDC would maintain a master list of questions for each test to be given, who submitted each question, when it was last reviewed, and then generate the test questions using a random selection method. The test would be changed annually. Once a test has been developed, PDC would submit the test questions (along with the answers) to the SCC for his/her use in certification.

Step Four: PDC will establish confidentiality, test and field verification protocol for the tests to ensure the integrity of the test and test validity are maintained. This is crucial given the wide scope of testing and the need to offer testing in every state. This ISWM test protocol and other successful test procedures should be studied to build on current successes. NCWM will print and issue certificates and provide recognition to certificate holders. The SCC in each state will be responsible for printing all test materials and instructions, giving the tests, and grading the tests; the SCC must monitor testing to see that test protocol is followed.

Certification program expected outcome: consistency of enforcement, uniformity, respect, integrity, and acceptance of end product. Inspectors will be able to compete in the marketplace for fair wages and be recognized as professionals in their field.

Other things to consider:

1. Each state must also ensure field competency along with certification.
2. Should certificates be required to be renewed?
3. Should there be a fee associated with certification to generate a revenue source or to cover the basic cost of administering the test?
4. Should study guides or workshops be developed as a revenue source for NCWM or as increased value to NCWM membership and attendance at meetings?

401-5   D   Recommended Topics for Conference Training (Carryover Item 401-10)

Source: The Committee (2003)

Background: Bill Sveum and Vince Orr's presentation, Net Content Control of Retail Products during Manufacturing, was added to the NCWM 2006 annual agenda as an educational session.

The Committee recommends the following topics for possible training seminars, round tables, or symposia suitable for presentation at the National Conference meetings:
- Risk-based inspections,
    Robert Williams, Tennessee, volunteered to present their state's RMFD testing program;
- Marketplace surveys;
- Auditing the performance of field staff,
    Will Wotthlie, Maryland, volunteered to lead a session on auditing field staff;
- Device inspections using a sampling model; and
- Emerging issues.

All members are encouraged to submit their ideas for topics to the Committee members and to volunteer to lead, present, or moderate a topic.

Action: PDC recommends that Maryland present a session on auditing of field staff activities and that Tennessee give a presentation on their state's RMFD testing program.

PDC recommends that the NCWM chairperson explore current motor-fuel trends and technology updates as a presentation at the next Annual Meeting. Due to the high cost of petroleum products, alternative fuels are growing in popularity. Inexperience with alternative fuels makes this a good topic to invite guest speakers to update the membership on these commodities.

Due to the importance of inspector safety, PDC sees value in safety discussion. The Committee is requesting that NCWM set aside one hour of conference time to devote to the sharing of best practice safety information or to consider a safety presentation. PDC will provide suggested speakers.

402 PROGRAM MANAGEMENT

402-1 I Safety Awareness (Carryover Item 402-3)

Source: The Committee (2003)

Background: In the past, the Committee's responsibility extended to the identification of safety issues in the weights and measures field and included efforts to increase safety awareness.

At the 2005 Annual Meeting, Past-Chairman Dennis Ehrhart recommended the Committee make training its highest priority. The Voluntary Quality Assurance Assessment Program, the NCWM Associate Membership Scholarships, and Safety Awareness efforts were carryover items from the Committee on Administration and Public Affairs and not the new direction of PDC.

Jurisdictions should send their safety reports and issues to their regional safety liaison, who in turn forwards them to Charles Gardner, the NCWM Safety Coordinator. Charles recommends the reports or summaries of them be published in the NCWM newsletter. At the 2005 Interim Meeting, a CD-ROM on safety produced for the U. S. Environmental Protection Agency was made available for review. The Committee will ensure that safety awareness is a part of every aspect of training for NCWM stakeholders.

Discussion: CWMA: Posting of the safety report to the website is recommended. Electronic submission is desirable. Safety training should be routinely incorporated into the conference agendas. The incident and accident report could be printed in the conference documents and e-mailed to state directors annually to facilitate access, submission, and discussion at meetings. Several topics for safety presentations were suggested, such as homeland security, preventing back injuries, and dealing with hostile situations.

There were no incident reports this year.

Action: Many states have changed their method of approach to conducting business to accommodate safety concerns. PDC believes that the sharing of this information has value and suggests that one hour of conference time be devoted to the sharing of best safety practices.

402-2 I Standard Categories of Weighing and Measuring Devices (Carryover Item 402-4)

Source: Western Weights & Measures Association (WWMA) (2005)

Background: The Western Weights and Measures Association (WWMA) Administration and Public Affairs (A&P) Committee recommended that standard categories of weighing and measuring devices be adopted to facilitate development of technical standards, inspector training, data collection, and program management.

The final report of the *Survey of Inspection Statistics Collected by State Weights and Measures Programs [2002]*, conducted during mid-2003, observed that the absence of standard categories for weighing and measuring devices was a serious obstacle to data collection. For example, the way weights and measures programs categorize scales by type, use, or capacity and capacity ranges often vary considerably. Retail motor-fuel dispensers are currently being counted either by dispenser, grade, or number of hoses or meters. The need for reliable weights and measures statistics is summarized in the final report conclusion as follows:

> Accurate statistics would be helpful in many ways at both the state and national level. For instance, performance measures are difficult to develop without statistics. Also, work plans require accurate and detailed statistics. In addition, budget, staffing, and other elements of each state program demand statistics on inspection workloads. Finally, neither individual states nor NCWM will be able to estimate and advertise the value of the nation's weights and measures programs unless reliable statistics are available.

To correct this problem, WWMA developed *Standard Categories for Weighing and Measuring Devices.* CWMA recommends that standard categories for weighing and measuring devices be adopted to facilitate the development of technical standards, inspector training, inspection data collection, and weights and measures program management.

At the 2005 Interim Meeting, the Committee agreed this item should remain informational at this time because standardized categories of weighing and measuring devices have merit and should be considered in the future.

Discussion: CWMA: PDC should clarify the intended purpose of this list. For example, compiling information for inspection time data would be different from compiling a device count. Add hopper as an example under large-scale category. Add GM for Grain Moisture Meters and MD for Multi Dimensional Devices. Add MV as a designation for a vehicle LPG meter and leave MG to designate Meter and LPG for a stationary meter.

NEWMA recommended use of the categories from Handbook 44 instead of creating new ones.

WWMA drafted the following recommendation for consideration by the Committee. The standard categories of weighing and measuring devices are based on capacity ranges rather than type or use. It is assumed that the inspection test procedures for scales and meters within these capacity ranges are generally similar. Weights and measures programs can adopt the recommended standard categories without changing the manner in which they presently keep records of device inspections by simply adding an extra data field.

Two-letter device category codes could be employed to categorize devices in weights and measures jurisdictions for reporting to NCWM during annual surveys. Otherwise, the data collection procedures already in place would be unaffected. It would be helpful to add the two-letter device category code to inspection reports.

Action: The NCWM Device Category Codes was updated.

NCWM DEVICE CATEGORY CODES

DEVICE CODE	CATEGORY	CAPACITY	EXAMPLES
SP	Scale, Precision	< 5 g scale division	jewelry, prescription scales
SS	Scale, Small	< 300 lb	retail computing scales
SM	Scale, Medium	300 to 5000 lb	dormant, platform scales
SL	Scale, Large	> 5000 lb	livestock, recycler scales, hopper scales, belt conveyor
SV	Scale, Vehicle	> 40 000 lb	vehicle, railway track scales
MS	Meter, Small	< 30 gpm[1]	retail motor fuel dispensers
MM	Meter, Medium	30 to 200 gpm	vehicle-tank meters
ML	Meter, Large >	200 gpm	agri-chemical meters, bulk oil meters, loading rack meters
MF	Meter, Mass Flow	All	heated tanks of corn syrup (soft drinks)
MW	Meter, Water	All	water sub-meters for mobile homes & apartments
MG	Meter, LPG	All propane	sales
MT	Meter, Taxi All Taximeters		
DT	Device, Timing	All	clocks in parking garages
DL	Device, Length Measuring	All cordage	meters
GM	Grain Moisture Meter All		
GA	Grain Analyzer	All	
MD	Multiple Dimension Measuring Device	All	
MC Meter,	Cryogenic	All	

[1] Retail motor-fuel dispenser counts should be based on meters except that mid-grades should be added for blenders.

PDC believes this item is ready to move forward as a voting item.

PDC 2006 Final Report

402-3 D PDC Publication

Source: The Committee (2005)

Discussion: The Committee recognized that many aspects of their work would need to be documented and presented. The Committee and Board should consider the publication of a handbook or similar document.

Action: Many of PDC items will continue to be carryover items from year-to-year. The Committee has created a PDC document archive. NCWM will be requested to maintain the archive. To eliminate the cost of reprinting the more lengthy items in their entirety and to preserve the important aspects of PDC work, a legacy document was developed. These documents are recommended to be archived on the web for easy access and downloading as needed.

The initial list of PDC work and documents will include:

History of PDC
Formal Scope of PDC
NCWM Board of Directors Charge to PDC
PDC's Role in the NCWM Strategic Plan
PDC's Strategic Plan
National Training Curriculum Outline
Suggested Topics for NCWM Annual Conference
Standard Categories of Weighing and Measuring Devices
Safety Liaison Contact Information
List of State Certification Coordinators and Contacts
NCWM Issued Certification Program
Voluntary Quality Assurance Assessment Program

Celeste Bennett, Michigan, Chair
Kenneth Deitzler, Pennsylvania
Agatha Shields, Franklin County, Ohio
Richard W. Wotthlie, Maryland
Michael Sarachman, Kraft Food Global, Associate Member
C. Gardner, New York, Safety Liaison
Linda Bernetich, NCWM Staff Liaison

Professional Development Committee

Appendix A

Strategic Direction for the Professional Development Committee

The Committee developed their strategic direction to define its roles and responsibilities to NCWM and the weights and measures community. The Committee members wrote principles to guide them in their deliberations and defined four main areas to focus their efforts. The Committee recognizes that its direction and responsibilities may be changed by the Board of Directors.

The guiding principles of the group were:

- Keep things simple,
- Develop programs that are realistic and achievable,
- Minimize redundancy and administrative tasks,
- Recognize that no one size fits all, and
- Meet the needs of W&M officials, service companies, industry and manufacturers.

The four main areas for focusing their efforts were:

National Training Program (NTP) – The focus of NTP would be to increase technical knowledge, strengthen credibility and improve the professionalism of the individual weights and measures official. A strong NTP will work to promote uniformity across the nation.

National Certification System – A national certification system would be developed to recognize or accredit weights and measures programs as competent or capable. The program would include requirements based on individual training, proper test standards, use of national handbooks, and a data gathering system.

Conference Training Topics – The Committee would be the focal point for gathering and recommending workshops or symposia on leadership, management, and emerging issues to be presented during the annual conference. These topics would provide a forum for the exchange of ideas and discussion of changes in the marketplace.

Uniformity of Data – The Committee would develop standard categories for devices and inspection areas so such things as the number of devices, compliance rates, frequency of inspection and other areas could be compiled and compared at the national level. These statistics could be used to benchmark organizations and to communicate the value of weights and measures to the public and to decision makers (see Item 402-4).

THIS PAGE LEFT INTENTIONALLY BLANK.

NTEP Committee 2006 Final Report

Report of the
National Type Evaluation Program (NTEP) Committee

Jim Truex
Chief
Ohio Department of Agriculture, Weights and Measures

Reference
Key Number

500 INTRODUCTION

The National Type Evaluation Program (NTEP) Committee (hereinafter referred to as "Committee") submits its report for consideration by the 91st National Conference on Weights and Measures (NCWM). This consists of the Interim Report presented in NCWM Publication 16 as amended in the Addendum Sheets issued during the Annual Meeting that was held July 9 - 13, 2006, in Chicago, Illinois. The Committee considered communications received prior to and during the 91st Annual Meeting that are noted in this report.

Table A identifies the agenda items in the report by Reference Key Number, Item Title, and Page Number. The item numbers are those assigned in the Committee's Interim Meeting Agenda. A voting item is indicated with a "V" after the item number or, if the item was part of the consent calendar, by the suffix " VC". An item marked with an "I" after the reference key number is an information item. An item marked with a "W" was withdrawn by the Committee and generally will be referred to the regional weights and measures associations because it either needs additional development, analysis, and input or does not have sufficient Committee support to bring it before the NCWM. Table B lists the appendices to the report, and Table C provides a summary of the results of the voting on the Committee's items and the report in entirety.

This report contains many recommendations to revise or amend National Conference on Weights and Measures (NCWM) Publication 14, Administrative Procedures, Technical Policy, Checklists, and Test Procedures or other documents. Proposed revisions to the publication(s) are shown in **bold face print** by ~~striking out~~ information to be deleted, and **underlining** information to be added. Requirements that are proposed to be nonretroactive are printed in *italics*.

Note: The policy of NIST is to use metric units of measurement in all of its publications; however, recommendations received by the NCWM technical committees have been printed in this publication as they were submitted and may, therefore, contain references to inch-pound units.

Table A
Index to Reference Key Items

Reference Key Number	Title of Item	Page
	Introduction	1
1.	Test Data Exchange Agreements	3
2.	Adoption of Uniform Regulation for National Type Evaluation by States (URNTE)	4
3.	NTEP Participating Laboratories and Evaluations Reports	4
4.	NTETC Sector Reports	5
5.	NTEP Participation in U.S. National Work Group on Harmonization of NIST Handbook 44, NCWM Publication 14 and OIML R 76 and R 60	7
6.	Software Sector	7
7.	Conformity Assessment Program (CAP)	9
8.	NTEP Certification of Residential-Type Water Meters	9

Table B
Appendices

Appendix	Title	Page
A	NTETC Grain Analyzer Sector Meeting Summary	A1
B	NTETC Measuring Sector Meeting Summary	B1
C	NTETC Weighing Sector Meeting Summary	C1

Table C
Glossary of Acronyms*

BIML	Bureau of International Legal Metrology	IR	International Recommendation
CD Committee	Draft[1]	MAA	Mutual Acceptance Arrangement
CIML	International Committee of Legal Metrology	OIML	International Organization of Legal Metrology
CPR	Committee on Participation Review	PTB	Physikalisch-Technischen Bundsanstalt
DD Draft	Document[2]	R Recommendation	
DR Draft	Recommendation[2]	SC Subcommittee	
DV Draft	Vocabulary[2]	TC Technical	Committee
DoMC	Declarations of Mutual Confidence WD Working		Document[3]

[1] CD: a draft at the stage of development within a technical committee or subcommittee; in this document, successive drafts are numbered 1 CD, 2 CD, etc.

[2] DD, DR, DV: draft documents approved at the level of the technical committee or subcommittee concerned and sent to BIML for approval by CIML.

[3] WD: precedes the development of a CD; in this document, successive drafts are number 1 WD, 2 WD, etc.

* Explanation of acronyms provided by OIML.

Table D
Voting Results

Reference Key Number	House of Representatives		House of Delegates		Results
	Yeas	Nays	Yeas	Nays	
500 (Report in Its Entirety) Voice Vote	All Yeas	No Nays	Al Yeas	No Nays	Passed

Details of All Items
(In Order by Reference Key Number)

1. Test Data Exchange Agreements

Background/Discussion: This item was included on the Committee's agenda in 1998 to provide an update on NTEP's work to establish bilateral and multilateral agreements. Under such agreements and arrangements, manufacturers would be able to submit their equipment to any of the participating countries for testing to OIML-recommended requirements. The resulting test data would be accepted by other participants as a basis for issuing each country's own type approval certificate. Following is a report on the three types of test data exchange agreements:

Mutual Acceptance Arrangement (MAA): NTEP Director, Stephen Patoray, attended an MAA Seminar for Assessors September 5 - 6, 2005. During this seminar, Mr. Patoray provided the attendees an overview of the additional requirements in the United States for both OIML R 76 and R 60. He updated the attendees at the 2006 NCWM Interim meeting regarding the current status of the MAA and other developments. The next scheduled meeting of the Committee on Participation Review (CPR) for R 76 and R 60 was held on March 7, 8, and 10, 2006, in Sydney, Australia.

The NTEP Committee discussed this item during the fall 2006 NTEP Committee meeting. Based on previous input from the NCWM membership and other discussion on this topic, the NTEP Committee believes the United States should be a Country A (issuing participant) with full laboratory capabilities for OIML R 76 "Non-automatic weighing instruments" and should not participate in a Declaration of Mutual Confidence (DoMC) as a Country B (utilizing participant) for R 76. However, the NTEP Committee recognizes that currently there are no identified resources available to be able to move forward with a laboratory for R 76 at this time. Based on this fact and given the realities of the NIST Force Group's position to not participate as a testing laboratory for OIML R 60 "Load cells", the NTEP Committee recommended that the NCWM Board of Directors consider signing the DoMC as a Country B for R 60 "Load cells" only.

The MAA is also in the NCWM Board of Directors' Committee Report.

Summary: During the 2006 NCWM Interim Meeting, the full NCWM Board carefully considered this issue and the recommendation of the NTEP Committee. Significant discussion was held on this issue with the primary focus on the desire to become a utilizing member (Country B) for the DoMC that will cover OIML R 60 load cells. Significant comments also came from the full membership during the 2006 NCWM Interim Meeting open hearings on this issue. In addition, a very large group attended a late evening meeting on this topic. The participants in this meeting asked many important questions and demonstrated a high level of interest in the NCWM's direction regarding MAAs. The NTEP Committee would like to acknowledge and thank this group of participants for their significant contributions in discussing this issue.

The decision of the Board was to accept the recommendation of the NTEP Committee and indicate the intention of signing on as a utilizing member of the DoMC for OIML R 60 Load Cells. The NCWM Board indicated no interest at this time in being a utilizing participant for OIML R 76 "Non-automatic weighing instruments (NAWI)." The intent is to investigate various alternatives and determine if a laboratory can be established that will allow NCWM to be an issuing participant in the DoMC for OIML R 76. It was clearly stated that this laboratory would have to be "viable" and that NCWM must fully understand the effect such a signing may have on NTEP, existing NTEP labs, and our standards development process in NCWM. It was also stated that it is not clear at this time if funding for such a laboratory is available.

Bilateral Agreements: No additional discussions have been held on this topic pending the outcome of the MAA discussions.

NTEP-Canada Mutual Recognition Program No additional areas of MRA activities have been identified.

NTEP Committee 2006 Final Report

2. Adoption of Uniform Regulation for National Type Evaluation by States (URNTE)

Background/Discussion: The Scale Manufacturers Association (SMA) has hosted NTEP adoption and implementation meetings for state directors at each regional weights and measures association conference. These meetings enable jurisdictions to share information about adopting and implementing NTEP in their respective jurisdictions, encourage non-NTEP jurisdictions to adopt the regulation, and allow current NTEP jurisdictions to share ideas on how to make enforcement more effective and uniform among the states. The meetings also provide NTEP management with information related to areas in which the operation and implementation of the program can be improved. Several questions have been posed at these meetings about issues associated with NTEP interpretation or practice. Comments from 1997 to 2005 have been summarized, without attribution and are available for review and download on the SMA website at http://www.scalemanufacturers.org.

During the most recent NCWM Annual Meeting, SMA Representative, Darrell Flocken, indicated SMA decided it would be more useful to show which states require NTEP certificates before allowing weighing and measuring devices to be certified as legal for trade regardless of their adoption of the NIST/NTEP URNTE. SMA developed a new map that shows that status. SMA, deciding that it would be more useful to show which states require Voluntary Registration of Service Agencies and Service Personnel (VRSA) regardless of their adoption of VRSA, developed separate maps that show that status. Such maps are available for review and download on the SMA website at http://www.scalemanufacturers.org.

Mr. Flocken will update the attendees on any future additional developments in this area. Based on comments from the NCWM membership, the NTEP Committee will make a final decision to discontinue this item from the NTEP report.

Summary: The NTEP Committee wishes to acknowledge and thank SMA for all of the work they have and continue to put into this item. The updated maps will be available on the SMA website for all to review. Based on comments from the NCWM membership, it was the decision of the NTEP Committee to discontinue reporting on this item as part of the NCWM Interim and Annual Meeting report agendas.

This item will be dropped as a standing item from future NTEP Committee agendas.

3. NTEP Participating Laboratories and Evaluations Reports

At the 2006 NCWM Interim Meeting, Stephen Patoray, NTEP Director, updated the Committee on NTEP laboratory and administrative activities since October 1, 2003. A report of NTEP Laboratory Activities was distributed at the 2006 NCWM Interim Meeting.

The NTEP weighing and measuring laboratories held a joint meeting in April 2006 in Annapolis, Maryland. The NTEP weighing laboratories also met September 25, 2005, before the meeting of the Weighing Sector in Columbus, Ohio. The NTEP measuring laboratories also met October 21, 2005, prior to the Measuring Sector meeting in Nashville, Tennessee.

The date and location of 2007 meeting of the NTEP Laboratories is to be determined.

Summary: During the 2006 NCWM Interim Meeting, the NTEP Director, Steve Patoray, reported that the number of the authorized NTEP labs has not changed within the last year. He also indicated that the NTEP Committee and he are watching the backlog at the NTEP laboratories closely. At the present time, the backlog at the NTEP laboratories has returned to more historical levels, after a period of months at a much higher level. Comments from the floor indicated interest in continuing to improve the length of time to complete an NTEP evaluation. It was noted, based on some random internal audit information provided by the California NTEP laboratory that a significant portion (up to 50 % of the total time) of the time spent during an evaluation may be due to delays by the manufacturer. There could be several factors, but lack of preparedness by the applicant, slow responses to laboratory inquiries, and need to correct device deficiencies lead to significant delays in completing an evaluation. The NTEP Committee will continue to monitor the laboratory backlog and also attempt to find additional solutions to improve the time to compete a device evaluation.

NTEP Director, Steve Patoray provided the Committee with the following updated report of the NTEP Laboratory and administrative activities from October 1, 2005 to June 2006.

NCWM Activity Report

Activity: NTEP

Date: June 13, 2006   Submitted By: NCWM Staff

NTEP Application Statistics:	2004-2005 10/1/04 - 6/13/05	2005-2006 10/1/05 - 6/7/06	Grand Total 10/1/00 - 6/7/06
Total Appls. Processed (Reactivations)	(2) 198	173	(49) 1403
Applications Completed	53	67	1097
New Certificates Issued:	131	185	1322
Certificates Distributed to State Directors	134	197	1312
Certificates Posted to Web Site	134	183	3857
Current Active NTEP Certificates:			1579

Time for NCWM to assign an evaluation:	Avg.: 8 days	Median: 8 days
Time for NCWM to review a draft CC:	Avg.: 8 days	Median: 6 days
Time for complete evaluation:	Avg.: 145 days	Median: 115 days

Upcoming meetings:

- Grain Analyzer Sector – August 23 - 24, 2006, Kansas City, Missouri
- Weighing Sector – September 26 - 28, 2006, Annapolis, Maryland
- Software Sector – October 18 - 19, 2006, Annapolis, Maryland
- Measuring Sector – October 20 - 21, 2006, Annapolis, Maryland

4. NTETC Sector Reports

The Committee heard an update on the activities of the National Type Evaluation Technical Committee (NTETC) Sectors at the 2006 NCWM Interim Meeting. Outlined below is a brief summary of Sector activities since the 2005 NCWM Annual Meeting.

Grain Analyzer Sectors: The NTETC Grain Analyzer Sector held a joint meeting in Kansas City, Missouri, August 24 - 25, 2005. A draft of the final summary was provided to the Committee prior to the 2006 NCWM Interim Meeting for review and approval.

The next meeting of the Grain Analyzer Sector is tentatively scheduled for August 2006 in Kansas City, Missouri. For questions on the current status of Sector work or to propose items for a future meeting, please contact the Sector technical advisors:

Diane Lee
NIST WMD
100 Bureau Drive – Stop 2600
Gaithersburg, MD 20899-2600
Phone: (301) 975-4405
Fax: (301) 975-8091
e-mail: diane.lee@nist.gov

Jack Barber
J.B. Associates
10349 Old Indian Trail
Glenarm, IL 62536
Phone: (217) 483-4232
e-mail: jbarber@motion.net

Measuring Sector: The NTETC Measuring Sector met October 21 - 22, 2005, in Nashville, Tennessee. A draft of the final summary was provided to the NTEP Committee prior to the 2006 NCWM Interim Meeting for review and approval.

NTEP Committee 2006 Final Report

The next meeting of the Measuring Sector is scheduled for October 2006 in conjunction with the Southern Weights and Measures Association's Annual Meeting. For questions on the current status of sector work or to propose items for a future meeting, please contact the Sector technical advisor:

> Richard Suiter
> NIST WMD
> 100 Bureau Drive – Stop 2600
> Gaithersburg, MD 20899-2600
> Phone: (301) 975-4406
> Fax: (301) 975-8091
> e-mail: rsuiter@nist.gov

Weighing Sector: The NTETC Weighing Sector met September 25 - 27, 2005, in Columbus, Ohio. A final draft of the meeting summary was provided to the Committee prior to the 2006 NCWM Interim Meeting for review and approval.

The next Weighing Sector meeting is scheduled for September 2006 in Annapolis, Maryland. For questions on the current status of Sector work or to propose items for a future meeting, please contact the Sector technical advisor:

> Steven Cook
> NIST WMD
> 100 Bureau Drive – Stop 2600
> Gaithersburg, MD 20899-2600
> Phone: (301) 975-4003
> Fax: (301) 975-8091
> e-mail: stevenc@nist.gov

NTETC Sector Summaries: The NTEP Committee received copies of the summaries prior to the 2006 NCWM Interim Meeting for their review and approval. Past NTETC Sector summaries are available upon request from NCWM and the NIST technical advisor:

> NCWM Inc. or   NIST WMD Technical Advisor, Steven Cook
> Phone: (240) 632-9454   (See contact information above)
> e-mail: ncwm@mgmtsol.com

Summary:
The NTEP Committee reviewed the recommendations of the Weighing, Measuring and Grain Analyzer Sectors. The recommended changes, based on the final summary reports of these sectors, were accepted by the NTEP Committee. The NTEP Committee instructed the NTEP director to amend NCWM Publication 14 accordingly and granted editorial privilege to the NTEP director.

In addition, the NTEP Committee heard that progress has been made by the work groups on the checklists for both Multiple Dimension Measuring Devices (MDMD) and Automatic Weighing Systems. The NTEP Committee accepted a recommendation from the NTEP director that these updated checklists, even though still in draft form, be placed in the current edition of NCWM Publication 14. The draft checklists will be used by the labs and reviewed by all applicants so that final comments can be received and these checklists may be finalized. It was noted that both the MDMD and the AWS work groups would need to meet again to finalize the changes to the appropriate checklists.

The NTEP Committee reviewed an *ad hoc* procedure for the evaluation of a device with an option for radio frequency communication. This brief checklist will be utilized to evaluate any devices that come into the NTEP labs with that option. This item was be reviewed by the NTEP labs at their April 2006 meeting and will also be reviewed by the 2006 NTETC Weighing and Measuring Sectors for further input.

Steve Patoray reported that the previous year's Sector reports can be found on the NCWM website. He also reported that, if contacted, he could supply anyone interested with all previous Sector reports.

5. NTEP Participation in U.S. National Work Group on Harmonization of NIST Handbook 44, NCWM Publication 14 and OIML R 76 and R 60

The Secretariat for OIML TC 9/SC 1 recently submitted the second Committee Draft (2 CD) of OIML R 76-1 "Non-automatic Weighing Instruments" to the participating members of TC 9/SC 1 for review, comment, and vote. The 2 CD was developed based on an analysis of the 1992 edition OIML R 76, answers from OIML TC 9/SC 1 members to a questionnaire distributed in May 2002, and comments on the December 2003 Working Draft (WD) for R 76. The 2 CD includes the changes to the December 2003 WD and the December 2004 1 CD based upon comments and recommendations of the U.S. National Work Group on R 76 (USNWG) and other countries.

The United States submitted twenty-seven recommendations and requests for clarifications to the Secretariat of TC 9/S C1 on the 1 CD and opposed the 1 CD being elevated to a Draft Recommendation. Eighteen of the U.S. recommendations and requests for clarification were accepted by the Secretariat, four recommendations resulted in alternate language proposed by the Secretariat, and five recommendations were not accepted by the Secretariat. The Secretariat provided the United States with a reason the remaining comments were not accepted.

The Secretariat has already registered the 2 CD of R 76-1 as a Draft Recommendation (DR) so as not to prolong the revision process at the technical committee level provided the 2 CD receives approval.

Summary: NIST WMD asked the USNWG for R 76 and other interested individuals, organizations, and associations to review the 2 CD and submit any comments, along with recommended language and technical justifications, to NIST WMD. During the 2006 NCWM Interim Meeting, Steven Cook, NIST WMD, provided the Committee with an update to the revision of R 76 and indicated that the United States will vote in favor of the 2 CD.

Although this current review of R 76 will likely be completed shortly, OIML has indicated a willingness to revisit the Recommendation and to consider including a large-capacity class similar to the current Handbook 44 Class III L and the Canadian Class III HD at some point in the future. WMD will be working with its Canadian counterparts to develop a North American Heavy-Duty Device Class.

6. Software Sector

Background: During the 2005 NCWM Annual Meeting, general comments from the floor were supportive of developing this issue further. The NTEP Committee discussed the pros and cons of software evaluation. General concerns related to difficulties identifying software and determining traceability to an NTEP Certificate of Conformance (CC) during field verification and providing NTEP laboratories with a meaningful and functional checklist for evaluating software security and functions. NCWM staff presented the costs involved with forming a sector and the costs to conduct a sector meeting. This information, along with a detailed action plan for the development of the sector charges, was presented and reviewed by the NCWM Board of Directors. Based on this information, a decision was made at the 2005 Annual Meeting to form a Software Sector. Funding was provided for this Sector in the 2006 Budget.

The first scheduled meeting of the Software Sector was held for April 5, 6, and 7, 2006, in Annapolis, Maryland.

Summary: During the 2006 NCWM Interim Meeting, the NTEP Committee Chair, Jim Truex, reported that the NTETC Software Sector was in the process of being formed. Interested parties have responded to a request to participate in this Sector and members will be appointed by the NTEP Committee Chair.

Excerpts from the "Request for Participation" in this Sector:

Without a doubt software is a major component of the weighing and measuring systems which are inspected today. NTEP evaluators need help. Weights and measures (W&M) field officials need help. Even manufacturers and designers are asking for help. The W&M community is asking for guidance on how to evaluate software, how to inspect software in the field, what to look for, what to inspect, what level of security is needed and what information should be marked and available on-site. We are looking for volunteers, the experts, and the software writers to assist us in this endeavor. As you may know, the NCWM Board of Directors has decided to create an NTETC Software Sector.

At this time the recommended scope of the Software Sector is to:

- Develop a clear understanding of the use of software in today's weighing and measuring instruments.

- Develop NIST Handbook 44 specifications and requirements, as needed, for software incorporated into weighing and measuring devices. This may include tools for field verification, security requirements, identification, etc.

- Develop NCWM Publication 14 checklist criteria, as needed, for the evaluation of software incorporated into weighing and measuring devices, including marking, security, metrologically significant functions, etc.

- Assist in the development of training guidelines for W&M officials in verifying software as compliant to applicable requirements and traceable to an NTEP certificate. Educational material for manufacturers, designers, service technicians and end users may also be considered.

Funding for public sector participants:

It is the current NCWM policy to provide funding to a sector meeting to one public sector participant from each state NTEP Laboratory that is active in evaluating the device type(s) which will be discussed at the particular sector meeting. For the Software Sector, initially NCWM will provide funding to one (1) participant from New York (weighing), one (1) participant from Ohio (weighing), two (2) participants from California (one weighing, one measuring), and two (2) participants from Maryland (one weighing and one measuring).

SOFTWARE SECTOR
Meeting Summary
Annapolis, Maryland
April 5, 6, 7, 2006

Action items:

1. Software identification D-SW 5.1.1 model/version, etc., help screen?
a. Built-for-Purpose
b. Not-Built-for-Purpose
   c. Version number or greater
2. Software protection/security D-SW 5.1.3
   a. Identification of unapproved/unauthorized software
3. Storage of data, D-SW5.2.3 and subsections, automatic storing and transmission
4. Software maintenance and reconfiguration D-SW5.2.6
5. D-SW Section 7. verification in the field needs work
6. Manufacturer documentation to be submitted, change to the NTEP application D-SW 6.1.1
7. Definitions Software-Based Device, etc.

Note: Underlined "D-SW" sections above refer to the document OIML D-SW, "General Requirements for Software Controlled Measuring Instruments."

The group agreed that Jim Truex should continue as Software Sector Chair.
Mr. Truex asked Steve Patoray to continue as technical advisor to the Software Sector. It was requested that NIST consider the role of technical advisor in the future, as they currently do with other Sectors.

The next meeting of the Software Sector is scheduled for Wednesday and Thursday, October 18 and 19, 2006, in Annapolis, Maryland, immediately prior to the Measuring Sector meeting.

For questions on the current status of Sector work or to propose items for a future meeting, please contact the Sector technical advisor.

7. Conformity Assessment Program (CAP)

At the fall 2005 NTEP Committee Meeting, the Committee discussed the current status of this project. The following items were noted:

Certificate Review: The question is how this would be accomplished given the limited resources of NCWM. It was suggested that this item may need to be put on a "back burner" until resources can be clearly identified to proceed with the project in an efficient, thorough and accurate manner.

Initial Verification: This part of the project is moving forward. The work group chair, Lou Straub, has sent out requests to several states to act in the pilot program for this area. Several of the states have responded positively. The work group is currently waiting for data. There are still questions on what will be done with this data and how it will be tabulated.

Verified Conformity Assessment Program (VCAP): It is the opinion of the NTEP Committee that additional information may be needed from the work group in order to move this area of the program forward. A request will be made to the work group chair for a report on the current status of this committee.

Summary: During the 2006 NCWM Interim Meeting:

The Chair of the Certificate Review work group, Don Onwiler, reported that the work in this area will not commence until there is adequate information available from the pilot being conducted by the Initial Verification Group. Once this information is available, the work to define the certificate requirements for price computing scales can begin.

The Chair of the Initial Verification work group, Lou Straub, reported that requests for assistance have gone out and have been accepted by several state and local jurisdictions. Currently, he has received some feedback on the draft checklist. At this time, no actual completed forms have been returned. Several states made a commitment to put a priority on getting completed checklists submitted.

The NTEP Committee Chair, Jim Truex, reported that he has had contact from the chair of the Verified Conformity Assessment Program (VCAP), Mark Knowles, stating that the work group has completed its initial work and will provide the NTEP Committee with a final report prior to the April timeframe. Based on this report, the NTEP Committee will notify members of its content, request comment, and determine the next steps that need to be taken.

The NCWM Board of Directors has received a final report from the co-chairs of the Verified Conformity Assessment work group (VCAP). This will be reviewed by the NCWM Board and further action will be identified.

The NCWM Board of Directors has received information from the chair of the Initial Verification (IV) work group that data has begun to come in from various states. The NTEP Committee authorized the IV work group to develop initial verification checklist for vehicle scales and retail motor-fuel dispensers. The NCWM Board will discuss this information further at its next scheduled Board Meeting.

8. NTEP Certification of Residential-Type Water Meters

New Item:

Summary: A request has come in from one state for NTEP to conduct evaluations and certify residential-type water meters. After discussions on this topic, the NTEP Committee made the decision to look into this item and determine the feasibility for NTEP to certify such devices. It was noted that currently there is a section in NIST Handbook 44 for these types of devices. It was also noted that California already conducts evaluation and certification under a state-type evaluation program on these types of devices based on the current specifications, tolerances and other technical requirements in NIST Handbook 44. It was the belief of the Committee that work to complete a checklist and set up testing on such devices would not be a major effort. It was noted that the OIML R 49 is currently undergoing review, and also that there are significant differences between the requirements in NIST Handbook 44 and the OIML recommendation on this type of device. The NTEP director will report to the NTEP Committee on findings into setting up this certification.

The NTEP Committee also discussed the potential for NTEP certification of vapor meters.

Both issues of NTEP certification of water meters and vapor meters will be discussed at the next Measuring Sector meeting in October 2006. The Sector will focus on reviewing existing checklists from various states and work toward a recommendation for the NTEP Committee to consider.

James Truex, Ohio, NTEP Committee Chair
Don Onwiler, Nebraska, NCWM Chair
Mike Cleary, California, NCWM Chair-Elect
Stephen Pahl, Texas
Charles Carroll, Massachusetts

NTEP Technical Advisor: S. Patoray, NTEP Director
NTEP Technical Advisor: S. Cook, NIST WMD
National Type Evaluation Program Committee

Appendix A

National Type Evaluation Technical Committee (NTETC)
Grain Analyzer Sector

August 24 - 25, 2005 – Kansas City, Missouri
Meeting Summary

Agenda Items

1. Report on GIPSA/NIST Interagency Agreement – Fee Increase..A1
2. Report on the 2005 NCWM Interim and Annual Meetings..A2
3. Report on NTEP Type Evaluations and OCP (Phase II) Testing..A3
4. Proposed Change to NCWM Publication 14 – Bias Tolerances for Test Weight per Bushel.............A3
5. Comparative NTEP On-going Calibration Program (OCP) Performance Data..................................A6
6. Review of On-going Calibration Program (Phase II) Performance Data..A6
7. Effective Dates for NTEP and GIPSA Calibration Changes...A7
8. "All-Class" Moisture Calibrations...A8
9. Editorial Correction to GMM Chapter of Publication 14 – Table in Appendix D............................A10
10. Evaluating GMM Moisture Accuracy as a Continuous Function across the Entire Moisture Range.........A11
11. Prescreening Grain Samples for GMM Type Evaluation..A12
12. Proposed Change to Publication 14 - Assigning Sample Data to Moisture Ranges for GMM Type Evaluation...A13
13. Report on OIML TC 17/SC 1 IR59 "Moisture Meters for Cereal Grains and Oilseeds"..................A14
14. Report on OIML TC 5/SC 2 Document D-SW, "General Requirements for Software Controlled Measuring Devices"...A15
15. Report on OIML TC 17/SC 8 Protein Draft Recommendation...A16
16. Naming Conventions for Near-Infrared Analyzer Calibrations...A16
17. Time and Place for Next Meeting..A19

1. Report on GIPSA/NIST Interagency Agreement – Fee Increase

The Grain Inspection Packers and Stockyards Administration (GIPSA) and the National Institute of Standards and Technology (NIST) signed an updated Interagency Agreement in March 2005 that provides funding for the Grain Moisture Meter On-going Calibration Program (OCP) for fiscal years 2005 through 2009. Under the terms of the updated agreement, NIST and GIPSA each will contribute one-third the cost of the program subject to an annual maximum of $26,500 each. The balance of costs is borne by manufacturers and depends on the number of meter models in the NTEP "pool" according to the fee schedule shown below. Implementation of this fee schedule became effective at the start of FY2005 (October 1, 2004). The fee schedule shown below was developed about two years ago using a modest estimate of likely increases in GIPSA's costs. Dr. Richard Pierce, GIPSA, reported that GIPSA's hourly rate for NTEP evaluations has risen to $83.20 and the fee for air oven moisture determinations has increased to $13.00 each. In spite of these increases, the OCP Fee Schedule is expected to remain as shown below through FY 2009.

NTEP On-going Calibration Program Fee Schedule for Fiscal Years 2005 - 2009								
(1) Total Meters (including official meter)	(2) Meters in NTEP Pool	(3) Cost per NTEP Pool Meter	(4) Total Program Cost	Funding Contribution from Participants				(8) Cost per Meter Type
				(5) NIST	(6) GIPSA	(7) Manufacturers (total funding from mfg's)	
2	1	$19,875	$19,875	$6,625	$6,625	$6,625	$3,315
3	2	19,875	39,750	13,250	13,250	13,250	4,415
4	3	19,875	59,625	19,875	19,875	19,875	4,970
5	4	19,875	79,500	26,500	26,500	26,500	5,300
6	5	19,875	99,375	26,500	26,500	46,375	7,730
7	6	19,875	119,250	26,500	26,500	66,250	9,465
8	7	19,875	139,125	26,500	26,500	86,125	10,765
9	8	19,875	159,000	26,500	26,500	106,000	11,775

2. Report on the 2005 NCWM Interim and Annual Meetings

The Interim Meeting of the 90th National Conference on Weights and Measures (NCWM) was held January 23 - 26, 2005, in Santa Monica, California. At that meeting, the NTEP Board of Directors accepted the Sector's recommendation to merge the Grain Moisture Meter Sector and the Near-Infrared Grain Analyzer Sector into a new Sector to be called the Grain Analyzer Sector. The NTEP Committee accepted the Sector's recommended amendments and changes to the 2004 Edition of the Grain Moisture Meter chapter of Publication 14. These changes appear in the 2005 Edition of NCWM Publication 14. For additional background refer to *Committee Reports for the 90th Annual Meeting*, NCWM Publication 16, April 2005.

Amendments and Changes to the 2004 Edition of the Grain Moisture Meter Chapter of Publication 14		
Section Number	Amendment/Change	Page
Section IV. Tolerances for Calibration Performance	Add Item c. to establish an overall calibration bias requirement based on up to three years of available data. Change wording in paragraph preceding Item a. and in paragraph following Item c. to reflect addition of Item c.	GMM-5 through GMM-6
Section VII.B. Accuracy, Precision, and Reproducibility	Change the Minimum Test Weight per Bushel Ranges in the table in §VII.B. to facilitate selection of test-set samples.	GMM-11
Section VII.B. Accuracy, Precision, and Reproducibility	Change tolerances for repeatability (precision) for corn and oats to more realistic value.	GMM-13

The 90th Annual Meeting of the NCWM was held July 10 - 14, 2005, in Orlando, Florida. No Grain Moisture Meter (GMM) or Near-Infrared (NIR) Grain Analyzer items appeared in the Specifications and Tolerances (S&T) Committee Interim Report for consideration by the NCWM at the 2005 Annual Meeting.

Steve Patoray, NTEP Director, expressed concern about declining attendance at the NCWM Interim and Annual Meetings. He encouraged Sector members to attend future meetings. At least one state weights and measures representative related that a lack of state funds (and withdrawal of NCWM travel support) had severely limited out-of-state travel to meetings.

Steve reported that an electronic version of NCWM Publication 14 is now available in Adobe Acrobat PDF format on compact disk (CD). Single CDs are priced at $135 plus postage and handling. Because of copyright issues, the PDF file is locked so it is not possible to print a hard copy of the document. It is possible, however, to add comments and highlight text. All four sections of Publication 14 are included on the CD. Order forms can be found on the updated NCWM website, http://www.ncwm.net/. Search capabilities for NTEP certificates have been greatly improved on the updated site. Steve cautioned that users must delete existing "bookmarks" to the old certificate database search page. The new certificate database cannot be reached using the old "bookmarks." The new database can be accessed easily from the new home page.

Steve briefed the Sector on the Verification Conformity Assessment Program (VCAP) under development for weighing devices or components of weighing devices. Initial verification will not repeat NTEP testing, but will involve field checking of model numbers and markings and will include some general testing to verify that the devices meet type. Additionally, there will be a third-party assessment of the manufacturer's quality system. The manufacturer must have a sampling plan and documented evidence to show that it is being used. The manufacturer must also comply with a sub-set of ISO/IEC 17025, **General requirements for the competence of testing and calibration laboratories** demonstrating that all the factors that may contribute to errors in the calibration process have been taken into account.

3. Report on NTEP Type Evaluations and OCP (Phase II) Testing

Cathy Brenner, GIPSA, the NTEP Participating Laboratory for Grain Analyzers, reported on NTEP Type Evaluation activity. In addition to regular grain moisture meter calibration updates, evaluations are currently underway for three additional devices: one for test weight per bushel (an add-on to a currently approved grain moisture meter); one new grain moisture meter with test weight capability; and one new NIR grain analyzer for miscellaneous constituents including moisture. Cathy also reported that the following devices would be enrolled in the OCP (Phase II) for the 2005 harvest:

[Note: Models listed on a single line are considered to be of the same "type."]
DICKEY-john Corporation   GAC2000, GAC2100, GAC2100a, GAC2100b
Foss   North America   Infratec   1241
Foss North America   Infratec 1227, Infratec 1229
Seedburo Equipment Company   1200A
The   Steinlite Corporation   SL95

4. Proposed Change to NCWM Publication 14 – Bias Tolerances for Test Weight per Bushel

Background: The Grain Moisture Meter (GMM) Chapter of Publication 14 calls for testing the automatic test weight per bushel (TW) measuring feature of GMMs for accuracy, repeatability (precision), and reproducibility using 12 selected samples of each grain type (for which the meter has a pending or higher moisture calibration). The two tests for accuracy are bias (meter versus the standard reference method) and the Standard Deviation of the Differences (SDD) between the meter and the standard reference method. Publication 14 states that, "The manufacturer may adjust the calibration bias to compensate for differences from the type evaluation laboratory in reference methods or sample sets."

Recent NTEP tests revealed that the results of the bias test, which uses only 12 selected samples, are sample set dependent. The following table illustrates this dependence. No changes were made to the meters between the tests using Sample Set 1 and Sample Set 2. The table also shows how those same meters compare against the most recent three crop years of Phase II test weight (TW) data.

NTEP Committee 2006 Final Report
Appendix A – NTETC Grain Analyzer Sector

Grain Type	GMM Model	Test Weight per Bushel Bias				
		Based on Phase II TW Data (3 crop-years)	Sample Set 1		Sample Set 2	
			Meter "A"	Meter "B"	Meter "A"	Meter "B"
Corn	1	–0.20 –0.02		+0.01	–0.36	–0.24
	2	+0.09 +0.79 +0.13 +0.82	+0.32			
Oats	1	–0.27 –0.06		+0.04	–0.29	–0.24
	2	–0.14 –0.04		+0.03	–0.14	–0.16
Six-Row Barley	1	–0.21 –0.01 –0.05 –0.01	–0.02			
Sunflower	1	–0.10	–0.02	–0.09	+0.10	+0.13

Because of the above-observed differences, the NTEP Lab did not list specific bias terms on the Certificate of Conformance (CC) for instruments recently evaluated for TW. Instead, the CC simply indicates that the meter is approved for Test Weight per Bushel measurements.

Discussion: The NTEP Lab proposed eliminating the bias tolerance requirement for test weight per bushel from the accuracy tests of the GMM Chapter of Publication 14. The test would still be conducted, and TW bias results would be provided to the manufacturer as is currently done with NIR grain analyzer protein and oil bias results.

Dr. Charles Hurburgh, Iowa State University, pointed out that based on data taken on only 12 samples, the bias differences between Sample Set "1" and Sample Set "2" did not appear to be statistically significant and asked if this might be a reproducibility issue. For these tests, Publication 14 specifies that samples will be dropped three times through each of two meters. He asked if more than three drops might be needed. He noted also that for corn there was an unusually large difference in biases between Meters "A" and "B" of Model 2 for both sets of samples. He suggested that the Sector consider adding a requirement to Publication 14 to specify that the difference in bias between the two instruments submitted for evaluation must not exceed the individual instrument tolerances for bias.

Dr. Richard Pierce, GIPSA, explained that there is a difference between the sample sets used for Phase I moisture evaluations and Phase I Test Weight per Bushel (TW) evaluations. Sample sets for moisture evaluations are carefully pre-screened. As a result, they have produced very similar results from year to year, although the individual grain samples that comprise a set vary from year to year. Conversely, the process for selecting samples for TW evaluations is somewhat random (except for moisture distribution criteria and the requirement that samples represent a distribution of TW that minimizes the correlation between TW and moisture). There is no reason to expect two different sets of TW samples to agree, and there is no way to determine if one set is better than another. Consequently, bias data obtained using a TW sample set is not suitable for determining what adjustment should be applied to minimize bias error on a large population of samples.

One Sector member asked if there might be a better way to pre-select TW samples to obtain a more reproducible sample set. Dr. Pierce replied that pre-screening is very difficult. Adding more criteria to the selection of TW samples will make sample selection even more difficult. The fact that in many years very low TW samples are not available further contributes to this difficulty.

Sean Bauer, Steinlite Corporation, mentioning that TW can change with time, asked if there was a significant time interval between determination of TW by the standard kettle method and the measurement of TW on the meters. Cathy Brenner, GIPSA, stated that these tests were conducted on either the same day or the next day. She added that operator uniformity had been verified and that data obtained by check test operators had been compared with data taken on the same samples for Phase II tests. It was determined that the procedures used did not contribute to the observed differences between the two TW test sets.

Jack Barber, Co-Technical Advisor to the Sector, expressed concern about not listing grain-dependent bias adjustment coefficients on the CC. He pointed out that NIST Handbook 44, Section 5.56.(a) Grain Moisture Meters Code, stipulates:

S.2.4.3. Calibration Transfer - *The instrument hardware/software design and calibration procedures shall permit calibration development and the transfer of calibrations between instruments of like models without requiring user slope or bias adjustments.*

This requirement applies to both moisture and TW calibrations. [*Editor's note:* For further background on the Sector's original intent regarding calibration transfer between grain moisture meters of like type, see Agenda Item 9 in the Grain Moisture Meter Sector March 1997 Meeting Summary.] In devices where grain-dependent TW calibration coefficients (including bias adjustment coefficients) are imbedded in the CC listing of grain moisture calibration coefficients, there is no problem. Any change in coefficients affecting TW will require a change in the moisture calibration and an amendment to the CC. The concern is with devices that do not treat a grain-dependent TW bias adjustment coefficient as part of the moisture calibration. In that case, unless grain-dependent bias adjustment coefficients are listed on the CC, there is no way for field inspectors to know if the most recent adjustment coefficients are being used for test weight. The Sector agreed that if the bias adjustment term is not part of the moisture calibration coefficients then it must be listed on the certificate.

The Sector was in general agreement that TW data from the OCP (Phase II) was the best measure of how closely a meter is biased to the standard quart kettle method. In response to a question of whether Phase II TW data for corn for the entire moisture range should be used or only data for a restricted (and lower) moisture range, Dr. Pierce replied that TW data above 20 % moisture would not be used.

The proposed use of Phase II TW data raised several questions:

1. What grain-dependent bias correction coefficient should be specified before the meter has been in the OCP for at least one year?
2. Should a TW calibration that has not been verified in the OCP be classified as "pending?"
3. Should the most recent three years of available data be used to determine if a bias adjustment is necessary? If so, what tolerance should be applied?

In the ensuing discussion, the Sector agreed that the manufacturer should specify the grain-dependent bias correction coefficients to be used initially, provided the devices could pass Phase I tests using those coefficients. Although no vote was taken, there was not enthusiastic support for classifying the initial TW calibration as "pending," and no one suggested what tolerance should be applied after the device had been in the OCP for a year or more.

Conclusion: The Co-Technical Advisor was requested to develop suggested wording for changes to Publication 14 to reflect the following:

1. The Bias test for TW Accuracy will be retained.
2. Data from the Phase II On-going Calibration Review Program may be used at the manufacturer's discretion to support a grain-specific TW bias-adjustment change in a TW calibration.
3. A new Phase I evaluation is NOT required for a grain-specific TW bias-adjustment change in a TW calibration supported by Phase II data.
4. Any change in a grain-specific TW calibration (including changes in grain-specific bias adjustments) must be reflected on the CC in a manner obvious to field inspectors.
5. The Bias results for TW accuracy for each of the two instruments of like-type submitted for evaluation must agree with each other by the same tolerance that they must agree with the reference method.

If possible, the proposed changes will be submitted to the Sector by letter ballot for approval in time to forward the item to the NTEP Committee for consideration at the NCWM Interim Meeting in January 2006.

NTEP Committee 2006 Final Report
Appendix A – NTETC Grain Analyzer Sector

5. Comparative NTEP On-going Calibration Program (OCP) Performance Data

Source: Seedburo Equipment Company

Background: At the Sector's August 2004 meeting, Dr. Richard Pierce, GIPSA (the NTEP Laboratory), presented graphical data showing the comparative performance of all NTEP meter types vs. the air oven. These data were based on the last three crop years (2001 - 2003) using calibrations updated for use during the 2004 harvest season. Because of the proprietary nature of OCP data, individual meters (including the Official Meter) were not identified by model or by manufacturer. There were lengthy discussions on these results, speculation about which instruments were which, and questions of whether calibration verification analysis was actually being conducted by some manufacturers. Some comments suggested that a meter manufacturer might not be aware of their relative position based on these comparisons. Examination of the comparative performance data led the Sector to recommend changes to the GMM Chapter of Publication 14 to set a limit on average calibration bias (with respect to air oven) to improve alignment between meter types.

Recommendation: To assist manufacturers in improving NTEP grain calibrations and to achieve better uniformity between meter types, the sector should annually review comparative OCP performance data identifying the USDA-GIPSA Official Meter and containing average bias data for each meter type on each grain.

Discussion: Some meter manufacturers have since expressed concern that the Official Meter was not identified in the presentation of comparative performance data. Even though the air oven is the standard reference against which NTEP meter performance is measured in the OCP, the Official Meter is the *de facto* standard for the grain trade. Other manufacturers want to know how their meters compare with the Official Meter.

Regular review of comparative OCP performance data by the Sector has definite advantages:

- Calibration performance problems not addressed by existing requirements are exposed.
- Manufacturers can see how their instruments compare with others.

To be of greatest value to manufacturers, the comparative OCP performance data must identify the Official Meter and list the average bias for each meter type on each grain. Accuracy of the Official Meter (average differences between the GAC 2100 and Air Oven as percent moisture) based on the U.S. nationwide sample set, 3 years' data, and most recent review, is already being published annually by USDA GIPSA/FGIS in Directive 9180.61. This is the OCP performance data for the Official Meter, so there should be no proprietary/confidentiality issues regarding identifying the Official Meter in the presentation of comparative OCP performance data.

Conclusion: The Sector agreed that the proposed comparative performance data should be available for annual review by the Sector. In the event that the Sector does not hold a formal meeting in any year, the data for that period can be distributed by e-mail for review. Note: The OCP data presented in Agenda Item 6 for 2002 - 2004 does specifically identify the Official Meter.

6. Review of On-going Calibration Program (Phase II) Performance Data

Background: This item was included on the Sector's agenda to provide information to the sector on the OCP meter performance data with calibrations updated for the 2005 grain season. Cathy Brenner of GIPSA, the NTEP Participating Laboratory for Grain Analyzers, presented data showing the performance of NTEP meters compared to the air oven. These data are based on the last three crop years (2002 - 2004) using calibrations updated for use during the 2005 harvest season. The Official Meter is the only meter specifically identified. The numerical identifiers were assigned randomly to the remaining meters except for sunflowers where, because only three devices are approved, the remaining meters are identified by the letters A and B. Meter 1 is the same instrument for all grains, etc. The moisture range covered by these graphs is the same moisture range listed on USDA GIPSA/FGIS in Directive 9180.61. As an example of the data presented, the graph for corn is shown below. The number in parentheses following the meter identification in the box beneath the graph indicates the average bias for that meter across the full moisture range represented by the graph. A PDF file with graphs of all NTEP grains is available from Co-Technical Advisor, Jack Barber. Send requests to jbarber@motion.net.

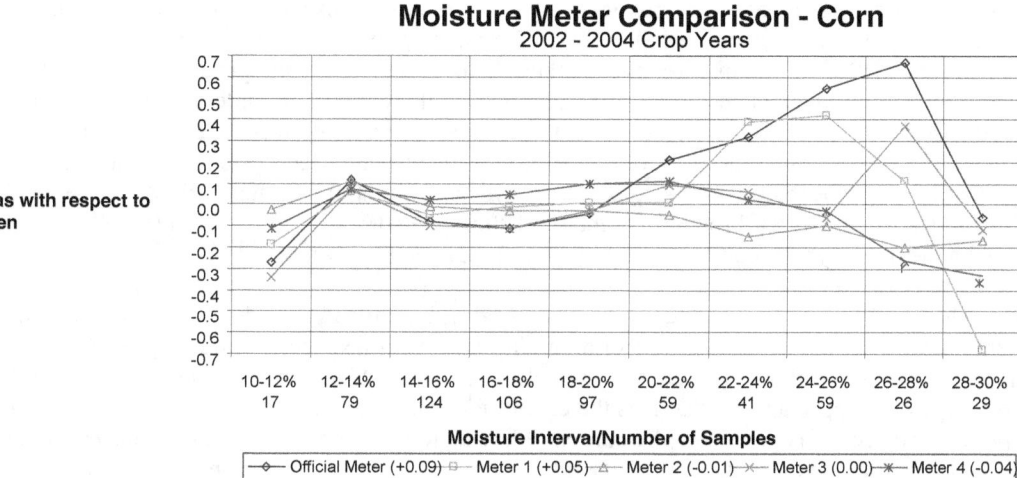

7. Effective Dates for NTEP and GIPSA Calibration Changes

Background: Grain Industry representatives have repeatedly stressed the importance of keeping NTEP calibration changes synchronized with GIPSA calibration changes. In the past, calibration changes for the Official Moisture Meter were made on a staggered schedule typically between May 1 and August 1, with dates chosen to coincide with the time at which stocks would be at their lowest level to minimize economic impact. Several years ago GIPSA reduced the number of dates for changing calibrations to two: May 1 for the NTEP grains wheat, barley, sorghum, rice, and oats; and August 1 for NTEP grains corn, soybeans, and sunflowers. These dates represent a compromise between making calibrations available prior to harvest and ensuring that grain stocks will be at their lowest levels. The present timeline for NTEP Phase II activities lists July 1 as the latest date for re-issuing the annual CC. However, because a July 1 date would miss the heat harvest in many states, the CC for the Official Moisture Meter is now re-issued no later than May 1 for all NTEP grain calibrations. The CC notes the effective dates for the calibrations to indicate when they will be put into use in the official system.

When this issue was discussed at the Sector's March 1998 meeting, one weights and measures representative wondered how to handle meter inspections performed in July, asking which calibration should be used, the one effective August 1 or the existing one. Opinions were divided on the best way to handle this situation. In one state, old calibrations may be used until the effective date of the new calibration, after which the device is re-inspected to verify that the new calibration has been installed. Others felt that this method of enforcement was not realistic, because it could result in requiring two or more trips per year to the majority of meters in their jurisdictions. They favored having the user install the new calibration at time of inspection. A manufacturing representative pointed out that the only purpose of specifying "effective dates" on a CC was to match the dates on which the new calibrations would be used in the official system. He suggested that W&M inspectors tell the user that the new calibration must be installed on the effective date if they want their meter to be in closer agreement with the Official Meter. It was recognized that the use of effective dates wasn't a new concept. Prior to the NTEP program, manufacturers had revised calibrations at various dates, sometimes without much warning, and often after a significant number of meters had already been inspected for the current season. States with inspection programs had already figured out how to deal with this situation. At that time, the Sector decided that the details of enforcement should be left to each state to decide based on their individual needs.

The issue of CCs showing only the current calibration details for calibrations with delayed (August 1) effective dates (when used on Official Meters) has come up again, this time in the case of cross-utilized meters. Under GIPSA's cross-utilization program, elevator or official agency-owned instruments can be "cross-utilized" between official inspection and commercial applications. Problems have arisen when such meters fail state inspections but fully comply with GIPSA directives and requirements. In April, an Illinois weights and measures inspector checked, and rejected, an official agency meter. The inspector correctly used the most recent CC that had been re-issued in February to reflect the addition of test weight per bushel testing features. Although the moisture measurement calibration constants remained the same as on the previous version of the CC, constants relating to Test Weight had been revised. The official agency meter contained the constants from the previous certificate, matching the constants of the then current GIPSA Program Directive. Although this situation was unique arising from the addition of NTEP approval for test weight and a February CC revision, there is still a problem when there is a difference between the issue date of a CC and the implementation dates for calibration changes shown on the CC. For example, this year the new CC (issued prior to May 1, 2005) for the Official Meter listed constants for soybeans that were not scheduled for implementation until August. The soybean calibration constants shown on the 2005 CC did not agree with those shown on GIPSA Program Directive 9180.61 (dated May 1, 2005) until GIPSA reissued the Program Directive with the new soybean constants on August 1, 2005.

Recommendation: The CC for the Official Meter is issued on May 1, but GIPSA introduces changes (if required) in the official system on two different dates: May 1 (for all grains except corn, soybeans, and sorghum) and August 1 for corn, soybeans, and sorghum. Unnecessary rejections of cross-utilized meters could be avoided if state inspectors retained a copy of the previous CC that lists the calibration constants for corn, soybean, and sorghum approved for use prior to August 1. To eliminate the burden of having to retain copies of old certificates and the possibility of using an old certificate by mistake, the NTEP Laboratory proposed an addition to the certificate showing the constants from the previous, superseded certificate for any grains with an implementation date later than May 1 (corn, soybean, and sorghum). Rich Pierce, GIPSA, commented that the FGIS Technical Services Division had proposed that all changes to the official system affecting NTEP grains be complete by May 1, so that calibration changes for any NTEP grain on the Official Meter are issued at the same time the CC is issued for the Official Meter.

Conclusion: The Sector rejected the proposal. Weights and Measures representatives were of the opinion that this was not a big issue in practice, and that it may be a training issue.

8. "All-Class" Moisture Calibrations

Background: The GMM type evaluation program is currently structured to deal with individual class calibrations for moisture. The NIR Grain Analyzer program allows for either individual class calibrations or "all-class" calibrations for constituents other than moisture. One currently certified GMM uses an "all-class" barley calibration that is listed separately on the certificate under two-row barley and six-row barley with different approved and pending moisture ranges for each of those classes. Two other instruments currently certified for grain moisture list the barleys, rough rices, and wheats separately on the certificate and have the meters set up with individual class calibrations. These two meters have a single equation and bias term for all classes of barley; another equation and bias term for all classes of rough rice; and a third equation for all classes of wheat with separate bias terms for all soft classes, all hard classes, and durum.

A grain moisture meter currently being evaluated has a single wheat calibration (excluding durum), which may be called an "all type" calibration because the calibration covers something other than all the grains in a class, single rice, and single barley calibration with a common equation and separate bias terms for each grouping. Another instrument being evaluated uses a single calibration and bias term for wheat (excluding durum).

Recommendation: Cathy Brenner, GIPSA (the NTEP Participating Laboratory for Grain Analyzers), asked the Sector to consider the following questions regarding the evaluation of grain analyzers using "all-class" or combined-grain moisture equations:

- How should such devices be evaluated?
- What should be placed on the certificate for approved and pending moisture ranges?

For type evaluation purposes, she suggested treating "all-class" moisture calibrations in a manner similar to the way "all-class" calibrations for other constituents are handled on NIR Grain Analyzers. "All-class" moisture calibrations would have to meet the accuracy, precision, and reproducibility requirements for the test sets of each included class in addition to meeting the "all-class" accuracy requirement when the data from all the included classes is pooled.

For example in the case of an "all-class" wheat moisture calibration covering 5 classes of wheat, the basic 6 % moisture range for evaluating a hard white wheat calibration is 8 % to 14 % moisture content while the basic 6 % range for evaluating calibrations for the other classes of Wheat is 10 % to 16 %. Thus, an "all-class" Wheat calibration would be tested over an 8 % moisture range of 8 % to 16 % rather than the standard 6 % range.

The "approved" moisture range for an "all-class" moisture calibration would cover the range from the absolute lower to the absolute upper 2 % moisture interval for which the meter meets individual class tolerances. If an individual class does not have samples available in a given 2 % moisture interval to meet the approved tolerances, the meter must meet the pending tolerances in order for that moisture interval to be listed as "approved" on the certificate.

The "pending" moisture range for an "all-class" moisture calibration would cover the ranges from the absolute lower to the absolute upper 2 % moisture interval for which the meter meets the individual class tolerances. If an individual class does not meet either the approved or pending tolerances in a given 2 % moisture interval, then the next lower or upper moisture interval for which the meter meets either the "approved" or "pending" tolerances for each individual class is listed as the "pending" moisture range on the certificate.

Rich Pierce, GIPSA, reminded the Sector that Phase I testing was originally intended to evaluate basic meter capability – to check permanence, accuracy, repeatability and reproducibility. Soybeans, hard red winter wheat (HRWW), and Corn were chosen as representative test media to demonstrate basic meter capability. These three grains could still be used to evaluate devices having an "all-class" or "all-wheat" calibration. NCWM Publication 14 stipulates that grains other than corn, soybeans, and HRWW will be checked for calibration bias before they can be listed on the CC. This implies that grains in an "all-class" or "all-wheat" calibration would be individually checked for bias against air oven prior to being listed on an original CC.

Discussion: The issue of "pending" and "approved" ranges for "all-class" or "all-type" calibrations led to a lengthy discussion. The Sector struggled with how to handle cases where Phase II data resulted in different approved or pending ranges on the individual grain types included in an "all-class" or "all-type" calibration. What range should appear on the CC? Again, the general opinion was that ranges should not be reduced due to lack of data. If one class of Wheat had insufficient samples in a 2 % interval to support a "pending" rating for that interval while another Wheat class had samples supporting a "pending" rating for the same 2 % interval, it seemed logical to allow the interval to have a "pending" rating in the "all-class" or "all-type" calibration. One member reasoned that the 2 % interval with insufficient Phase II samples to support a "pending" rating was also unlikely to see many market samples in that moisture interval.

In a related issue, Rich Pierce mentioned that the NTEP Laboratory is having problems increasing and decreasing ranges of the meter depending on the data available in the most recent three-year period. Most Sector members agreed that it didn't seem reasonable to reduce a range solely because data previously used to justify the range classification had to be dropped from the most recent 3-year period.

Conclusion: A final decision on this issue was postponed until specific wording for Publication 14 could be developed to address the handling of cases where Phase II data resulted in different approved or pending ranges on the individual grain types included in an "all-class" or "all-type" calibration. The Sector agreed that existing Phase I test methodology was adequate for "all-class" and "all-type" calibrations. Phase I testing will be performed only with corn, soybeans, and HRWW. If an "all-wheat" (except durum) calibration is submitted, HRWW will be used for the Phase I tests. Until one or more years of Phase II data are available, grains other than corn, soybeans, and HRWW will be checked for calibration bias before they are listed on the CC.

Diane Lee, NIST, Co-Technical Advisor to the Sector, agreed to send manufacturers a request for additional suggestions/comments on this issue. Comments are due by the end of October. Co-Technical Advisor, Jack Barber, will consider these comments in developing wording for changes to NCWM Publication 14. A letter ballot on the final wording is to be circulated in time to be considered by the NTEP Committee at the NCWM Interim Meeting in January 2006.

9. Editorial Correction to GMM Chapter of Publication 14 – Table in Appendix D

Background: At its August 2003 meeting the GMM Sector recommended changing the hard white wheat moisture range from "10 % to 16 %" to "8 % to 14 %" in the table **Moisture Ranges and Tolerances for Sample Temperature Sensitivity** in Appendix D of the 2003 Edition of the GMM Chapter of Publication 14. The Sector also noted that missing quotation marks needed to be added in the table's heading and that medium grain rough rice with a moisture range of 10 % to 16 % and tolerance limit of 0.45 (as approved at the Sector's September 1997 meeting) needed to be added to the table; this entry to the table was inadvertently omitted from the 2001 and 2002 editions of Publication 14.

The 2004 Edition of the GMM Chapter of Publication 14 incorporated the following changes to the Table in Appendix D:

- The missing quotation marks were added to the table heading in Appendix D
- The hard white wheat moisture range in the table was changed to "8 % to 14 %".
- Medium grain rough rice with a moisture range of 10 % to 16 % and tolerance limit of 0.45 was added to the table.

However, the row for long grain rough rice was mistakenly deleted from the table. This error was addressed at the Sector's August 2004 meeting and the Sector was advised that because this was an editorial error, it could be corrected without making the issue a formal Agenda Item. Unfortunately, the error was not corrected in the 2005 Edition of the GMM Chapter of Publication 14.

Recommendation: Correct the **Moisture Ranges and Tolerances for Sample Temperature Sensitivity** Table on page 43 of Appendix D of the 2005 Edition of the GMM Chapter of Publication 14 by inserting a row for grain type long grain rough rice (with Moisture Range 10 % to 16 % and Tolerance Limit 0.45) between the rows for oats and medium grain rough rice.

Conclusion: The Sector agreed unanimously to the proposed correction as shown in the following table.

Moisture Ranges and Tolerance for Sample Temperature Sensitivity (for the "Other 12" NTEP Grains)		
Grain Type	**Moisture Range for Test**	**Tolerance Limit (Bias at Temperature Extremes)**
Durum Wheat	10 % to 16 %	0.35
Soft White Wheat	10 % to 16 %	0.35
Hard Red Spring Wheat	10 % to 16 %	0.35
Soft Red Winter Wheat	10 % to 16 %	0.35
Hard White Wheat	8 % to 14 %	0.35
Sunflower seed (Oil)	6 % to 12 %	0.45
Grain Sorghum	10 % to 16 %	0.45
Two-rowed Barley	10 % to 16 %	0.35
Six-rowed Barley	10 % to 16 %	0.45
Oats	10 % to 16 %	0.45
Long Grain Rough Rice	10 % to 16 %	0.45
Medium Grain Rough Rice	10 % to 16 %	0.45

10. Evaluating GMM Moisture Accuracy as a Continuous Function across the Entire Moisture Range

Source: Charles R. Hurburgh, Jr., Iowa State University

Background/Discussion: Section III of the GMM Chapter of NCWM Publication 14 calls for testing device accuracy over a 6 % moisture range using 10 samples selected from each 2 % moisture interval. The two tests for accuracy are bias (meter versus oven) and the Standard Deviation of the Differences (SDD) between the meter and the air oven for each of the 2 % moisture intervals. The bias of all samples in each 2 % moisture interval of the full moisture range is also the basis for evaluating GMM calibration performance annually using data collected as part of the on-going national calibration program.

The evaluation of accuracy (for moisture) in two percentage point intervals, with an independent evaluation in each interval, assumes that the performance of a device is not continuous and can be adjusted in each of the increments independently of the others. This is not a true assumption, and so the individual increment evaluations, particularly in cases where fewer than 20 samples (not enough to encompass the full 95 % confidence interval (CI) that the tolerances are based upon) become partially dependent on the properties of the samples in the increments. Naturally all samples cannot be tested in all increments, so there is automatically a nested design. Instrument performance is a continuous function. As an alternative to the present evaluation method, data interpretation (not the design of the lab work) could require that the overall bias (across all samples) not be statistically significant (p = 0.05) and that there be no significant slope (Δ error / Δ oven moisture) across the range of data. The variability test (SDD) could remain the same as it is now. The NIR program is essentially this way now, because there are no ranges for the constituents. A second alternative for consideration is to use a moving average (across ranges) to test bias and standard deviation.

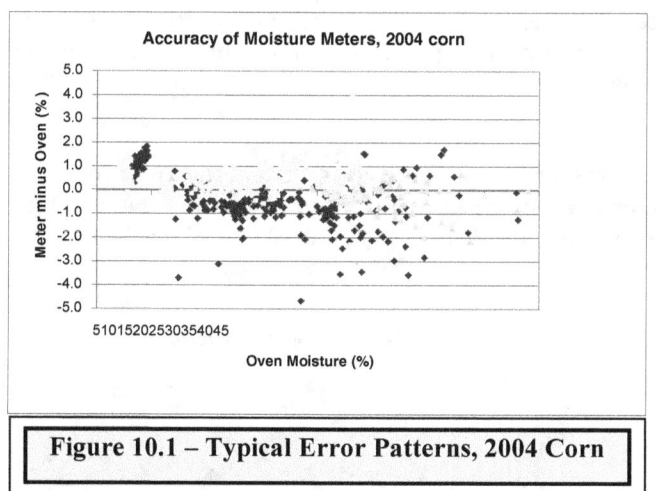

Figure 10.1 – Typical Error Patterns, 2004 Corn

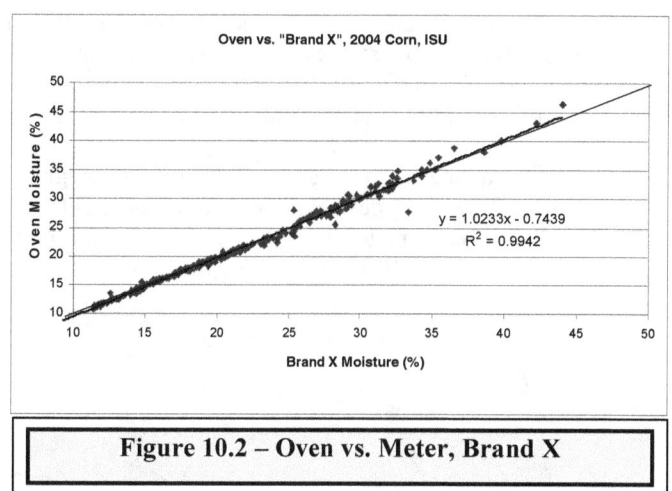

Figure 10.2 – Oven vs. Meter, Brand X

Figure 10.1 shows typical moisture error patterns (meter minus air oven) for three device types based on 2004 corn crop data. Figure 10.2 illustrates the continuous nature of meter performance when measured over the full range of operation.

Dr. Hurburgh commented that the study of error functions was mostly applicable to Phase II evaluations, but because of the small number of samples involved in Phase I testing, the study might provide suggested improvements for interpreting Phase I data.

Recommendation: The Sector was asked to review this issue and consider making it a work project for the coming year with formation of an *ad hoc* study group composed of interested Sector members and non-member statistician(s).

Conclusion: Dr. Hurburgh volunteered to chair an *ad hoc* study group to review the issues outlined in Agenda Items 10 and 11. He will send a questionnaire to Sector members and interested parties to determine who is interested in joining the group.

11. Prescreening Grain Samples for GMM Type Evaluation

Source: Charles R. Hurburgh, Jr., Iowa State University

Background: Grain samples used in the accuracy, precision, and reproducibility tests of Section III. **Accuracy, Precision, and Reproducibility Requirements** in the Grain Moisture Meter (GMM) Chapter of *NCWM Publication 14* are selected according to the following procedure:

> The sample set will be screened using the GIPSA official meter model and the air oven. Samples where the official meter model disagrees from the air oven by more than the Handbook 44 acceptance tolerance will be deleted and another sample selected to replace it. No sample set will be used where the standard deviation of the differences between the GIPSA official meter model and the air oven for the 10 samples in a moisture interval exceed one-half the Handbook 44 acceptance tolerance minus 0.1, (i.e., in the 12 % to 14 % interval for corn, the standard deviation of the differences should not exceed (0.4 to 0.1) = 0.3). Finally, any sample that is not within three standard deviations of the mean for the test meter (for either the 2 % or 6 % moisture interval) will be dropped before analysis of the data.

Discussion: The prescreening of samples to eliminate poor predictors is an attempt to remove outliers in advance, so that the test lab does not have to make judgments about outliers. The problem is that samples prescreened on one device will likely have larger rather than smaller variability in the device under test. Error patterns of devices, even when accurately calibrated on average to the reference, will not be the same on individual samples and often will be in opposite directions. The effect is to increase the chances of outliers on the tested device and effectively lessen the chances of the second device passing. Multivariate NIR units are especially prone to this problem. In test categories that have few samples (10 or less) with low tolerances, the impact is quite large and drives calibrations to model the NTEP data rather than the universe of samples.

The following figures illustrate this problem. Figure 11.1 shows air oven moisture vs. meter moisture for two different device types based on data from the 2003 corn crop covering typical market-range moistures. Figure 11.2 shows the error patterns for the two devices, and Figure 11.3 shows that there is no relationship between the two devices on an individual sample error basis.

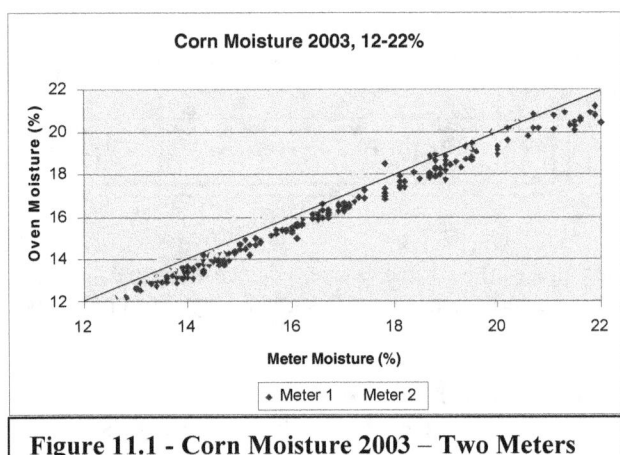

Figure 11.1 - Corn Moisture 2003 – Two Meters

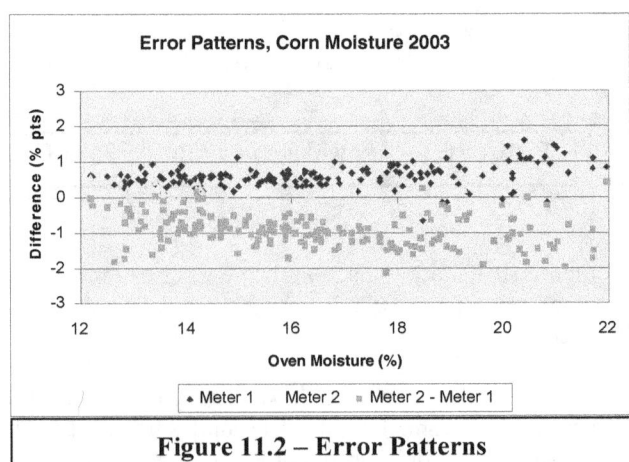

Figure 11.2 – Error Patterns

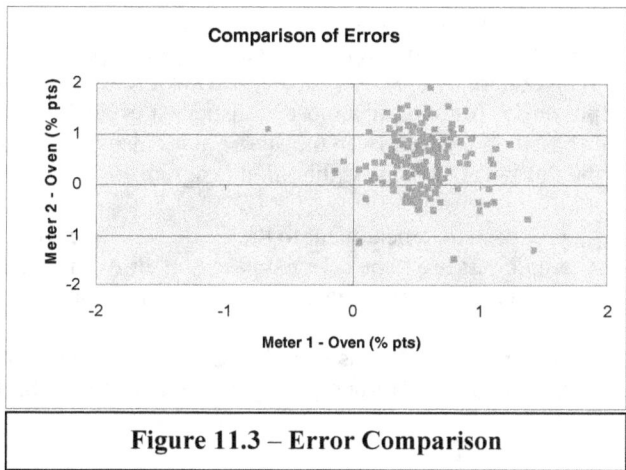

Figure 11.3 – Error Comparison

To overcome this effect, the following options might be considered, recognizing that there has to be a tradeoff between "fairness" and lab procedure complexity:

- Choose the test samples randomly and use statistical outlier tests that incorporate the variability of the reference method data as well as the device data.
- Choose the special set samples (temperature stability) after the accuracy test so these samples can be reasonable predictors on the device being tested. The purpose of temperature samples is to test response to temperature only.
- Choose field inspection samples based on all approved devices.

Dr. Hurburgh remarked that this is an emerging problem that will become more acute as more instruments of different technologies are introduced into the system.

Rich Pierce, GIPSA, reported that the present method of prescreening samples has worked well with test set results agreeing well over time. He said that virtually no samples can be found that will fit all instruments. He has concerns that the topics of Agenda Items 10 and 11 are too general and wonders what impact they might have on NTEP evaluation procedures.

Recommendation: The Sector is asked to review this issue and consider making it a study item for the coming year with formation of an *ad hoc* study group composed of interested Sector members. Because this issue has a major effect on type evaluation, especially when alternative technologies are involved, manufacturers are urged to seriously consider becoming an active participant in this *ad hoc* group should the Sector decide to form one.

Conclusion: Dr. Hurburgh volunteered to chair an *ad hoc* study group to review the issues outlined in Agenda Items 10 and 11. He will send a questionnaire to Sector members and interested parties to determine who is interested in joining the group.

12. Proposed Change to Publication 14 - Assigning Sample Data to Moisture Ranges for GMM Type Evaluation

Source: Charles R. Hurburgh, Jr., Iowa State University

Background: Many of the tests specified in the GMM chapter of NIST Publication 14 require using a defined number of samples in each of three 2 % moisture intervals. For ease of selection, the samples are tested on the Official meter and are assigned to the 2 % moisture intervals based on the Official meter's moisture result. It is simpler to assign ranges in advance based on prescreening because the sample set is defined before the test; however, assignment of sample data to moisture ranges can be a critical item for device evaluation, in that one sample shifted from one range to another can actually affect the pass/fail status of the device in both ranges, depending on the performance of the device on the other samples in the two ranges. Assigning the samples to 2 % moisture intervals based on air oven moisture results (or, in the case of sample temperature sensitivity tests, based on moisture determined at room temperature by the device under test) will reduce sample set dependence and lessen the impact of individual sample properties resulting in a more realistic test of device characteristics. Assigning samples to 2 % moisture intervals based on their air oven moisture values also matches the basis on which sample data are grouped for analysis in the Phase II On-going Calibration Program.

Recommendation: Dr. Hurburgh proposed an amendment to the Grain Moisture Meter chapter of NIST Publication 14 to specify that test sample sets are to be selected based on air oven moisture values or, in the case of sample temperature sensitivity tests, based on moisture determined at room temperature by the device under test.

Discussion: A question was raised regarding what basis would be used to decide which samples to discard in the event that all extra samples were not needed. Dr. Hurburgh suggested that one possibility was to use only the first 10 samples that fell within the range.

Rich Pierce, GIPSA, was not in favor of changing the existing laboratory procedure. He explained that deliberately selecting samples that are distributed across each 2 % range provides for a better test set. The NTEP Laboratory was not eager to change a procedure that has worked well for years. Dr. Pierce did not see a problem with what is being done procedurally at the present time.

Conclusion: The Sector failed to reach a consensus on the proposed change.

13. Report on OIML TC 17/SC 1 IR59 "Moisture Meters for Cereal Grains and Oilseeds"

Background: This item was included on the Sector's agenda to provide a summary of the activities of OIML TC 17/SC 1. Since June 22, 2001, a TC 17/SC 1 work group has been meeting to review revision to OIML R 59. The most recent meeting of the TC 17/SC 1 work group was held on September 20 - 21, 2004, at the Laboratory National D'Essais (LNE) in Paris, France.

Discussion: The most recent draft of OIML R 59 is the 3rd Committee Draft of OIML R59 "Moisture Meters for Cereal Grain" dated April 2005. This has been submitted by the Secretariat to participating and observing countries for review, comment, and approval of the changes. Copies of the 3rd Committee Draft of OIML R59 and the minutes of the TC 17/SC 1 September 2004 meeting can be found on the NIST Weights and Measures Division website at: http://ts.nist.gov/ts/htdocs/230/235/R59draft.htm.

Diane Lee, NIST Weights and Measures Division, reviewed some of the changes included in the draft and asked Sector members to forward comments to her by September 8, 2005. She reported that concerns relating to the temperature requirements were addressed by inserting the following sentence into Paragraph 5.7.1.:

> If the moisture meter is not able to measure sample temperature, then the operating temperature range shall be defined by national responsible bodies.

And Paragraph 5.7.2. was modified by inserting the sentences:

> The moisture meter shall be able to take into account a temperature difference of at least 10 °C. If the moisture meter is not able to measure sample temperature, the maximum allowable temperature difference between the meter and the sample shall be defined by national responsible bodies.

To address the concerns relating to sample size requirements, Paragraph 6.1.5. was modified to remove the explicit minimum sample size requirements, leaving only the sentence:

> "Meters shall be designed to measure the moisture content of representative size grain samples."

A test section checklist has been added to the draft. It is not a detailed "checklist" like the one in Publication 14.

Ms. Lee also reported that China (the Secretariat of TC 17/SC 1) has indicated that a meeting of TC 17/SC 1 would not be held in 2005. A date for a future meeting has not yet been set.

Steve Patoray, NTEP Director, answered Sector concerns that changes in the 3rd Committee Draft might ultimately allow approval of grain moisture meters that did not meet current Handbook 44 requirements. Mr. Patoray stated that these differences could be dealt with when (and if) the United States enters into a mutual acceptance agreement (MAA) with OIML, the EU or other body.

14. Report on OIML TC 5/SC 2 Document D-SW, "General Requirements for Software Controlled Measuring Devices"

Background: This item was included on the Sector's agenda to provide a summary of the activities of OIML TC 5/SC 2. In December 2004 the Secretariats, Germany and France, for OIML TC 5/SC 2 submitted a pre-draft of the OIML Document "General Requirements for Software-Controlled Measuring Instruments." The Document is intended as guidance for technical committees when addressing software requirements in future OIML Recommendations for software-controlled measuring instruments.

According to the Secretariat, the pre-draft was developed based on responses of OIML TC 5/SC 2 members to a questionnaire, the analysis of existing OIML Recommendations and Documents, the analysis of existing regional software requirements (including the European Measurement Instrument Directive and U.S. Food and Drug Guidance Documents), and ISO/IEC software standards.

Noting that Sections 7, 8, and 9 of the pre-draft document were incomplete, Wayne Stiefel, NIST, Weights and Measures Division, solicited comments on the pre-draft. Interested parties from the United States were asked to review the document in terms of the general approach being proposed and what is practical and applicable in a type approval setting and also to provide detailed comments on specific sections. NIST was particularly interested in comments related to the general and specific requirements for measuring instruments in Section 5, and the type approval examination and evaluation procedures in Section 6. Comments were to be returned to Mr. Stiefel by February 1, 2005, to allow NIST to prepare a collated set of comments by February 28, 2005, for the Secretariat.

The pre-draft document prescribes in Section 5 general requirements for measuring instruments, including:

1. Information display;
2. Means of fraud protection;
3. Hardware features supporting fault detection and durability protection; and
4. Specific requirements for:
   a. Design of interfaces;
   b. Separation of software models performing functions subject to legal control from other functions;
   c. Display or printouts;
   d. Storage of data and transmission via communication systems;
   e. Compatibility of operating systems and hardware portability;
   f. Conformity of production-line devices and software with approved type;
   g. Verification of software updates; and
   h. Procedures for loading updated software and maintaining audit trail.

In addition, the document provides in Section 6 type approval procedures to be used in examination and evaluation of the software including the following items:

1. Software documentation to be supplied;
2. A set of validation methods for software examination, which a Recommendation may use to specify the details of the procedure to assure that the instrument complies with the Recommendation. Software specific validation methods include: examination of the software documentation and specification and validation of design; functional testing of metrological features; functional testing of software features; data flow analysis; code inspection walk-through; and software module testing.

NTEP Committee 2006 Final Report
Appendix A – NTETC Grain Analyzer Sector

The pre-draft software document, the Secretariat's Response to TC 5/SC 2 Member Comments, and electronic forms for submitting comments are still available on the web at: http://ts.nist.gov/ts/htdocs/230/235/TC5-SC2.htm.

Discussion: Diane Lee, NIST/WMD, reported that a first working draft Recommendation is being prepared by the Secretariats to address comments received on the outline draft. Another meeting of TC 5/SC 2 has tentatively been scheduled for the end of 2005. Commenting on the possible impact of the proposed Recommendation, one manufacturer stated that his company would be opposed to the recommendation if it meant that calibration parameters would need to be made available. Sector members are asked to review this document, especially in terms of its possible impact on OIML R59 "Moisture Meters for Cereal Grain," and with emphasis on what is practical and applicable in a type approval setting.

15. Report on OIML TC 17/SC 8 Protein Draft Recommendation

Background: This item was included on the Sector's agenda to provide a summary of the activities of OIML TC 17/SC 8. Australia, Secretariat of TC 17/SC 8, developed an outline of the Recommendation on Protein Measuring Instruments for Cereal Grain (March 2004) that was circulated to participating nations (Australia, Brazil, Canada, Czech Republic, Germany, Japan, Poland, Republic of Korea, Russia, and the United States) for comments. In the United States the document was circulated to the U.S. National Work Group (USNWG) for comments. OIML TC 17/SC 8, charged with developing an International Recommendation (IR) for Protein Measuring Instruments for Cereal Grain, held its first meeting May 31 – June 1, 2004, in Sydney, Australia. Representatives from Australia, Japan, New Zealand, and the United States attended the meeting. Comments received from the United States and Germany were discussed at the TC 17/SC 8 meeting in Australia. The comments for the most part were accepted. The scope was expanded to include wheat, barley, corn, soybeans, and rice, and changes were made to allow the national measurement authority to determine moisture basis, reference method, instrument monitoring process, and whether or not to test non-indirect measuring devices.

A revised outline of the Recommendation on Protein Measuring Instruments for Cereal Grain, incorporating the changes agreed upon at the 2004 meeting in Sydney, was distributed with the agenda for the Near-Infrared Grain Analyzer Sector's August 2004 meeting for further review and comment. The U.S. work group members provided limited comments to this draft. The comments that were provided to the Secretariat related to parts of the document that appeared to be in conflict with U.S. metrological practice and procedures.

Discussion: A meeting of TC 17/SC 8 was hosted by PTB in Berlin, Germany, June 27 - 28, 2005, to review the May 2005 version of the "Outline of the Recommendation on Protein Measuring Instruments." Diane Lee, NIST/WMD, reported that the first working draft may be available by end of September 2005. Diane will distribute the draft to the sector members along with a request for comments when the first working draft is available. Diane also requested that the Sector review the tolerances in the current draft and provide comments as soon as possible.

16. Naming Conventions for Near-Infrared Analyzer Calibrations

Background: Both the Grain Moisture Meters Code and the Near-Infrared Grain Analyzer Code of NIST Handbook 44 specify that a device must be capable of displaying either calibration constants, a unique calibration name, or a unique calibration version number. The relevant paragraphs are shown below:

    Sec. 5.56.(a) Grain Moisture Meters
        S.2.4.1. Calibration Version. - A meter must be capable of displaying either calibration constants, a unique calibration name, or a unique calibration version number for use in verifying that the latest version of the calibration is being used to make moisture content and test weight per bushel determinations. (Added 1993) (Amended 1995 and 2003)

    Sec. 5.57. Near-Infrared Grain Analyzers
        S.2.5.2. Calibration Version. - *An instrument must be capable of displaying either calibration constants, a unique calibration name, or a unique calibration version number for use in verifying that the latest version*

of the calibration is being used to make constituent determinations, and that the appropriate instrument settings have been made for the calibration being used.
[Nonretroactive as of January 1, 2003]
(Amended 2001)

Because the constituent calibrations used on near-infrared (NIR) instruments typically consist of many multi-digit constants, manufacturers of these devices normally elect to identify the calibration version by means of "a unique calibration version number."

Some devices currently use a combination of terms to identify the calibration. For example, the Foss Infratec 1241 uses two levels of calibration identification. At the most basic level, a prediction model (PM) identifier is used for each individual constituent calibration. The PM contains the coefficients used to actually determine constituent content. Prediction models for various constituent calibrations are combined to form application models (AM). AM identifiers appear on the analyzer screen and are also the calibration identifiers used in the audit trail. The AM identifiers may be different for each instrument based on the customer's requirements (e.g., the AM may include constituents not covered by NTEP, such as wheat gluten, or possibly an alternate moisture basis). The PM identifiers, which may be displayed by moving deeper into the menu system, are the same for all instruments.

Two other Foss instruments, Infratec 1227 and Infratec 1229, also make use of AM identifiers which may be different for each instrument depending on the specific combination of prediction models they contain. However, the PM identifiers cannot be displayed on these two instruments.

Discussion/Recommendation: GIPSA implemented the NTEP wheat protein calibration in May and the NTEP barley calibration in July. Foss Infratecs are being used in both the official system and the commercial system. Anticipating that the uniqueness of AM identifiers based on user requirements could lead to field inspection problems on cross-utilized instruments, GIPSA met with Foss last December to discuss how "unique calibration version numbers" might be listed to meet the needs of both the NTEP program and GIPSA, with the objective being to make it obvious that the current NTEP protein and moisture calibrations are being used. The proposed solution would first appear on Foss Certificates of Conformance 95-063A9 and 01-063A5.

The solution proposed by GIPSA is to list the calibrations using the following code:

ABYYMMxx

where AB is the grain identifier
YY is the year the calibration is issued
MM is the month the calibration is issued
xx would be a "version" number from 00 to 99

The ABYYMM part of the calibration would be the unique identifier to ensure that the current calibrations listed on the CC for moisture, oil, and protein are being used. The xx would then be customer specific and it could include constituents not covered by NTEP such as wheat gluten or possibly an alternate moisture basis.

For example, the calibration for durum wheat protein and moisture would be listed as WU050101. The unique identifier of the calibration would be WU0501 to let the field inspector quickly see on any Infratec 1227, 1229, or 1241 that it has the current NTEP moisture and protein calibrations. The 01 would be a version number that is assigned from 00 to 99 that is customer specific and it includes constituents not covered by the NTEP such as wheat gluten or possibly an alternate moisture basis.

The ABYYMMxx is the designation the user and field inspector would see when they walk up to the instrument. The field inspector could go into the instrument menu structure to see the specific moisture equation name, protein equation name, etc., that are bundled together to make up the ABYYMMxx calibration version on the Infratec 1241 with the xx suffix unique to each instrument.

NTEP Committee 2006 Final Report
Appendix A – NTETC Grain Analyzer Sector

The Sector was asked to consider if there would be any pitfalls or problems with using the above GIPSA proposal to list the calibrations on the CC by the AM number, using this scheme, e.g. WU0501xx, with the note that xx can be any number between 00 and 99.

One Sector member pointed out that the PM calibrations making up the bundle had been approved, but not the AM bundle itself. Several members favored using the proposed naming convention, listing only PM identifiers on the CC for the Infratec 1241 and listing both the AM identifier and, if possible, the included PM identifiers on the CC for the Infratec 1227 and 1229. The Foss representative noted that the Infratec 1227 and 1229 were NTEP approved only for moisture and had not been available for sale for a number of years. It was also pointed out that the AM contains metrologically significant instrument set-up data (the number of replicates for example), so it must appear on the CC in addition to the PM's.

Conclusion: The CC for the Infratec 1241 will list both AM identifiers and the identifiers of all NTEP-approved PM's included in each AM. The CC for the Infratec 1227 and 1229 will list only the AM identifier (in this case called "Calibration Version"). For all of these models, the AM identifier will appear in the form proposed above with only the last two digits, shown as "xx," varying. Examples of the listings for hard red spring wheat and corn as they appear on the CC's are shown below.

From CC 01-063A5 (Infratec 1241)	From CC 95-063A9 (Infratec 1227 and 1229)
Hard Red Spring Wheat Designation: HRS WHEAT Application Model: WS0501xx Moisture Prediction Model: WBMO0024 Moisture Range - Approved: 8 % to 20 % Moisture Range - Pending: 6 % to 24 % Protein Prediction Model: WBPR0028 Native Moisture Basis: 0 % Subsamples: 7 (or more) Slope: 1.0 for all instruments Intercept (Bias): Varies by instrument	**Hard Red Spring Wheat** Designation: HRS WHEAT Calibration Version: WS0501xx Moisture Range - Approved: 8 % to 20 % Moisture Range - Pending: 6 % to 24 % Subsamples: 10 Path Length: 18 mm Slope: 1.0 for all instruments Intercept (Bias): Varies by instrument
Corn Designation: CORN Application Model: CO0501xx Moisture Prediction Model: COMO0011 Moisture Range - Approved: 8 % to 40 % Moisture Range - Pending: 8 % to 46 % Oil Prediction Model: COOI0006 Protein Prediction Model: COPR0007 Native Moisture Basis: 0 % Subsamples: 7 (or more) Slope: 1.0 for all instruments Intercept (Bias): Varies by instrument	**Corn** Designation: CORN Calibration Version: CO0501xx Moisture Range - Approved: 8 % to 44 % Moisture Range - Pending: 8 % to 46 % Subsamples: 10 Path Length: 30 mm Slope: 1.0 for all instruments Intercept (Bias): Varies by instrument

17. Time and Place for Next Meeting

The next meeting is tentatively planned for Wednesday, August 23, and Thursday, August 24, 2006, in the Kansas City, Missouri, area. Sector members are asked to hold both these days open pending determination of exact meeting times and meeting duration. Meetings will be held in one of the meeting rooms at the National Weather Service Training Center if available. Final meeting details will be announced by late April 2006.

If you would like to submit an agenda item for the 2006 meeting, please contact Steve Patoray, NTEP Technical Director, at spatoray@mgmtsol.com, G. Diane Lee, NIST Technical Advisor, at diane.lee@nist.gov, or Jack Barber, Technical Advisor, at jbarber@motion.net by April 1, 2006.

Change Summary

Recommended Amendments and Changes to the Grain Moisture Meters Chapter in the 2005 Edition of Publication 14			
Section Number	Amendment/Change	Page	Source
Appendix D	Correct the Table titled: **Moisture Ranges and Tolerances for Sample Temperature Sensitivity** by inserting a row for Grain Type Long Grain Rough Rice (with Moisture Range 10 % to 16 % and Tolerance Limit 0.45) between the rows for Oats and Medium Grain Rough Rice (see corrected Table).	GMM-43	08/05 Grain Analyzer Sector Item 9

Appendix B

National Type Evaluation Technical Committee
Measuring Sector

October 21 - 22, 2005 – Nashville, Tennessee
Meeting Summary

National Type Evaluation Technical Committee..B2
1. Recommendations to Update NCWM Publication 14 to Reflect Changes to NIST Handbook 44.......B2
   A. Checklist and Test Procedures for Retail Motor-Fuel Dispensers...B2
   B. Checklist and Test Procedures for Specific Criteria for Vehicle-Tank Meters...........................B3
   C. Checklist and Test Procedures for Specific Criteria for Vehicle-Tank Meters...........................B3
   D. Field Evaluation and Permanence Test for Vehicle Tank Meters..B4

Carry-over Items...B6
2. Product Family Tables for MAG Meters, Ultrasonic Meters, and Turbine Meters.............................B6
3. Acceptable Symbols or Wording to Identify Unit Price, Total Price, and Quantity on a Retail Motor-Fuel Dispenser..B6

New Items B8
4. Product Families for Positive Displacement (PD) Meters..B8
5. Permanence Test for "Wholesale Meters" in Publication 14...B21
6. NTEP Tolerances for Meters with Different Flow Rates when Using Different Sized Provers..........B22
7. Marking Requirements for 3.32. LPG and Anhydrous Ammonia Liquid-Measuring Devices...........B25
8. Marking Requirements for 3.37. Mass Flow Meters..B26
9. Value of the Smallest Unit for Liquid Measuring Devices (LMD) Code..B27
10. Value of the Smallest Unit for Vehicle-Tank Meters (VTM) Code..B28
11. Add Fluid Ounce to NIST Handbook 44, Section 3.30. Liquid-Measuring Devices, Paragraph S.1.2. Units...B29
12. Reorganize Publication 14 to Clarify Tests of Electronic Cash Registers (ECR) for Retail Motor-Fuel Dispensers (RMFD)..B29
13. Next Meeting...B30
14. Multi-point Calibration (linearization) for Meters...B30
15. Audit Trail Remote Configuration...B31
16. New Product Application for Meters and Formula for the Proper Calculation of Relative Error......B31

NTEP Committee 2006 Final Report
Appendix B – NTETC Measuring Sector

National Type Evaluation Technical Committee

1. Recommendations to Update NCWM Publication 14 to Reflect Changes to NIST Handbook 44

Source: NIST/WMD

Background: At its Annual Meeting in July 2005, the National Conference on Weights and Measures (NCWM) adopted the following new or modified requirements that will be reflected in the 2006 Edition of NIST Handbook 44 and NCWM Publication 14. These items are part of the agenda to inform the Measuring Sector of the NCWM actions and to recommend changes to NCWM Publication 14.

Recommendation: The Sector was asked to review and, if acceptable, recommend to the NTEP Committee adoption of the following changes to Publication 14 based on changes to NIST Handbook 44:

 A. Checklist and Test Procedures for Retail Motor-Fuel Dispensers
   Code Reference: S.1.6.1. Indication of Delivery: Electronic Devices

	Code Reference: S.1.6.1. Indication of Delivery			
7.25.	Retail devices shall automatically show their initial zero condition and amount delivered up to the nominal capacity of the device. **For electronic devices manufactured on or after January 1, 2006, the measurement, indication of delivered quantity, and the indication of total sales price shall be inhibited until the fueling position reaches conditions necessary to ensure the delivery starts at zero.**	Yes	No	N/A
7.26.	~~The initial indication on digital indicators may be "suppressed" or not indicated up to a maximum of 0.03 liter or 0.009 gallon.~~ **For electronic devices manufactured prior to January 1, 2006, the first 0.03 L (or 0.009 gal) of a delivery and its associated total sales price need not be indicated.**	Yes	No	N/A

Discussion/Conclusion: The Sector reviewed the proposal and agreed that the change was consistent with the requirements in NIST Handbook 44; however, a manufacturer stated that a test method was needed to provide uniform evaluations by various NTEP laboratories of the ability of a device to meet the requirement. That manufacturer and an NTEP Laboratory official agreed to develop a test method for review by the Sector on the second day of the meeting. The Sector reviewed the proposed method and agreed to add the following test method immediately following Section 7.26 currently on page LMD 26 of NCWM Publication 14 and to forward the amended proposal to the NTEP Committee as written for consideration.

NTEP Committee 2006 Final Report
Appendix B – NTETC Measuring Sector

Test Method:

Step	Description		
1	Set unit price on dispenser.		
2	Pressurize system.		
3	Turn the dispenser off		
4	Create void in dispenser hydraulics by opening the fuel nozzle to provide a zero internal pressure. Then close the fuel nozzle.		
5	Activate the dispenser and let the system reset to 8's, blanks then 0's.		
6	With the nozzle closed, watch the main sales display for advancement of total sales and total volume for at least 5 seconds and no more than 10 seconds.		
7	No advancement constitutes a passing test.		
8	Advancement constitutes a failed test.		
9	Replace the fuel nozzle and turn off the dispenser.		
10	Repeat this test 2 more times. Note: The evaluator must be aware that a time delay for this feature may be incorporated		
11	Device passes test	Yes ☐ No	☐

    B. Checklist and Test Procedures for Specific Criteria for Vehicle-Tank Meters
       Code Reference S.1.4.1. Display of Unit Price

Code Reference: S.1.4.1. Display of Unit Price		
25.1.	Means must be provided to display the unit price at which the device is set to compute in proximity to the total computed price display. **(In a device of the computing type, means shall be provided for displaying, in a manner clear to the operator and an observer, the unit price at which the device is set to compute. The unit price is not required to be displayed continuously.)**	Yes No N/A
25.2.	The unit price shall be expressed in dollars and decimals of dollars using a dollar sign. A common fraction shall not appear in the unit price (e.g., $1.299 not $1.29 9/10).	Yes No N/A

Discussion/Conclusion: No comments were received on Agenda Item B; therefore, the proposal will be forwarded to the NTEP Committee as written for consideration.

    C. Checklist and Test Procedures for Specific Criteria for Vehicle-Tank Meters
       Code Reference S.2.4. Zero Set-Back Interlock, Vehicle-Tank Meters, Electronic

Code Reference: S.2.4. Zero Set-Back Interlock, Vehicle-Tank Meters, Electronic		
26.4.	Except for vehicle-mounted metering systems used solely for the delivery of aviation fuel, a device shall be so constructed that after individual or multiple deliveries at one location have been completed, an automatic interlock system shall engage to prevent a subsequent delivery until the indicating and, if equipped, recording elements have been returned to their zero position. For individual deliveries, if there is no product flow for 3 minutes, the transaction must be completed before additional product flow is allowed. The 3-minute timeout shall be a sealable feature on an indicator.	Yes No N/A

Discussion/Conclusion: No comments were received on Agenda Item C; therefore, the proposal will be forwarded to the NTEP Committee as written for consideration.

D. Field Evaluation and Permanence Test for Vehicle Tank Meters

Code Reference: N.4.2. Special Tests (except Milk-Measuring Systems), N.4.5. Product Depletion Test, and T.4. Product Depletion Test

Product Depletion Test

Before vehicle-mounted applications are listed on an NTEP Certificate of Conformance, the meter must pass a product depletion test. This policy applies to all meter technologies (e.g., Coriolis mass flow meters, turbine meters, and positive displacement meters) even if the meter will never be installed on trucks with more than a single compartment. The permanence test still applies ~~to~~ includ~~e~~ing the throughput and ~~with~~ a duration of at least 20 days. Ideally, this test should be performed with a multiple-compartment vehicle; however, a single-compartment vehicle may be used to simulate the product depletion test by running the tank empty ~~, if a multiple-compartment vehicle is unavailable, a single-compartment vehicle may be used~~ to simulate the product depletion ~~test by running the tank empty.~~

Purpose: A product depletion test verifies the proper operation of air elimination means when the storage tank for the product being measured is pumped dry. This test is necessary for meters that may drain a tank completely, such as a vehicle-tank meter.

Test Procedure:

For a multi-compartment tank:

Begin the test from a compartment (ideally the largest compartment) containing an amount of fuel equal to or less than one-half the nominal capacity of the prover being used. Operate the meter at the normal full flow rate until the compartment is empty. There are several methods for determining that the compartment is empty. There may be a significant change in the sound of the pump. ~~Someone may visually watch for~~ There may be visual evidence that the compartment ~~to~~ has run dry. The meter may stop entirely or may begin to move in jumps (pause, resume running, then pause, then run again.)

Continue the test until the meter indication stops entirely for at least 10 seconds. If the meter stops for 10 seconds or more, proceed to Step 3. If the meter indication fails to stop entirely for a period of 10 seconds, continue to operate the system for 3 minutes.

Close the valve from the empty compartment, and, if top filling, close the nozzle or valve at the end of the delivery hose. Open the valve from another compartment containing the same product. Carefully open the valve at the end of the delivery hose. Pockets of vapor or air may cause product to splash out of the prover. The test results may not be valid if product is splashed out of the prover. Appropriate eye protection is required, but caution is still necessary.

Continue delivering product at the normal full flow rate until the liquid level in the prover reaches the nominal capacity of the prover.

Close the delivery nozzle or valve, stop the meter, allow any foam to settle, then read the prover sight gauge as quickly as practical.

Compare the meter indication with the actual delivered volume in the prover.

Calculate the meter error, apply ~~special~~ **Product Depletion** test tolerance, and determine whether or not the meter error is acceptable.

Test Procedure:

For a single-compartment tank:

The test of a single-compartment tank is easier to accomplish if there is a quick-connect hose coupling between the compartment valve and the pump that supplies product to the meter. If the system does not have a quick-connect coupling between the compartment and the meter, an additional source of sufficient product at the test site is required.

Without a quick-connect coupling:

1. Begin the test with the compartment containing an amount of fuel equal to or less than one-half the nominal capacity of the prover being used. Operate the meter at the normal full flow rate until the supply tank is empty. There are several methods for determining that the tank is empty. There may be a significant change in the sound of the pump. Someone may visually watch for the tank to run dry. The meter may stop entirely or may begin to move in jumps (pause, resume running, then pause, then run again).

Continue the test until the meter indication stops entirely for at least 10 seconds. If the meter stops for at least 10 seconds, proceed to Step 3. If the meter indication fails to stop entirely for at least 10 seconds, continue to operate the system for 3 minutes.

Close the compartment valve and the delivery nozzle or valve if top filling. Stop the pump and load sufficient product from the alternate source into the supply compartment for the meter being tested. Allow the product to stand in the compartment for a brief time to allow entrained vapor or air to escape.

Open the compartment valve and restart the pump without resetting the meter to zero. Carefully open the nozzle or valve at the end of the delivery hose. Pockets of vapor or air may cause product to splash out of the prover. The test results may not be valid if product is splashed out of the prover. Appropriate eye protection is required, but caution is still necessary.

Continue delivering product at the normal full flow rate until the liquid level in the prover reaches the nominal capacity of the prover.

Close the delivery nozzle or valve, stop the meter, allow any foam to settle, then read the prover sight gauge as quickly as practical.

Compare the meter indication with the actual delivered volume in the prover.

Calculate the meter error, apply ~~special~~ **Product Depletion** test tolerance, and determine whether or not the meter error is acceptable.

With a quick-connect coupling:

2. During a normal full flow test run, close the compartment valve at approximately one-half of the nominal prover capacity. Then slowly and carefully disconnect the quick-connect coupling allowing the pump to drain the supply line.

3. Continue the test until the meter indication stops entirely for at least 10 seconds. If the meter fails to stop entirely for at least 10 seconds, continue to operate the system for 3 minutes.

4. If the meter stops for at least 10 seconds or after 3 minutes, close the delivery nozzle or valve at the end of the delivery hose if top filling.

5. Reconnect the quick-connect coupling and open the compartment valve.

6. Carefully open the nozzle or valve at the end of the delivery hose. Pockets of vapor or air may cause product to splash out of the prover. The test results may not be valid if product is splashed out of the prover. Appropriate eye protection is required, but caution is still necessary.

7. Continue delivering product at the normal full flow rate until the liquid level in the prover reaches the prover's nominal capacity.

8. Close the delivery nozzle or valve, stop the meter, allow any foam to settle, then read the prover sight gauge as quickly as practical.

9. Compare the meter indication with the actual delivered volume in the prover.

10. Calculate the meter error, apply ~~special~~ **Product Depletion** test tolerance, and determine whether or not the meter error is acceptable.

Discussion/Conclusion: The Sector reviewed this item and agreed that the term "special test" should be changed to "product depletion test" throughout the Product Depletion Test procedure of Section "C" Field Evaluation and Permanence Test For Vehicle-Tank; Except for LPG, Cryogenic, and CO_2 Meters, on pages LMD 65 through LMD 68 in the 2005 Edition of NCWM Publication 14, to be consistent with NIST Handbook 44 Paragraphs N.4.5. and T.4. A manufacturer of aircraft refueling equipment suggested that the exception in N.4.5. for devices used exclusively for the delivery of aircraft fuel should be added to the checklist. The Sector agreed that the first paragraph of the Product Depletion Test should be modified as follows and the modified proposal be forwarded to the NTEP Committee for consideration:

Except for devices used exclusively for the delivery of aircraft fuel, Bb~~efo~~**re vehicle-mounted applications are listed on an NTEP Certificate of Conformance, the meter must pass a product depletion test. This policy applies to all meter technologies (e.g., Coriolis mass flow meters, turbine meters, positive displacement meters) even if the meter will never be installed on trucks with more than a single compartment. The permanence test still applies to include the throughput and with a duration of at least 20 days. Ideally, this test should be performed with a multiple-compartment vehicle; however, a single-compartment vehicle may be used to simulate the product depletion test by running the tank empty if a multiple-compartment vehicle is unavailable.**

Carry-over Items

2. Product Family Tables for MAG Meters, Ultrasonic Meters, and Turbine Meters

Source: Turbine Meter Work Group

At the meeting this Agenda Item was combined with Agenda Item 4. (See Agenda Item 4 for the conclusion.)

3. Acceptable Symbols or Wording to Identify Unit Price, Total Price, and Quantity on a Retail Motor-Fuel Dispenser

Source: Maryland NTEP Laboratory

Background: At the June 2002 NTEP Laboratory Meeting, one of the participating laboratories requested guidance on acceptable symbols or wording to identify the unit price, total sale, and quantity delivered on a retail motor-fuel dispenser. The laboratories recommended the question be added to the 2002 Measuring Sector Agenda.

At the 2002 Sector Meeting, a work group was formed to address this issue. No input has been received from the work group assigned to develop this issue following the 2002 Sector Meeting.

At its 2004 Meeting, the Sector agreed the NTEP laboratories should develop a list of acceptable symbols at the next laboratory meeting.

NTEP Committee 2006 Final Report
Appendix B – NTETC Measuring Sector

Recommendation: The NTEP laboratories submitted to the Sector the following list of acceptable words and symbols for price and volume declarations on RMFDs for inclusion in Publication 14:

List of Price and Quantity Markings on RMFDs		
Total Sale	**Unit Price**	**Delivered Quantity**
Acceptable	Acceptable	Acceptable
Total Sale $ 000.00 (Preferred) Total $ 000.00 This Sale $ 000.00 Purchase $ 000.00 Total Purchase $ 000.00 Sale $ 000.00	Price Per Gallon $ 0.000 Price/Gallon $ 0.000 $/Liter $0.000 Price Per Unit $ 0.000 Price/Unit $0.000 Unit Price $0.000 (Preferred) $/Gal $0.000 $/L $0.000	Gallons (Preferred) Gal Liters (Preferred) L
Unacceptable	Unacceptable	Unacceptable
$ 000.00	Price Per Vol Price/Vol $/G $0.000 $/l $0.000	G l (lower case L for liter) Unit Volume Vol

Discussion/Conclusion: The Sector reviewed the proposed table and agreed with the concept; however, some members believed that the letter "l" (lower case L for liter) should be acceptable because it is recognized and allowed in NIST Handbook 44, General Code Table 1. Representation of Units. Another member was concerned that if something was identified in the List of Price and Quantity Marking for RMFDs as preferred, some NTEP laboratories might allow only those markings. The Sector modified the table containing the List of Price and Quantity Markings for RMFDs as shown below and recommended the modified table be forwarded to the NTEP Committee for consideration.

List of Price and Quantity Markings on RMFDs[1]		
Total Sale	**Unit Price**	**Delivered Quantity**
Acceptable	*Acceptable*	*Acceptable*
Total Sale $ 000.00 Total $ 000.00 This Sale $ 000.00 Purchase $ 000.00 Total Purchase $ 000.00 Sale $ 000.00	Unit Price $0.000 Price Per Gallon $ 0.000 Price/Gallon $ 0.000 Price Per Liter $ 0.000 Price/ Liter $ 0.000 Price Per Unit $ 0.000 Price/Unit $0.000	Gallons Gal Liters L or l
Unacceptable	*Unacceptable*	*Unacceptable*
$ 000.00	Price Per Vol Price/Vol $/G $0.000 $/Gal $0.000 $/Liter $0.000 $/L $0.000 $/l $0.000	G Unit Volume Vol

[1] Does not apply to receipt format

New Items

4. Product Families for Positive Displacement (PD) Meters

Source: Murray Equipment, Tuthill and Turbine Meter Work Group

Background/Discussion: During several NTEP evaluations conducted since the last Sector meeting, concerns were expressed by manufacturers that the product families table for positive displacement meters need to be revised and updated to reflect changes in metering designs submitted for evaluation and products currently found in the marketplace. One meter manufacturer questioned the appropriateness of keeping aviation fuel as a separate "Product Subgroup" when the physical characteristics of those products are so similar to other refined products. Another manufacturer wanted to know what testing was required to include "biodiesel" on a CC (Certificate of Conformance). Another question asked whether or not the evaluation must be conducted using biodiesel fuel with the highest specific gravity available or could testing be conducted using a product with very similar characteristics that is available in the manufacturer's test facility.

Recommendation: Agenda Item 2 of the meeting agenda distributed prior to the meeting contained a proposal for a family products table for turbine meters. Agenda Item 4 contained two proposals for changes to the product family table for PD meters. At the Sector meeting Items 2 and 4 were combined for discussion and consideration. The Sector reviewed and discussed two alternative proposals for PD meters and the proposal for turbine meters to determine if any of the proposals contained appropriate recommendations for modifications to Section "C" and the Product Family Table for Positive Displacement Meters in the LMD Technical Policy of Publication 14. Two proposals were received to address some of the issues for PD meters. The first proposal submitted by Paul Glowacki (Murray Equipment, Inc.) is shown below as proposal alternative number 1. The second proposal submitted by Maurice Forkert (Tuthill Transfer System) is shown below as proposal alternative number 2. The proposed family products table submitted by the turbine meters work group is shown following proposal alternative number 2.

Proposal Alternative Number 1:

Proposal Overview

The driving factor behind this proposal is simplification of the Positive Displacement (PD) Meter Product Family chart to more accurately reflect the reality that PD meters are not sensitive to the differences between typical products, but rather that viscosity and specific gravity are the determining metrological considerations.

Thus, the product families are simplified to group liquids in one large category (Normal Liquids) and several additional categories for specialized liquids where other factors are considered.

There are four components to this proposal. Part I is the revised product family table itself to replace the one currently in Pub 14. Part II contains revised language that covers the requirements for testing meters for new certificates according to the table. Part III provides language for the requirements to convert existing certificates to the new proposed categories. Part IV provides revised language to harmonize certain requirements for vehicle-tank meters and stationary meters.

Part I
Proposed Product Table Group

PRODUCT GROUP TABLE				
Product Groups	**Typical Products**	**Viscosity (Centipoise [cP])**	**Specific Gravity**	**Minimum Test Requirements to Cover Products in Group***
Normal Liquids	Water; Alcohols; Glycols; Water Mixes thereof; Agricultural Liquid Fertilizers, Liquid Feeds, Crop Chemicals; Chemicals: Petroleum Products; Solvents; Suspensions; Vegetable Oils	0.3 to 2500	to 2.5	* All products in this group within the range of lowest specific gravity/viscosity to the highest specific gravity/viscosity tested are covered
Compressed Liquids	Propane, Butane, Ethane, Freon 11, Freon 12, Freon 22, NH3, etc.	0.1 to 0.5	0.3 to 0.68	Test with one product in the group to cover all products in this group
Compressed Gases	CNG	0.1 to 0.5	0.6 to 0.8	Test with one product in the group to cover all products in this group
Cryogenic Liquids (BP 152 C) and Liquefied Natural Gas	Liquefied Oxygen, Nitrogen, etc.	0.1 to 0.5	0.07 to 1.4	Test with one product in the group to cover all products in this group
Heated Products (above 50 C)	Bunker C, Asphalt, etc.	25 to 2420	0.8 to 1.2	* All products in this group within the range of lowest specific gravity/viscosity to the highest specific gravity/viscosity tested are covered

*If only a single product is selected for test in Normal Liquids or Heated Products groups, the resulting CC will cover only that product.

NOTE: The Typical Products listed in this table are not limiting or all-inclusive; there may be other products and product trade names, which fall into a product family and product subgroup.

Part II
Proposed Language For Product Family Requirements

C. Product Families for All Meters

When submitting a meter for evaluation, the applicant must specify the product or product group for which the meter is being submitted. To cover a product group, NTEP tests must be conducted with two liquids within the product group. Upon test completion, a range of specific gravities/viscosities between the specific gravities/viscosities of the two liquids attained within the product group will be covered on the Certificate of Conformance (CC). The specific gravity/viscosity range within the product group can be expanded by conducting an NTEP test with a liquid of higher or lower specific gravity/viscosity than is covered on the existing CC.

The above does not apply to the following product groups: compressed gasses, compressed liquids, and cryogenic liquids. In case of these product groups, only one liquid within each of these groups is required to undergo an NTEP evaluation and, upon completion, the entire product group will be covered on the CC.

> Multi-product applications in which the meter is to be used without a change to zero or calibration to dispense different products must include a multi-product test if:
>
> (1) specific gravity varies by more than 0.1 for devices measuring in mass; or
> (2) viscosity varies by more than 1 cP (below 25 cP) for devices measuring in volume.
>
> The multi-product initial test will be performed on the meter without a change to zero or calibration using multiple products having a difference in specific gravity of at least 0.2 for devices measuring in mass and 2 centipoise for devices measuring in volume. For mass measuring devices which will be used to dispense products having a specific gravity range greater than 0.2 and for volume measuring devices which will be used for products having a viscosity range greater than 2 cP, the multi-product testing must be performed over the anticipated range before multi-product applications will be included on the CC. For the multi-product testing, throughput testing will be performed on one or more combinations of products; testing for the subsequent test will be conducted on all products used during the initial test without a change to zero or calibration. Multi-product testing requirements do not apply to devices used to dispense a product such as propane in which the product varies in normal operation.

Part III
Proposed Requirements for Conversion of Pre-existing NTEP Certificates of Conformance to New Requirements

NTEP Liquid Measuring Device Certificates of Conformance issued before 2006, will be reclassified according to specific gravity and viscosity ratings matching the Product Groups and corresponding Sub-Groups listed on the existing manufacturer's Certificate of Conformance:

NTEP Committee 2006 Final Report
Appendix B – NTETC Measuring Sector

Current Certificate Product Family and Subgroup Listing	2006 Certificate Product Group Table Classification

Fuel, Lubricant, Oil Products, and Edible Oil Products
   Refined Products
   Aviation Fuels
   Vegetable Oils
	Normal Liquids:
	Specific Gravity 0.70 to 2.5
	Viscosity 0.3 cP to 2500 cP

Solvents
   General Solvents
   Chlorinated Solvents	

Alcohol & Glycols Alcohols, Glycols, Water Mixes	
Water Water	

Agricultural Liquids
   Clear Liquid Fertilizer, Crop Chemicals, Flowables,
   Crop Chemicals, Suspension Fertilizer, Liquid Feed	

Chemicals Chemicals	

Liquefied Compressed Gases
   Fuels and Refrigerants
   NH3
	Compressed Liquids:
	Specific Gravity 0.3 to 0.68
	Viscosity 0.1 cP to 0.5 cP

Liquefied Compressed Gases
   Fuels and Refrigerants
   CNG
	Compressed Gases
	Specific Gravity 0.6 to 0.8
	Viscosity 0.1 cP to 0.5 cP

Liquefied Compressed Gases
   Fuels and Refrigerants
   Liquefied Oxygen, Nitrogen
	Cryogenic Liquids and Liquefied Natural Gas
	Specific Gravity 0.7 to 1.4
	Viscosity 0.1 cP to 0.5 cP

Fuel, Lubricant, Oil Products, and Edible Oil Products
   Refined Products
   Bunker C, Asphalt
	Heated Products:
	Specific Gravity 0.8 to 1.2
	Viscosity 25 cP to 2420 cP

NOTE: In the event pre-2006 NTEP Liquid-Measuring Device testing was performed on a single meter with products having a Specific Gravity and/or Viscosity greater or lower than the Specific Gravity and Viscosity of the reclassification, the product's actual Specific Gravity and Viscosity can be used to meet the requirements for the 2006 manufacturer's Liquid Measuring Device Certificate of Conformance.

NOTE: A table of sample specific gravity and viscosity values for typical products would be included in Pub 14. This is not included in the proposal and would have to be developed at some point for inclusion with the other changes.

EXAMPLES:

1) Current Certificate lists a meter model approved for Solvents. The 2006 classification is: Normal Liquids Specific Gravity 0.70 to 2.5 and Viscosity 0.3 cP to 2500 cP.

2) Current Certificate lists a meter model approved for Solvents and Agricultural Liquids. The 2006 Classification is: Normal Liquids Specific 0.70 to 2.5 Viscosity 0.3 cP to 2500 cP.

3) Current Certificate lists a meter model approved for Solvents, Agricultural Liquids and Asphalt. 2006 Classification is Normal Liquids and Heated Products Specific 0.70 to 2.5 Viscosity 0.3 cP to 2500 cP.

4) Current Certificate lists a meter model approved for Asphalt and Solvents. The 2006 Classification is Normal Liquids Specific Gravity 0.70 to 2.5 Viscosity 0.3 cP to 2500 cP and Heated Products Specific Gravity 0.8 to 1.2 Viscosity 25 cP to 2420 cP.

Part IV
Revised Language for Vehicle-Mounted and Stationary Meter Application Requirements

Publication 14 LMD Section R, page 8

Vehicle-Mounted and Stationary Applications of the Meter

If a meter evaluation is conducted in a vehicle-mounted **or** stationary application and the meter successfully meets the NTEP accuracy and performance requirements for both vehicle-mounted and stationary applications, then both applications can be included on the NTEP Certificate of Conformance.

Proposal Alternative Number 2:

This proposal is based on several factors:

A) Level playing field. The regulation should not be dependent on the type of liquid-measuring device. All types of liquid-measuring devices should be required to meet the same regulation or not be approved. I am proposing this Family of Liquids for all types of liquid-measuring devices.

B) End use of a liquid is not a metrological issue. It is not an issue of measurement if vegetable oil ends up on the dinner table or in the crankcase. My proposal does not recognize the end use of a liquid. The marketplace regulations take care of that aspect.

C) The effect of a measuring device on a liquid is not a metrological issue. The viscosity/specific gravity can affect the performance of a meter. It is a marketplace issue if the liquid is Newtonian, Thixotropic, Dilatant, Colloidal, or Rheopectic.

D) Liquid-measuring devices that are approved for a range of viscosities/specific gravities may encounter liquids with solids in that range. The marketplace will be quick to eliminate the measuring device if the measuring device is not able to handle the solids.

E) This is a move to bring our regulations closer in alignment with Canada and OIML regulations.

C. Product Families for All Meters

When submitting a meter for evaluation, the applicant must specify the product or product group for which the meter is being submitted. To cover a product group, NTEP tests must be conducted with two liquids within the product group. Upon test completion, a range of specific gravities/viscosities between the specific gravities/viscosities of the two liquids attained within the product group will be covered on the Certificate of Conformance (CC). The specific gravity/viscosity range within the product group can be expanded by conducting an NTEP test with a liquid of higher or lower specific gravity/viscosity than is covered on the existing CC.

The above does not apply to the following product groups: compressed gasses, compressed liquids, and cryogenic liquids. In case of these product groups, only one liquid within each of these groups is required to undergo an NTEP evaluation and, upon completion, the entire product group will be covered on the CC.

Multi-product applications, in which the meter is to be used without a change to zero or calibration to dispense different products, must include a multi-product test if:

a) specific gravity varies by more than 0.1 for devices measuring in mass;
b) viscosity varies by more than 1 cP (below 25 cP) for devices measuring in volume.

The multi-product initial test will be performed on the meter without a change to zero or calibration using multiple products having a difference in specific gravity of at least 0.2 for devices measuring in mass and 2 cP for devices measuring in volume. For mass measuring devices which will be used to dispense products having a specific gravity range greater than 0.2 and for volume measuring devices which will be used for products having a viscosity range greater than 2 cP, the multi-product testing must be performed over the anticipated range before multi-product applications will be included on the CC. For the multi-product testing, throughput testing will be performed on one or more combinations of products; testing for the subsequent test will be conducted on all products used during the initial test without a change to zero or calibration. Multi-product testing requirements do not apply to devices used to dispense a product such as propane in which the product varies in normal operation.

Product Group Table				
Product Groups	**Typical Products**	**Viscosity (Centipoise [cP])**	**Specific Gravity**	**Minimum Test Requirements to Cover Products in Group***
Normal Liquids	Water;Alcohols; Glycols; Water Mixes thereof; Agricultural Liquids, Fertilizers, Seeds, and Herbicides; Chemicals:Petroleum Products; Solvents; Suspensions	0.3 to 2500	0.7 to 2.5	* All products in this group within the range of lowest specific gravity/viscosity to the highest specific gravity/viscosity tested are covered
Compressed Liquids	Propane, Butane, Ethane, Freon 11, Freon 12, Freon 22, NH3, etc.	0.1 to 0.5	0.3 to 0.68	Test with one product in the group to cover all products in this group
Compressed Gases	CNG	0.1 to 0.5	0.6 to 0.8	Test with one product in the group to cover all products in this group
Cryogenic Liquids (BP 152 C) and Liquefied Natural Gas	Liquefied Oxygen, Nitrogen, etc.	0.1 to 0.5	0.07 to 1.4	Test with one product in the group to cover all products in this group
Heated Products (above 50 C)	Bunker C, Asphalt, etc.	25 to 2420	0.8 to 1.2	* All products in this group within the range of lowest specific gravity/viscosity to the highest specific gravity/viscosity tested are covered
*If only a single product is selected for test in Normal Liquids or Heated Products groups, the resulting CC will cover only that product.				
NOTE: The Typical Products listed in this table are not limiting or all-inclusive; there may be other products and product trade names, which fall into a product family and product subgroup.				

The turbine meters work group proposed amending Section "P" of the LMD Technical Policy in Publication 14 to add the following:

P. Product Families for Turbine Meters

To facilitate the certification of turbine meters, product family groups have been created to eliminate the necessity of testing each product individually. Turbine meter product groups are defined by viscosity, density, lubricity, and chemical/physical compatibility.

When submitting a turbine meter for evaluation, the applicant must specify the product or product group(s) for which the meter is being submitted. A meter that is successfully tested on one product will be approved for use with that product only. If the meter is successfully tested on a lower viscosity product and then successfully tested on a higher viscosity product in the same product group, then all products in that group falling within the range of viscosities can be included on the Certificate.

Bi-directional turbine meters must be tested in "forward" and "reverse" flow directions. Turbine meters must be tested in the mounting orientation(s) required. Horizontal/vertical-mounted turbine meters must be tested in both horizontal and vertical orientation, and in "forward" and "reverse" flow, if they are bi-directional. Vertically-mounted turbine meters that flow in only one direction must be described in the Certificate.

The flow range of turbine meters is affected by line size, viscosity, and specific gravity. Therefore, the criteria for inclusion of meters from 50 % to 200 % min/max flow rate of the meter tested cannot be applied to all line size, viscosity, and specific gravity requirements, with respect to turbine meters.

One method to include smaller line sizes with higher viscosities is to use multiple meter factors to linearize the performance curve.

Another method to include smaller line sizes with higher viscosities is to increase the minimum flow rate.

The following calculation can be used to determine if a smaller line size needs adjustment because of viscosity. The method of adjustment must be described in the Certificate.

Sizing Ratio = Liquid Viscosity (centistokes) / Nominal Line Size (inches)

Sizing Ratio = 1 or less, use the normal 10 % minimum flow rate. (10:1 turndown)
   = Above 1 to 1.5 use 20 % minimum flow rate. (5:1 turndown)
   = Above 1.5 exceeds the Minimum Discharge Rate of Wholesale Devices and cannot be included.

Multiple meter factors can also be used to achieve extended flow rate and to linearize the performance curve with low and high specific gravity applications. This use must be described in the Certificate.

The product or product group(s), meter orientation, and flow directions covered by the Certificate are to be identified on page 1 of the Certificate of Conformance. More detailed information, including typical products to be covered, number of meter factors required for smaller line size, higher viscosity, low/high specific gravity and extended flow rate are to be included in the application section of the Certificate.

Turbine Meter Product Group Table				
Product Groups	**Typical Products[1]**	**Viscosity (centistokes [cSt])**	**Specific Gravity[2]**
Refined Petroleum Products	diesel[3], gasoline[4], kerosene, jet fuel	0.5 to 200	0.64 to 1.1
	distillate, fuel oil, stove oil		
Alcohols & Glycols	ethanol, methanol, butanol,	0.6 to 54	0.6 to 1.6
	isopropyl, isobutyl		
	ethylene glycol, propylene, glycol		
Compressed Liquefied Gases	LPG, anhydrous-ammonia,	0.2 to 0.6	0.3 to 0.68
	propane, butane, freon		
Cryogenic Liquids (BP 152 C) and Liquefied Natural Gas	Liquefied Argon, Oxygen, Nitrogen	0.1 to 0.4	0.8 to 1.4

[1]NOTE: The Typical Products listed in this table are not limiting or all-inclusive; there may be other products and product trade names, which fall into a Product Group.
[2]The specific gravity of a liquid is the ratio of its density to that of water at standard conditions, usually 4 °C (or 20 °C) and 1 atmosphere. The density of water at standard conditions is approximately 1 000 kg/m3 (or 998 kg/m3).
[3]Diesel fuel blends (biodiesel) with up to 20 % vegetable or animal fat/oil.
[4]Gasoline includes oxygenated fuel blends with up to 15 % oxygenate.

The source for some of the viscosity value information is in the Industry Canada – Measurement Canada "Classification of Liquids for the Approval of Liquid Meters", Bulletin V-16 (rev. 2), Issue Date: 2005-05-13, Effective Date: 2005-07-01.

Discussion: On the first day of the meeting, because of the common issue presented in the proposals, the Sector agreed to combine Agenda Items 2 and 4 for discussion. One manufacturer of RMFDs stated that the proposals in Item 4 to include alcohols in the product group of "normal liquids" that also included water, petroleum products, chemicals, and vegetable oils was not appropriate. Another manufacturer stated that if a company could make a single device that can pass type evaluation for both alcohols and petroleum products, that company should not be penalized because another company must submit different models to measure each product. After considerable discussion it was apparent that while each of the proposals had merit, no individual proposal satisfied all of the concerns of the members. It was suggested that the parties responsible for each of the proposals and other interested parties meet after the conclusion of the first day of the Sector Meeting to work on a compromise document that would satisfy all participants.

Conclusion: On the second day of the meeting the volunteer group presented a proposal for consideration by the entire Sector membership present at the meeting. After a few minor editorial changes, the Sector agreed to forward proposed revisions to NCWM Publication 14 Section "C" Product Families for Positive Displacement (PD) Meters, Section "D" Product Families for Mass Flow Meters (MFM), and a new Product Families Table designed to include product family testing requirements for PD meters, MFM, and Turbine Meters in a single table, as shown below, to the NTEP Committee for consideration.

NTEP Committee 2006 Final Report
Appendix B – NTETC Measuring Sector

C. Product Families for ~~Positive Displacement~~ Meters

When submitting a ~~positive displacement~~ meter for evaluation, the manufacturer must specify the product family and ~~subgroup(s)~~ <u>critical parameters</u> for which the meter is being submitted. ~~From the list of liquids constituting a product family and subgroup, at least two liquids representing of the high and low key characteristics of that subgroup are to be selected for use in the test. If the meter successfully completes all accuracy and permanence tests with these products, the resulting Certificate of Conformance will cover the entire subgroup of the product family.~~

The product family and the specific product subgroup covered by the Certificate are to be identified on Page 1 of the Certificate of Conformance. More detailed information, including the typical product types found in the subgroup, is to be included in the Application section of the Certificate.

Tests to be Conducted

Test A – Products must be individually tested and noted on the Certificate of Conformance.

Test B – To obtain coverage for a range of products within a family: Test with one product having a low specific gravity; test with a second product having a high specific gravity. The Certificate of Conformance will cover all products in the family within the specific gravity range tested.

Test C – To obtain coverage for a range of products within a family: Test with one product having a low viscosity; test with a second product having a high viscosity. The Certificate of Conformance will cover all products in the family within the viscosity range tested.

Test D – To obtain coverage for a product family: Test with one product in the product family.

Test E – To obtain coverage for a range of products within a family: Test with one product having a low kinematic viscosity; test with a second product having a high kinematic viscosity. The Certificate of Conformance will note coverage for all products in the family within the kinematic viscosity range tested.

Mass Meter Product Family & Test Requirements (Test B unless otherwise noted)	PD Product Family & Test Requirements (Test C unless otherwise noted)	Turbine Product Family & Test Requirements (Test A unless otherwise noted)	Typical Products[1]	Viscosity[5] (Centipoise [cP]) (Centistokes [cSt])	Specific Gravity[2]
Normal Liquids	Fuels, Lubricants, Industrial and Food Grade Liquid Oils	Fuels, Lubricants, Industrial and Food Grade Liquid Oils (Test E permitted)	Diesel Fuel[3], Distillate, Gasoline[4], Fuel Oil, Kerosene, Light Oil, Spindle Oil, Lubricating Oils, SAE Grades, Bunker Oil, 6 Oil, Crude Oil, Asphalt, Vegetable Oil, Biodiesel above B20, AVgas, Jet A, Jet A-1, Jet B, JP4, JP5, JP7, JP8, Cooking Oils, Sunflower Oil, Soy Oil, Peanut Oil, Olive Oil, etc.	0.3 to 2500 0.44 to 2270	0.68 to 1.1
	Solvents General	Solvents General (Test E permitted)	Acetates, Acetone, Esters, Ethylacetate, Hexane, MEK, Naphtha, Toluene, Xylene, etc.	0.3 to 7 0.5 to 4.38	0.6 to 1.6
	Solvents Chlorinated	Solvents Chlorinated	Carbon Tetra-Chloride, Methylene-Chloride, Perchloro-Ethylene, Trichloro-Ethylene, etc.	0.3 to 7 0.5 to 4.38	0.6 to 1.6
	Alcohols, Glycols, & Water Mixes Thereof	Alcohols, Glycols, & Water Mixes Thereof (Test E permitted)	Ethanol, Methanol, Butanol, Isopropyl, Isobutyl, Ethylene glycol, Propylene glycol, etc.	0.3 to 7 0.5 to 4.38	0.6 to 1.6

NTEP Committee 2006 Final Report
Appendix B – NTETC Measuring Sector

Mass Meter Product Family & Test Requirements (Test B unless otherwise noted)	PD Product Family & Test Requirements (Test C unless otherwise noted)	Turbine Product Family & Test Requirements (Test A unless otherwise noted)	Typical Products[1]	Viscosity[5] (Centipoise [cP]) (Centistokes [cSt])	Specific Gravity[2]
	Water (Test D permitted)	Water (Test D permitted)	Tap Water, Deionized, Demineralized, Potable, Nonpotable	1.0 1.0	1.0
	Clear Liquid Fertilizers	Clear Liquid Fertilizers	Nitrogen Solution; 28 %, 30 % or 32 %; 20 % Aqua-Ammonia; Urea; Ammonia Nitrate; N-P-K solutions; 10-34-0; 4-10-10; 9-18-9; etc.	10 to 400 10 to 275	1.0 to 1.45
	Crop Chemicals	Crop Chemicals	Herbicides: Round-up, Touchdown, Banvel, Treflan, Paraquat, Prowl, etc	4 to 400 5.7 to 333	0.7 to 1.2
	Crop Chemicals	Crop Chemicals	Fungicides, Insecticides, Adjuvants, Fumigants	0.7 to 100 1 to 83	0.7 to 1.2
	Flowables	Flowables	Dual, Bicep, Marksman, Broadstrike, Doubleplay, Topnotch, Guardsman, Harness, etc.	20 to 900 20 to 750	1 to 1.2
	Crop Chemicals	Crop Chemicals	Fungicides		
	Crop Chemicals	Crop Chemicals	Micronutrients		
	Suspensions Fertilizers	Suspensions Fertilizers	3-10-30; 4-4-27, etc.	20 to 900 20 to 560	1.0 to 1.6
	Liquid Feeds	Liquid Feeds	Liquid Molasses; Molasses plus Phos Acid and/or Urea; etc.	10 to 50 000 8 to 33 000	1.2 to 1.5
	Chemicals	Chemicals	Sulfuric Acid, Hydrochloric Acid, Phosphoric Acid, etc	1.0 to 296 0.9 to 160	1.1 to 1.85
Heated Products (above 50 °C)	Heated Products (above 50 °C)	Heated Products (above 50 °C)	Bunker C, Asphalt, etc.		0.8 to 1.2

Mass Meter Product Family & Test Requirements (Test B unless otherwise noted)	PD Product Family & Test Requirements (Test C unless otherwise noted)	Turbine Product Family & Test Requirements (Test A unless otherwise noted)	Typical Products[1]	Viscosity[5] (Centipoise [cP]) (Centistokes [cSt])	Specific Gravity[2]
Compressed Liquids – (Test D)	Fuels and Refrigerants	Fuels and Refrigerants – (Test E)	LPG, Propane, Butane, Ethane, Freon 11, Freon 12, Freon 22, etc.	0.1 to 0.5 0.3 to 0.77	0.3 to 0.65
	NH[3]	NH[3]	Anhydrous Ammonia Note: If a meter is certified for anhydrous ammonia the same meter type may also be certified for LPG without further testing	0.1 0.2	0.56 to 0.68
Compressed Gases – (Test D)	Note: CNG is only included in Section 3.37 Mass Flow Meters of Handbook 44		CNG		0.6 to 0.8
Cryogenic Liquids and Liquefied Natural Gas – (Test D)	Cryogenic Liquids and Liquefied Natural Gas – (Test A)	Cryogenic Liquids and Liquefied Natural Gas – (Test D)	Liquefied Oxygen, Nitrogen, etc.		0.07 to 1.4

[1] NOTE: The Typical Products listed in this table are not limiting or all-inclusive; there may be other products and product trade names, which fall into a product family. Water and a product such as stoddard solvent or mineral spirits may be used as test products in the fuels, lubricants, industrial, and food- grade liquid oils product family.

[2] The specific gravity of a liquid is the ratio of its density to that of water at standard conditions, usually 4 °C (or 40 °F) and 1 atm. The density of water at standard conditions is approximately 1000 kg/m3 (or 998 kg/m3)

[3] Diesel fuel blends (biodiesel) with up to 20 % vegetable or animal fat/oil.

[4] Gasoline includes oxygenated fuel blends with up to 15 % oxygenate.

[5] Kinematic viscosity is measured in centistokes. $Centistokes = \dfrac{Centipoise}{Specific\ Gravity}$

Source for some of the viscosity value information is in the Industry Canada - Measurement Canada "Liquid Products Group, Bulletin V-16-E (rev. 1), August 3, 1999."

D. **Additional Criteria for** Product Families for Mass Flow Meters

~~When submitting a direct mass flow meter for evaluation, the manufacturer must specify the product or product group for which the meter is being submitted. To cover a product group, NTEP tests must be conducted with two liquids within the product group.~~ When two liquids of different densities are tested, the Certificate of Conformance (CC) for the mass flow meter will cover approved liquids with a specific gravity range from 0.1 above the highest specific gravity tested to 0.1 below the lowest specific gravity tested. The specific gravity range within the product group can be expanded by conducting an NTEP test with a liquid of higher or lower specific gravity than is covered on the existing CC.

~~The above does not apply to the following product groups: compressed gases, compressed liquids, and cryogenic liquids. In the case of these product groups, only one liquid within each group is required to undergo an NTEP evaluation and, upon completion, the entire product group will be covered on the existing CC.~~

Multi-product applications (that is, applications in which the meter will be used without a change to zero or calibration to dispense different products which vary in specific gravity by more than 0.1) must include a multi-product test. The multi-product initial test will be performed on the meter without a change to zero or calibration using multiple products having a difference in specific gravity of at least 0.2. For devices which will be used to dispense multiple products having a specific gravity range greater than 0.2, the multi-product testing must be performed over the anticipated range before multi-product applications will be included on the CC. For the multi-product testing, throughput testing will be performed on one or a combination of the products; testing for the subsequent test will be conducted on both products without a change to zero or calibration. The CC for a mass flow meter will cover multi-product applications where the specific gravity of a single product, or multiple products, varies by the amount tested throughout the entire approved specific gravity range of the meter. Example: Where a meter has been tested and a certificate issued for multi-product with one liquid having a specific gravity of 0.7 and another liquid having a specific gravity of 1.0 and the meter is subsequently tested to expand the range with a liquid having a specific gravity of 1.6, the allowed variation of gravities covered by the CC will be from 0.7 through 1.6. Multi-product testing requirements do not apply to meters used to dispense a product such as propane in which the density varies in normal operation.

5. **Permanence Test for "Wholesale Meters" in Publication 14**

Source: NTEP Laboratories

Background/Discussion: At the 2005 meeting of the NTEP laboratories, it was noted that Publication 14 does not contain permanence test criteria for wholesale positive displacement meters. The NTEP labs developed the following proposal for submission to the Sector for review.

Recommendation: The Sector reviewed the following proposal for possible forwarding to the NTEP Committee for approval and addition to the 2006 edition of Publication 14.

Proposal: Modify Section D of the Publication 14 LMD Checklist as follows:

D. <u>**Initial Evaluation and Permanence Tests for Wholesale Positive Displacement (PD) Meters**</u>

<u>**The following tests are considered to be appropriate for metering systems on Wholesale PD Meters:**</u>

1. <u>**Four test drafts at each of five flow rates.**</u>

2. <u>**Only one meter is required for the initial test, after which the meter will be reevaluated for permanence. The minimum throughput criterion for these meters is the maximum rated flow in units per minute x 2000**</u>

3. <u>**Following the period of use, the tests listed above are to be repeated. All results must be within acceptance tolerances.**</u>

Tests of Automatic Temperature Compensating Systems on Wholesale Meters (Code Reference T.2.3.4.)

The difference between the meter error for results determined with and without the automatic temperature compensating system activated shall not exceed:

1. 0.2 % of the test draft for mechanical automatic temperature compensating systems; and

2. 0.1 % of the test draft for electronic automatic temperature compensating systems.

The results of each test shall be within the applicable "acceptance" or maintenance tolerance.

Repeatability on Wholesale Meters (Code Reference T.2.3.3.)

When multiple tests are conducted at approximately the same flow rate, the range of the test results for the flow rate shall not exceed 40 % of the absolute value of the maintenance tolerance, and the results of each test shall be within the applicable tolerance. This tolerance does not apply to the test of the automatic temperature compensating system.

Tests for repeatability shall include a minimum of three consecutive test drafts of approximately the same size and be conducted under controlled conditions where variations in factors, such as temperature, pressure, and flow rate, are reduced to the extent that they will not affect the results obtained.

Discussion/Conclusion: A mass flow meter manufacturer suggested that the throughput requirement should be replaced with a time requirement of 60 days between the initial evaluation and the permanence test. The NTEP laboratories were opposed to that change because it did not include any criteria for an amount of use between tests. After some discussion the proposal for a 60-day time frame was withdrawn. Another member suggested that the reference to the Canadian throughput requirement should be removed because at this time there is no mutual recognition program between the United States and Canada for meters. The Sector agreed that the reference to Canadian throughput requirements should be editorially removed from all permanence test section in NCWM Publication 14. The Sector agreed to forward the proposal for test requirements for wholesale meters to the NTEP Committee for consideration.

6. NTEP Tolerances for Meters with Different Flow Rates when Using Different Sized Provers

Source: Maryland NTEP Laboratory

Background: During an evaluation of a high-gallonage RMFD with marked flow rates of 60 gpm maximum and 12 gpm minimum, the Maryland NTEP laboratory found that the actual flow rate on the lowest setting of the automatic nozzle was 6 GPM. Several questions need to be addressed regarding this situation.

N.4.2.2 (b) in the LMD Code states "Devices with a marked minimum flow rate shall have a "special" test performed at or near the marked minimum flow rate."

If a 10-gal test measure is used, what is the appropriate tolerance applicable? Table T.2. in the LMD Code stipulates that the special test tolerance is 0.5 %, which is 11.55 cu in on a ten-gal test draft; however, there is a footnote that states that the applicable acceptance tolerance for a special test when using a 10-gal test draft is 5.5 cu in. Which tolerance should be applied during an NTEP evaluation? If a prover with a capacity greater than 10 gallons is used, does it provide a tolerance advantage over tests conducted with a 10-gal test measure?

G-T.1. (e) states that acceptance tolerances apply to all equipment undergoing type evaluation. Does that mean that special test tolerances are not applicable during NTEP testing?

At its 2005 meeting the Sector agreed to forward a proposal to modify G-T.1. as shown below to the NCWM and Southern Weights and Measures Association S&T Committees for consideration.

Proposal: Modify H44 Sec. 1.10 Paragraphs G-T.1. Acceptance Tolerances (e) and N.4.2.2. Retail Motor-Fuel as follows:

G-T.1. Acceptance Tolerances. - Acceptance tolerances shall apply to:

(a) equipment to be put into commercial use for the first time;

(b) equipment that has been placed in commercial service within the preceding 30 days and is being officially tested for the first time;

(c) equipment that has been returned to commercial service following official rejection for failure to conform to performance requirements and is being officially tested for the first time within 30 days after corrective service;

(d) equipment that is being officially tested for the first time within 30 days after major reconditioning or overhaul; and

(e) equipment undergoing type evaluation <u>(special test tolerances are not applicable)</u>.

At the 2005 NCWM Annual Meeting, the Meter Manufacturers Association (MMA) indicated that they had not understood that the proposal submitted to the Committee from the Measuring Sector would only apply to all types of liquid-measuring devices submitted for NTEP evaluation. The MMA stated that without special test tolerances most meters, especially those installed in vehicle-mounted applications, would not meet tolerances for low flow tests during both field and NTEP evaluations. The Committee agreed to make the proposal an information item to allow the MMA and the Measuring Sector time to further develop the proposal and resubmit it to the Committee for consideration.

Prior to the addition of Table T.2. to the Handbook 44 LMD Code in 2002, the applicable tolerances in T.2.1. for "retail devices" including RMFDs were the same for normal and special tests. Special test tolerances were only applicable to "wholesale devices" measuring liquids other than agri-chemicals and asphalt. The Sector was asked to consider a recommendation that limits the application of special test tolerances in the LMD code to only those devices where it was appliclble prior to 2002.

Recommendation: The Sector reviewed the following proposal for possible forwarding to the NCWM S&T Committee for consideration along with a recommendation that the NCWM S&T Committee General Code item to amend G-T.1. be withdrawn.

Proposal: Modify Table T.2. Accuracy Classes for Liquid-Measuring Devices Covered in NIST Handbook 44 Section 3.30. as follows:

| \multicolumn{5}{c}{**Table T.2. Accuracy Classes for Liquid Measuring Devices Covered in NIST Handbook 44 Section 3.30.**} |

Accuracy Class	Application	Acceptance Tolerance	Maintenance Tolerance	Special Test Tolerance[1]
0.3	Petroleum products delivered from large capacity (flow rates over 115 L/min (30 gal/min))** devices including motor fuel devices, heated products at or greater than 50 °C asphalt at or below temperatures 50 °C, all other liquids not shown where the typical delivery is over 200 L (50 gal)	0.2 %	0.3 %	0.5 %
0.3A	Asphalt at temperatures greater than 50° C	0.3 %	0.3 %	0.5 %
0.5*	Petroleum products delivered from small capacity (at 4 L/min (1 gal/min) through 115 L/min (30 gal/min))** motor-fuel devices, agri-chemical liquids, and all other applications not shown where the typical delivery is # 200 L (50 gal)	0.3 %	0.5 %	0.5%
1.1	Petroleum products and other normal liquids from devices with flow rates** less than 1 gal/min and devices designed to deliver less than 1 gal	0.75 %	1.0 %	1.25%

*For 5 gal and 10 gal test drafts, the tolerances specified for Accuracy Class 0.5 in the table above do not apply. For these test drafts, the maintenance tolerances on normal and special tests for 5 gal and 10 gal test drafts are 6 cu in and 11 cu in, respectively. Acceptance tolerances on normal and special tests are 3 cu in and 5.5 cu in.

** Flow rate refers to designed or marked maximum flow rate.

[1] **Special Test Tolerances are not applicable to Retail Motor-fuel Dispensers or to devices used for the measurement of agri-chemical liquids and asphalt.**

(Added 2002)

Discussion/Conclusion: The Sector reviewed the proposal that would remove the special test tolerance for retail motor-fuel dispensers and wholesale meters measuring agri-chemicals and asphalt. The Sector agreed that some devices measuring agri-chemicals and asphalt should have a special test tolerance. The current definition of "retail" in Handbook 44 now applies to devices that, prior to 2004 when the definition of "retail" was changed, would have met the definition for a wholesale device because of their rated flow. When the wholesale devices measuring agri-chemicals and asphalt were classified as "wholesale," they were permitted to have a special test tolerance. Those same devices may now meet the criteria to be classified as "retail"; however they should still be allowed to have a special test tolerance. The Sector agreed to limit the proposal to only RMFDs and to forward the modified proposal shown below to the NCWM S&T Committee for consideration.

Table T.2. Accuracy Classes for Liquid-Measuring Devices Covered in NIST Handbook 44 Section 3.30.					
Accuracy Class	Application	Acceptance Tolerance	Maintenance Tolerance	Special Test Tolerance[1]
0.3	Petroleum products delivered from large capacity (flow rates over 115 L/min (30 gal/min))** devices including motor fuel devices, heated products at or greater than 50 °C asphalt at or below temperatures 50 °C, all other liquids not shown where the typical delivery is over 200 L (50 gal)	0.2 %	0.3 %	0.5 %
0.3A	Asphalt at temperatures greater than 50 °C	0.3 %	0.3 %	0.5 %
0.5*	Petroleum products delivered from small capacity (at 4 L/min (1 gal/min) through 115 L/min (30 gal/min))** motor-fuel devices, agri-chemical liquids, and all other applications not shown where the typical delivery is # 200 L (50 gal)	0.3 %	0.5 %	0.5%
1.1	Petroleum products and other normal liquids from devices with flow rates** less than 1 gal/min and devices designed to deliver less than 1 gal	0.75 %	1.0 %	1.25%

*For 5 gal and 10 gal test drafts, the tolerances specified for Accuracy Class 0.5 in the table above do not apply. For these test drafts, the maintenance tolerances on normal and special tests **(except for retail motor-fuel dispensers)** for 5 gal and 10 gal test drafts are 6 cu in and 11 cu in, respectively. Acceptance tolerances on normal and special tests **(except for retail motor-fuel dispensers)** are 3 cu in and 5.5 cu in. [1] **Special Test Tolerances are not applicable to retail motor-fuel dispensers.**
** Flow rate refers to designed or marked maximum flow rate.

(Added 2002)**(Amended 200X)**

7. **Marking Requirements for 3.32. LPG and Anhydrous Ammonia Liquid-Measuring Devices**

Source: NTEP Laboratories

Background/Discussion: At the 2005 meeting of the NTEP laboratories it was recommended that the location of markings requirement from the LMD code be added to Sections 3.32. LPG and Anhydrous Ammonia Liquid-Measuring Devices and 3.37. Mass Flow Meters.

Recommendation: The Sector was asked to review the following proposal and, if it agreed, to forward it to the NCWM S&T Committee for consideration.

Proposal: Add a new paragraph S.4.3. Location of Marking Information; Retail Motor-Fuel Dispensers to Handbook 44 Section 3.32. LPG and Anhydrous Ammonia Liquid-Measuring Devices and renumber subsequent paragraphs as follows:

S.4. Marking Requirements.

S.4.1. Limitation of Use. - If a device is intended to measure accurately only products having particular properties, or to measure accurately only under specific installation or operating conditions, or to measure accurately only when used in conjunction with specific accessory equipment, these limitations shall be clearly and permanently stated on the device.

S.4.2. Discharge Rates. - A device shall be marked to show its designed maximum and minimum discharge rates. The marked minimum discharge rate shall not exceed:

(a) 20 L (5 gal) per minute for stationary retail devices, or

(b) 20 % of the marked maximum discharge rate for other retail devices and for wholesale devices.
(Amended 1987)

Note: See example in Section 3.30. Liquid-Measuring Devices Code, Paragraph S.4.4.1.
(Added 2003)

~~**S.4.3. Location of Marking Information; Retail Motor-Fuel Dispensers.** - The required marking information in the General Code, Paragraph G.S.1. Identification shall appear as follows:~~

(a) ~~within 60 cm (24 in) to 150 cm (60 in) from the base of the dispenser;~~

(b) ~~either internally and/or externally provided the information is permanent and easily read; and~~

(c) ~~on a portion of the device that cannot be readily removed or interchanged (i.e., not on a service access panel).~~

~~**Note:** The use of a dispenser key or tool to access internal marking information is permitted for Retail Liquid-Measuring Devices.~~
~~[*Nonretroactive as of January 1, 200X]~~

S.4.~~3~~4. Temperature Compensation. - If a device is equipped with an automatic temperature compensator, the primary indicating elements, recording elements, and recorded representation shall be clearly and conspicuously marked to show that the volume delivered has been adjusted to the volume at 15 °C (60 °F).

Conclusion: There was no discussion on agenda Item 7 to add a new paragraph S.4.3. and renumber subsequent paragraphs. The Sector agreed to forward the proposal to the NCWM S&T Committee for consideration.

8. Marking Requirements for 3.37. Mass Flow Meters

Source: NTEP Laboratories

Background/Discussion: At the 2005 meeting of the NTEP laboratories it was recommended that the location of markings requirement from the LMD Code be added to Sections 3.32. LPG and Anhydrous Ammonia and 3.37. Mass Flow Meters

Recommendation: The Sector was asked to review the following proposal and, if it agreed, to forward the proposal to the S&T Committee for consideration.

Proposal: Add a new paragraph S.5.1. Location of Marking Information; Retail Motor-Fuel Dispensers to Handbook 44 Section 3.37. Mass Flow Meters and renumber subsequent paragraphs as follows:

S.5. Markings. - A measuring system shall be legibly and indelibly marked with the following information:

(a) pattern approval mark (i.e., type approval number);

(b) name and address of the manufacturer or his trademark and, if required by the weights and measures authority, the manufacturer's identification mark in addition to the trademark;

(c) model designation or product name selected by the manufacturer;

(d) nonrepetitive serial number;

(e) *the accuracy class of the meter as specified by the manufacturer consistent with Table T.2.;**
(Added 1994)

(f) maximum and minimum flow rates in pounds per unit of time;

(g) maximum working pressure;

(h) applicable range of temperature if other than –10 °C to +50 °C;

(i) minimum measured quantity; and

(j) product limitations, if applicable.

[*Nonretroactive as of January 1, 1995]

~~**S.5.1. Location of Marking Information; Retail Motor-Fuel Dispensers.** - The required marking information in the General Code, Paragraph G.S.1 Identification shall appear as follows:~~

~~(d) within 60 cm (24 in) to 150 cm (60 in) from the base of the dispenser;~~

~~(e) either internally and/or externally provided the information is permanent and easily read; and~~

~~(f) on a portion of the device that cannot be readily removed or interchanged (i.e., not on a service access panel).~~

~~**Note:** The use of a dispenser key or tool to access internal marking information is permitted for Retail Liquid-Measuring Devices.~~
~~[*Nonretroactive as of January 1, 200X]~~

S.5.~~1~~2. Marking of Gasoline Volume Equivalent Conversion Factor. -   A device dispensing compressed natural gas shall have either the statement "One Gasoline Liter Equivalent (GLE) is Equal to 0.678 kg of Natural Gas" or "One Gasoline Gallon Equivalent (GGE) is Equal to 5.660 lb of Natural Gas" permanently and conspicuously marked on the face of the dispenser according to the method of sale used.
(Added 1994)

Conclusion: There was no discussion on agenda Item 8 to add a new paragraph S.5.1. and renumber subsequent paragraphs. The Sector agreed to forward the proposal to the NCWM S&T Committee for consideration.

9. **Value of the Smallest Unit for Liquid Measuring Devices (LMD) Code**

Source: WMD

Background/Discussion: In 2004 the definition of a "retail device" in Handbook 44 was modified to include all devices used to measure product for the purpose of sale to the end user. At that time the S&T Committee believed all affected parties were aware of the proposal and there was no opposition to the change. However, after the 2005 Edition of Handbook 44 was published and distributed, WMD received a comment from a weights and measures jurisdiction that routinely tests large meters used to deliver fuel to fishing fleets and other large ocean-going boats. The jurisdiction stated that the average delivery is approximately 300 000 gal and may be as much as 1 000 000 gal. At the present time value of the smallest unit of the indicated delivery for these devices is 1 gal. Because the fuel is being delivered to the end user, the jurisdiction believes this is a retail delivery and that Handbook 44 now requires a smallest unit of delivery of not more than 0.5 L (1 pt) for these devices. WMD recommends a change to Handbook 44 is appropriate to recognize a larger minimum unit of delivery for large fuel deliveries.

Recommendation: The Sector was asked to review the following proposal and if it agreed, to forward it to the S&T Committee for   consideration. It was also suggested that as an alternative, the Sector could decide it was more appropriate to form a work group to develop suitability criteria for all meters, including such things as minimum and maximum flow rate, minimum resolution, minimum measured quantity, etc., for an application and forward the concept to the S&T Committee as a developing issue.

Proposal: Modify Handbook 44, Section 3.30., S.1.2.3. Value of Smallest Unit as follows:

> **S.1.2.3. Value of Smallest Unit.** - The value of the smallest unit of indicated delivery, and recorded delivery if the device is equipped to record, shall not exceed the equivalent of:
>
> (a) 0.5 L (~~1 pt~~ 0.1 gal) on ~~retail~~ devices <u>making a delivery of less than 1000 gal;</u>
>
> (b) 5 L (1 gal) on ~~wholesale~~ devices <u>making a delivery of 1000 gal or more.</u>
>
> This requirement does not apply to manually operated devices equipped with stops or stroke-limiting means. (Amended 1983 and 1986)

Discussion/Conclusion: The Sector supported the concept of the proposal; however, during the discussion of the item, a recommendation was made to base the smallest unit requirement on meter size (marked flow rate) rather than the size of the delivery. The Sector agreed and modified the proposal as shown below. The Sector agreed to forward the modified proposal to the NCWM S&T Committee for consideration.

Proposal: Modify Handbook 44, paragraph S.1.2.3. as follows:

> **S.1.2.3. Value of Smallest Unit.** - The value of the smallest unit of indicated delivery, and recorded delivery if the device is equipped to record, shall not exceed the equivalent of:
>
> (a) 0.5 L (~~1 pt~~ **0.1 gal**) on ~~retail~~ devices <u>**with a maximum rated flow rate of 750 L/min (200 gal/min) or less.**</u>
>
> (b) 5 L (1 gal) on ~~wholesale~~ devices <u>**with a maximum rated flow of more than 750 L/min (200 gal/min).**</u>
>
> This requirement does not apply to manually operated devices equipped with stops or stroke-limiting means. **(Amended 1983, ~~and~~ 1986, and 200X)**

10. Value of the Smallest Unit for Vehicle-Tank Meters (VTM) Code

Source: Maryland NTEP Laboratory

Background/Discussion: Paragraph S.1.1.3. in the VTM Code requires the smallest unit of indicated delivery to be not greater than 0.5 L (0.1 gal) for deliveries on meters with a rated maximum flow rate of 500 L/min (100 gal/min) or less used for retail deliveries of liquid fuel and 5 L (1 gal) for all other meters (except milk-metering systems). VTMs with rated maximum flow rates greater than 100 gal/min are being introduced into the marketplace; however, the amount of the increase in flow rate and the amount of product being delivered do not warrant a tenfold increase in the required value of the smallest unit of measurement.

Recommendation: The Sector was asked to review the following proposal and consider forwarding it to the NCWM S&T Committee for consideration.

Proposal: Modify Handbook 44, Section 3.31., Paragraph S.1.1.3. Value of the Smallest Unit. as follows:

> **S.1.1.3. Value of Smallest Unit.** - The value of the smallest unit of indicated delivery, and recorded delivery if the meter is equipped to record, shall not exceed the equivalent of:
>
> (a) 0.5 L (0.1 gal) or 0.5 kg (1 lb) on milk-metering systems
>
> (b) 0.5 L (0.1 gal) on meters with a rated maximum flow rate of ~~500~~ **750** L/min (~~100~~ **200** gal/min) or less used for retail deliveries of liquid fuel, or

(c) 5 L (1 gal) on other meters.

Discussion/Conclusion: The Sector reviewed a proposal to increase the rated maximum flow rate criteria in S.1.1.3. from 100 gal/min to 200 gal/min. Some manufacturers of aviation refueling systems suggested that these systems need a separate criterion due to the unique nature of their application. The Sector agreed with the aviation refueler manufacturers and agreed to forward the modified proposal shown below to the NCWM S&T Committee for consideration.

Proposal: Modify Paragraph S.1.1.3. as follows:

> **S.1.1.3. Value of Smallest Unit.** - The value of the smallest unit of indicated delivery, and recorded delivery if the meter is equipped to record, shall not exceed the equivalent of:
>
> (a) 0.5 L (0.1 gal) or 0.5 kg (1 lb) on milk-metering systems,
>
> (b) 0.5 L (0.1 gal) on meters with a rated maximum flow rate of ~~500~~ **750** L/min (~~100~~ **200** gal/min) or less used for ~~retail~~ deliveries of liquid fuel, or
> (**Amended 200X)**
>
> **(c) 5 L (1 gal) on meters with a rated maximum flow of 575 L/min (150 gal/min) or more used for aviation refueling systems.**
> **(Added 200X)**
>
> (~~c~~**d**) 5 L (1 gal) on other meters.

11. Add Fluid Ounce to NIST Handbook 44, Section 3.30. Liquid-Measuring Devices, Paragraph S.1.2. Units

Source: NTEP Laboratories

Background: NTEP issued a CC for a liquid-measuring device that displays its deliveries in fluid ounces. The device currently in use always makes a delivery of 4 fl oz. A weights and measures jurisdiction would not approve the use of the device stating that it did not comply with S.1.2. in the LMD Code. Paragraph S.1.2. allows binary submultiples of the liter or gallon; therefore an indication of 1/32 gallon would be acceptable. The laboratories agreed that consumers would understand 4 fl oz better than 1/32 of a gallon and suggested the Measuring Sector review the following proposal and consider recommending it to the NCWM S&T Committee for adoption into Handbook 44.

Recommendation: Modify Handbook 44, Section 3.30, S.1.2. Units, as follows:

> **S.1.2. Units.** - A liquid-measuring device shall indicate, and record if the device is equipped to record, its deliveries in liters, gallons, quarts, pints, **fluid ounces** or binary-submultiples or decimal subdivisions of the liter or gallon. (Amended 1987, 1994)

Conclusion: The Sector supported the proposal to modify S.1.2. and agreed to forward the proposal a recommended to the NCWM S&T Committee for consideration.

12. Reorganize Publication 14 to Clarify Tests of Electronic Cash Registers (ECR) for Retail Motor-Fuel Dispensers (RMFD)

Source: NTEP Laboratories

Background: At the 2005 NTEP Laboratory Meeting, one of the Measuring labs stated that the LMD section of Publication 14 was not well organized. During an NTEP evaluation the evaluator must continuously flip from one section of the publication to another to find all the requirements applicable to the device under test. The lab also stated

NTEP Committee 2006 Final Report
Appendix B – NTETC Measuring Sector

that the evaluation of an ECR interfaced with a RMFD required the use of both the ECR Checklist and the LMD Checklist in order to find all the applicable requirements. The California laboratory volunteered to provide a draft reorganization of LMD Checklist and a draft of a revised ECR checklist with the applicable requirements added from the LMD checklist. Drafts of the reorganized LMD checklist and the revised ECR checklist are available from NIST WMD upon request.

Recommendation: The Sector was asked to review the drafts submitted and, if agreeable, to forward them to the NTEP Committee for approval as revisions to the 2006 version of Publication 14.

Conclusion: The Sector supported the concept provided all NTEP laboratories and other interested parties conduct a thorough review of the proposed changes before they are incorporated in NCWM Publication 14. The NTEP Director, Steve Patoray, agreed to post the draft changes as shown in Appendices A and B on the NCWM website.

13. Next Meeting

The Sector discussed the time and location for its next meeting. The Sector supported having its next meeting immediately prior to the Annual Meeting of the Southern Weights and Measures Association which will be held in Annapolis, Maryland. Maryland Weights and Measures offered to host a tour of the Maryland NTEP facility in the morning of the first day of the meeting.

14. Multi-point Calibration (linearization) for Meters

Source: NTEP Laboratories

Background/Discussion: At the 2005 NTEP Laboratory Meeting, one of the labs noted a concern that some meter manufacturers are using multi-point calibration (linearization) to expand the range of flow rates for a meter submitted for type evaluation. Neither Handbook 44 nor Publication 14 prohibit or provide requirements for the use of multi-point calibration for meters. The laboratories agreed that, if multi-point calibrations are used during an evaluation, it must be noted on the CC for the device and that installations must include that feature. The laboratories also agreed that multi-point calibration should only be used to extend the range of flow rates beyond a turn-down ratio of 5 to 1. Any meter submitted for evaluation utilizing multi-point calibration must be able to meet test requirements over a turn-down ratio of 5 to 1 without multi-point calibration and then would be tested using multi-point calibration to expand the range of flow rates beyond a ratio of 5 to 1.

At the time of distribution of this agenda a specific proposal for addition to Handbook 44 or Publication 14 had not been submitted by any of the NTEP laboratories. This item is included on the agenda to alert the members of a concern and to solicit input on the subject that may appear as an agenda item at the next Sector Meeting.

Conclusion: The Sector discussed the concerns of the NTEP laboratories and agreed that the use of multi-point calibration should be restricted to only extending the turn-down range to a ratio of greater than 5 to 1. During the meeting the Sector developed a modification to Section "G" of the technical policy on page LMD – 6 of the 2005 edition of NCWM Publication 14 as shown below and agreed to forward the recommended change to the NTEP Committee for consideration.

Modify Publication 14 Technical Policy Section G. Range of Data Points as follows:

G. Range of Data Points

The number and types of tests to be run on devices covered under this checklist are specified in the Checklist and Test Procedures section and the Field Evaluation and Permanence Tests for Metering Systems section of this checklist. However, if the NTEP laboratory feels that there is a performance or other Handbook 44 related problem and provides reasons to support this belief, the laboratory is given the latitude to require additional testing.

Multi-point calibration shall be blind and integral (programmed during manufacture and not accessible in the field) to the measuring element or it shall not be used to establish the minimum flow range required (5:1 or 10:1, etc., as required). Programmable multi-point calibration can be used to extend the range of a system beyond the minimum range required for the measuring element. The use of multi-point calibration to extend the range will be noted on the CC.

15. Audit Trail Remote Configuration

Source: NTEP Laboratories

Background/Discussion: At the 2005 NTEP Laboratory Meeting, one of the labs noted a concern that some retail motor-fuel dispensers do not meet the sealing requirements for Category 1 devices because of the definition of remote configuration capability in Handbook 44. Remote configuration capability is defined as "the ability to adjust a weighing or measuring device or change its sealable parameters from or through some other device that is not itself necessary to the operation of the weighing or measuring device or is not a permanent part of that device." The mechanism for changing blend ratios on some dispensers, while not required for normal operation of the device, is not a "permanent" part of the device.

At the time of distribution of the agenda a specific proposal for addition to Handbook 44 or Publication 14 had not been submitted by any of the NTEP laboratories. This item was included on the agenda to alert the members of a concern and to solicit input on the subject that may appear as an agenda item at the next Sector Meeting.

The Sector discussed NIST Handbook 44 codes for liquid-measuring devices that do not have specific provisions for electronic sealing (i.e., audit trails) in the code, such as the Vehicle-Tank Meters Code or the LPG and Anhydrous Ammonia Metering-Devices Code. At the meeting, manufacturers of these devices stated that they have designed metering systems with electronic sealing capability with remote configuration capability. They are currently seeking an NTEP Certificate of Conformance (CC) for these systems. Currently the specific NIST Handbook 44 code for these devices does not address electronic sealing, but it is recognized in the General Code and under the provisions of G-A.3. Special and Unclassified Equipment. Accordingly, NTEP has made an *ad hoc* decision to apply the criteria in the LMD Code to these devices; however, the manufacturers would prefer specific language similar to that in the Liquid-Measuring Devices (LMD) Code. During the discussion, the Sector concluded that some of these new applications and other applications currently in use would have been classified as the former device Category 2 device.

Conclusion: The Sector agreed that the decision to remove Category 2 from the LMD Code and the Mass Flow Meters Code should be reversed and that provisions for electronic sealing should be added to liquid-measuring devices codes 3.30. Liquid-Measuring Devices, 3.31. Vehicle-Tank Meters, 3.32. LPG and Anhydrous Ammonia Liquid-Measuring Devices, 3.34. Hydrocarbon Gas Vapor-Measuring Devices, 3.35. Milk Meters, and 3.38. Carbon Dioxide Liquid-Measuring Devices and agreed to forward that proposal to the Committee for consideration. The technical advisor, Dick Suiter, NIST, will develop the specific proposal for the recommended change to each of the codes listed above.

16. New Product Application for Meters and Formula for the Proper Calculation of Relative Error

(Note: This item was added to the agenda during the Sector meeting.)

Source: FMC Smith Meter

Recommendation: Amend Section "F" of the LMD Technical Policy in Publication 14 as shown in the proposal below:

Proposal: If a manufacturer wants to add a new product to an existing family of meters, the following criteria will be applied:

1. If the accuracy class in NIST Handbook 44 for the new product falls within the same NIST Handbook 44 accuracy class or a more strict accuracy class than the most strict accuracy class covered on the Certificate of Conformance, the entire range of meters sizes will be covered for product tested.

2. If the accuracy class in NIST Handbook 44 for the new product falls within a less strict NIST Handbook 44 accuracy class than the most strict accuracy class covered by the Certificate, the new product will only be covered for meters meeting the requirements of paragraph E, Meters Sizes to be included on a Certificate of Conformance.

   If the product being added is from a family of products that has been previously subjected to the permanence test, then the requirement for a permanence test may be waived provided the initial test of the product being added meets following conditions:

   a) the results of the initial test were not questionable; and
   b) multi-point calibration may not be used to add the new product.

Make the following editorial change to NCWM Publication 14 LMD Checklists to add the formula for the proper calculation of relative error

Percent Error = [(Indicated – Actual) / Actual] x 100

Where "Actual" = the amount delivered corrected for appropriate influence factors.

Discussion/Conclusion: At the Sector meeting, FMC Smith Meter requested that Section "F" be modified, as shown above, to allow the addition of a new product to a CC that already includes product(s) from the same product family as the product to be added. FMC Smith Meter also suggested that the formula for proper calculation of relative error should be added to all of the LMD checklists to provide uniformity between the NTEP laboratories when calculating errors during NTEP evaluations. The Sector reviewed the proposed change to Section "F" and agreed to forward the proposal to the NTEP Committee for consideration. The Sector also agreed that the formula for proper calculation of relative error should be added to all of the LMD checklists to provide uniformity between the NTEP laboratories when calculating errors during NTEP evaluations.

Appendix A
2005 Measuring Sector Meeting Attendees

Name	Company/Agency	Address	Telephone #	E-Mail Address
Beattie, Dennis	Measurement Canada	4th Floor 400 St Mary Avenue Winnipeg, Manitoba, Canada R3C 4K5	(204) 983-8910	Beattie.dennis@ic.gc.ca
Belue, Mike	Belue Associates	1319 Knight Drive Murfreesboro, TN 37128	(615) 867-1010	bassoc@aol.com
Beyer, Joseph	Liquid Controls	105 Albrecht Drive Lake Bluff, IL 60044	(847) 283-8300	jbeyer@idexcorp.com
Butler, Jerry W.	North Carolina Dept of Agriculture	1050 Mail Service Center Raleigh, NC 27699-1050	(919) 733-3313	Jerry.butler@ncmail.net
Buxton, Joe	Daniel Measurement Control	19267 Hwy 301 N Statesboro, GA 30461	(912) 489-0253	Joe.buxton@emersonprocess.com
Castro, Gary	State of California Meas Stds	8500 Fruitridge Road Sacramento, CA 95826	(916) 229-3049	gcastro@cdfa.ca.gov
Cleary, Michael	California Div of Meas Stds	6790 Florin Perkins Road Ste 100 Sacramento, CA 95828	(916) 229-3000	mcleary@cdfa.ca.gov
Cook, Steven	NIST/OWM	Stop 2600 100 Bureau Drive Gaithersburg, MD 20878	(301) 975-4003	steven.cook@nist.gov
Cooper, Rodney	Actaris Neptune	1310 Emerald Road Greenwood, SC 29646	(864) 942-2226	rcooper@greenwood.actaris.com
DeMarco, Stephen	Dresser Wayne	3814 Jerrett Way Austin, TX 78728	(512) 388-8601	steve.demarco@wayne.com
Forkert, Maurice	Tuthill Transfer Systems	8825 Aviation Drive Ft. Wayne, IN 46809	(260) 747-7529	mforkert@tuthill.com
Frailer, Michael	Maryland Department of Agriculture	50 Harry S. Truman Parkway Annapolis, MD 21401	(410) 841-5790	michaelfrailer@comcast.net
Gallo, Mike	Clean Fuel Technologies	140 Market Street Georgetown, TX 78626	(512) 942-8304	mike.gallo@cleanfuelusa.com
Glowacki, Paul	Murray Equipment, Inc.	2515 Charleston Place Fort Wayne, IN 46808	(260) 484-0382	pglowacki@murrayequipment.com
Hoffman, David	Toptech Systems	280 Hunt Park Cove Longwood, FL 32750	(407) 332-1774	dhoffman@toptech.com
Johnson, Gordon	Marconi Commerce Systems Inc	7300 W. Friendly Avenue Greensboro, NC 27420	(336) 547-5375	gordon.johnson@gilbarco.com
Katalinic, Allen	North Carolina Dept of Agriculture	1050 Mail Service Center Raleigh, NC 27699-1050	(919) 733-3313	None available
Katselnik, Yefim	Dresser Wayne	3814 Jarrett Way Austin, TX 78728	(512) 388-8763	Phil.katselnik@wayne.com
Keilty, Mike	Endress & Hauser Flowtech AG	2350 Endress Place Greenwood, IN 46143	(317) 535-2745	michael.keilty@us.endress.com
Lachance, Christian	Measurement Canada	Stds Bldg #4 Tunney's Pasture Ottawa, Ontario, Canada K1AOC9	(613) 952-3528	lachance.christian@ic.gc.ca
Long, Douglas	RDM Industrial Electronics	850 Harmony Grove Road Nebo, NC 28761	(828) 652-8346	doug@wnclink.com
Miller, Richard	FMC Measurement Solutions	1602 Wagner Ave, Box 10428 Erie, PA 16514	(814) 898-5286	rich.miller@fmcti.com
Murnane, Robert	Seraphin Test Measure	P.O. Box 227 Rancocas, NJ 08073	(609) 267-0922	rmurnane@pemfab.com
Numrych, Charlene	Liquid Controls LLC	105 Albrecht Drive Lake Bluff, IL 60044	(847) 283-8330	cnumrych@idexcorp.com
Onwiler, Don	Nebraska Div of Weights & Meas	301 Centennial Mall South P.O. Box 94757 Lincoln, NE 68509	(402) 471-4292	donlo@agr.ne.gov
Parrish, Johnny	Brodie Meter Co., LLC	19267 Highway 301, North Statesboro, GA 30461	(912) 489-0203	Johnny.parrish@brodiemeter.com

Appendix A
2005 Measuring Sector Meeting Attendees

Name	Company/Agency	Address	Telephone #	E-Mail Address
Patoray, Steve	NTEP/NCWM	1239 Carolina Drive Tryon, NC 28782	(828) 859-6178	spatoray@mgmtsol.com
Rajala, David	Veder-Root Company	P.O. Box 1673 Altoona, PA 19906-1673	(814) 696-8125	drajala@veeder.com
Suiter, Richard C.	NIST/OWM	Stop 2600 100 Bureau Drive Gaithersburg, MD 20878	(301) 975-4406	rsuiter@nist.gov
Truex, James C.	Ohio Department of Agriculture	8995 E. Main Street Bldg. 5 Reynoldsburg, OH 43068-3399	(614) 728-6290	truex@mail.agri.state.oh.us
Wotthlie, Richard	State of Maryland	50 Harry S. Truman Parkway Annapolis, MD 21771	(410) 841-5790	wotthlrw@mda.state.md.us

Appendix C

National Type Evaluation Technical Committee
Weighing Sector Annual Meeting

September 25 - 27, 2005 – Columbus, Ohio
Meeting Summary

Carry-over Items C3

   1. Recommendations to Update NCWM Publication 14 to Reflect Changes to NIST Handbook 44.......C2
      (a) Footnote to S.1.8.4..C3
      (b) Automatic Zero-Setting Mechanism (Zero-tracking)..C3
      (c) Table S.6.3.b. Note 3 – Nominal Capacity and Value..C3
      (d) Time Dependence (Creep Test) for Scales..C4
      (e) Time Dependence (Creep Test) for Load Cells..C5
   2. Identification: Built-for-Purpose Software-based Devices..C5
   3. S.1.1.c. Zero Indication (Marking Requirements)...C6
   4. Bench/Counter Scale Shift Test and Definitions..C8
   5. Publication 14 Force Transducer (Load Cell) Family and Selection Criteria......................................C8
   6. Compatibility of Indicators Interfaced with Weighing and Measuring Elements................................C9
   7. Handbook 44 Computing Scales Interfaced with an Electronic Cash Register..................................C10
   8. Publication 14 - New Items in Computing Scale Section...C11
   9. CLC Type Evaluation Tests on Railway Track/Vehicle Scales – Technical Policy............................C12
   10. Tare on Multiple Range Scales..C13
   11. Performance and Permanence Tests for Railway Track Scales Used to Weigh Statically..................C15
   12. Cash Acceptors or Card-activated Systems...C17
   13. Ranges Covered on the CC for a Railway Track Scale Based on the Device Evaluated....................C19

New Items C19

   14. CLC for Combination Railway Track/Vehicle Scales...C19
   15. Abbreviations for Carat and Count in Publication 14 Sections 38. and 76...C20
   16. Performance and Permanence Test for Bench and Counter Scales...C21
   17. Minimum Height of Weight and Units Indications...C22
   18. Automatic Weighing Systems Influence Factor Temperature Ranges that Exceed –10 °C to 40 °C..C23
   19. Criteria for Railway Track Scales With a Rotary Dump Option...C26
   20. Permanence Tests for Identification Information..C26
   21. Next Sector Meeting...C26

Appendix A. Recommendations C27

   Agenda Item 1 (a) Footnote to S.1.8.4...C29
   Agenda Item 1 (b) Automatic Zero-Setting Mechanism (Zero-tracking)..C29
   Agenda Item 1 (c) and 20. Table S.6.3.b. Note 3 – Nominal Capacity and Value & Permanence Tests
      for Identification Information..C30
   Agenda Item 1 (d) Time Dependence (Creep Test) for Scales..C38
   Agenda Item 1 (e) Time Dependence (Creep Test) for Load Cells...C41
   Agenda Item 11. Performance and Permanence Tests for Railway Track Scales Used to Weigh
      Statically...C44

Agenda Item 12. Cash Acceptors or Card-activated Systems...C47
Agenda Item 14. CLC for Combination Railway Track/Vehicle Scales....................................C48
Agenda Item 15. Abbreviations for Carat and Count in Publication 14 Sections 38 and 76......C49
Agenda Item 16. Performance and Permanence Test for Bench and Counter Scales.................C50
Agenda Item 18. AWS Influence Factor Temperature Ranges that Exceed –10 °C to 40 °C....C50

Appendix B. Meeting Attendees C52

Carry-over Items

1. Recommended Changes to Publication 14 Based on Actions at the 2005 NCWM Annual Meeting

The NTEP technical advisor provided the Sector with specific recommendations for incorporating test procedures and checklist language based upon actions of the 2005 Annual Meeting of the National Conference on Weights and Measures (NCWM). The Sector was asked to briefly discuss each item and provide general input on the technical aspects of the issues.

(a) Footnote to S.1.8.4.

Background: See the Report of the 90 [th] NCWM, Specifications and Tolerances (S&T) Committee Agenda Item 320-1 for additional background information. During its 2005 Annual Meeting, the NCWM agreed to amend NIST Handbook 44 Scales Code paragraph footnote to S.1.8.4. Recorded Representations, Point-of-Sale Systems to nonretroactively prohibit the use of the "#" symbol.

Discussion: The Weighing Sector considered a proposal from the NIST Technical Advisor to amend NCWM Publication 14 Weighing Devices Technical Policy, Checklists, Test Procedures Digital Electronic Scales (DES) Section 76. List of Acceptable Abbreviations and Symbols and Electronic Cash Registers Interfaced with Scales (ECRS) Section 11 Recorded Representation Point-of-Sale Systems.

Recommendation: **The Sector recommends that amendments proposed in Appendix A-Agenda Item 1(a) be incorporated into NCWM Publication 14 DES Section 76. List of Acceptable Abbreviations and ECRS Section 11. Recorded Representation Point-of-Sale Systems.**

(b) Automatic Zero-Setting Mechanism (Zero-tracking)

Background: See the Report of the 90 [th] NCWM, Specifications and Tolerances (S&T) Committee Agenda Item 320-4 for additional background information. During its 2005 Annual Meeting, the NCWM agreed to amend NIST Handbook 44 2.20. Scales Code paragraph S.2.1.3. Scales Equipped with an Automatic Zero-Setting Mechanism (AZSM), add new paragraphs S.2.1.3.1. Zero-Tracking for Scales Manufactured between January 1, 1981, and January 1, 2007, and S.2.1.3.2. Zero-Tracking for Scales Manufactured on or After January 1, 2007, and renumber paragraph S.2.1.3.3. Means to Disable Zero-Tracking on Class III L Devices.

Discussion: The Weighing Sector considered a proposal from the NIST Technical Advisor to amend NCWM Publication 14 Weighing Devices Technical Policy, Checklists, Test Procedures Digital Electronic Scales (DES) Section 43. The NIST Technical Advisor responded to a question on the AZSM requirements for Class III vehicle scales, Class III L scales, and Class IIII scales. The language that was adopted by the NCWM states that the AZSM limit for vehicle, axle-load, and railway track scales is 3.0 scale divisions for both Class III and III L Vehicle Scales. Wheel-load weighers must meet the same requirements as other scales in paragraph S.2.1.3.2. (b).

Recommendation: **The Sector recommends that amendments proposed in Appendix A-Agenda Item 1(b) be incorporated into NCWM Publication 14 DES Section 43. Automatic Zero-Setting Mechanism.**

(c) Table S.6.3.b. Note 3 – Nominal Capacity and Value

Background: See the Report of the 90 [th] NCWM, Specifications and Tolerances (S&T) Committee Agenda Item 320-5 for additional background information on the location and content for the marking of nominal capacity by division. During its 2005 Annual Meeting, the NCWM agreed to amend NIST Handbook 44 2.20. Scales Code Table S.6.3.b. Note 3 – Nominal Capacity and Value.

Discussion: The Weighing Sector considered a proposal from the NIST Technical Advisor to amend NCWM Publication 14 Weighing Devices Technical Policy, Checklists, Test Procedures Digital Electronic Scales (DES) Sections 1 and 2, and Electronic Cash Registers Interfaced with Scales (ECRS) Sections 5 and 7.

NTEP Committee 2006 Final Report
Appendix C – NTETC Weighing Sector - Appendix A. Recommendations

The Sector requested clarification on what is meant by the phrase "readily apparent by the design of the device" in the previous editions of Handbook 44 Scales Code Table S.6.3.b. Note 3. They also reported that field officials, in both the United States and Canada, have repeatedly raised questions and suggested that pictures or diagrams be included in Publication 14 that demonstrate the meaning of the existing language. The Sector also suggested that examples of acceptable "capacity by value" markings and that the terms "Max," "min," and "e" be included in Publication 14 as examples of acceptable markings for "capacity by value."

Recommendation: **The Sector recommends that amendments in Appendix A-Agenda Item 1(c) be incorporated into NCWM Publication 14 DES with the three drawings from the Report of the 90 th NCWM, S&T Committee Agenda Item 320-5 and an example using the international markings such as "Max", "e $_{min}$", and "d" be included in Publication 14 [1]. Additionally, the Sector recommended that examples such as single revolution dials, beam scales[2] (excluding tip weights) be added to Publication 14 to demonstrate what is meant by the phrase "readily apparent by the design of the device."**

NIST Technical Advisor's Notes:

1. The Sector recommendation to amend the capacity markings sections of Publication 14 in **Appendix A-Agenda Item 1(c)** have been consolidated with the Sector recommend changes in Agenda Item 20. Permanence Tests for Identification Information.

2. WMD disagrees with the recommendation to exclude beam scales with tip weights from the capacity by division marking requirements. The example of a portable platform scale with supplemental weights should be required to be marked with a capacity by division statement since the sum of the supplemental weights are not readily apparent when viewing the reading face of the scale. Additionally, supplemental weights that are normally furnished with the scale may have been removed or additional weights may have been added which, according to the definition of "nominal capacity" in Handbook 44 Appendix D, would change its "nominal capacity". If supplemental weights are added in addition to the weights normally supplied with the scale, the scale would be overloaded beyond its intended capacity for both shift and increasing load tests. If weights were removed, shift tests would not be conducted with the appropriate amount of weight based on the intended scale capacity. Markings that included the nominal capacity would make the field inspector and user aware of the intended capacity of the scale for both use and test whether or not supplemental weights have been added to or removed from the scale.

During the discussion of this item the Sector noted that the use of "d" and "e" are used interchangeably in NIST Handbook 44. This can lead to the incorrect application of requirements applied to weighing devices where the scale division "d" is different than the verification division "e." Additionally, the terms graduation, interval, and division are not consistently used throughout the Scale Code. A small work group consisting of Darrell Flocken (Mettler Toledo), Gary Lameris (Hobart Corporation), the Ohio NTEP Lab, and Paul Lewis (Rice Lake Weighing) will review the entire Scales Code and develop a recommendation to amend Handbook 44 so that the abbreviations, terms, and definitions are used correctly and consistently in the code.

(d) Time Dependence (Creep Test) for Scales

Background: See the 2005 NCWM Publication 16 Committee Reports of the 90 th National Conference on Weights and Measures, Specifications and Tolerances Committee Agenda item 320-8 for additional background information. During its 2005 Annual Meeting, the NCWM agreed to amend NIST Handbook 44 Scales Code paragraph T.N.4.5. Time Dependence and add new paragraphs T.N.4.5.1. Time Dependence Class II, III, and IIII Non-automatic Weighing Instruments, and T.N.4.5.2. Time Dependence; Class III L Non-automatic Weighing Instruments.

Discussion: The Weighing Sector considered a proposal from the NIST Technical Advisor to amend NCWM Publication 14 Weighing Devices Technical Policy, Checklists, Test Procedures Digital Electronic Scales (DES) Section 58. Time Dependence Test. Some members of the Sector requested clarification on the ambient test conditions and automatic zero-tracking information in the proposed test form. The NIST Technical Advisor reported that the ambient test conditions recorded on the test form are the same as the test forms used in OIML R 76-2. The information on the test form regarding the operational status of the AZSM was considered as optional information and is not on the equivalent OIML test form and will be removed from the proposed test form. The Sector questioned the meaning of some of the symbols in the proposed test form and suggested that they be defined on the test form.

There were additional discussions that existing test procedures in Publication 14 requires that the creep test be performed at 20 °C, –10 °C, and 40 °C. OIML R 76 states that only one influences factor be tested at one time and that performing creep test at the various temperatures is considered as combining the influence factors of time and temperature. Members of the Sector believed that this subject should be submitted to Sector as a new agenda item, or be considered by the NCWM Specifications and Tolerance Committee.

Recommendation: The Sector recommends that amendments in Appendix A-Agenda Item 1(d), with changes to the test form recommended by the Sector, be incorporated into NCWM Publication 14.

  (e) Time Dependence (Creep Test) for Load Cells

Background: See the 2005 NCWM Publication 16 Committee Reports of the 90th National Conference on Weights and Measures, Specifications and Tolerances Committee Agenda item 320-8 for additional background information regarding load cell creep test tolerances during type evaluation. During its 2005 Annual Meeting, the NCWM agreed to add NIST Handbook 44 Scales Code paragraph T.N.4.6. Time Dependence for Load Cells During Type Evaluation and Table T.N.4.6. Maximum Permissible Error (mpe) for Load Cells During Type Evaluation.

Discussion: The NIST Technical Advisor reported that NIST Weights and Measures Division (WMD) will be submitting a proposal to a regional weights and measures association S&T committee to add creep recovery test procedures that were inadvertently omitted from the proposal to add the Time Dependence requirements and <u>lower</u> the apportionment factors to better align NIST Handbook 44 with the 2005 Edition of NCWM Publication 14.

The Weighing Sector also considered a proposal from the NIST Technical Advisor to amend NCWM Publication 14 Weighing Devices Technical Policy, Checklists, Test Procedures for Force Transducers Section L. II Determination of Creep.

Recommendation: The Sector recommends that the proposed language provided by the NIST Technical Advisor with editorial corrections to the language as recommended by the Sector in Appendix A-Agenda Item 1(e) be included in the 2006 Edition of NCWM Publication 14 Force Transducers (Load Cells).

The NIST Technical Advisor has submitted a proposal to the Southern Weights and Measures Association S&T Committee that would correct the tolerances applied to Class III L load cells and add the creep recovery tolerances that were inadvertently omitted in the 2005 NCWM S&T Committee agenda item 320-8.

Pending action by the 91st NCWM Specification and Tolerances Committee in 2006 on this WMD proposal, the Sector recommends that no corresponding changes should be made to Table T.N.4.6. in the proposal to amend Publication 14 and that the creep test recovery procedures be deleted from the language submitted by the NIST Technical Advisor.

2. Identification: Built-for-Purpose Software-based Devices

Background: See the 2005 Report of the 90th National Conference on Weights and Measures, Specifications and Tolerances Committee Agenda Item 320-1 in NCWM Publication 16 for additional background information and the proposed software identification language considered by the S&T Committee.

At the 2005 Annual Meeting of the NCWM, the S&T Committee heard no support for this item in its present form and agreed to withdraw the item from is agenda. The S&T Committee encouraged the regional Weights and Measures Associations, and associations of device manufacturers to develop and resubmit a new proposal if they think it is appropriate.

Additionally, the NCWM Board of Directors agreed to establish an NTETC Software Sector. That Sector will tentatively meet in April 2006. The charge of the Software Sector is to:

NTEP Committee 2006 Final Report
Appendix C – NTETC Weighing Sector - Appendix A. Recommendations

- Develop a clear understanding of the use of software for the operation of today's weighing and measuring instruments. This first step is important to permit the direction of the efforts mentioned in the next steps.
- Develop Handbook 44 specifications as needed to provide appropriate requirements for software incorporated into weighing and measuring devices and adequate tools for field verification and enforcement of such devices to include security requirements, simple identification means, etc.
- Revise existing or develop new Publication 14 checklists to provide NTEP laboratories the capability of identifying and certifying software or software components as being metrologically compliant with Handbook 44 requirements including, but not limited to its functions, marking, and security.
- Consider the development of guidelines for and promote training of weights and measures officials in proper application of Handbook 44 in verifying software as compliant and traceable to a NTEP Certificate of Conformance (CC).

Individuals interested in participating as members of the Software Sector were requested to contact Jim Truex, NTEP Committee Chairman.

Discussion: The Weighing Sector reviewed the background information and heard comments from Don Onwiler, NCWM Chairman, that the first meeting of the Software Sector will be held in conjunction with the 2006 meeting of the NTEP Participating Laboratories. The NTEP Committee has requested volunteers to participate in the Sector, including people who are experienced in developing metrological software. WMD recommended that the Software Sector consider soliciting input from foreign metrological regulatory agencies that have experience with regulating metrological software used in weighing and measuring devices and other U.S. Government Agencies that have experience in verifying the performance and security of software. Mettler Toledo reported that they have had some contact with the Western European Legal Metrology Cooperation (WELMEC) and experience with WELMEC Guide 2.3. Guide for Examining Software (Weighing Instruments). A copy of the WELMEC publication can be downloaded from their website at www.welmec.org/publications/2-3.pdf. The NTEP Director also suggested investigating the existence of software standards written by other U.S. standards writing organizations (e.g., ANSI) and that any volunteers to the Sector be willing to actively participating in the Sector and be committed to following through with assigned tasks.

Recommendation: **The NIST Technical Advisor included this item on the agenda only to provide the Weighing Sector with an update the status of the S&T Committee Agenda item 320-1 in NCWM Publication 16 Identification: Built-for-Purpose Software-based Devices and recommends no further action on this item since it was withdrawn from the S&T Committee agenda.**

3. **S.1.1.c. Zero Indication (Marking Requirements)**

Source: 2004 Weighing Sector Agenda Item 4 - S.1.1. (c). Zero Indication (Marking Requirements).

Background: See the 2005 Report of the 90th National Conference on Weights and Measures, Specifications and Tolerances Committee Report, the 2003 NTETC Weighing Sector Meeting Summary agenda item 19, and the 2005 NCWM Publication 16 S&T Committee Report Item 320-1 for additional background information on the proposal to clarify marking requirements for scales that display unloaded scale conditions with other than digital zero indications.

During the 2004 NCWM Interim Meeting, the S&T Committee was briefed on some ongoing discussions about zero indications within the Weighing Sector for the past several years. The Committee agreed that its interpretation of paragraph S.1.1. (c) is consistent with the original intent of the 78th NCWM Report of the Specifications and Tolerances Committee. The Committee agreed that additional language is needed to clarify that no marking is required if operator intervention is necessary to verify a zero condition before the start of a transaction. The Committee believed this will provide a record of how the requirement should be applied and proposed changes to paragraph S.1.1. (c) to clarify that no marking is required if operator intervention is necessary to verify a zero condition before the start of a transaction.

At the 2005 Annual Meeting of the NCWM, the S&T Committee changed the status of the item from "voting" to "information" to allow additional time to assess whether or not the markings could be displayed as part of the indication rather than being physically marked on the device and to gather more information on whether or not self-service systems are providing the necessary information about the zero-load condition of the scale prior to each weight determination.

Discussion: A couple of the scale manufacturers provided weighing instruments during the meeting and demonstrated how they operate with in the current requirements of S.1.1.(c). The purpose of the demonstration was to see the operation; have the opportunity to operate the scale; help other members of the Sector to understand the issue better; and show that the units have "an effective automatic means..." to satisfy the requirement without additional labels or markings.

NIST WMD restated that they continue to support the language recommended in the S&T Committee's agenda item 320-1 that clarifies the intent of the 78th NCWM S&T Committee. Furthermore, parties that disagree with the 2004 Committee's interpretation and oppose the proposed language in 320-1 should develop an alternate proposal to clarify that additional markings **are not required** for devices that have "an effective automatic means" to inhibit a weighing operation or return the device to a continuous digital indication when the scale is in an out-of-balance condition.

Mettler Toledo stated that they continue to oppose the proposed language to amend Scales Code paragraph S.1.1. (c). since effective means are provided to inhibit a weighing operation when zero indications are indicated by other than a digital zero when the scale is in an out-of-balance condition. That is, the scale will not go into a "sleep" mode if there scale is not at zero and will return to an active weight display if the scale senses that the scale is no longer at zero. In situations where the scale display turns off with the scale in an out-of-balance condition, operator intervention is required to turn on the scale, in which case the scale will automatically be rezeroed or indicate an error condition.

Mettler Toledo further stated that their position is based on the language in NIST Handbook 44. WMD responded that the proposal is intended to clearly state the position of the 78th NCWM S&T Committee in NIST Handbook 44.

Other manufacturers supported the Mettler Toledo position and discussed other methods that provide effective means to inhibit weighing transactions and display other than digital zero indications such as center-of-zero annunciators, RFID (radio frequency identification device) would reactivate the scale displays when the product is in close proximity to the scale, touch screen display scale activation that would automatically activate when the scale was in an out-of-balance condition, weight displays visible to the operator when the customer display indicates promotions or other non weight information.

The Maryland NTEP laboratory and NIST WMD stated that the proposed language represents what is already covered by NTEP evaluation and test criteria. The problem is that field officials do not know if or when additional markings are required, and that customers need the zero information (either by a digital zero or other indication that the scale is at zero) along with the weight, and pricing information in a computing type device, in order to make an informed decision on whether or not to accept the weight (and total price) determination.

The Ohio NTEP laboratory disagreed with the WMD and Maryland positions and reported that they have not heard of any problems by field officials and that they have received no customer complaints on this subject.

Additional comments were made that supported the Ohio position and that customers do not look at the zero condition of the scale and that they are only concerned about the price they have to pay. WMD and Maryland responded that the Sector should not be making that assumption and that there are customers that want to make sure that the scale starts at zero in order to receive an accurate transaction.

Recommendation: The discussion was concluded since there was no clear consensus on a position that the Sector could report to the NCWM S&T Committee on the agenda item. The Sector Chairman held two votes on this subject. The results of the vote will be forwarded to the NCWM S&T Committee.

The first vote was to determine if the Sector agreed with the proposal on the NCWM S&T agenda to amend Handbook 44 paragraph S.1.1. (c) to clarify that additional markings are required for devices that have an effective automatic means to inhibit a weighing operation or return the device to a continuous digital indication when the scale is in an out-of-balance condition. Two Sector members voted to support the S&T Committee proposal and eleven Sector members voted against supporting the proposal.

The second vote was to establish a Sector position that states that additional markings should not be not required during type evaluation on devices that have an effective automatic means to inhibit a weighing operation, or return

NTEP Committee 2006 Final Report
Appendix C – NTETC Weighing Sector - Appendix A. Recommendations

the device to a continuous digital indication when the scale is in an out-of-balance condition. The results of the second vote: two Sector members voted to oppose this position and twelve Sector members voted to support this position.

The result of the second vote means that such markings would not be required during type evaluation. It should be noted that WMD continues to believe that field officials may require such markings citing General Code paragraph G-S.6. Marking Operational Controls, Indications, and Features and the interpretation of the 78th NCWM S&T Committee unless Scales Code paragraph S.1.1. (c). is amended to clearly state that no additional markings are required when a device, where zero is indicated by other than a continuous digital zero, has effective means to inhibit a weighing transaction when the scale is in an out-of-balance condition.

4. **Bench/Counter Scale Shift Test and Definitions**

Source: NIST WMD

Background: See the 2004 NTETC Weighing Sector Meeting Summary agenda item 5 and the 2005 NCWM Publication 16 S&T Committee Report agenda item 320-6 for additional background information.

At the 2005 Annual Meeting of the NCWM, the S&T Committee agreed with the Scale Manufacturers Association to modify Figure 2, test positions for test loads located in the corners of the scale platform but kept the proposal as an information item to enable weights and measures officials and the NTEP Laboratories to continue forwarding data on the proposed and current shift test to the NIST Technical Advisor.

Discussion/Recommendation: WMD has received limited data from one state and no data from the NTEP laboratories. WMD requests that any data from the participating NTEP laboratories be submitted by November 1, 2005, in order that the results can be compiled and presented to the S&T Committee during the January 2006 NCWM Interim Meeting.

Jim Truex, Chief Ohio Department of Agriculture Weights and Measures, reported that their field officials and the Ohio NTEP laboratory have collected data, and the data will be submitted to WMD by November 1, 2005. Jim added that preliminary results indicate that they have not found any significant problems.

There is no action required by the Sector at this time.

5. **Publication 14 Force Transducer (Load Cell) Family and Selection Criteria**

Source: NTEP Committee Technical Advisor

Background: See the 2004 NTETC Weighing Sector Meeting Summary agenda item 11 for additional background information regarding a recommendation to amend the family selection criteria for load cells to be listed on an NTEP Certificate of Conformance.

During its 2004 Meeting, the Weighing Sector agreed to assign a work group (Stephen Patoray (NTEP), Steven Cook (NIST), the NIST Force Group, Joseph Antkowiak (Flintec), Frank Rusk (Coti), and the California NTEP laboratory) to complete the following tasks:

1. Develop the definition of a family, determine load cell selection criteria, and develop an example of a load cell selection for the 2005 NCWM Interim Meeting.
2. Review and adapt OIML R 60 language developed by John Elengo for incorporation into Publication 14 for the 2005 meeting of the Weighing Sector.

Discussion: Stephen Patoray, NTEP Director, updated the Sector on the status of the project. He described a proposal that has been forwarded to the small work group. In summary, the proposal has the potential for an applicant to submit only one load cell for a basic load cell family to be covered on an NTEP CC. However, taking into consideration possible groups within the family (e.g., material construction, methods of mounting, strain gauge bonding, output rating, input impedance, supply voltage, cable details, etc.), there will be no significant difference in the number of load cells that have to be submitted for evaluation.

One of the questions that must be addressed in any proposed change to the selection criteria is how the criteria will affect applications to amend and expand existing CC.

Recommendation: **The Sector agreed that no actions are required by the Sector at this time since the work group has not finalized a specific proposal to modify load cell selection criteria.**

6. Compatibility of Indicators Interfaced with Weighing and Measuring Elements

Source: NTETC Measuring Sector and NCWM S&T Committee

Background: This issue proposed to change what requirements and evaluation criteria must be met to interface an indicating element and a weighing or measuring element that have not been previously evaluated together on a single NTEP CC, but which have their own NTEP CC listing compatible communication specifications. See the 2004 Report of the 89th NCWM, Specifications and Tolerances (S&T) Committee Agenda Item 310-2 and the 2004 NTETC Weighing Sector Meeting Summary Agenda Item 12 for additional background information.

At its 2004 meeting, the Weighing Sector stated that the proposal as written is not appropriate for weighing devices since the language could require all combinations of devices and communications to be evaluated. The Weighing Sector agrees with the Measuring Sector that this is not the intent of the proposed language. The NCWM S&T Committee decided to withdraw Item 310-2 from the S&T Committee Agenda until it is further developed and resubmitted with the support of the NTETC Weighing and Measuring Sectors.

The Sector supported a joint meeting of the NTETC Weighing and Measuring Sector members attending the 2004 Southern Weights and Measures Technical Conference (SWMA). The Weighing Sector agreed that, if both the Weighing and the Measuring Sectors could agree on the issues and proposal, then the proposed language could be proposed to the NCWM S&T Committee for placement in the General Code; otherwise, any proposed language should be proposed for inclusion in the specific codes. If there were no agreement between the Weighing and Measuring Sectors, the Measuring Sector could request a separate work group to develop a proposal to address the compatibility of multiple elements issue for the NIST Handbook 44 Liquid-Measuring Devices Codes.

At its 2004 meeting, the Measuring Sector generally agreed that the language added to Publication 14 in a new Section T. Testing Required To Interface Components With Individual CC's That Were Not Previously Tested Together was sufficient to address the original concerns of manufacturers regarding when additional testing is necessary to determine compatibility between components. The Measuring Sector did not propose any new language for Handbook 44 to be submitted to the NCWM S&T Committee for consideration. The Sector agreed that the item should be dropped from the Measuring Sector's Agenda. As a result of the Measuring Sector's conclusion, for a joint discussion between the Weighing and Measuring Sectors to develop a proposal to address the compatibility of multiple elements was no longer necessary.

Discussion/Recommendation: **The NIST Technical advisor has received no additional input on this item and recommended that it be withdrawn from the Weighing Sector's agenda until a proposal has been developed to address the apportionment of errors for separable weighing, load-receiving, and indicating elements. The proposal should also include testing and reporting the minimum sensitivity of indicating elements (i.e., smallest voltage per scale division). It should also be noted that the proposed revision of OIML R 76 for Non-automatic Weighing Instruments includes recommendations for the apportionment of errors and a proposed Annex E for checking the compatibility of modules of non-automatic weighing instruments. The OIML definition for the term "module" is nearly identical to the Handbook 44 definition of "element".**

The Weighing Sector agreed that the compatibility of weighing modules is not clearly defined in NIST Handbook 44 and NCWM Publication 14 evaluation and test criteria for digital electronic scales and that any proposal to define such criteria would be a major project.

NTEP Committee 2006 Final Report
Appendix C – NTETC Weighing Sector - Appendix A. Recommendations

The Sector recommends no further action on this item and that it be removed from future agendas unless a specific proposal to establish criteria for determining the compatibility of weighing, indicating, and other elements has been developed.

7. Handbook 44 Computing Scales Interfaced with an Electronic Cash Register

Background: See the 2005 Reports for the 90th National Conference on Weights and Measures, Specifications and Tolerances Committee Agenda item 320-3 and the 2004 NTETC Weighing Sector Meeting Summary agenda item 13 for additional background information on a proposal to amend NIST Handbook 44 that would list specific requirements for electronic cash registers that are interfaced with scales.

At its 2004 meeting, the Weighing Sector agreed not to recommend a proposal to NIST Handbook 44 to add new device-specific code requirements to the Scales Code to address the proper interface of computing scales with electronic cash registers (ECR). The Sector generally agreed that there are currently appropriate means in Handbook 44, including General Code paragraphs G-S.5. Indicating and Recording Elements and G-S.2. Facilitation of Fraud, and the examination procedure outlines to address the proper interface of computing scales with ECRs during field evaluation.

At the 2005 NCWM Annual Meeting, the S&T Committee expressed concerns that the proposal is not fully developed for multiple reasons.

- Manufacturers indicate the proposed subparagraphs are too restrictive when a point-of-sale system reads UPC codes and recomputes prices for frequent shopper discounted prices.
- The Committee heard comments that NTEP verifies the requirement in the proposed new paragraph (d) to ensure that the electronic cash register does not have any input to the computing scale in the process of determining the total price of a weighed item. However, the Committee believes that the term "input" should be expanded to clarify the requirement for field officials.
- The proposal does not address computing scales with multiple sales accumulation capability.
- Further work is also required to make certain that an examination procedure outline is available to provide field procedures for use in determining that the interface complies with the requirement.
- The current definition of point-of-sale system (POS) may also require some modification to clarify the specific type of weighing element that is permitted as part of the POS assembly.

The Committee also heard that there are instances in which a computing scale may be inappropriately interfaced with an ECR to create a point-of-sale system contrary to the intended device application covered on the device's CC. The Committee believes this becomes a design issue rather than one involving the user; however, a user requirement might also be appropriate. Because of these questions and unresolved issues, the Committee changed the item status from "voting" to "information" and recommends the original submitter rework the proposal as a specification that (1) provides more detail to the field official about how the cash register must function, and (2) is readily available in NIST Handbook 44 to assist device manufacturers who are considering design modifications to a computing scale or cash register. The Committee also asked the SWMA to determine if a user requirement is needed as a companion paragraph to a device specification, and review any proposed language to ensure there are no conflicts with requirements in related paragraphs such as S.1.8.4. Recorded Representations, Point-of-Sale Systems.

Discussion: The NIST technical advisor recommended no action on this item pending further action and work by the original submitter. It was reported the Western Weights and Measures Association at their 2005 Technical Conference recommended that this item be withdrawn from the NCWM S&T Committee agenda. The Central Weights and Measures Association (CWMA) also reported that there were no comments on this item and that they did not provide the S&T Committee with a recommendation during the 2005 CWMA Technical Conference Interim Meeting.

The Maryland NTEP laboratory stated that weights and measures officials are not uniformly applying existing requirements since it is easy to miss language that is located in multiple places in Handbook 44 and that the proposal to amend NIST Handbook 44 is being modified.

Recommendation: The Sector recommends no action on this item and that it not is placed on the 2006 Sector agenda as a carryover item.

8. Publication 14 - New Items in Computing Scale Section

Source: Maryland Participating Laboratory

Background: See the 2004 NTETC Weighing Sector Meeting Summary agenda item 16 for additional background information regarding the display of product code information in the total price display on a computing scale.

The Maryland NTEP laboratory reported on a computing scale (see picture below) that used the "Total Price" display to indicate the product code prior to a load being placed on the scale and a calculation of total price. They reported that the product code (PLU) is indicated by illuminating all " " segments and turning off the decimal point in the "Total Price" portion of the display. This PLU indication in this example may cause a customer to believe that the PLU number is the total price to pay if a load was already on the platform and the product code was entered.

Many of the sector members did not believe the above example provided by the Maryland laboratory was a problem since the product code did not use a decimal point similar to a representation of money.

The 2004 Weighing Sector concluded that the example provided by the Maryland NTEP laboratory did not demonstrate that there is a problem and that the proposed language may cause additional confusion. The Maryland NTEP Lab was requested to further develop the language and submit such to the Sector for discussion and ballot approval.

Discussion: The Maryland NTEP laboratory updated the Sector on the status of their proposal. The NTEP laboratories and manufacturers stated that any language proposed for NIST Handbook 44 and/or NCWM Publication 14 should address the following:

- Price computing scales with Weight, Unit Price, and Total Price information displayed from top to bottom,
- Total Price information should be located on the right for horizontal layouts,
- New products are likely to have panel type liquid crystal or matrix displays that can be configured in multiple or customer designed formats,
- Once the Unit Price is displayed on the scale, the PLU should be replaced by the Total Price (the example above example indicated both a Unit Price with the PLU number in the Total Price position),
- Weight and pricing information, regardless of the order it is presented should be adequately identified and easily read, and
- Product code or other information should not interfere with the weight display

Some of the manufacturers noted that transactions frequently happen too fast for a customer to understand what is happening during the weighing and pricing procedures and only pay attention to the Total Price. The NIST technical advisor responded that the Sector should not be making that assumption that all customers do not look at or care about the net weight and unit price information.

A few of the Sector members noted that the example shown above could be confusing to the customer if the PLU number has three of more digits. Other Sector members replied that the leading digital zeros in the above example are not permitted to be part of the "Total Price" to pay. The NTEP Director questioned whether this prohibition is in Publication 14 or Handbook 44.

Recommendation: There was no consensus on a recommendation for this item among the voting and non voting members of the Sector. The Sector Chairman took a vote of the voting members to determine if the Sector believed there was a problem with the language on the format of the displays on price computing scales in NCWM Publication 14. The Sector voted 15 (agreed) to 1 (disagree) that no language is needed to address the format of price computing scale displays.

Gary Lameris volunteered to review NIST Handbook 44 Scales Code and NCWM Publication 14 to determine if language is needed to address "other than weight information" that may be indicated in the weight display. Any recommendations will be forwarded to the participating laboratories at their 2006 spring meeting and to the 2006 NTETC Weighing Sector Meeting.

9. **CLC Type Evaluation Tests on Railway Track/Vehicle Scales – Technical Policy**

Source: Brechbuhler Scales Inc.

Background: At its 2004 meeting, the Weighing Sector could not reach a consensus on the request that vehicle weighing applications (e = 20 lb) be added to existing railway track scale CCs (e = 50 lb) that have been designed to Cooper E-80 standards and tested using the GISPA test car (or other railroad test cars and additional test weights).

Brechbuhler Scales stated that they would develop and submit a proposal for testing for railroad track scales that would include procedures to include highway vehicle applications with d = 20 lb on CC for railway track scales that were evaluated with d = 50 lb without additional testing for consideration at the 2005 meeting of the Weighing Sector.

Publication 14 Technical Policy Section 8 paragraph "c." states that a CC will apply to all models that have scale division values equal to or greater than the value of the scale division used in the scale that was evaluated. Brechbuhler Scales recommends that the technical policy in 8.c. should not apply to combination railway track/vehicle scales that already have an active CC for weighing railway track cars. That is, the CC for a railway track scale with d = 50 lb can include vehicle-weighing weighing application with d = 20 lb without additional testing provided that the GISPA test car, or suitable field standard weight carts are used for the evaluation of the railway track scale. The recommendation for amending the technical policy for modular combination railway track/vehicle scales is included in the 2nd recommendation to Agenda Item 14, CLC for Combination Railway Track/Vehicle Scales.

Discussion: The NTEP Director requested clarification on whether this agenda item is intended to address the issue of what is required to be tested for new device types or if the issue is to address what can be covered on existing certificates. If a device is tested with d = 50 lb, the certificate cannot cover scales with d = 20 lb without additional testing. Additionally, the performance and permanence tests for vehicles are different than the performance and permanence test for railway track scales. A railway track scale permanence test does not meet the requirements of the vehicle scale permanence test. The NIST technical advisor stated that the subject of agenda item 11 is intended to draft language for the permanence and performance testing the style that has been drafted for vehicle scales and other large capacity scales. There will be remaining differences in the number of test loads for the increasing/decreasing load tests and the amount of test weights and test loads needed for each test.

Brechbuhler Scales stated that it would be best to test the scale with a multiple range indicating element where d = 20 lb in the weighing range of typical vehicle weights and with d = 50 lb in the weighing range for railway cars.

Many of the NTEP laboratories remain concerned that vehicles on combination railway track/vehicle scale applications do not roll on to the scale in the same path as railroad cars since vehicles can drive on either the right or left side of the railroad car traffic pattern. Compliance with loading along the sides of the scale that simulates vehicle traffic (wandering loads from side to side) should be verified during an NTEP evaluation. Additionally, testing at weights in the vehicle weighing range and railway car weighing range should also be performed at the same time since span calibrations at the lower weighing range does not guarantee accuracy at the higher range, or vice versa.

The NTEP Director stated that there is no well-defined test procedure or technical policies in NCWM Publication 14 for combination railway track/vehicle scale NTEP evaluations and recommends that such language be developed. The Ohio NTEP laboratory supports such a project. Other comments included that the procedures should include discussions about Cooper E 80 design requirements.

Another NTEP laboratory cautioned that some of the Cooper E 80 requirements are not suitable for NTEP evaluation and subsequent verification by field officials such as approaches to railway track scales. NTEP evaluations should be limited verifying the compliance with the metrological and installation requirements in NIST Handbook 44. A manufacturer also recommended that the NTEP application form include a space for an applicant to request the vehicle weighing option on the railway track scale application.

Recommendation: **The Sector agreed that NCWM Publication 14 Technical Policies and Test Criteria for vehicle scales and railway scales should be reviewed and that separate test criteria should be developed for combination vehicle/railway track scales. The new criteria should include technical policies and test procedures for:**

1) **New NTEP applications,**
2) **Amendments to existing CCs for railway track scales to include the vehicle weighing feature including;**
   a. **CLC ratings,**
   b. **CLC testing using field standard weight (center vs. off-center),**
   c. **Permanence tests for amending railway track CCs to include vehicle weighing option, and**
3) **Test using the vehicle scale e_{min} for new NTEP applications and existing CCs.**

Ed Luthy agreed to develop a draft proposal and distribute it for review and comment to Stephan Langford, Darrell Flocken, and Bob Feezor. Develop procedures and technical policies are due to the NIST Technical Advisor by March 1, 2006, in order that the proposal can be reviewed by the NTEP laboratories prior to it being submitted to the NTETC Weighing Sector for their September 2006 meeting.

10. Tare on Multiple Range Scales

Source: NTEP Participating Laboratories:

Background: See the 2004 NTETC Weighing Sector Meeting Summary agenda item 22 for additional background information on the discussion for the rounding of tare on single and multiple range, and multi-interval scales.

The NIST Technical Advisor requested clarification on the rounding of tare on multiple range scales from the Secretariat to OIML R 76 as part of the U.S. comments to the Working Draft (WD) revision of R 76. The Secretariat responded by including several examples of tare rounding for single and multiple range scales with both tare weighing (pushbutton tare) and preset tare (keyboard tare) in the 1st Committee Draft (1 CD) revision. To summarize the exampled, tare must be round to the nearest division of the higher weighing range when the gross weight goes to the higher weighing range. However, the Secretariat did not include examples where the tare would round to zero when the gross weight entered a higher range. The United States followed up on this question in their comments on the 1 CD in April 2005. The Secretariat will address this question in the 2nd Committee Draft (2 CD), which will be distributed in October 2005.

The Sector was requested to:

(1) Discuss the rounding up of tare for multiple range and multi-interval scales in NCWM Publication 14 section 31 and 32. The rounding up of tare conflicts with NIST Handbook 44 General Code paragraph G-S.5.2.2. (c), which requires that digital values round off to the nearest minimum unit that can be indicated or recorded, and Publication 14 section 48.2.2., which requires that keyboard tare weight entries be rounded to the nearest displayed scale division.

NTEP Committee 2006 Final Report
Appendix C – NTETC Weighing Sector - Appendix A. Recommendations

(2) Review the of examples of tare rounding from the 1 CD of the revision to OIML R 76 for possible inclusion into Publication 14 once the revision to R 76 has been completed.

Discussion: The Sector reviewed the examples or tare rounding from the 1st Draft Revision of OIML R 76. The examples indicated that in the examples where tare was determined by actual weighing, tare and gross weights could be taken to the internal resolution of the scale and that the rounding after the net weight was calculated from the internal resolution of the gross and tare weights and that printed tare values could be off by 1 e. Other examples showed that the net weight, calculated as the difference between gross and tare weights) could have a least significant digit that was not the same as the weighing range of the net weight.

The Sector also reviewed the NCWM Publication 14 paragraphs that discuss the rounding of tare. There were several points made on the rounding of tare including:

- Always rounding tare in the upward direction always benefits the customer to the detriment of the scale seller.
- Tare rounding procedures should be clear and well documented in NIST Handbook 44 and NCWM Publication 14 for consistent type evaluations and field enforcement activities.
- Past Sector discussions concluded that tare would round up to facilitate compliance with NIST Handbook 130 Model Uniform Weights and Measures Law Section 15. Misrepresentation of Quantity which states that, "no person shall sell, offer, or expose for sale a quantity less than the quantity represented..."
- A proposal has been submitted to the 2005 Southern Weights and Measures Association Specifications and Tolerance Committee to require that tare always rounds up. It is intended for the seller to include the cost of the packaging in the price of the product as opposed to paying the same unit price for the package as the product.
- Some states disagree that rounding to the nearest scale division is in violation with Uniform Weights and Measures Law
- NCWM Publication 14 tare rounding requirements for multi-interval and multiple range scales is in conflict with NIST Handbook 44 General Code paragraph G-S.5.2.2. (c).
- Handbook 44 does not support the Publication 14 requirement that zero tare entries are not permitted.
- Rounding tare to zero when the gross weight goes to the next segment or range in multi-interval or multiple range scales should not be allowed.
- Why does Publication 14 specify different methods for rounding tare between single range and multi-interval, multiple range scales?

Recommendation: The Sector voted 13 to 4 to modify Publication 14 to make tare rounding consistent with Handbook 44 General Code paragraph G-S.5.2.2.(c) Digital Indication and Representation for multi-interval and multiple range scales. The NIST Technical Advisor will work on develop amendments to Publication 14 sections 31, 32, and 45-51 for Tare and other possible sections that will consistently apply the rounding of tare throughout the digital electronic scales checklist. The Sector will then be balloted on the proposed modifications to Tare in Publication 14.

The Sector also agreed to consider the OIML R 76 examples of tare rounding at a later date once the revision of the R 76 has been completed.

> **NIST Technical Advisor Note:** During the development of the letter ballot language, it was noted that there were some items (e.g., tare annunciators and terminology) that requires further discussion by the Sector. Additionally, there is a developing (D) item in the 2006 NCWM S&T Interim Agenda that may have an impact on the Sector recommendation. An alternate proposal was also developed that would address the operation of the "tare entered" annunciators, examples demonstrating tare rounding in different scenarios, and add definitions clarifying the differences between semi-automatic tare and preset tare. Based on these concerns, the NIST Technical Advisor does not believe that the language to amend Publication 14 is sufficiently developed to be submitted to the Sector as a letter ballot.
>
> The NIST Technical Advisor consulted with the NCWM Chairman, NTEP Committee Chairman, Sector Chairman, and NCWM Technical Advisor on both proposals to amend Publication 14 tare requirements. As a result, it is recommended that a small work group review the proposals, review tare operation and requirements in general, and make recommendations on how this is applied to single range, multiple range and multi-interval scale operation. The work group should develop a recommendation(s) for changes to Handbook 44 and Handbook 130 (if necessary), and provide the Weighing Sector guidance on checklist requirements. It is anticipated that the group could perform the tasks though the use of e-mail correspondences and conference calls.

11. Performance and Permanence Tests for Railway Track Scales Used to Weigh Statically

Source: NTEP Participating Laboratories

Background: See the 2004 NTETC Weighing Sector Meeting Summary agenda item 23 for additional background information on performance test criteria, permanence test requirements, and application of tolerances for railway track scales. At the 2004 meeting of the Weighing Sector, the NIST technical advisor and Ed Luthy (Brechbuhler Scales) volunteered to submit this issue at the October 2004 meeting of American Railway Engineering and Maintenance of Way Association (AREMA) Committee 34-Scales.

AREMA Committee 34 responded with the following statements to comments and questions from the summary of the 2004 meeting of the Weighing Sector.

1. The railroads agree that, when conducting NTEP testing of railroad scales, acceptance tolerances must be applied regardless of the interval between the initial test and the permanence test.
2. The railroads do not agree that there is a poor "As Found" compliance rate *when railroad track scales are designed and installed per the requirements of the AAR Scale Handbook.*
3. NCWM Publication 14 (DES-109 68.7 Permanence Test) allows the permanence test to be conducted with alternative test weights, such as railroad scale test cars. With sufficient coordination between GIPSA and the railroad upon which the scale is located, delays should be minimal and controllable.
4. The railroads do not agree with removing permanence testing from the NTEP test. This is an important part of the NTEP process.

GISPA has also provided some additional comments regarding permanence testing on railroad track scale NTEP evaluations. GISPA recommended that new installations should be set up and calibrated using a railroad test car after GIPSA inspects the installation for compliance with railroad bridge specifications; and then the scale should be subjected to a "break-in" period of a month or two. GIPSA would then come in and perform the initial NTEP test. GIPSA would come back as soon as possible, but no sooner than 20 or 30 days following the initial NTEP test and do the final test for permanence; the scale would be held to acceptance tolerances. If GIPSA can't get back for some reason, a single 100 000 lb (minimum) railroad scale test car or two 80 000 lb cars with current NIST traceable calibrations can be used for the permanence test.

Discussion: The Sector reviewed a proposal to amend the 2005 Edition of Publication 14, Section 69. Performance and Permanence Tests for Railway Track Scales Used to Weigh Statically submitted by the NIST technical advisor based upon the comments of the 2004 Weighing Sector, GIPSA, and AREMA Committee-34.

NTEP Committee 2006 Final Report
Appendix C – NTETC Weighing Sector - Appendix A. Recommendations

The Sector also reviewed additional comments dated September 23, 2005, from Ron Mueller, stating that the Canadian National Railway does not agree with GIPSA's recommendations concerning Performance and Permanence Tests for Railway Track Scales Used to Weigh Statically and that NTEP should initially approve all new types of devices. The reasons for the Canadian National Railway's position are that many railroads will not be willing to oversee installation or evaluate railway track scale design and that the length of minimum and maximum time for the recommended break-in period prior to the start of the official NTEP testing is too subjective and not adequately defined. Ron Mueller also stated that the task of type approving a weighing device is, and should remain, that of NIST, NTEP, and GIPSA combined.

Ron Mueller stated that NIST, NTEP, and GIPSA have relied on the servicing railroads to do engineering tasks assigned for their approval procedures and suggested that an independent organization with the expertise and desire to inspect and evaluate these design criteria be allowed to perform this task (e.g., Mr. Ronald W. Kaye, Senior Transportation Engineer, Patric Engineering, Joliet, Illinois at (630) 795-7265). The cost for such design and engineering approval could become part of the NTEP process. He further added that no consideration should be given to performing a type approval of a railway track scale at a manufacturer's site."

Robert Feezor, Northfolk Southern Corporation, amended the language submitted by the NIST Technical Advisor based on comments from the Canadian National Railway and submitted it for review by the Sector. The Sector reviewed the proposal as amended by Bob Feezor and discussed the possible use of 80 000 lb field standard weight carts where and additional 20 000 lb could <u>safely</u> be added to the weight carts for the tests. Additionally, the Sector discussed the permanence test language that permitted one or more railroad test cars to be used for the permanence test in lieu of the GIPSA type weight cart. The railroads believe that the length of suitable railroad test cars precludes using two cars on a single scale and that it is unlikely that two railroad test cars would be available for the tests. Other Sector members believed that it would be acceptable to use any combination of field standards, field standard weight carts, and railroad test cars to perform the permanence test.

Recommendation: The Sector agreed to amend the language developed by the NIST technical advisor as recommended by Bob Feezor with additional changes recommended by the Sector. The modified proposal with Sector comments were forwarded to AREMA Committee-34 for their October 24 - 24, 2005, meeting. The modified proposed language and comments from AREMA Committee-34 were then be forwarded to the Sector for a vote on the final language that will be recommended for incorporation into the 2006 Edition of Publication 14.

Technical Advisor's Note: The following is a summary of AREMA Committee-34 suggestions from their October 2005 meeting to modify to the Sector's recommendation.

Delete the language that allows permanence testing at the applicant's manufacturing site.
- Justification: It is unlikely that the applicant's manufacturing facility will have a suitable on-site location and loads at their site. The railroads are concerned that a manufacturer's site may not represent typical customer installations where the scale design and various aspects of the installation are evaluated and approved by the serving railroad prior to the railroads accepting weights from the scale. Additionally, the loads may not represent actual usage when railcars are not used for the weighing operations.

Change the minimum number of weighing operations from 300 to 150.
- Justification: Unlike in-motion scales, some static railway track scale installations may only have 3 to 5 weighing operations per day. At that rate, it could easily take a year or longer between tests. Even with the minimum 150 weighing operations recommended by the railroads it would take 30 to 50 days to complete the minimum number of weighing operations. The railroads added that it could cost at least $6000 or more to perform additional weighing operations that were not part of an installations normal operation.

Change the minimum time to conduct the permanence test after the initial test from 20 days to 30 days. Note that this does not agree with the Sector recommendation.
- Justification: The railroads believe that 20 days is too short a time between that initial and subsequent test for permanence even at a high volume test site. Adding the extra time provides the railroads with additional assurance that the scale can perform within tolerance between normal subsequent tests.

Technical Advisor's Note: The proposed language and comments from AREMA Committee-34 were then forwarded

to the Sector for a vote on the final language that will be recommended for incorporation into the 2006 Edition of Publication 14.

The following information is a summary of the voting results during the balloting process. A copy of this summary, comments on the ballot language, and the amended proposed language were forwarded to the NCWM NTEP Committee for their consideration during the January 22 - 25, 2006, NCWM Interim Meeting in Jacksonville, Florida.

ITEM NO.	SUB. NO.	ITEM AFFIRM		NEGAT.	ABST.
1		Approve the 2005 Weighing Sector recommendations to amend NCWM Publication 14 Section 69. Performance and Permanence Tests for Railway Track Scales Used to Weigh Statically.	7 *(3 private 4 public)*	1 *(public)*	3 *(2 private 1 public)*
2		Approve the following additional modifications recommended by the American Association of Railroads AREMA Committee-34.			
	a.	Delete the language that allows permanence testing at the applicant's manufacturing site.	4 *(1 private 3 public)*	3 *(2 private 1 public)*	4 *(3 private 1 public)*
	b.	Change the minimum the number of weighing operations from 300 to 150.	3 *(private)*	3 *(public)*	5 *(3 private 2 public)*
	c.	Change minimum time to conduct the permanence test after the initial test from 20 days to 30 days.	4 *(3 private 1 public)*	2 *(public)*	5 *(3 private 2 public)*

Based upon the ballot results and comments received during the balloting process, the language in Appendix A-Agenda Item 11 was amended to delete the language that allows permanence testing at the applicant's manufacturing site, to change the minimum time to conduct the permanence test from 20 days to 30 days, and clarify that 100 000 lb of field standard test weights and/or field standard weight carts are required for the initial test of a railway track scale. Additionally, language is added to clarify that a railroad test car(s) may be used in lieu of, or in conjunction with field standard test weights and/or field standard weight during the permanence test.

Additional editorial suggestions are proposed to clarify the documentation required to verify certification of field standards and railway track scale test cars, and clarify term "standard rail car" since the railroads use this term to describe a type of railway scale test equipment.

12. Cash Acceptors or Card-activated Systems

Source: NTEP Participating Laboratories

Background: At its 2004 meeting, the Weighing Sector recommended cash acceptor checklist language. After the meeting, a device incorporating cash acceptors was submitted for evaluation. During the evaluation, it became evident to the NTEP laboratory evaluator that some items in the recommended checklist were either vague or missing from the proposed Publication 14 language. The items identified by the laboratory were:

(1) insufficient paper to print a receipt and complete a transaction, and
(2) insufficient funds to return the correct change or return the correct amount inserted into the machine should a transaction be canceled.

Additional language was proposed by WMD and reviewed by the NTEP Director and the NTEP laboratory that was conducting the evaluation. The *ad hoc* language attempts to ensure that customers receive printed or displayed

NTEP Committee 2006 Final Report
Appendix C – NTETC Weighing Sector - Appendix A. Recommendations

instructions directing them to contact a store attendant or manager to retrieve correct change or a copy of the transaction information printed on a separate recording element in case of insufficient funds or receipt paper.

During the 2005 NCWM Interim Meeting, the NTEP Committee agreed to add the additional language as *ad hoc* language in the 2005 update of NCWM Publication 14 (below). The NTEP Committee discussed several additional "cash acceptor" issues that may require clarification or additional checklist requirements. The NTEP Committee also requested that this item be presented during the 2005 meeting of the Weighing Sector to address these issues and noted that these items may also need to be addressed in other sections of NCWM Publication 14.

The NTEP Committee asked the Weighing Sector to:
1. Review the procedures and ad hoc language in the agenda for addition to Publication 14 Electronic Cash Registers Interfaced with Scales Section 13.
2. Discuss the need for a definition of card-activated and/or cash acceptor systems. Some of the questions that need to be answered include:
   a) Are they limited to ECR/POS interfaced with scales?
   b) Are they self-service customer card-activated/cash acceptor systems and does the checklist apply to store clerk card-activated/cash acceptor systems?
3. Discuss other possible scenarios involving cash acceptors and card activated systems that may affect the accuracy of the transaction, including issues such as the ability for the customer to receive sufficient information to make informed decisions about their transaction, and to receive correct change, credits, discounts, and suitable receipts.

The NTEP Participating Laboratories for Weighing Devices reviewed the *ad hoc* language, explored the possibilities of additional cash acceptor problems, and developed Publication 14 language to be recommended to the Weighing Sector. This information has been forwarded to the NTEP Liquid-Measuring Devices (LMD) Participating Laboratories and NTETC Measuring Sector for their review for potential amendments to the Publication 14 LMD Checklist.

Discussion: The Weighing Sector reviewed the *ad hoc* modifications to the checklist. It was acknowledged by the Weighing Sector that there are differences between cash and card acceptors interfaced with weighing devices and liquid-measuring devices. For example, cash and card acceptors used in liquid-measuring devices issue receipts with a fixed length so that the device can easily predict when it will run out of paper. Cash and card acceptors interfaced with weighing devices are predominantly used in point-of-sale interfaces with scales where the receipts can significantly vary in length. The cash acceptors at attended locations may also accept cash in large denominations where the customer is provided with a mechanism to receive all of their change. The *ad hoc* language was developed to include these types of applications. Additional applications include self-service vehicle scales where card acceptors are used to initialize the weighing of a vehicle and to issue printed tickets. Several Sector members stated that the current and *ad hoc* language in Publication 14 is sufficient for these applications.

The Weighing Sector also suggested some minor editorial changes to the language including replacing the term "terminated" with "canceled" since the latter term indicated that the transaction was stopped by a conscious decision of the customer as opposed to being automatically stopped by the device.

Conclusion/Recommendation: The Weighing Sector recommends that the language to amend NCWM Publication 14 Electronic Cash Registers Interfaced with Scales in Appendix A-Agenda Item 12 be incorporated into the 2006 Edition of NCWM Publication 14.

The Weighing Sector did not recommend new definitions of card-activated and/or cash acceptor systems for NIST Handbook 44.

13. Ranges Covered on the CC for a Railway Track Scale Based on the Device Evaluated

Source: 2005 NTEP Committee

Background: During the 2005 NCWM Interim Meeting, the NTEP Committee discussed an issue brought forward by a manufacturer regarding the title of Section 8.2 of NCWM Publication 14 Digital Electronic Scales, "Additional Criteria For Vehicle Scales, Railway Track Scales, Combination Vehicle/Railway Track Scales, and Other Platform Scales Greater Than 200 000 lb." The NTEP Committee reviewed information from the 1998 and 2000 Weighing Sector meetings that indicated that the Sector, during its 2000 meeting, recommended that an NTEP CC would apply to all models having nominal capacities no greater than the capacity of the scale submitted for evaluation. The Sector made no recommendations to change the length criteria from 135 % to 100 % of the scale submitted for evaluation in either the 1998 and 2000 meetings. However, the 2001 edition of Publication 14 included a change to the length criteria that limits the length of the family of scale to that of the device submitted for evaluation. The NTEP Committee instructed the NTEP Director to correct the Publication 14 language to reflect previous decisions of the sectors, identify the changes clearly in Publication 14, and place this item on the agenda for the 2005 meeting of the Weighing Sector for additional comments and recommendations.

The NTEP Participating Laboratories discussed this item during their April 2005 meeting in Columbus Ohio. The laboratories agreed with the changes recommended by the NTEP Committee. Additionally, they agreed that there are two remaining issues should be reviewed to determine if changes are needed to the criteria for (1) the allowable span between sections, and (2) platform widths based upon the device submitted for evaluation).

Discussion: The Weighing Sector reviewed issues on this topic in past Sector summaries. Don Onwiler, NTEP Committee, added that the NTEP Committee's changes to Publication 14 were based on the Sector summaries. The changes did not reflect the Committee's position on what is to be covered on the certificate for a railway track scale based on the device evaluated. He also stated that NCWM Publication 14 Administrative Policy J.4. Amending a pre-NTEP Certificate was modified based on the NTEP Committee discussion of an appeal that initiated review of the past Sector recommendations.

The Sector also discussed the criteria for the allowable span between sections and platform widths based upon the device submitted for evaluation that were identified by the NTEP Participating Laboratories during their April 2005 meeting. However, no specific language was discussed to amend Publication 14 Section 8.2.

Recommendation: The Weighing Sector agreed with the changes approved by the 2005 NTEP Committee regarding the ranges to be covered on a CC. The Sector made no recommendations to amend that language in the 2005 Edition of Publication 14 Section 8.2. and no further action is recommended by the Sector at this time. Future recommendations to amend NCWM Publication 14 Section 8.2 should be submitted to the Sector for consideration.

New Items

14. CLC for Combination Railway Track/Vehicle Scales

Source: Mettler Toledo – Scott Davidson

Background/Discussion: Mettler Toledo submitted a proposal to amend CLC requirements in section 8.3. by requiring a minimum CLC of 60 000 lb for the vehicle portion of a combination railway track/vehicle scale.

When using higher capacity load cells (e.g., by using load cells with larger mv/V ratings) within an approved load cell family, the manufacturer is forced to increase the CLC to meet 40 % of the summed capacity for two load cells required in NCWM Publication 14 paragraph 8.3.1 b (DES-7). Increasing the CLC requires additional NTEP testing even if the manufacturer does not want to increase the CLC rating, increase the structural strength of the weighbridge, or increase the scale capacities.

The minimum 60 000 lb CLC requirement was derived from NIST Handbook 44 Scales Code Table UR.3.2.1. Span Maximum Load and looking at 3 axles in 8 feet between the extremes of the axles at 17 000 lb per axle. It shows an "r" factor of 1.00. This means that there are 3 axles within a space of 8 ft, for a total of 51 000 lb for the maximum legal weight for a group of 3 axles. This value was rounded to 60 000 lb since many highway enforcement agencies allow a 10 % tolerance to axle-load weights and provides an additional factor for axle groups that exceed legal highway limits.

The v_{min} calculations for load cell suitability show that when using higher capacity load cells, the v_{min} is required to remain within the necessary values to meet the 20 lb increment size for the family of scales if the vehicle scale portion has a CLC that is no less than 60 000 lb.

Discussion - Part 1: The Sector reviewed a proposal from Mettler Toledo that recommended amending Publication 14 Digital Electronic Scales Part B, Section 8.3 Modular Load-Cell Vehicle, Livestock, or Railroad Track Scales, paragraph 8.3.1. (b) and adding a new paragraph 8.3.1. (c).

The Sector also reviewed recommendations from the NIST Technical Advisor for editorial changes to Publication 14 paragraph 8.3.1.(a) that are intended to avoid confusion and to clarify what is meant by structural strength (load cell or weighbridge), capacity (nominal or concentrated load), and family (scale or load cells).

Prior to the Sector meeting, Darrell Flocken, Mettler Toledo, had questioned the origin and purpose of the original language in Publication 14 paragraph 8.3.1.b. He made some inquiries and reported that the language was intended to address the loading of CLC and that it was possibly a cautionary note to prevent overloading of the load cells with a capacity less that 40 % of the CLC. Other Sector members stated that 8.3.1.b. is not needed since the CLC is calculated by the manufacturer based on the maximum load that can be applied by vehicles with tandem axles according to Handbook 44 Table UR. 3.2.1. Span Maximum Load and not load cell capacity. Another Sector member cautioned that paragraph 8.3.1.b. should not be removed until the reason for the existing language is understood.

After the meeting, the NIST Technical Advisor did some additional research in to the origin of the NTEP Technical Policy Section 8 paragraph 8.3.1.b. The language was originally developed and recommended during the June 1990 meeting of the NTETC Weighing Sector under agenda item VIII Criteria for Modular Vehicle Scale Parameters. A letter dated June 21, 1990, from Terry James, Vice-president Engineering Services at Cardinal Scale Manufacturing Company, stated that the "40 % of the sum of the capacity of two load cells" value for the minimum CLC was selected using the 50 000 lb load cell to establish a capacity with some safety factor based on the legal highway tandem axle load of 34 000 lb. The maximum CLC is the rated nominal capacity of the pair of load cells that comprise a section.

Recommendation Part 1: **The Sector recommends that the language submitted by Mettler Toledo, as amended by the Sector in Appendix A-Agenda Item 14, be incorporated into the 2006 Edition of NCWM 14.**

Discussion/Recommendation Part 2: **Brechbuhler Scales stated that their proposal in Sector Agenda Item 14 part 1 was no longer necessary based on the Sector discussion and recommendation for agenda item 14 part 1. No further action was recommended by the Sector.**

15. Abbreviations for Carat and Count in Publication 14 Sections 38. and 76.

Source: NIST Weights and Measures Division (WMD)

Background: WMD is in the process of developing an EPO and inspector's training manual for Class I and Class II precision balances. During this process, WMD reviewed NIST Handbooks 44 and 130, NCWM Publication 14, and several CC as sources for potential examples for metrological criteria such as methods of sealing, units of measurement, identification, and marking requirements that an inspector might find during a field inspection.

Research into the subject revealed that NIST Handbook 44 only recognizes the "c" as an acceptable abbreviation for carat in Section 2.23 Weights paragraph S.4.5. Carat Weights and in Appendix C General Table of Units of Measurement, Units of Mass (page C-17). NIST Handbook 130 Packaging and Labeling Regulations paragraph 6.7.1. Symbols and Abbreviations recognizes the "ct" as an acceptable abbreviation for count.

During the review of NCWM Publication 14, Section 76. List of Acceptable Abbreviations/Symbols, it was noted that the abbreviation "ct" is acceptable for both "carat" and for "count." This raises the question about Class I or II scales that may have an approved counting feature for prescription filling applications and also the "carat" as a unit of measurement since "ct" is listed in Publication 14 as an exception to the General Tables of W&M, in NIST Handbook 44. Problems would arise if the abbreviation "ct" were to be used on a device with both the "count" and the "carat" unit of measurement. An Internet search for the "abbreviation of carat" indicates that the jewelry industry uses both "c" and "ct" (c or ct = 200 mg) and the term "carat" is synonymous "carat troy." The abbreviation for "count" is also "ct" according to many dictionaries and Internet searches and was listed as an acceptable abbreviation in NCWM Publication 14 for "carats" and abbreviation for pieces on receipts and labels for items sold by count.

The abbreviation "ct" in Publication 14 was originally intended for scales that could display indications and print labels and receipts for items sold by count. The term "count" and its abbreviation "ct" was not intended to be used on a scale with an operational counting feature since the counting feature was, until 2003, prohibited in NIST Handbook 44.

The Sector was asked to consider amending the NCWM Publication 14 paragraphs 38.3.1. and 38.4., and Section 76. to eliminate any potential confusion between indications of carat weights and count when the carat weight unit and counting feature are enabled on the same scale.

Discussion: The NTEP laboratories stated that the abbreviation "ct" carat was not in Handbook 44 when it was recommended as an acceptable abbreviation for both carat and count in NCWM Publication 14. The "ct" abbreviation for carat is commonly used in the jewelry industry and language in Publication 14 paragraph 38.3.2 does not permit the abbreviation to be the same if a scale has both carat units and the counting option.

Some of the manufacturers state that they use the term "pieces" or the abbreviation "pcs" to identify count on their devices. Based on that comment, some of the Sector members suggested that Publication 14 language should encourage the use of this term and its abbreviation in Publication 14, Section 76.

The NTEP Director noted that the abbreviation "ct" for carat is not listed in NIST Handbook 44 and that NCWM Publication 14 allows the "ct" for carat, and that Handbook 44 should support the requirements and policies in Publication 14. Several laboratory members stated that the industry should not be penalized by not allowing the customary business practice of using "ct" as the abbreviation for carat. They felt that it would be obvious to the customer and user since a carat weight will include decimal values whereas a display of count will be in whole numbers.

Measurement Canada stated that their regulations recognize the "ct" for carat and that the "c" for carat is not accepted.

Recommendation: The majority of the Sector agreed that "ct" is an acceptable abbreviation for the term carat since: the abbreviation is in common usage by the jewelry industry, "ct" has been listed in NCWM Publication 14 Table 76 List of Acceptable Abbreviations and Symbols since it was developed by the Sector at their December 8, 1992 meeting, "c" in not an acceptable abbreviation for count, and the obvious indication that carats are displayed decimal values and pieces or count are displayed as whole numbers.

The Sector agreed to recommend that the amendments to NCWM Publication 14 submitted by the NIST technical advisor with changes recommended by the Sector in Appendix A-Agenda Item 15 be incorporated in the 2006 edition of Publication 14.

16. Performance and Permanence Test for Bench and Counter Scales

Source: Ohio NTEP Participating Laboratory

Background: The 2002 edition of NCWM Publication 14 Section 62. Performance and Permanence Test for Bench and Counter Scales paragraph 62.9.5. Test Load stated that 50 % of the maximum capacity, not to exceed 500 lb, of the bench or counter scale is to be repeatedly applied to the scale. The phrase "not to exceed 500 lb" was inadvertently omitted from subsequent editions of Publication 14.

NTEP Committee 2006 Final Report
Appendix C – NTETC Weighing Sector - Appendix A. Recommendations

The Sector was asked to review amendments to NCWM Publication 14 Section 63., paragraph 63.6.5.1. (Section 62. was renumbered to Section 63. in 2004) to include language that limits the test load to 500 lb for scales with a capacity greater than 1 000 lb.

Discussion: Two of the five NTEP laboratories authorized to conduct type evaluations on scales below 2000 lb (1000 kg) have the ability to test 2000 lb scales with 1000 lb on their repetitive test equipment. The other laboratories test for permanence on these scales with loads not to exceed 500 lb. Measurement Canada's test equipment applies loads not to exceed 250 kg for scales no greater than 2000 kg. The Sector agreed that any changes to Publication 14 should be compatible with Measurement Canada and NTEP-Canada Mutual Acceptance Program. Many of the manufacturers stated that they believe the severity of the test should be the same for all evaluations of these devices. There were also suggestions that the language should include metric capacities.

Recommendation: **The Sector voted (12 in favor and 1 opposed) to amend the Ohio proposal and change the "load not to exceed 500 lb" to "load not to exceed 250 kg (550 lb)" and recommended that the amended language Appendix A-Agenda Item 16 be incorporated into the 2006 Edition of NCWM Publication 14.**

17. Minimum Height of Weight and Units Indications

Source: New York NTEP Participating Laboratory

Background: The New York NTEP Participating Laboratory reported the height of the indications of weight and the corresponding units of measure on recent several scales submitted for NTEP evaluations are getting smaller and questioned when displays are too small. Neither NIST Handbook 44 nor NCWM Publication 14 have requirements or suggestions for the evaluation of these displays. New York submitted an example of a scale with a unit of measure display that is 4 mm (incorrectly reported as 2 mm in the Sector agenda) in height.

The Weighing Sector discussed a similar item in 1999 and submitted a proposal to add language to the General Code the that would establish a minimum height requirement for primary measurement indication to the customer (see the 2000 85th NCWM Annual Meeting Report of the S&T Committee Item 310-4). The S&T Committee withdrew the proposal because of opposition and asked the Weighing Sector to conduct additional work to clarify the intent of the requirement and ensure it applies to the appropriate applications.

Discussion: The Sector was asked to review the background information and an example from the New York NTEP laboratory demonstrating the height of the units display compared to the weight display.

The Sector also reviewed a proposal from the New York and Maryland NTEP laboratories for a new NIST Handbook 44 specification paragraph that specifies the minimum height requirements for primary weight indications and units of measure.

> **G-S.5.2.3. Size and Character.**
>
> (a) In any series of graduations, indications, or recorded representations, corresponding graduations and units shall be uniform in size and character. Graduations, indications, or recorded representations that are subordinate to or of a lesser value than others with which they are associated shall be appropriately portrayed or designated. [Retroactive as of January 1, 1975]
>
> (b) The display of primary measurement indications on both the operator and the customer side shall be clear and at least 9.5 mm in height.
> [Nonretroactive as of January 1, 200X]
>
> (c) The display of the character size of the units of mass, on both the operator and the customer side, shall be no less than a factor of 0.6 times the width and 0.6 times the height of the numeric values.
> [Nonretroactive as of January 1, 200X]

The NIST Technical Advisor provided the following information for consideration during the discussion of this item.

Handbook 44 Section 5.54 Taximeters, Sections 5.56.(a) and 5.56.(b) Grain Moisture Meters, and Section 5.57. Near-Infrared Grain Analyzers already include specifications for the minimum height of figures, words and symbols.

OIML R 76 Non Automatic Weighing Systems states that the minimum height of weight indications is 9.5 mm, and 2 mm for capital letters on required markings.

OIML R 117 Measuring Systems for Liquids Other Than Water states that the minimum height of the quantity indication on fuel dispensers 10 mm (4 mm for other liquid-measuring devices) with the minimum height of the price indication no less than 4 mm.

Additionally, "unit of measurement" should replace "unit of mass" in the proposed paragraph G-S.5.2.3. to be consistent with Handbook 44 language since the requirement would apply to all weighing and measuring devices. For example, paragraph G-S.5.3.1. On Devices That Indicate in More that One Unit. refers to the "unit of measurement."

One of the manufacturers stated that the proposal is more restrictive than the language in OIML R 76 since OIML R 76 states that the height requirement applies to <u>direct sale applications</u> and prefers that the height of the analog weight indications be based on the distance between the customer and the indicting device, and that R 76 OIML also states a minimum 2 mm for marked information. Additionally, annunciators such as " ▲ " that point to the units of measures are often smaller than 2 mm in height and manufacturers are limited to the display heights from their vendors. Other manufacturers stated that the marketplace will decide what is an acceptable height for weight displays. They added that the costs for a vendor to tool up for a custom display would be prohibitive. The manufacturers were also concerned about indicating elements such as video display monitors where the height of the weight values may change with the height of the display (monitor). The NIST technical advisor suggested that a user requirement could be developed for users that replace indicating elements with indicating elements that are not from the original equipment manufacturer.

The Maryland NTEP laboratory stated that the New York laboratory's (The New York Sector member was unable to attend the meeting) concern was primarily with the height of the lettering of the unit of measure in their example and that both the Maryland and New York laboratories are agreeable to limit the language for minimum height requirements to direct sales to the public applications. Don Onwiler, Nebraska NTEP laboratory, stated that there will be some applications where the device complies with the minimum requirements but may still be difficult to read because of the distance or the brightness and contrast of the display. Don Onwiler added that officials may have to be educated that the proposal does not conflict with Handbook 44 General Code G-S.5.1. General (Indicating and Recording Elements), G-UR.2.2. Installation of Indicating or Recording Elements, G-UR.3.3. Position of Equipment when the device complies with the specific height requirements in the Scales Code but is still not clear and easily read because of the individual circumstances of the installation.

Recommendation **The Sector agreed that any proposal to specify the height of the weight display and units indications in NIST Handbook 44 should be limited to the Scales Code and should align with OIML R 76 to the extent possible. The size requirements should be limited to weight indications visible to the customer in direct sale applications, the weight display should be no smaller than 9.5 mm, and the units display or marking should be no smaller that 2 mm.**

The NIST technical advisor, the New York and Maryland laboratories, and Jesus Zapien (A&D Engineering) were asked to rework the proposal in the agenda based on the recommendations of the Sector. The Sector will be balloted on the language developed by the small work group and submitted, if acceptable, for consideration to the Southern Weights and Measures Association at their 2005 annual meeting and the NCWM Review panel during the week of October 23, 2005.

18. Automatic Weighing Systems Influence Factor Temperature Ranges that Exceed –10 °C to 40 °C

Source: Ohio NTEP Participating Laboratory

Background: The Ohio NTEP Participating Laboratory has received NTEP applications to evaluate automatic weighing systems (AWS) with temperature ranges that exceed the standard temperature range of –10 °C to 40 °C. The applicant made the request on behalf of their customer since the AWS may be used in environments that are warmer than 40 °C

(104 °F). Handbook 44 Section 2.28 Automatic Weighing Systems Table S.7.b., footnote 5 states that the temperature range shall be marked "only on automatic weighing systems if the range is other than –10 °C to 40 °C (14 °F to 104 °F)."

The laboratory stated that testing above 40 °C or below –10 °C puts an unnecessary strain on both the environmental chamber and the NTEP technician who has to go into the chamber to perform the tests. There are some CC already issued with a stated temperature higher than 40 °C, but the vast majority of these are "Provisional" CCs for Wheel Load Weighers where no temperature testing has ever been performed by NTEP. If the NTEP laboratories ever acquire the capability to temperature test these devices in order to change the status of the CC from "Provisional" to "Full", they will most likely revert to the standard temperature range. There is at least one CC for a Class III scale that has a temperature higher than 40 °C stated on it (CC 92-213A2) and was tested at that temperature.

The laboratory is also concerned that other manufacturers will very likely decide that their device would be more marketable to a customer if it has been tested at 50 °C. This would turn the NTEP CC into an advertising tool and may initiate a never-ending escalation of temperature test requests from manufacturers.

The NIST Technical Advisor reported that OIML R 76 Non-automatic Weighing Systems paragraph 3.9.2.1. Prescribed temperature and 3.9.2.2. Special temperature limits and OIML R 51 Automatic Catchweighing Instruments and other OIML Recommendations have similar temperature marking requirements as the AWS code and other Handbook 44 codes.

Discussion: The Sector was asked to review the background information and consider submitting a proposal from the Ohio NTEP Participating Laboratory to amend Handbook 44 Section 2.28 Automatic Weighing Systems Table S.7.b. footnote 5 to the next meeting of the Southern Weights and Measures Association. The proposed language is identical to Handbook 44 Section 2.20. Scales Code Table S.6.3.b. Notes for Table S.6.3.a. footnote 5.

Table S.7.b. **Notes for Table S.7.a.**
5. Required only on automatic weighing systems if the range on the NTEP CC is narrower ~~other~~ than and within –10 °C to 40 °C (14 °F to 104 °F).

The NIST Technical Advisor recommended that Handbook 44 Sections 2.21. Belt-Conveyor Scale Systems paragraph S.4.e. Markings Requirements, 2.22. Automatic Bulk Weighing Systems paragraph S.5. Markings Requirements, and 5.58. Multiple Dimension Measuring Devices Table S.1.4.b. Notes for Table S.1.4.a. be amended to be consistent with the Scales Code.

The Sector commented that the language for the influence factor temperature requirements is worded differently among the various weighing device codes even though the range of temperatures is consistent (–10 °C to 40 °C). Unlike the Handbook 44 Scales Code paragraph T.N.2.3. Subsequent Verifications, not all of the weighing device codes in Handbook 44 include the language that states that tolerance values apply regardless of the influence factors in effect at the time of the conduct of the examination. Additionally, weighing devices that are marked with a temperature range may not be suitable to the installations if it is used in applications where the ambient temperature exceed that temperature range that is marked on the device Handbook General Code paragraphs G-UR.1.2. Environment (Selection Requirement) and G-UR.3.1. Method of Operation states that equipment shall be suitable for the environment in which it is used and operated only in a manner that is indicated by instructions on the device.

The NTEP Director stated that the AWS Code marking requirements are restrictive because the suitability of the device can be determined by the marking on the device. For example, Handbook 44 Scales Code Table S.6.3.a. Marking Requirements Note 5 states that the temperature range shall be marked on the device if the range is **narrower than** –10 °C to 40 °C, whereas AWS Code Table S.7.a. Marking Requirements Note 5. states that the markings are required if the temperature range is **other than** –10 °C to 40 °C. The NTEP Director is also concerned by the use of the term "temperature limit" in Scales code paragraph T.N.8.1.1. and T.N.8.1.2. and similar language in the other weighing device codes, and that the "limits" could be misinterpreted as a consideration for the suitability of a device at a particular installation.

The manufacturers believe that the range of temperature testing needs to be the same among the NTEP laboratories, otherwise, applicants will select the NTEP laboratories that have a greater temperature testing capabilities creating an uneven workload for all the NTEP Participating Laboratories. The manufacturers also believe that the testing for compliance with temperature influence factor requirement should not be below –10 °C or above 40 °C to avoid expanded temperature ranges listed on the CC being used by applicants for marketing purposes. One manufacturer suggested that the range of testing should be specified in Handbook 44. The NTEP Director added that Handbook 44 does not specifically state that temperatures tests are required if the device is marked with a temperature range that is wider or other than –10 °C to 40 °C.

The NTEP laboratories were concerned that a device may be marked with a temperature range wider than the temperature tests listed in the test conditions in the CC since the CC only lists the temperatures that were tested on the device (Note: This is not a concern for devices with a marked temperature range that is narrower than –10 °C to 40 °C since compliance with the narrower temperature range is verified during NTEP evaluation).

A question was asked if an applicant could request that the CC be listed with a temperature range wider than –10 °C to 40 °C if the applicant provided credible data that the device complies with the expanded temperature range. The Sector believed that a policy listing a wider temperature range on the CC than what was larger that the temperature range verified by NTEP would lead to applicants taking advantage of the larger temperature range and inferring that the quality of the device was better than other devices that were listed with the standard temperature range. Darrell Flocken, Mettler Toledo, added that influence factor testing for temperature should not be a quality or marketing issue, temperature tests verify compliance with Handbook 44, and that applicants can demonstrate the knowledge and the ability to comply the requirements. Russ Wykoff, Oregon NTEP laboratory, asked what will happen if a manufacturer marks the device with a larger temperature range than the –10 °C to 40 °C that was evaluated during type evaluation. The manufacturers responded that NTEP cannot control additional identification information marked on the device since the manufacturer must also comply with the marking requirements of other agencies that may be different than the temperature markings for other purposes than the accuracy requirements in Handbook 44.

Recommendation: The Sector agreed that the range of temperatures over which the NTEP laboratories will conduct temperature tests are –10 °C for the lowest temperature tested and +40 °C as the highest temperature. The Sector recommends that that NCWM Publication 14 Technical Policy B.1. Influence Factor Requirements and K. 59. Tests Procedures for Influence Factors, be amended and shown in Appendix A-Agenda Item 18 to limit the scope of temperature test that will be conducted by the NTEP laboratories.

The Sector did not provide a recommendation to amend NIST Handbook 44 AWS Code Table S.7.b. Note 5 at this time. The Sector believes that a more thorough review of Handbook 44 paragraph G-UR.1.2. Environment, and Scales Code Table S.6.3.b. Note 5 and paragraphs T.N. 2.3. Subsequent Verification and T.N.8.1. Temperature is needed in order to assure that suitability, marking, and performance requirements are consistent throughout Handbook 44 weighing sections, and that the temperature limits specified in the handbook are correctly applied by field officials in determining the suitability of a weighing device in various installations. Darrell Flocken will ask the SMA to take on this assignment and bring a recommendation back to the NTEP laboratories and the Weighing Sector during their 2005 Fall meeting.

Todd Lucas, (NCWM S&T Committee) agreed to update the 2006 NCWM S&T Committee about the sector discussions and recommendations and that "clean-up" work has been identified regarding Handbook 44 language for subsequent tests, temperature limits, and marking requirements in order that the language is consistent throughout in NIST Handbook 44 Section 2.

Lou Straub, Fairbanks Scales, agreed to notify the NCWM Review Panel at their next meeting that the SMA and Weighing Sector may be developing future proposals to amend NIST Handbook 44 temperature marking, performance, and suitability requirements.

Juana Williams (NIST), Steven Cook (NIST), and Darrell Flocken (Mettler Toledo) agreed to develop a summary paragraph, with points that need to be addressed (e.g., temperature testing at the time of the NTEP evaluation vs. ambient temperature during subsequent verifications and the marked temperature range).

NTEP Committee 2006 Final Report
Appendix C – NTETC Weighing Sector - Appendix A. Recommendations

19. Criteria for Railway Track Scales With a Rotary Dump Option

Submitted by: Bob Feezor, Norfolk Southern Corporation

Background: Manufacturers of rotary dump mechanisms for railway track cars offer a weighing option where a railway track scale is built into, or installed in the rotary dump mechanism. The manufacturers of these systems frequently believe that the railway track scale is approved for this application (or in some cases, just the load cells and indication elements), and is covered by an NTEP CC. Additionally, there are many existing rotary dump mechanisms that were installed prior to the formation of NTEP that are nearing the end of their useful life and the users of these devices are requesting that the railway track scales be covered by NTEP CCs. The submitter of this item is concerned there are no documented policies and test criteria for these devices, and therefore promotes inconsistent enforcement of the NTEP requirements on these devices.

NTEP and the laboratories have consistently stated that a railway track scale CCs must include the rotary dump mechanism must be verified by NTEP and subsequently listed on the CC. The problem is that this policy is not documented in NCWM Publication 14, nor are there any documented procedures to test the rotary dump scales.

Robert Feezor recommend recommended that *ad hoc* policies and test criteria should be developed to add the rotary dump mechanism as a feature on the.

Recommendation: The Sector agreed with the submitter that the rotary dump option should be included on CCs for railway track scales, and that NTEP Technical Policies and test criteria are needed for Pub 14. Robert Feezor and Steve Cook agreed to draft technical policies and test criteria will be developed and submitted for the 2006 meetings of the NTEP Labs and Weighing Sector.

20. Permanence Tests for Identification Information

Submitted by: Stephen Patoray, NTEP Director

Background: NCWM Publication 14 Section 1. Marking Complete Scales addresses permanence testing of identification information on complete scales. The sections for indicating elements, weighing/load-receiving elements, and livestock, vehicle, and railway track scales do not have any requirements for the permanence testing of the identification information and do not refer to the procedures in section 1.

Recommendation: The Sector recommends that the sections for marking requirements be consolidated and reorganized. The NIST technical advisor has worked on a proposed consolidation of the marking requirements that removes language that is repeated in Sections 2 though 5 and referenced the general requirements in Section 1; the proposed consolidation that has been re-titled as 1. Marking- Applicable to Indicating, Weighing/Load-Receiving Elements and Complete Scales. The NIST technical advisor will also ballot the Sector on the proposed changes in Appendix A-Agenda Item 1(c) and report the results to the NTEP Committee prior to the 2006 NCWM Interim Meeting.

> **NIST Technical Advisor's Note:**
>
> The Sector recommendation to amend the capacity markings sections of Publication 14 in **Appendix A-Agenda Item 1(c)** have been consolidated with the Sector recommend changes in Agenda Item 20. Permanence Tests for Identification Information.

21. Next Sector Meeting

Discussion: The locations for Weighing Sector meetings are typically rotated among the participating NTEP laboratories. If this schedule is followed, the location for the 2006 Weighing Sector meeting would be at the Maryland NTEP Participating Laboratory in Annapolis, Maryland. The Sector received a recommendation to hold the 2006 meeting in conjunction with the 2006 Western Weights and Measures Association Technical Conference. Another recommendation is to hold the meeting on a Tuesday through Thursday, since many airlines no longer have Saturday night layover restrictions. Lou Straub, Fairbanks Scales, cautioned that there are large annual boat shows and Naval Academy events in the fall that may affect the cost of lodging during the Sector meeting.

Recommendation: The Sector recommends that the next 2006 Sector meeting be held in Annapolis, Maryland, and that it start on a Tuesday. The Sector also recommended that NCWM headquarters look into holding the 2007 meeting of the Weighing Sector in conjunction with the WWMA Technical Conference in Lake Tahoe, Nevada.

Appendix A

Recommendations for Amendments to Publication 14

General Note. Unless otherwise noted, the following language from the 2005 edition of NCWM Publication 14 language that includes proposed changes are highlighted in gray. Revisions recommended by the Sector are shown by ~~crossing out~~ information to be deleted and <u>underlining</u> information to be added.

Agenda Item 1 (a) Footnote to S.1.8.4.

Digital Electronic Scales Section 76.   List of Acceptable Abbreviations/Symbols

Device Application	Term	Acceptable Not	Acceptable
ECRs, Recorded Representations:	net weight indication in pounds	"pound" or "lb" ~~the symbol "#" should be discouraged~~	<u>the "#" symbol for pound</u>

Electronic Cash Registers Interfaced with Scales Section 11.   Recorded Representation Point-of-Sale Systems

11.1. Customer's   receipts must contain:

11.2.   Net weight identified by the word "pound", "lb", "kilogram", "kg", "gram", "g", "ounces", ~~or~~ "oz". The use of the symbol "#" for pound <u>is not acceptable</u> ~~discouraged~~.   Yes   No   N/A

Agenda Item 1 (b) Automatic Zero-Setting Mechanism (Zero-tracking)

43. Automatic Zero-Setting Mechanism (AZSM) (Zero Tracking)

Code References: S.2.1.3., <u>S.2.1.3.1., S.2.1.3.2., and S.2.1.3.3</u>~~1~~.

A scale may be equipped with an AZSM capability to automatically correct for weight variations near zero within specified limits. To reduce the potential for weighing errors, the AZSM may operate only under limited conditions as indicated in the specific type evaluation criteria.

Class III L and III/III L devices equipped with AZSM, shall be designed with a sealable means to allow the AZSM to be disabled during the inspection and test of the device.

The limits for AZSM are: (a) for bench, counter, and livestock scales <u>manufactured prior to January 1, 2007 *</u>: 0.6 d
(b) for vehicle, axle-load, and railway track scales: 3.0 d; ~~and~~
<u>(c) for all other scales manufactured prior to January 1, 2007 *: 1.0 d, and</u>
<u>(d) for all other scales including bench, counter, and livestock scales manufactured on or after January 1, 2007 *: 0.5 d.</u>

<u>Note: Applicants for new weighing device and load-receiving elements are encouraged (but not required) to submit their devices to the 2007 criteria. September 2006 is the cutoff date for new submissions for devices that limit the AZSM to 0.6 d and/or 1.0 d *. All scales of this category manufactured after 2007 must comply with the 0.5 d requirement.</u>

<u>*(date of manufacture and sections (a) and (c) to be deleted in the 2007 edition of Publication 14)</u>

Record the AZSM capability provided.

NTEP Committee 2006 Final Report
Appendix C – NTETC Weighing Sector - Appendix A. Recommendations

    No AZSM capability.
    AZSM is always operational. (except for Class III/III L and III L devices)
    AZSM activated or deactivated by an external switch.
    AZSM activated or deactivated by an internal switch or selected by programming at the time of installation.
    The magnitude of the AZSM increment is selectable.

For ~~devices~~ bench, counter, and livestock scales falling under S.2.1.3.1. (a) and S.2.1.3.2 (b), ~~for that is, bench, counter, and livestock scales,~~ AZSM may be operable with the device at a gross load zero, at a net load zero, or at a negative net weight indication resulting from a tare weight entry having been made with the scale at zero gross load.

For scales other than bench, counter, and livestock scales falling under S.2.1.3.1. (a) and S.2.1.3.2. (b), and vehicle, axle-load and railway track scales, AZSM may be operable only at a gross load zero.

Indicate where AZSM is operational.

    Gross Zero
    Net Zero
    Negative with Tare

> Test Procedure for AZSM: With the scale at zero balance, place a load in excess of the AZSM range for the scale, e.g., 10d. Add error weights that are slightly in excess of the specified AZSM limit for the device or the AZSM setting. Remove the load, (e.g., 10d) but leave the error weights on the scale. Observe whether or not the scale automatically zeroes the error weights. Repeat this procedure by decreasing or increasing the amount of error weights to determine the zeroing range of the AZSM. Perform this test in an analogous manner on the negative side of zero to determine the zero range of AZSM on the negative side of zero.

If the device has an AZSM capability, record the maximum amount (in scale divisions) that can be zeroed at one time.

    AVOIRDUPOIS: _____ d
    METRIC: _____ d
    OTHER UNITS Identify units_____ d

43.1.	This amount must comply with S.2.1.3. for the intended application.		Yes	No	N/A
43.2.	AZSM shall not be operable on any hopper scale.		Yes	No	N/A
43.3.	For vehicle, axle-load, and railway track scales, and ~~devices~~ scales other than bench, counter, and livestock scales ~~falling under S.2.1.3. (b) and (c)~~ AZSM may be operable only at a gross load zero.		Yes	No	N/A
43.4.	AZSM shall not be operational when the scale is displaying a positive weight value greater than the maximum AZSM quantity allowed.		Yes	No	N/A
43.5.	~~Devices falling under S.2.1.3.1.~~ Hopper scales used in automatic bulk-weighing systems and all Class III L scales shall be equipped with a sealable means to enable/disable or set the AZSM window to zero (0) for testing and inspection.		Yes	No	N/A

Agenda Item 1 (c) and 20. Table S.6.3.b. Note 3 – Nominal Capacity and Value & Permanence Tests for Identification Information

Note: The following proposed amendments to Publication 14 includes the changes recommended in Agenda Item 1 (c) and Agenda Item 20 and includes the language that approved by the Sector in Ballot number 91-04 with changes recommended by NIST WMD that deletes the example of a portable beam scale from the example of scales that did not need capacity markings.

NTEP Committee 2006 Final Report
Appendix C – NTETC Weighing Sector - Appendix A. Recommendations

The results of the vote were forwarded to the NTEP Committee prior to the 2006 NCWM Interim Meeting.

1. Marking- Applicable to Indicating, Weighing/Load-Receiving Elements and Complete Scales
   Code References: G-S.1. and G-S.7.: General Code Requirements, Identification

   -
   -
   -

Marking - Accuracy Class, Verification Scale Division, and Temperature Limits
Code References: S.6., Table S.6.3.a., and Table S.6.3.b.

   -
   -
   -

Marking Nominal Capacity, Value of the Scale Division, Special Applications
   Code References: S.6., S.6.6., Table S.6.3.a., and Table S.6.3.b.

This requirement applies to digital indicating elements and to both the operator's and customer's indications on complete scales. The lettering must be permanent as described in S~~s~~ec~~t~~ion 1, but the attachment of any badge or decal is slightly less stringent than for the G-S.1. information. In terms of attachment, any badge or decal must be "durable," that is, it must be difficult to remove (at all temperatures). Remote weight displays (except "scoreboard" displays), the customer's weight display provided for scales interfaced with electronic cash registers (ECRs), and weight displays which are built into ECRs must be marked with the scale capacity and scale division. The nominal capacity shall be shown together with the value of the scale division (e.g., 15 x 0.005 kg, 30 x 0.01 lb, or capacity = 15 kg, d = 0.005 kg) in a clear and conspicuous manner and be readily apparent when viewing the reading face of the scale indicator.

The system must be clearly and permanently marked on an exterior surface, visible after installation, as follows:

1.1	The name, initials, or trademark of the manufacturer or distributor. A remote display is required to have the manufacturer's name or trademark and model designation. (Code Reference G-S.1.)	Yes	No	N/A
1.13.	The nominal capacity by minimum scale division shall cl~~early and conspicuously be~~ marked in a clear and conspicuous manner and be readily apparent when viewing the reading face of the scale indicator unless already apparent by the design of the device ~~adjacent to the weight display (acceptable location depends on conspicuousness).~~ This applies to mechanical scales, such as portable platform scales, with removable counterpoise weights marked since; 1) the markings on the weights are not readily apparent by viewing the reading face of the scale, 2) the additional weights are not a permanent part of the scale, and 3) additional weights can be added to the scales to incorrectly increase the capacity of the scale.	Yes	No	N/A
1.14.	The capacity by division size shall be marked for all weight units that can be displayed such as in both pounds and kilograms.	Yes	No	N/A

1.15.	If equipped with variable resolution, the scale shall be marked with the weight ranges and corresponding scale division sizes.
	
	Example: 0-3 kg (6 lb) x 1 g (0.002 lb) 0-6 lb x 0.002 lb
	                 3-6 kg (15 lb) x 2 g (0.005 lb) or 6-15 lb x 0.005 lb
	                 6-15 kg (33 lb) x 5 g (0.01 lb) 15-33 lb x 0.01 lb
		Yes	No	N/A

NTEP Committee 2006 Final Report
Appendix C – NTETC Weighing Sector - Appendix A. Recommendations

1.16. If the capacity by division statement is displayed on a video terminal with the weight values, then the capacity by division statement must be indicated in a clear and conspicuous manner and be readily apparent when viewing the reading face of the scale indicator unless already apparent by the design of the device adjacent to the weight display and displayed whenever the system is in the weighing mode.　　Yes　No　N/A

The following examples represent capacity and value markings that are conspicuous and readily apparent when viewing the reading face. Each scale division value or weight unit shall be marked on multiple range or multi-interval scales. The capacity by division statement may be part of the scale display or marked adjacent to the display.

The capacity by value markings are not required if they are already apparent by the design of the device such as the largest weight value that is defined on a single revolution scale, fan scale, and beam scales and balances.

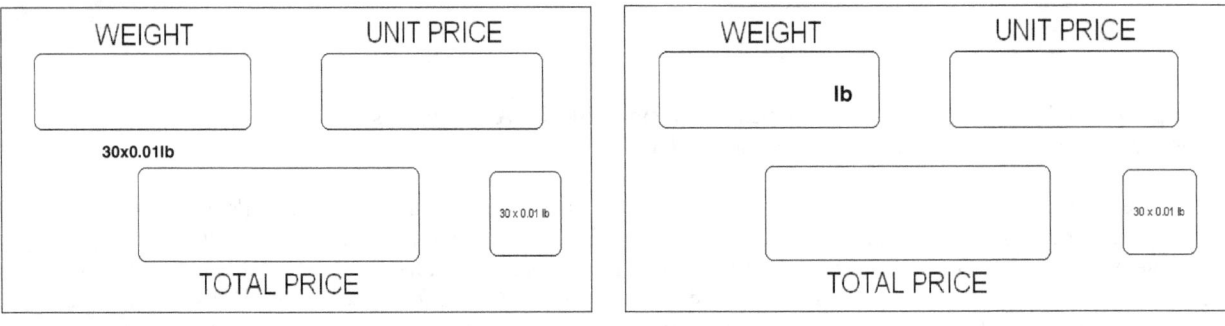

Example 1　　　　　　　　　　　　　　Example 2

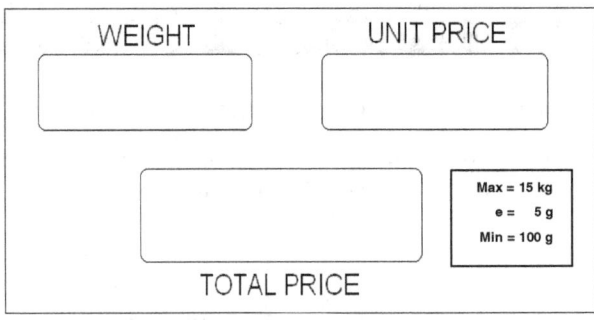

Example 3

NTEP - C32

NTEP Committee 2006 Final Report
Appendix C – NTETC Weighing Sector - Appendix A. Recommendations

==The following examples are types of scales where the capacity by scale division is readily apparent since the graduations, and beam capacities are marked with their respective values.==

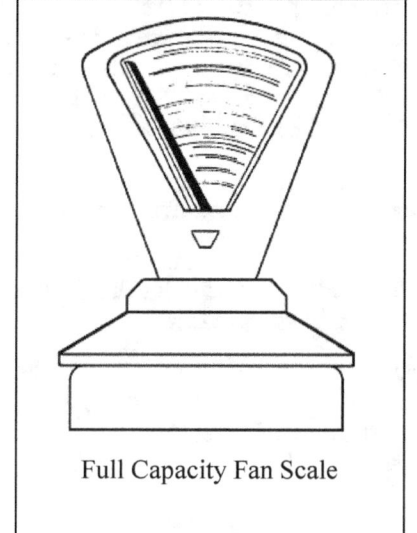
Full Capacity Fan Scale

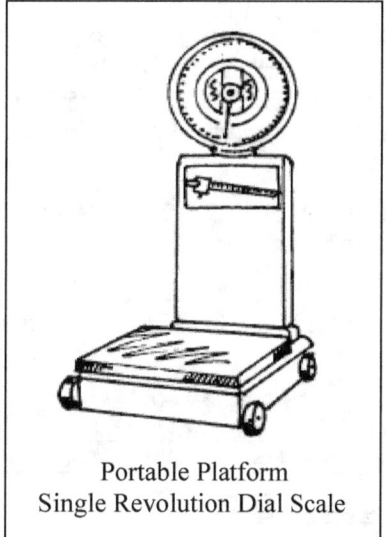
Portable Platform Single Revolution Dial Scale

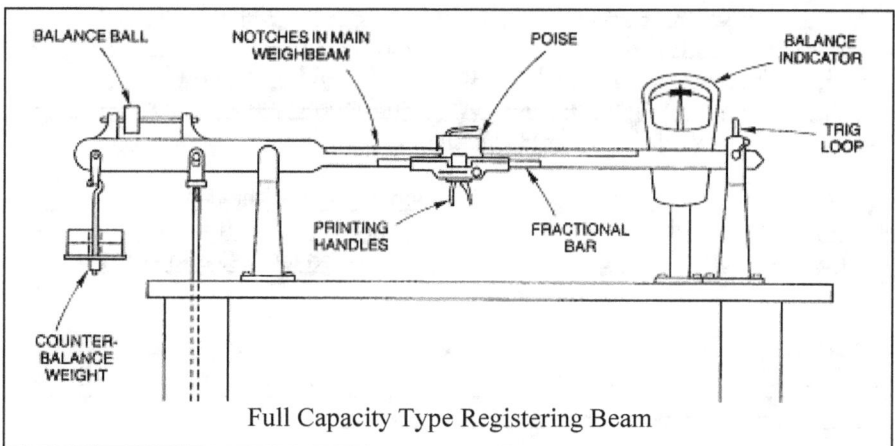
Full Capacity Type Registering Beam

1.17. Scales designed for special applications must be conspicuously marked to limit their use.   Yes   No   N/A
Special marking used: _____

1.23.3. The indicator is electronically linked to the weighing/load-receiving element and cannot be replaced without calibration.   Yes   No   N/A

2. ==Additional== Marking ==Requirements-== Indicating Elements

Weighing/load-receiving elements and indicators that are; (1) in the same housing, or (2) permanently hard wired together, or (3) sealed with a physical seal or an electronic link, shall have markings that comply with Section 1 Markings - ==Applicable to Indicating, Weighing/Load-Receiving Elements and== Complete Scales.

Code References: S.6., Table S.6.3.a., and Table S.6.3.b.

Since the United States permits indicating and weighing/load-receiving elements …

NTEP- C33

NTEP Committee 2006 Final Report
Appendix C – NTETC Weighing Sector - Appendix A. Recommendations

2.1.	~~The name, initials, or trademark of the manufacturer. A remote display is required to have the manufacturer's name or Trademark and model designation. (Code Reference G-S.1.)~~	~~Yes~~	~~No~~	~~N/A~~
2.2.	~~The manufacturer's model designation that positively identifies the type or design. The Model designation shall be prefaced by the word "Model," "Type," or "Pattern." These terms may be followed by the term "Number or an abbreviation of that word. The abbreviation for the word "Number" shall, as a minimum, begin with the letter "N" (e.g., No or No.) The abbreviation for the word "Model" shall be "Mod" or Mod." (Code Reference G-S.1.)~~	~~Yes~~	~~No~~	~~N/A~~
2.3	~~Except for equipment with no moving or electronic component parts, a non-repetitive serial number. (Code Reference G-S.1.)~~	~~Yes~~	~~No~~	~~N/A~~
2.4.	~~The serial number shall be prefaced by words, an abbreviation, or a symbol, that clearly identifies the number as the required serial number. (Code Reference G-S.1.)~~	~~Yes~~	~~No~~	~~N/A~~
2.5.	~~The serial number shall be prefaced by the words "Serial Number" or an abbreviation of that term. Abbreviations for the word "Serial" shall, as a minimum, begin with the letter "S," and abbreviations for the word "Number" shall, as a minimum, begin with the letter "N" (e.g., S/N, SN, Ser. No, and S No.). (Code Reference G-S.1.)~~	~~Yes~~	~~No~~	~~N/A~~
2.6.	~~[Code Reference G-S.1. (g).]~~ ~~The NTEP Certificate of Conformance (CC) Number or a corresponding CC addendum number for devices that have (or will have) a CC. The number shall be prefaced by the terms "NTEP CC," "CC," or "Approval." These terms may be followed by the word "Number" or an abbreviation for the word "Number." The abbreviation shall as a minimum begin with the letter "N" (e.g., No or No.).~~ ~~The device must have an area, either on the identification plate or on the device itself, suitable for the application of the Certificate of Conformance Number. If the area for the CC number is not part of an identification plate, note its intended location and how it will be applied.~~ ~~Location of CC Number if not located with the identification information: _____~~	~~Yes~~	~~No~~	~~N/A~~
2.7.	~~If the information required by G-S.1. is placed on a badge or plate, the badge or plate must be permanently attached to the device. (See criteria above for permanence of Attachment of Badge.)~~	~~Yes~~	~~No~~	~~N/A~~
2.8	~~Identifying information shall be so located that it is readily observable without the necessity of the disassembly of a part requiring the use of any means separate from the device.~~	~~Yes~~	~~No~~	~~N/A~~
2.9.	~~The indicator is marked with its accuracy class. Indicate class: _____~~	~~Yes~~	~~No~~	~~N/A~~
2.10.	~~The device meets all the parameters for the accuracy class.~~	~~Yes~~	~~No~~	~~N/A~~
2.11.	The indicator is marked with the maximum number of scale divisions (for each accuracy class) for which it complies with requirements.	Yes	No	N/A
2.12.	The system shall be marked with the operating temperature range if the temperature range is other than 14 °F to 104 °F (−10 °C to 40 °C).	Yes	No	N/A
2.13.	~~The nominal capacity by minimum scale division shall be clearly and conspicuously marked adjacent to the weight display (acceptable location depends on conspicuousness).~~	~~Yes~~	~~No~~	~~N/A~~

~~2.14.~~	~~The capacity division size shall be marked for all weight units that can be displayed, such as, both lb and kilograms.~~	~~Yes~~	~~No~~	~~N/A~~
~~2.15.~~	~~If equipped with variable resolution, the scale shall be marked with the weight ranges and corresponding scale division sizes.~~	~~Yes~~	~~No~~	~~N/A~~
~~2.16.~~	~~If the capacity by division statement is displayed on a video terminal with the weight values, then the capacity by division statement must be adjacent to the weight display and displayed whenever the system is in the weighing mode.~~	~~Yes~~	~~No~~	~~N/A~~
~~2.17.~~	~~All markings must be clear and easily readable.~~	~~Yes~~	~~No~~	~~N/A~~
~~2.18.~~	~~The lettering must be permanent (use the procedures outlined in section 1 for "Permanence of Lettering"). Record the grade for the permanence of markings:~~	~~Yes~~	~~No~~	~~N/A~~

2.3. The badge or decal must be durable (difficult to remove at all temperatures).   Yes   No   N/A

2.4. If the indicator is for Class III/III L applications, the "CLC" (concentrated load capacity) shall be marked on or adjacent to the identification markings or nomenclature plate that is attached to the system. (or space provided to include the CLC).   Yes   No   N/A

2.5. The section capacity of a railway track and livestock scale-indicating element shall be marked on or adjacent to the identification badge on the indicating element. The section capacity shall be prefaced by the words "Section Capacity" or an abbreviation of that term. Abbreviations shall be "Sec Cap" or "Sec C." All capital letters and periods may be used.   Yes   No   N/A

3. Additional Marking Requirements- Not Built-for-Purpose Software-Based Devices

Code Reference: G.S.1.1.

3.1. At least one of the following methods must be used:

     3.1.1. The manufacturer or distributor and the model designation are marked on the device according to Section 1 Markings - Applicable to Indicating, Weighing/Load-Receiving Elements and Complete Scales.   Yes   No   N/A

4. Additional Marking Requirements – Weighing/Load-Receiving Elements

Code References: S.6., Table S.6.3.a., and Table S.6.3.b.

Weighing/load-receiving elements and indicators that are; (1) in the same housing, or (2) permanently hard wired together, or (3) sealed with a physical seal or an electronic link, shall have markings that comply with section "1 Markings - Applicable to Indicating, Weighing/Load-Receiving Elements and Complete Scales." This does not apply…

~~4.1.~~	~~The name, initials, or trademark of the manufacturer or distributor. A remote display is required to have the manufacturer's name or trademark and model designation.~~	~~Yes~~	~~No~~	~~N/A~~
~~4.2.~~	~~A model designation that positively identifies the pattern or design of the device. The Model designation shall be prefaced by the word "Model," "Type," or "Pattern." These terms may be followed by the term "Number or an abbreviation of that word. The abbreviation for the word "Number" shall, as a minimum, begin with the letter "N" (e.g., No or No.)The abbreviation for the word "Model" shall be "Mod" or "Mod." (Code Reference G-S.1.)~~	~~Yes~~	~~No~~	~~N/A~~

~~4.3.~~	~~Except for equipment with no moving or electronic component parts, a Non-repetitive serial number. (Code Reference G-S.1.)~~	~~Yes~~	~~No~~	~~N/A~~	
~~4.4.~~	~~The serial number shall be prefaced by words, an abbreviation, or a symbol, that clearly identifies the number as the required serial number. (Code Reference G-S.1.)~~	~~Yes~~	~~No~~	~~N/A~~	
~~4.5.~~	~~The serial number shall be prefaced by the words "Serial Number" or an abbreviation of that term. Abbreviations for the word "Serial" shall, as a minimum, begin with the letter "S," and abbreviations for the word "Number" shall, as a minimum, begin with the letter "N" (e.g., S/N, SN, Ser. No, and S No.). (Code Reference G-S.1.)~~	~~Yes~~	~~No~~	~~N/A~~	
~~4.6.~~	~~[Code Reference G-S.1. (e).]~~	~~Yes~~	~~No~~	~~N/A~~	
	~~The NTEP Certificate of Conformance (CC) Number or a corresponding CC addendum number for devices that have (or will have) a CC. The number shall be prefaced by the terms "NTEP CC," "CC," or "Approval." These terms may be followed by the word "Number" or an abbreviation for the word "Number."~~				
	~~The abbreviation shall as a minimum begin with the letter "N" (e.g., No or No.).~~				
	~~The device must have an area, either on the identification plate or on the device itself, suitable for the application of the Certificate of Conformance Number. If the area for the CC number is not part of an identification plate, note its intended location and how it will be applied.~~				
	~~Location of CC Number if not located with the identification information: _____~~				
~~4.7.~~	~~If the information required by G-S.1. is placed on a badge or plate, the badge or plate must be permanently attached to the device. (See criteria above for permanence of Attachment of Badge.)~~	~~Yes~~	~~No~~	~~N/A~~	
~~4.8.~~	~~Identifying information shall be so located that it is readily observable without the necessity of the disassembly of a part requiring the use of any means separate from the device.~~	~~Yes~~	~~No~~	~~N/A~~	
4.1~~9~~.	The nominal capacity of the weighing/load-receiving element.	Yes	No	N/A	
4.2~~10~~.	Its accuracy class. Indicate class: _____	Yes	No	N/A	
~~4.11.~~	~~The device meets all the parameters for the accuracy class.~~	~~Yes~~	~~No~~	~~N/A~~	
4.3~~12~~.	The maximum number of scale divisions for which it complies with requirements.	Yes	No	N/A	
4.4~~13~~.	The minimum verification scale division for which it complies with requirements.	Yes	No	N/A	
4.5~~14~~.	The weighing/load-receiving element shall be marked with the operating temperature range if the temperature range is other than 14 °F to 104 °F (−10 °C to 40 °C).	Yes	No	N/A	
4.6~~15~~.	The lettering must be permanent. Record the grade for the permanence of markings: (Use procedures in section 1.)	Yes	No	N/A	
4.7~~16~~.	If the information is placed on a badge or plate, the badge or plate must be permanently attached to the device. If a badge, label, or plate made of a metal or plastic is used, then it must be riveted, welded, or attached to the scale by an adhesive so that a tool is required to remove it (bolts or removable screws are not acceptable).	Yes	No	N/A	
4.8~~17~~.	The information must be mounted on a protected surface such as the side of the weighing/load-receiving element, behind a ramp or under a cover plate. Access to the marking should be available with minimum effort.	Yes	No	N/A	

NTEP Committee 2006 Final Report
Appendix C – NTETC Weighing Sector - Appendix A. Recommendations

Location of the required identification information:

4.9 18.	The information must be on a surface that is an integral part of the chassis.	Yes No N/A
4.19.	~~All markings must be clear and easily readable.~~	~~Yes No N/A~~
4.10 20.	The identification information for the weighing/load-receiving elements of vehicle, axle-load, livestock, and railway track scales shall be located:	Yes No N/A
	4.10 20.1. Near the point where the signal leaves the weighing/load-receiving element. This would be the transverse lever on a mechanical scale.	Yes No N/A
	4.10 20.2. The information shall be on or near the junction box nearest the point where the signal leaves the scale on an above-ground scale.	Yes No N/A

5. Additional Marking Requirements - Livestock, Vehicle, and Railway Track Scales

Code References: G-S.1., G-S.5.1., ~~and~~ S.6.3, S.6.4., and S.6.5.

No additional changes to this section.

6. Additional Marking Requirements - Force Transducers (Load Cells)

Code References: S.6., Table S.6.3.a., and Table S.6.3.b.

No additional changes to this section.

Proposed changes to ECRS Sections 5 and 7.

5. Identification
Code References: G-S.1., G-S.5.1., and S.6.3

Example Modular System: Point of sale systems may consist of a file server, CPU, keyboard, printer, display, and cash drawer. A file server, which performs metrological functions such as price computations, must be marked with the system make, model, and unique serial number with required prefix. File servers, which only store information processed by other components in the system, need not be marked in accordance with S.6.3.

"Dumb" indicators with no intelligence (such as remote displays on point-of-sale systems) do not require marking in accordance with S.6.3. unless they are the primary indicator for the system. Primary indicators must be marked with or display ~~have~~ a manufacturer's ID, model designation, serial number and prefix, accuracy class, and n_{max}. The capacity by division statement must be indicated in a clear and conspicuous manner and be readily apparent when viewing the reading face of the scale indicator ~~and capacity and division size (adjacent to the weight display)~~.

7. Marking Requirements

Code References: ~~S.6.1.,~~ S.6.2., S.6.3., ~~S.6.5.,~~ Table S.6.3.a. and Table S.6.3.b.

The weight display in a point-of-sale system must be marked with the scale capacity and the displayed scale division, regardless of the location of the weight display in the system. If the analog-to-digital converter for the scale is located in

NTEP Committee 2006 Final Report
Appendix C – NTETC Weighing Sector - Appendix A. Recommendations

the ECR, then the ECR must also be marked with the accuracy class and the operating temperature range of the weighing system if different from −10 °C to 40 °C (14 °F to 104 °F).

The lettering must be permanent as described in section 1, but the attachment of any badge or decal is slightly less stringent than for the G-S.1. information. In terms of attachment, any badge or decal must be "durable," that is, it must be difficult to remove (at all temperatures).

7.1. The capacity and value of the scale division shall be marked or indicated in a clear and conspicuous manner and be readily apparent when viewing the reading face of the scale indicator ~~adjacent to the weight display.~~   Yes   No   N/A

There are no additional changes recommended for Section 7.

Agenda Item 1 (d) Time Dependence (Creep Test) for Scales

58. Time Dependence Test for Scales and Separable Load-receiving Elements

Code References: T.N.4.5.1. and T.N.4.5.2.

This test shall be conducted on Class II, III, and IIII complete scales and weighing/load-receiving elements in a laboratory. The applied load shall be between 90 % and 100 % of capacity for scales with capacities of 2000 lb or less. For scales with capacities greater than 2000 lb, the load cell or load cells shall be tested individually. The test shall be conducted at the temperature extremes specified for the device under test (DUT).

For Class III L scales that cannot be tested in the laboratory, the load cell or load cells shall have an NTEP Certificate of Conformance and be suitable for the device(s) submitted for evaluation with respect to n_{max} V_{min} nominal capacity, maximum capacity, accuracy class, temperature limits, single or multiple load cell application, minimum dead load, and safe load limit.

58.1. ~~After the application of the load at constant test conditions, the indications after 20 seconds and 1 hour shall not differ by more than the absolute value of the applicable tolerance.~~   Yes   No   N/A

Load the instrument close to Max. Take one reading as soon as the indication has stabilized and then note the indication in one hour intervals while the load remains on the instrument for a period of four hours. During this test the temperature should not vary more than 2 °C.

The test may be terminated after 30 minutes if the indication differs less than 0.5 e during the first 30 minutes and the difference between 15 and 30 minutes is less than 0.2 e.

If these conditions are not met, the difference between the indication obtained immediately after placing a load on the instrument and the indication observed during the following four hours shall not exceed the absolute value of the maximum permissible error at the load applied.

58.2. The deviation in the zero indication before and after a period of loading with a load close to Max for half an hour, shall be determined. The reading shall be taken as soon as the indication has stabilized.   Yes   No   N/A

For multiple range instruments, continue to read the zero indication during the following 5 minutes after the indication has stabilized.

If the instrument is provided with zero-tracking it shall not be in operation during the test.

TIME DEPENDENCE TEST FORM
Code Reference: T.N.4.5.1

Control No.: _____
Pattern designation: _____
Date: _____
Observer: _____
Verification scale interval e: _____
Resolution during test (smaller than e): _____

	At start	At max	At end	
Temp:				°C
Rel. h:				%
Time:				
Bar. Pres: (Only Class I)				hPa

Zero-tracking device is:
[ ] Non-existent   [ ] Not in operation   [ ] Out of working range

$E = I + 0.5\,e - \Delta L - L$

Load L	Time of Reading	Indication I	Add. Load ΔL	Error	mpe
	Initial + 20 sec				
	5 min				
	15 min				
	30 min				
	If the difference between the indication obtained at 15 minutes and that at 30 minutes exceeds 0.2 e, the difference between the indication obtained immediately after placing the load on the instrument and the indication observed during the following four hours shall not exceed the absolute value of the maximum permissible error at the load applied.				
	1 hr				
	2 hr				
	3 hr				
	4 hr				

15 to 30 min [ ] Passed [ ] Failed
0 to 30 min   [ ] Passed [ ] Failed
0 to 4 hr   [ ] Passed [ ] Failed   [ ] Not Applicable

Time Dependence Zero Return

Zero-tracking device is:
[ ] Non-existent   [ ] Not in operation   [ ] Out of working range

$P = I + 0.5\,e - \Delta L$

Time of Reading	Load L_0	Indication of zero I_0	Add. load ΔL	P
After loading for 30 minutes Load =				

Change of indication $\Delta P =$ _____

Check that $|\Delta P| \leq |MPE|$ for Class III L devices
Check that $|\Delta P| \leq 0.5\,e$ for Class II, III, and IIII devices

[ ] Passed   [ ] Failed

Meaning of symbols:
I = Indication
I_0 = Indication of no-load reference at the start of the test
L = Load
L_0 = Mass of no-load reference at the start of the test
Add. load ΔL = Additional load to next changeover point
P = Digital indication prior to rounding = $I + 1/2\,e - \Delta L$
E = Error = I - L or P - L
mpe = Maximum permissible error
EUT = Equipment under test

Remarks:

Agenda Item 1 (e) Time Dependence (Creep Test) for Load Cells

J. Tests to be Performed

1. Force transducer (load cell) error with respect to temperature.
2. Repeatability based on results of test 1.
3. Temperature effect on minimum dead load output.
4. Creep (~~30-minute one hour~~ test per HB-44 or 30-minute test per OIML R 60).
5. Barometric pressure effect if the cell is sensitive to barometric pressure changes as determined by guidelines discussed in the section titled "Barometric Pressure Tests."

L. Tolerances

Handbook 44 Reference	Table 3 Tolerance for Class III Force transducers (load cells)			
	Single Cell Requirement		**Multiple Cell Requirement**	
Force transducer (load cell) Error Table 6, Class III; T.N.3.2., T.N.8.1.1.	0.7 Factor Applied		1.0 Factor Applied	
	Load	Tolerance	Load	Tolerance
	0 to 500 v	0.35 v	0 to 500 v	0.50 v
	501 to 2000 v	0.70 v	501 to 2000 v	1.00 v
	2001 to 4000 v	1.05 v	2001 to 4000 v	1.50 v
	4001 to 10 000 v	1.75 v	4001 to 10 000 v	2.50 v
Repeatability Error; T.N.5., T.N.8.1.1	0.7 Factor Applied		1.0 Factor Applied	
	Load	Tolerance	Load	Tolerance
	0 to 500 v	0.70 v	0 to 500 v	1.00 v
	501 to 2000 v	1.40 v	501 to 2000 v	2.00 v
	2 001 to 4000 v	2.10 v	2 001 to 4000 v	3.00 v
	4001 to 10 000 v	3.50 v	4001 to 10 000 v	5.00 v
~~Creep (test at 90-100% of force transducer (load cell) capacity); T.N.4.5.~~	~~1.0 Factor Applied~~		~~1.0 Factor Applied~~	
	~~Load~~	~~Tolerance~~	~~Load~~	~~Tolerance~~
	~~0 - 500 v~~	~~0.50 v~~	~~0 - 500 v~~	~~0.50 v~~
	~~501 - 2000 v~~	~~1.00 v~~	~~501 - 2000 v~~	~~1.00 v~~
	~~2001 - 4000 v~~	~~1.50 v~~	~~2001 - 4000 v~~	~~1.50 v~~
	~~4001 - 10 000 v~~	~~2.50 v~~	~~4001 - 10 000 v~~	~~2.50 v~~
Temperature Effect on Minimum Dead Load Output; T.N.8.1.3. T.N.8.1.1	0.7 v_{min} /5 °C		0.7 v_{min} /5 °C	
Effects of Barometric Pressure; T.N.8.2.	Applicable only to specified force transducers (load cells) 1 v_{min} /1kPa		Applicable only to specified force transducers (load cells) 1 v_{min} /1kPa	

Table 4
Tolerance for Class III L Force transducers (load cells)

Handbook 44 Reference	Single Cell Requirement		Multiple Cell Requirement	
Force transducer (load cell) Error Table 6, Class III L; T.N.3.2., T.N.8.1.1.	0.7 Factor Applied		1.0 Factor Applied	
	Load	Tolerance	Load	Tolerance
	0 v to 500 v	0.35 v	0 v to 500 v	0.50 v
	501 v to 1 000 v[1]	0.70 v	501 v to 1 000 v[2]	1.00 v
	[1]Add 0.35v to the tolerance for each 500v of load or fraction thereof up to a maximum load of 10 000v		[2]Add 0.50v to the tolerance for each 500v of load or fraction thereof, up to a maximum load of 10 000v	
Repeatability Error; T.N.5., T.N.8.1.1.	0.7 Factor Applied		1.0 Factor Applied	
	Load	Tolerance	Load	Tolerance
	0 v to 500 v	0.70 v	0 v to 500 v	1.00 v
	501 v to 1 000 v	1.40 v	501 v to 1 000 v	2.00 v
	9001 v to 9500 v	13.30 v	9001 v to 9500 v	19.00 v
	9501 v to 10 000 v	14.00 v	9501 v to 10 000 v	20.00 v
	[3]Add 0.70v to the tolerance for each 500 v of load or fraction thereof up to a maximum load of 10 000v		[4]Add 1.00v to the tolerance for each 500v of load or fraction thereof up to a maximum load of 10 000v	
~~Creep (test at 90-100% of force transducer (load cell) capacity); T.N.4.5.~~	~~1.0 Factor Applied~~		~~1.0 Factor Applied~~	
	~~Load~~	~~Tolerance~~	~~Load~~	~~Tolerance~~
	~~0 – 500v~~	~~0.25v~~	~~0 – 500v~~	~~0.25v~~
	~~501 – 1000v~~	~~0.50v~~	~~501 – 1000v~~	~~0.50v~~
	~~9001 – 9500v~~	~~4.75v~~	~~9001 – 9500v~~	~~4.75v~~
	~~9501 – 10 000v~~	~~5.00v~~	~~9501 – 10 000v~~	~~5.00v~~
	~~[5]Add 0.25v to the tolerance for each 500v of load or fraction thereof up to a maximum load of 10 000v~~			
Temperature Effect on Minimum Dead Load Output; T.N.8.1.3. T.N.8.1.1	2.1 v_{min} /5 °C		2.1 v_{min} /5 °C	
Effects of Barometric Pressure; T.N.8.2.	Applicable only to specified force transducers (load cells) 1 v_{min} /1kPa		Applicable only to specified force transducers (load cells) 1 v_{min} /1kPa	

II. Determination of Creep

1. At 20 °C ambient, insert the force transducer (load cell) into the force generating system and load to the minimum dead load. If Procedure I. (which includes increasing and decreasing load tests) has just been completed, wait 1 hour. If a separate creep test is being conducted, exercise the force transducer (load cell) as in Procedure I.5 and then wait 1 hour.

2. If the indicating element for the force transducer (load cell) is provided with a convenient means for checking itself, conduct the self-test at this time.

3. Monitor minimum load output until stable.

4. ~~There are two test methods to determine the creep characteristics of force transducers (load cells). The 1-hour creep test at the maximum load (step 4. (a)) is the preferred form of the creep test; run the return-to-zero creep test (step 4. (b)) only when justified by limitations in the test equipment. The NTEP will conduct step 4. (a) creep tests whenever possible.~~

~~Take readings at 1-minute time intervals for the first 10 minutes and every 10 minutes thereafter.~~

   a. **Test for Creep:** Apply a load equal to 90 % to 100 % of the maximum capacity of the force transducer (load cell) and record the indication 20 seconds after reaching the load. The time to load test weights and read the indicator shall be as short as possible and shall not exceed the time specified in Table 5. With the load remaining on the load cell, cContinue to record indications periodically, thereafter at time intervals over a 30 minute ~~1 hour~~ period.

   Note: A 30-minute test is acceptable if the creep test is performed in accordance to OIML R 60 tolerances.

   b. Remove a load equal to 90 % to 100 % of the maximum capacity of the force transducer (load cell) that has been applied for ~~1 hour~~ 30 minutes. Record the indication after 20 seconds. The time to unload test weights and read the indicator shall be as short as possible and not exceed the time specified in Table 5. Continue to record indications periodically thereafter at time intervals over a 1 hour period (or 30 minutes if the creep test is conducted according to OIML R 60 requirements).

Table 5 Loading Times		
Load		**Time**
Greater than	**To and including**	
0 kg	10 kg	10 s
10 kg	100 kg	15 s
100 kg	1 000 kg	20 s
1 000 kg	10 000 kg	30 s
10 000 kg	100 000 kg	50 s
100 000 kg	------------	60 s

5. Repeat the operations described in steps 2 through 4 at the high and low temperature limits for the accuracy class~~. If~~ the manufacturer has specified a smaller or a larger range, repeat operations at the limits marked on the cell, provided the temperature range is at least the range required for the accuracy class.

6. With the resulting data, and accounting for the effect of barometric pressure changes, determine the magnitude of the creep and compare it to the tolerance in NIST Handbook 44 Scales Code Table T.N.4.6.2.

NTEP Committee 2006 Final Report
Appendix C – NTETC Weighing Sector - Appendix A. Recommendations

Table T.N.4.6.
Maximum Permissible Error (mpe) * for Load Cells
During Type Evaluation

Class	\[mpe in Load Cell Verifications Divisions (v) = p_{LC} x Basic Tolerance in v\]		
	p_{LC} x 0.5 v	p_{LC} x 1.0 v	p_{LC} x 1.5 v
I	0 v to 50 000 v	50 001 v to 200 000 v	200 001 v +
II	0 v to 5 000 v	5 001 v to 20 000 v	20 001 v +
III	0 v to 500 v	501 v to 2 000 v	2 001 v +
IIII	0 v to 50 v	51 v to 200 v	201 v +
III L	0 v to 500 v	501 v to 1 000 v	(Add 0.5 v to the basic tolerance for each additional 500 v or fraction thereof up to a maximum load of 10 000 v)

v represents the load cell verification interval
p_{LC} represents the apportionment factors applied to the basic tolerance
p_{LC} = 0.7 for load cells marked with S (single load cell applications)
p_{LC} = 1.0 for load cells marked with M (multiple load cell applications)
* mpe = p_{LC} x Basic Tolerance in load cell verifications divisions (v)

Agenda Item 11. Performance and Permanence Tests for Railway Track Scales Used to Weigh Statically

The Weighing Sector recommendation to amend Publication 14 Performance and Permanence Testing for Railway Track Scales in Agenda Item 11 was modified as follows according to the results of a November 10, 2005.

The NIST Technical Advisor reported the results of the ballot, including comments, to the Sector and NTEP Committee prior to the 2006 NCWM Interim Meeting.

69. Performance and Permanence Tests for Railway Track Scales Used to Weigh Statically

(NOTE: For combination vehicle/railway track scales, see also additional test considerations under "Test Considerations for Other Scales" in the application.)

It is desirable, but not required, that a new installation should be calibrated by a railroad test car after a representative of the railroad has inspected the installation for compliance with railroad design and construction specifications. A 100 000 lb field standard weight cart, or a combination of field standard weights safely added to a field standard weight cart for a total of 100 000 lb, will be used to conduct the initial NTEP calibration and test.

The permanence test shall not be conducted sooner than thirty (30) days after the initial NTEP test. If a 100 000 lb field standard weight cart, or a combination of field standard weights safely added to a field standard weight cart for a total of 100 000 lb, is not available for the subsequent permanence verification a 100 000 lb capacity railroad scale test car of may be used.

NOTE: A field standard weight cart shall have a footprint no greater than 7', which is the size of the footprint of railway track test weight cars. [The Association of American Railroad Scale (AAR) Handbook 2005 Revision © requirements for "standard railway track scale test weight car" can be found in AAR Handbook for Scales Sections 1.5 through 1.5.5. A standard rail car, as described in AAR Handbook Section 1.5.6, is not suitable for use during NTEP evaluations since the entire load of the rail car can not be concentrated in a footprint no greater than 7".]

Performance tests are conducted to determine compliance with the tolerances and, in the case of nonautomatic indicating scales, the sensitivity requirements specified in NIST Handbook 44. The tests described here apply primarily to the weighing/load-receiving element. It is assumed that the indicating element used during the test has already been examined and found to comply with applicable requirements. If the design and performance of the indicating element is to be determined during the same test, the applicable requirements for weighbeams, poises, dials, electronic digital indications, etc., must also be referenced.

69.1. Influence Factors

If tests are necessary to determine compliance with influence factors, individual main elements and components tests must be conducted according to NTEP Policy that is outlined in NCWM Publication 14, Section B.1. Influence Factor Requirements.

69.2. Test Standards

A 100 000 lb field standard weight cart or a 100 000 lb combination of field standard weights safely added to a field standard weight cart shall be used for the initial test using known test weights, in increments of 10 000 lb. Railroad test weight cars shall not be used for the initial test.

69.3. Sensitivity and Discrimination Tests

69.3.1. Weighbeams

The sensitivity test is conducted at zero load and at maximum load. The sensitivity test is conducted by determining the actual test weight value necessary to bring the beam from a rest point at the center of the trig loop to rest points at the top and bottom of the trig loop. The maximum load at which the sensitivity test is conducted need not be comprised of known test weight.

69.4. Digital Indications

Width-of-zero, zone of uncertainty, and automatic-zero-setting mechanism (if so equipped) tests shall be conducted as specified in other sections of NCWM Publication 14.

69.5. Increasing Load and Section Tests

69.5.1.
A minimum of three observations shall be made at test weight loads of at least 30 000 lb, 40 000 lb, and 50 000 lb moving test cart across the scale in both directions. [12] Readings may be taken at 10 000 lb and 20 000 lb increments. Additional observations shall be made with a 50 000 lb test weight load. Remove test weight load from scale before moving in opposite direction and record any zero balance change. Zero the scale if necessary, and repeat this test moving the weights in the opposite direction. When the weights have been returned to the starting point, apply additional loads, making observations in increments equal to the value of each test weight (10 000 lb) up to 100 000 lb at each end if practical. Repeat tests with the load concentrated to the right and left over each section and midway between sections in both directions.

69.5.2. The results shall be within acceptance tolerance.

69.6. Strain Load Tests

The minimum test load for a strain-load test for single-load-receiving element platforms greater than 35 feet and for multiple-load-receiving element scale systems designed to weigh railroad cars in a single draft is 200 000 lb.

69.6.1. Place a strain load on the scale so that the test load can be placed on one end section and observe the weight to the smallest increment practical. Add a test weight load(s) to end section. If practical, repeat this test on the other end section.

Remove the test load, observing any balance change, then remove the strain load. If practical, repeat this test on the other end section. Conduct any sensitivity and discrimination tests at maximum load.

~~69.6.2. Place the strain load and the empty GIPSA or GIPSA-type test car on the load-receiving element platform so that the weights can be incrementally loaded from the weight cart, which remains off the platform. Observe weight to the smallest increment practicable. Load the test car with the test weights. Observe weight indications in increments equal to each added test weight (10 000 lb). At this maximum load, sensitivity and discrimination tests should be conducted.~~

~~69.6.3.~~ 69.6.2. The results of all observations shall be within acceptance tolerance.

69.7. Permanence Test

~~The permanence test shall be conducted after a minimum of 20 days after successful completion of the initial performance test.~~ It is recommended that the performance tests described above be repeated. However, it if ~~the~~ original test cart (and additional field standards if applicable) is not available, the test may be conducted to the extent possible with a ~~t~~ standard railway track scale test weight car with at least a 100 000 lb capacity and a suitable and current calibration report. ~~least two railroad test weight cars.~~ The results of this test must be within acceptance tolerance. ~~If~~ If the device does not meet these tolerance limits the scale will be rejected and the entire test must be repeated, including successful initial performance testing and a subsequent test after a minimum of 30 days.

69.7.1 Minimum Use Requirements for the Field Permanence Test

69.7.1.1 There must be at least 300 weighing operations executed over the scale prior to conducting the type evaluation permanence test. The permanence test should be performed at a customer location to be able to evaluate "normal" use.

69.7.1.2 The minimum time period of use is 30 days with a minimum of 300 weighing operations as described below. The subsequent permanence test should be tentatively scheduled when the initial test is started. If the 300 weighing operations have not been completed by that time, the time for the field permanence test shall be extended until at least 300 weighing operations have been completed. The second phase of the permanence test can be conducted as soon as 300 weighing operations have been achieved, but no sooner than 30 days after the initial test of the field permanence test. Acceptance tolerances apply regardless of the length of the test.

69.7.1.3 Only loads, which reflect "normal" use, will be counted during the permanence-testing period.
• 100 % of the loads must be above 20 % of scale capacity; and
• 50 % of the loads must be above 50 % of scale capacity.

The scale may be used to weigh other loads, but only the loads specified above are counted as part of the permanence test.

69.7.2 Subsequent Type Evaluation (Field) Permanence Test

A minimum of two increasing-load, two decreasing-load, and two section tests are to be conducted a minimum of 30 days after the initial tests. However, if the original field standard weight cart is not available, the test may be conducted to the extent possible with at least one railroad test cars. Strain load tests shall be conducted with a minimum 200 000 lb test load. If the test results are at or near acceptance tolerance limits, at least one more set of tests should be conducted immediately to verify the test results and determine device repeatability.

Repeat width-of-zero, zone of uncertainty, sensitivity, and discrimination tests near zero (outside the range of the AZSM) and at or near capacity on the subsequent tests.

If the device does not meet these tolerance limits, the entire test must be repeated, including successful initial performance testing and a subsequent test after a minimum of 30 days and an additional 300 weighing operations as described in the criteria above.

[12] Do not exceed section capacity

~~If the subsequent performance test cannot be completed within 30 days because of the unavailability of test cars, maintenance tolerance will be applied.~~

Agenda Item 12. Cash Acceptors or Card-activated Systems

Publication 14 ECRS, Section 13. Cash Acceptors or Card-activated Systems

Code References: G-S.2., G-S.5.1., G-S.6

(Note: Language changes and additions approved by the 2005 NTEP Committee are indicated in shaded, ~~strike-out, and~~ underlined text. Language changes and additions recommended by the Weighing Sector are indicated in **bolden, ~~strike-out,~~ and underlined** text.)

13.6.	Printed Receipt - A printed receipt must be available to the customer from the device at the completion of the transaction.	Yes	No	N/A
13.7.	~~Because the customer must be provided with a receipt, t~~T**he** system must not accept cash if sufficient paper is not available to complete the transaction.	Yes	No	N/A
13.8	The cash acceptor must not initiate a cash **or card** transaction if **one** ~~either~~ of the following conditions are true:	~~Yes~~	~~No~~	~~N/A~~
	• no paper is in the receipt printer of the cash **or card** acceptor;	Yes	No	N/A
	• insufficient paper is available to complete a transaction; or	Yes	No	N/A
	• the ECR receipt must be capable of being recalled and printed on a different printer. Instructions shall be displayed on the customer display or printed (if there is sufficient paper) directing the customer to see the store attendant or manager for a printed copy of the receipt.	Yes	No	N/A
13.9.	Instructions must be marked on the device to inform the customer how to operate the cash **or card** acceptor.	Yes	No	N/A
13.10.	Means must be provided for the customer to cancel the transaction at any point.	Yes	No	N/A
	13.10.1. If the customer cancels the transaction by pressing the cancel key (or equivalent key(s)), after the cash has been accepted, the device must either:			
	13.10.1.1. be equipped with means for the customer to retrieve the cash inserted from the device, AND	Yes	No	N/A
	automatically issue a printed receipt indicating the amount of cash tendered and the amount returned, OR			
	13.10.1.2. display instructions (such as "sale **canceled** ~~terminated~~," see attendant," "sale **canceled** ~~terminated~~, get receipt" or similar wording) for the customer to see the attendant, AND	Yes	No	N/A
	automatically issue a printed receipt showing the amount of cash inserted by the customer, a statement indicating that the sale was **canceled** ~~terminated~~, and instructions for the customer to see the attendant.			
13.11.	Means must be provided for the customer to retrieve correct change if the device has insufficient money to return to the customer.	Yes	No	N/A
	The device must display instructions (such as "insufficient change, see			

attendant." or similar wording) directing the customer to see the attendant, AND

Automatically issue a printed receipt showing the amount of cash inserted by the customer, a statement indicating that the sale was canceled ~~terminated~~, and instructions for the customer to see the attendant.

Note: It is acceptable for different messages to be used ~~when providing instructions to the customer~~. This depends upon whether the transaction is terminated by use of the cancel key, insufficient receipt paper, or insufficient change (e.g., "sale terminated, get receipt~~,~~" or "sale terminated, see cashier~~,"~~ or "change due, see cashier").

Agenda Item 14. CLC for Combination Railway Track/Vehicle Scales

8.3.   Modular Load-Cell Vehicle, Livestock, or Railroad Track Scales

NOTE: *These criteria apply if the scale is fully electronic (i.e., load cells comprise the sensors of the weighing/load-receiving element) and is of a modular design.*

Modular Scale. A vehicle, livestock, or railroad track scale made up of individual load-receiving elements of like design, which can be joined together to form a larger integral load-receiving element and can be separated at any time without structurally changing the individual load-receiving elements. This definition is to be applied for all new type evaluations and for applications to add new devices to an existing CC (see Figure 3).
(Effective January 2001)

8.3.1.   Modular Scale to be Tested

The following criteria must be satisfied in the scale design and the scale to be tested:

a. Load cells of the same design and capacity that consists of simply attaching modules together must be used throughout the family. If load cells of different capacities are used for scales of different structural design ~~weighbridge~~ strength and nominal capacity in the family of scales, then the module using the higher capacity load cells must be evaluated.

~~b. CLC in the family must be not less than 40 percent of the sum of the capacity of two load cells or 80 percent of the capacity of one cell.~~

~~c.~~ b. A scale with at least two modules must be tested. The module with the largest CLC is to be tested. If the longest span between sections is not tested, the CC will include up to 120 % of the span between sections that was tested. Arrangements regarding the specific scale in the family to be tested will be established in consultation with NTEP representatives.

NTEP Committee 2006 Final Report
Appendix C – NTETC Weighing Sector - Appendix A. Recommendations

Agenda Item 15. Abbreviations for Carat and Count in Publication 14 Sections 38 and 76.

38. Counting Feature on Class I or II Scales Used in Prescription Filling Applications

38.3.	The scale display differentiates between count indications and weight indications. (See Section 76 for acceptable abbreviations and symbols)	Yes No N/A
38.3.1.	The abbreviation or symbol "pc(s)," "ct," or "cnt" may be used to identify count or pieces.	Yes No N/A
38.3.2.	If abbreviation or symbol "ct" is used to identify count, in a ~~separate display for other than weight information, the "ct" or "c" shall not be it~~ is not used to identify carat in the ~~weight display~~ weighing mode.	Yes No N/A
~~38.3.3.~~	~~If symbol "ct" is used to identify count in a shared or combined display, the same abbreviation "ct" or "c" for carat shall not be used to identify the carat unit of measure and count.~~	Yes No N/A
38.4.	Values must be identified with an adequate ~~the~~ word, abbreviation, or symbol for ~~pieces (pcs) or count (ct). If~~ the symbol ∴ shown in Section 76. Table of Acceptable Abbreviations/Symbols is used and is intended for the customer, it cannot be used without additional description, marks, or directions displayed or marked on the device).	Yes No N/A

76. List of Acceptable Abbreviations/Symbols

Device Application	Term	Acceptable	<u>Not</u> Acceptable
General:	Piece(s)	Pieces, pc, or pcs	
	Count	count, cnt, or pc(s), is encouraged for symbol for pieces. ct is acceptable (HB-130)	c
Values Defined:	Other symbols	General Table of Weights And Measures, HB-44*	
Values Defined (cont)	carat carat or carat troy = 200 mg	c (HB-44 and NIST Guide for the Use of the International System of Units (SI) by B. N. Taylor) ct (common jewelry industry terminology and is only acceptable by Canada)	ct (is not permitted if used as the abbreviation for carat and count on a scale with an enabled count feature)
*Exceptions to Gen'l Tables of W&M, HB-44:	carat carat or carat troy = 200 mg	ct, ~~c~~ (common jewelry industry terminology)	ct (is not permitted if used as the abbreviation for carat and count on a scale with an enabled count feature)
	U.S. short ton	Ton or TN	

NTEP Committee 2006 Final Report
Appendix C – NTETC Weighing Sector - Appendix A. Recommendations

Agenda Item 16. Performance and Permanence Test for Bench and Counter Scales

63. Performance and Permanence Tests for Counter (Bench) Scales (Including Computing Scales)

63.6.5. Test load:

63.6.5.1. For laboratory tests of scales with a capacity of 1 000 lb or less, the test load required for the permanence test is 50 % of maximum capacity, distributed uniformly over the load points of the scale.

63.6.5.2. For laboratory tests of scales with a capacity greater than 1 000 lb, the test load required for the for the permanence tests is 250 kg (550 lb), distributed uniformly over the load points of the scale.

63.6.10. Step 4: Apply a test load of 50 % capacity, not to exceed 250 kg (550 lb), approximately 25 000 times. It is recommended that the frequency and speed of application of the load shall allow the instrument to come to rest both when loaded and unloaded.

Agenda Item 18. AWS Influence Factor Temperature Ranges that Exceed –10 °C to 40 °C

B. Certificate of Conformance Parameters

1. Influence Factors Requirements

Although NIST Handbook 44 contains a set of influence factors requirements, not all devices must be tested for all of the influence factors. The following table identifies the influence factor tests to be conducted on various devices. The main elements and components (indicating elements and load cells) of scales with a capacity greater than 2000 lb must be tested separately for compliance with the influence factors requirements.

Devices To Be Tested For Influence Factors							
Device Type	Temperature Accuracy	Temp. Zero Drifts	Barometric Pressure	Warm-up Time	Voltage[4]	Power Interruption[5]	Time Dependence
Scales ≤ 2000 lb	X X X		[1]	X X X X			
...							
Load Cells							
...							

[1] Testing is limited to some canister load cells.
[2] Compliance with influence factors requirements will be determined according to existing NTEP policy.
[3] Test limited to power switch only, not to initial plug-in of the device.
[4] Voltage test is 130 and 100 VAC and low battery test on DC. (See Section K 60.)
[5] Power interruption is pulling the plug for 10 seconds. (See Section K.19.)
[6] Indicating elements processing only digital information do not have to be tested for compliance with the influence factors.
[7] Compliance with temperature requirements by NTEP is limited to temperatures that are no lower that –10 °C and no higher than 40 °C.

59. Test Procedures for Influence Factors

Introduction

Influence factors are variables in the environment that might affect the performance of a scale, especially the accuracy and sensitivity (or discrimination) of the device. The T.N.8. section of the Scales Code in Handbook 44 specifies performance requirements for scales over given ranges. The test equipment, (e.g., thermometers, hygrometers, timing devices) must be sufficiently accurate that their errors do not contribute significantly to the measurement results. The environmental chamber must satisfy specified conditions. In general, good laboratory practices must be followed.

The test procedures of the International Electrotechnical Commission are excellent background material and provide guidance for performing the influence factors tests. The use of these documents is encouraged. Compliance with temperature requirements by NTEP is limited to temperatures that are no lower that −10 °C and no higher than 40 °C.

Not all devices are affected…

Appendix B
2005 Weighing Sector Meeting Attendees

Cary Ainsworth c/o USDA GIPSA
75 Spring Street, #230
Atlanta, GA 30303-3309
(404) 562-5840, FAX: (404) 562-5848
e-mail: L.Cary.Ainsworth@usda.gov

Joseph Antkowiak Flintec, Inc.
18 Kane Industrial Drive
Hudson, MA 01749
(978) 562-7800, FAX: (978) 562-0008
e-mail: jantkowiak@flintec-us.com

William E. Bates
USDA,GIPSA, FMD, PPB
1400 Independence Avenue SW/STOP 3630
Washington, DC 20250-3630
(202) 690-0961, FAX: (202) 720-1015
e-mail: william.e.bates@usda.gov

Andrea P. Buie
Maryland Dept. of Agriculture
50 Harry S Truman Parkway
Annapolis, MD 21401
(410) 841-5790, FAX: (410) 841-2765
e-mail: buieap@mda.state.md.us

Luciano Burtini
Measurement Canada
2008 Matera Avenue
Kelowna, British Columbia, Canada V1V 1W9
(250) 862-6557, FAX: (250) 712-4215
e-mail: burtini.luciano@ic.gc.ca

Gary Castro
California Division of Measurement Standards
6790 Florin Perkins Road, Suite 100
Sacramento, CA 95828
(916) 229-3049, FAX: (916) 229-3026
e-mail: gcastro@cdfa.ca.gov

Steven E. Cook
NIST, Weights & Measures Division
100 Bureau Drive MS 2600
Gaithersburg, MD 20899-2600
(301) 975-4003, FAX: (301) 926-0647
e-mail: steven.cook@nist.gov

Scott Davidson
Mettler-Toledo, Inc.
1150 Dearborn Drive
Worthington, OH 43085
(614) 438-4387, FAX: (614) 781-7484
e-mail: scott.davidson@mt.com

Terry Davis
Kansas Dept. of Agriculture
PO Box 19282/Forbes Field Building 282
Topeka, KS 66619-0282
(785) 862-2415, FAX: (785) 862-2460
e-mail: tdavis@kda.state.ks.us

Robert K. Feezor
Norfolk Southern Corporation
1200 Peachtree, Box 142
Atlanta, GA 30309
(404) 527-2537, FAX: (404) 527-2589
e-mail: rkfeezor@mindspring.com

Darrell E. Flocken
Mettler-Toledo, Inc.
1150 Dearborn Drive
Worthington, OH 43085
(614) 438-4393, FAX: (614) 438-4355
e-mail: darrell.flocken@mt.com

Sara Garverick
Air Force Metrology & Calibration
813 Irving Wick Drive W., Bldg. 2
Heath, OH 43056
(740) 788-5009, FAX: (740) 788-5036
e-mail: sara.garverick@afmetcal.af.mil

Scott Henry
NCR Corporation
2651 Satellite Blvd
Duluth, GA 30096
(770) 623-7543, FAX: (770) 479-1174
e-mail: scott.henry@ncrcom

Michael Kelley
Ohio Department of Agriculture
8995 East Main Street, Building 5
Reynoldsburg, OH 43068-3399
(614) 728-6290, FAX: (614) 728-6424
e-mail: kelley_laptop@mail.agri.state.oh.us

Gary Lameris
Lameris Consulting
220 Burgess Avenue
Dayton, OH 45415
(937) 274-1812
e-mail: glameris@yahoo.com

Stephen Langford
Cardinal Scale Manufacturing Co.
203 East Daugherty, P.O. Box 151
Webb City, MO 64870
(417) 673-4631, FAX: (417) 673-5001
e-mail: slangford@cardet.com

Paul A. Lewis, Sr.
Rice Lake Weighing Systems
230 West Coleman Street
PO Box 272
Rice Lake, WI 54868-2404
(715) 234-3494, FAX: (715) 234-6967
e-mail: paulew@rlws.com

Todd R. Lucas
Ohio Dept. of Agriculture
8995 East Main Street, Building 5
Reynoldsburg, OH 43068
(614) 728-6290, FAX: (614) 728-6424
e-mail: lucas@mail.agri.state.oh.us

L. Edward Luthy
Brechbuhler Scales Inc
1424 Scale Street
SW Canton, OH 44706
(330) 458-2424, FAX: (330) 458-3068
e-mail: eluthy@brechbuhler.com

Angelique McCoy
Ohio Department of Agriculture
8995 East Main Street, Building 5
Reynoldsburg, OH 43068-3399
(614) 728-6290, FAX: (614) 728-6424
e-mail: mccoy@mail.agri.state.oh.us

Don Onwiler
Nebraska Division of Weights & Measures
301 Centennial Mall South, Box 94757
Lincoln, NE 68509
(402) 471-4292, FAX: (402) 471-2759
e-mail: donlo@agr.state.ne.us

Stephen Patoray
National Conference on Weights & Measures
1239 Carolina Drive
Tryon, NC 28782
(828) 859-6178, FAX: (828) 859-6180
e-mail: spatoray@mgmtsol.com

Frank Rusk Coti, Inc.
122 Export Circle
Huntsville, AL 35806
(256) 859-6010, FAX: (256) 859-5024
e-mail: frankjrusk50@hotmail.com

Milton Smith
Measurement Canada Standards Bldg #4,
Tunney's Pasture, Holland Ave.
Ottawa, Ontario, Canada K1A OC9
(613) 952-0656, FAX: (613) 952-1754
e-mail: smith.milton@ic.gc.ca

Louis E. Straub
Fairbanks Scales, Inc.
3056 Irwin Drive
SE Southport, NC 28461
(910) 253-3250, FAX: (910) 253-3250
e-mail: strauble@yahoo.com

James C. Truex
Ohio Department of Agriculture
8995 East Main Street, Building 5
Reynoldsburg, OH 43068-3399
(614) 728-6290, FAX: (614) 728-6424
e-mail: truex@mail.agri.state.oh.us

William West
Ohio Department of Agriculture
8995 East Main Street, Building 5
Reynoldsburg, OH 43068-3399
(614) 728-6290, FAX: (614) 728-6424
e-mail: west@mail.agri.state.oh.us

Juana Williams NIST
100 Bureau Drive MS 2600
Gaithersburg, MD 20899-2600
(301) 975-3989, FAX: (301) 926-0647
e-mail: juana.williams@nist.gov

Russ Wyckoff
Oregon Dept. of Agriculture
635 Capitol Street, N.E.
Salem, OR 97301-2532
(503) 986-4767, FAX: (503) 986-4784
e-mail: rwyckoff@oda.state.or.us

Jesus P. Zapien
A&D Engineering Inc
1555 McCandless Drive Milpitas, CA 95035
(408) 518-5114, FAX: (408) 635-2314
e-mail: jzapien@andweighing.co

NCWM 91st Annual Meeting
July 9 - 13, 2006 – Chicago, IL

Attendee List

Ross Andersen
New York Bureau of Weights & Measures
10B Airline Drive
Albany, NY 12235
Ph: (518) 457-3146
Fax: (518) 457-5693
Email: ross.andersen@agmkt.state.ny.us

Lanny Arnold
Kentucky Department of Agriculture
107 Corporate Drive
Frankfort, KY 40601
Ph: (502) 573-0282
Fax: (502) 573-0303
Email: lanny.arnold@kyagr.com

Todd Barrows
Elkhart County Weights & Measures
117 N 2nd, Room 107
Goshen, IN 46526-3231
Ph: (574) 535-6472
Fax: (574) 535-6622
Email: elwtmeas@npcc.net

Steven Beitzel
Systems Associates, Inc.
1932 Industrial Drive
Libertyville, IL 60048
Ph: (847) 367-6650
Fax: (847) 367-6960
Email: sjbeitzel@systemsassoc.com

F. Michael Belue
Belue Associates
Court View Towers, Suite 111A
201 North Pine
Florence, AL 35630
Ph: (256) 768-9917
Fax: (256) 768-9912
Email: Bassoc@aol.com

Joe Benavides
Texas Department of Agriculture
1700 North Congress Avenue,
Stephen F. Austin Building, 11th Floor
Austin, TX 78711
Ph: (512) 463-7401
Fax: (512) 463-8225
Email: joe.benavides@agr.state.tx.us

Stephen Benjamin
North Carolina Department of Agriculture
1050 Mail Service Center
Raleigh, NC 27699-1050
Ph: (919) 733-3313
Fax: (919) 715-0524
Email: steve.benjamin@ncmail.net

Celeste Bennett
Michigan Department of Agriculture
940 Venture Lane
Williamston, MI 48895-2451
Ph: (517) 655-8202
Fax: (517) 655-8303
Email: bennettc9@michigan.gov

Linda Bernetich
National Conference on Weights & Measures
15245 Shady Grove Road, Suite 130
Rockville, MD 20850
Ph: (240) 632-9454
Fax: (301) 990-9771
Email: lbernetich@mgmtsol.com

Doug Biette
Sartorius North America
6542 Fig Street
Arvada, CO 80004
Ph: (303) 403-4690
Fax: (303) 423-4540
Email: doug.biette@sartorius.com

Tom Bloemer
Kentucky Department of Agriculture
107 Corporate Drive
Frankfort, KY 40601
Ph: (502) 573-0282
Fax: (502) 573-0303
Email: tom.bloemer@ky.gov

Jonelle Brent
Illinois Department of Agriculture
PO Box 19281
Springfield, IL 62794-9281
Ph: (217) 785-8301
Fax: (217) 524-7801
Email: jbrent@agr.state.il.us

Kerry Brimmer
Wisconsin Dept. of Ag & Consumer Protection
879 Paetsch Lane
Mosinee, WI 54455-9589
Ph: (715) 693-1160
Fax: (608) 224-4939
Email: kerry.brimmer@datcp.state.wi.us

Gary Brown
Fort Wayne Weights & Measures
1903 St Mary's Avenue
Fort Wayne, IN 46808
Ph: (260) 427-1157
Fax: (260) 427-5789
Email: gbtbmb@yahoo.com

Norman R. Brucker
Precision Measurement Standards, Inc.
1665 135th Street West
Rosemount, MN 55068
Ph: (651) 423-3241
Fax: (651) 322-7938
Email: sharnoma@frontiernet.net

NCWM 91st Annual Meeting
July 9 - 13, 2006 – Chicago, IL

Attendee List

Mark Buccelli
State of Minnesota, Weights and Measures
2277 Highway 36, Suite 150
St. Paul, MN 55113
Ph: (651) 215-5821
Fax: (651) 639-4014
Email: mark.buccelli@state.mn.us

Jerry Butler
North Carolina Department of Agriculture
1050 Mail Service Center
Raleigh, NC 27699-1050
Ph: (919) 733-3313
Fax: (919) 715-0524
Email: jerry.butler@ncmail.net

Marc Buttler
Emerson Process Management
Micro Motion
7070 Winchester Circle
Boulder, CO 80301
Ph: (303) 530-8562
Fax: (303) 530-8459
Email: marc.buttler@emersonprocess.com

Joe Buxton
Daniel Measurement & Control
P.O. Box 2709
Statesboro, GA 30459
Ph: (912) 489-2383
Fax: (912) 489-2390
Email: joe.buxton@emersonprocess.com

James Byers
San Diego County Dept. of Agriculture, Weights & Measures
5555 Overland Ave, Suite 3101
San Diego, CA 92123-1256
Ph: (858) 694-2778
Fax: (858) 505-6484
Email: james.byers@sdcounty.ca.gov

Judy Cardin
Wisconsin Dept. of Ag & Consumer Protection
PO Box 8911, 2811 Agriculture Drive
Madison, WI 53708-8911
Ph: (608) 224-4945
Fax: (608) 224 4939
Email: judy.cardin@datcp.state.wi.us

Loretta Carey
U. S. Food and Drug Administration
5100 Paint Branch Parkway
College Park, MD 20740
Ph: (301) 436-1799
Fax: (301) 436-2639
Email: loretta.carey@fda.hhs.gov

Stacy K. Carlsen
Marin County Weights & Measures
1682 Novato Boulevard, Ste 150-A
Novato, CA 94947-7021
Ph: (415) 499-6700
Fax: (415) 499-7543
Email: scarlsen@co.marin.ca.us

Charles Carroll
Massachusetts Division of Standards
One Ashburton Place, Room 1115
Boston, MA 02108
Ph: (617) 727-3480
Fax: (617) 727-5705
Email: Charles.Carroll@state.ma.us

James Cassidy
Cambridge Weights & Measures
831 Massachusetts Ave
Cambridge, MA 02139
Ph: (617) 349-6133
Fax: (617) 349-6134
Email: jcassidy@CambridgeMA.gov

Phillip Chase
AssetSmart
2800 28th Street, Suite 109
Santa Monica, CA 90405
Ph: (310) 450-2566
Fax:
Email: miranda.groboske@assetsmart.com

Tim Chesser
Arkansas Bureau of Standards
4608 West 61st Street
Little Rock, AR 72209
Ph: (501) 570-1159
Fax: (501) 562-7605
Email: tim.chesser@aspb.ar.gov

Mike Cleary
California Division of Measurement Standards
6790 Florin Perkins Road, Suite 100
Sacramento, CA 95828
Ph: (916) 229-3000
Fax: (916) 229-3026
Email: mcleary@cdfa.ca.gov

William Cobb
West Virginia Weights & Measures, Division of Labor
570 McCorkle Avenue West
St. Albans, WV 25177
Ph: (304) 722-0602
Fax: (304) 722-0605
Email: wcobb@labor.state.wv.us

Ed Coleman
Tennessee Department of Agriculture
PO Box 40627 Melrose Station
Nashville, TN 37204
Ph: (615) 837-5109
Fax: (615) 837-5015
Email: ed.coleman@state.tn.us

NCWM 91st Annual Meeting
July 9 - 13, 2006 – Chicago, IL

Attendee List

Belinda Collins
NIST
100 Bureau Drive, MS 2000
Gaithersburg, MD 20899
Ph: (301) 975-4500
Fax: (301) 975-2183
Email: belinda.collins@nist.gov

Rodney Cooper
Actaris Neptune
1310 Emerald Road
Greenwood, SC 29646
Ph: (864) 942-2226
Fax: (864) 223-0341
Email: rcooper@greenwood.actaris.com

Richard L. Davis
Georgia-Pacific
1915 Marathon Avenue
Neenah, WI 54957-0899
Ph: (920) 729-8174
Fax: (920) 729-8089
Email: richard.davis@gapac.com

Vicky Dempsey
Montgomery County Weights & Measures
451 West Third Street P.O. Box 972
Dayton, OH 45422-1027
Ph: (937) 225-6309
Fax: (937) 224-3927
Email: dempseyv@mcohio.org

Kathryn Dresser
NIST, Weights & Measures Division
100 Bureau Drive MS 2600
Gaithersburg, MD 20899-2600
Ph: (301) 975-3289
Fax: (301) 975-8091
Email: kathryn.dresser@nist.gov

Isabel Esparza
Dept. of Consumer Services,
City of Chicago
Richard J. Daley Center, Room 208; 50 West Washington Street
Chicago, IL 60602
Ph: (312) 744-2355
Fax:
Email:

Steven Cook
NIST, Weights & Measures Division
100 Bureau Drive MS 2600
Gaithersburg, MD 20899-2600
Ph: (301) 975-4003
Fax: (301) 975-8091
Email: steven.cook@nist.gov

Richard Cote
New Hampshire Department of Agriculture Markets & Food
PO Box 2042
Concord, NH 03302-2042
Ph: (603) 271-3700
Fax: (603) 271-1109
Email: rcote@agr.state.nh.us

Kenneth Deitzler
Bureau of Ride & Measurement Standards
2301 North Cameron Street
Harrisburg, PA 17110-9408
Ph: (717) 787-9089
Fax: (717) 783-4158
Email:

G.W. (Wes) Diggs
Virginia Product & Industry Standards
PO Box 1163 Rm 402
Richmond, VA 23218
Ph: (804) 786-2476
Fax: (804) 786-1571
Email: Wes.Diggs@vdacs.virginia.gov

Dennis Ehrhart
Arizona Department of Weights & Measures
4425 West Olive Avenue, Suite 134
Glendale, AZ 85302
Ph: (623) 463-9937
Fax: (602) 255-1950
Email: dehrhart@azdwm.gov

Robert K. Feezor
Norfolk Southern Corporation
1200 Peachtree, Box 142
Atlanta, GA 30309
Ph: (404) 527-2537
Fax: (404) 527-2589
Email: rkfeezor@mindspring.com

Clark Cooney
Oregon Department of Agriculture
635 Capitol Street, N.E.
Salem, OR 97301-2532
Ph: (503) 986-4677
Fax: (503) 986-4784
Email: ccooney@oda.state.or.us

Mark Coyne
Brockton Weights & Measures
45 School Street, City Hall
Brockton, MA 02301-9927
Ph: (508) 580-7120
Fax: (508) 580-7173
Email: sealer@ci.brockton.ma.us

Donald Delorme
Virginia Product & Industry Standards
PO Box 1163 Rm 402
Richmond, VA 23218
Ph: (804) 786-2476
Fax: (804) 786-1571
Email: donald.delorme@vdacs.virginia.gov

Kimberly Dorsey
National Conference on Weights & Measures
15245 Shady Grove Road, Suite 130
Rockville, MD 20850
Ph: (240) 632-9454
Fax: (301) 990-9771
Email: kdorsey@mgmtsol.com

Chuck Ehrlich
NIST, Weights & Measures Division
100 Bureau Drive MS 2600
Gaithersburg, MD 20899-2600
Ph: (301) 975-4834
Fax: (301) 975-8091
Email: charles.ehrlich@nist.gov

Albert Fischer
Wal-Mart Stores, Inc.
608 SW 8th Street
Bentonville, AR 717616
Ph: (479) 277-7277
Fax: (479) 277-8195
Email: al.fischer@wal-mart.com

NCWM 91st Annual Meeting
July 9 - 13, 2006 – Chicago, IL

Attendee List

Darrell Flocken
Mettler-Toledo, Inc.
1150 Dearborn Drive
Worthington, OH 43085
Ph: (614) 438-4393
Fax: (614) 438-4355
Email: darrell.flocken@mt.com

Kurt Floren
County of Los Angeles
12300 Lower Azusa Road
Arcadia, CA 91006
Ph: (626) 575-5451
Fax: (626) 575-5451
Email: kurtf@acwm.co.la.ca.us

Maurice J. Forkert
Tuthill Transfer Systems
8825 Aviation Drive
Fort Wayne, IN 46809
Ph: (260) 747-7529
Fax: (260) 747-7064
Email: Mforkert@tuthill.com

Roger Frazier
Arkansas Bureau of Standards
4608 West 61st Street
Little Rock, AR 72209
Ph: (501) 570-1159
Fax: (501) 562-7605
Email: roger.frazier@astb.ar.gov

Cary Frye
International Dairy Foods Assn
1250 H St NW Ste 900 PO Box 549
Washington, DC 20005
Ph: (202) 737-4332
Fax: (202) 331-7820
Email: cfrye@idfa.org

Carol Fulmer
South Carolina Department of Agriculture
PO Box 11280
Columbia, SC 29211
Ph: (803) 737-9690
Fax: (803) 737-9703
Email: cfulmer@scda.sc.gov

Randy Fulmer
Alabama Department of Agriculture & Industry
PO Box 3336
Montgomery, AL 36109-0336
Ph: (334) 240-7133
Fax: (334) 240-7175
Email: randyf@agi.state.al.us

John Gaccione
Westchester County Weights & Measures
112 East Post Road, 4th Floor
White Plains, NY 10601
Ph: (914) 995-2160
Fax: (914) 995-3115
Email: jpg4@westchestergov.com

Regine Gaucher
OIML
11 Rue Turgot
Paris, 75009
France
Ph: 33 1 48 78 17 27
Fax: 33 1 48 78 17 27
Email: regine.gaucher@oiml.org

Thomas Geiler
Town of Barnstable
200 Main Street
Hyannis, MA 02601
Ph: (508) 862-4670
Fax: (508) 778-2412
Email: Tom.Geiler@town.barnstable.ma.us

Steve P. Gill
Missouri Department of Agriculture
P.O. Box 630
Jefferson City, MO 65102-0630
Ph: (573) 751-4278
Fax: (573) 751-0281
Email: steve.gill@mda.mo.gov

Gary R. Gist
Howard County Weights & Measures
100 S Union-City Hall Floor 1
Kokomo, IN 46901
Ph: (765) 456-7466
Fax: (765) 456-7571
Email:

Jason Glass
Kentucky Department of Agriculture
107 Corporate Drive
Frankfort, KY 40601
Ph: (502) 573-0282
Fax: (502) 573-0303
Email: jason.glass@kyagr.com

Paul Glowacki
Murray Equipment, Inc.
2515 Charleston Place
Fort Wayne, IN 46808
Ph: (260) 484-0382
Fax: (260) 484-9230
Email: pglowacki@murrayequipment.com

Joe Gomez
New Mexico Department of Agriculture
MSC 3170, PO Box 30005
Las Cruces, NM 88003-8005
Ph: (505) 646-1616
Fax: (505) 646-2361
Email: jgomez@nmda.nmsu.edu

Steven Grabski
Division of Measurement Standards
2150 Frazer Avenue
Sparks, NV 89431
Ph: (775) 688-1166
Fax: (775) 688-2533
Email: sgrabski@govmail.state.nv.us

Christopher Guay
Procter & Gamble Co
1 Procter & Gamble Plaza
Cincinnati, OH 45202
Ph: (513) 983-0530
Fax: (513) 983-8984
Email: guay.cb@pg.com

Brett Gurney
Utah Department of Agriculture & Food
P.O. Box 146500
Salt Lake City, UT 84114-6500
Ph: (801) 538-7158
Fax: (801) 538-4949
Email: bgurney@utah.gov

NCWM 91st Annual Meeting
July 9 - 13, 2006 – Chicago, IL

Attendee List

Charles Hackett
City of Kokomo Weights and Measures
100 South Union Street
Kokomo, IN 46901
Ph: (765) 456-7466
Fax: (765) 456-7571
Email: chackett@cityofkokomo.org

Melvin Hankel
MCH Engineering Associates Inc
6926 Balmoral Drive
Fort Wayne, IN 46804-1442
Ph: (260) 436-9234
Fax: (260) 436-0196
Email: melvin.hankel@juno.com

Ronald G. Hayes
Missouri Department of Agriculture
P.O. Box 630
Jefferson City, MO 65102-0630
Ph: (573) 751-2922
Fax: (573) 751-8307
Email: Ron.Hayes@mda.mo.gov

Marilyn Herman
Herman and Associates
3730 Military Road NW
Washington, DC 20015
Ph: (202) 362-9520
Fax: (202) 362-9523
Email: mherman697@aol.com

Jason Hoar
AgriFuels
34 22nd Street
Cayucos, CA 93430
Ph: (805) 995-1972
Fax: (866) 466-2764
Email: jasonhoar@agrifuels.com

Jeff Humphreys
Los Angeles County Weights & Measures
11012 Garfield Avenue, Building A
South Gate, CA 90280
Ph: (562) 940-8922
Fax: (562) 861-0278
Email: jeffh@acwm.co.la.ca.us

Ethan A. Halpern
Maryland Department of Agriculture
50 Harry S. Truman Parkway
Annapolis, MD 21401
Ph: (410) 841-5790
Fax: (410) 841-2765
Email:

Krister K. Hard af Segerstad
IKEA Wholesale Inc.
496 West Germantown Pike
Plymouth Meeting, PA 19462
Ph: (610) 834-0180
Fax: (610) 834-0872
Email: krister@memo.IKEA.com

Jess Helmlinger
Mettler-Toledo, Inc.
2549 Richmond Road
Lexington, KY 40509
Ph: (859) 266-3000 x22
Fax:
Email: jess.helmlinger@mt.com

Tom Herrington
Nestle USA - Prepared Foods Division
5750 Harper Rd
Solon, OH 44139-1880
Ph: (440) 264-6467
Fax: (440) 248-1709
Email: Thomas.Herrington@us.nestle.com

Carol Hockert
NIST, Weights & Measures Division
100 Bureau Drive MS 2600
Gaithersburg, MD 20899-2600
Ph: (301) 975-5507
Fax: (301) 975-8091
Email: carol.hockert@nist.gov

Charles Hunt
COSA Instrument
84G Horseblock Road
Yaphank, NY 11980
Ph: (631) 345-3434 x108
Fax:
Email: chunt@cosaic.com

Jonathan Handy
Colorado Department of Agriculture
3125 Wyandot Street
Denver, CO 80211
Ph: (303) 477-4220
Fax: (303) 477-4248
Email: Jonathan.Handy@ag.state.co.us

Ronald Hasemeyer
Alameda County Dept. of Agriculture, W&M
333 5th Street
Oakland, CA 94607
Ph: (510) 268-7343
Fax: (501) 444-3879
Email: ron.hasemeyer@acgov.org

Scott Henry
NCR Corporation
2651 Satellite Blvd
Duluth, GA 30096
Ph: (770) 623-7543
Fax: (770) 479-1174
Email: scott.henry@ncr.com

Tyler Hicks
Oklahoma Dept. of Agriculture
P.O. Box 528804
Oklahoma City, OK 73152
Ph: (405) 205-2697
Fax: (405) 522-5885
Email: thicks@oda.state.ok.us

Steve Howell
National Biodiesel Board
101 E. Main Street, Suite 2
Kearney, MO 64060
Ph: (816) 903-6272
Fax: (816) 635-4836
Email: showell@marciu.com

Grace L. Jan, CMP
National Conference on Weights & Measures
15245 Shady Grove Road, Suite 130
Rockville, MD 20850
Ph: (240) 632-9454
Fax: (301) 990-9771
Email: gjan@mgmtsol.com

NCWM 91st Annual Meeting
July 9 - 13, 2006 – Chicago, IL

Attendee List

Dr. William A. Jeffrey
NIST
100 Bureau Drive
Gaithersburg, MD 20899-2600
Ph: (301) 975-5507
Fax: (301) 975-8091

Rafael Jimenez
Association of American Railroads
P.O. Box 11130, 55500 D.O.T. Road
Pueblo, CO 81001
Ph: (719) 584-0691
Fax: (719) 584-0770
Email: rafael_jimenez@ttci.aar.com

Dennis Johannes
California Division of Measurement Standards
6790 Florin Perkins Road, Suite 100
Sacramento, CA 95828
Ph: (916) 229-3000
Fax: (916) 229-3026
Email: DJohannes@cdfa.ca.gov

Andrea Johnson
American Petroleum Institute
1220 L Street, NW
Washington, DC 20005
Ph: (202) 682-8107
Fax: (202) 962-4797
Email: johnsona@api.org

Gordon Johnson
Gilbarco, Inc.
7300 West Friendly Avenue
Greensboro, NC 27420
Ph: (336) 547-5375
Fax: (336) 547-5079
Email: Gordon.Johnson@gilbarco.com

Raymond Johnson
New Mexico Department of Agriculture
MSC 3170, PO Box 30005
Las Cruces, NM 88003-8005
Ph: (505) 646-1616
Fax: (505) 646-2361
Email: rjohnson@nmda.nmsu.edu

Alan Johnston
Measurement Canada
Main Bldg. No. 3 Tunney's Pasture
Ottawa, Ontario K1A0C9
Canada
Ph: (613) 952-0655
Fax: (613) 957-1265
Email: johnston.alan@ic.gc.ca

John Junkins
West Virginia Weights & Measures, Division of Labor
570 McCorkle Avenue West
St. Albans, WV 25177
Ph: (304) 722-0602
Fax: (304) 722-0605
Email: jjunkins@labor.state.wv.us

Jack Kane
Montana Bureau of Weights & Measures
P.O. Box 200516
Helena, MT 59620-0516
Ph: (406) 841-2240
Fax: (406) 841-2060
Email: jkane@mt.gov

Michael Keilty
Endress & Hauser Flowtec AG
2350 Endress Place
Greenwood, IN 46143
Ph: (317) 535-2745
Fax: (317) 535-1341
Email: michael.keilty@us.endress.com

Jackie Kerper
National Conference on Weights & Measures
15245 Shady Grove Road, Suite 130
Rockville, MD 20850
Ph: (240) 632-9454
Fax: (301) 990-9771
Email: jkerper@mgmtsol.com

Ted Kingsbury
Measurement Canada
Standards Bldg #4, Tunney's Pasture, Holland Ave.
Ottawa, Ontario K1A0C9
CANADA
Ph: (613) 941-8919
Fax: (613) 952-1736
Email: kingsbury.ted@ic.gc.ca

Dennis Kolsun
H.J. Heinz Company
357 6th Avenue
Pittsburgh, PA 15222
Ph: (724) 778-4503
Fax: (412) 237-5922
Email: dennis.kolsun@hjheinz.com

Gary Lameris
Lameris Consulting
220 Burgess Avenue
Dayton, OH 45415
Ph: (937) 274-1812
Fax:
Email: glameris@yahoo.com

Leon Lammers
Avery Weigh-Tronix
1000 Armstrong Drive
Fairmont, MN 56031-1439
Ph: (800) 533-0456
Fax: (507) 238-8255
Email: leon.lammers@weigh-tronix.com

Stephen Langford
Cardinal Scale Manufacturing Co.
203 East Daugherty, P.O. Box 151
Webb City, MO 64870
Ph: (417) 673-4631
Fax: (417) 673-5001
Email: slangford@cardet.com

Cindy Lease
Wisconsin Dept. of Ag & Consumer Protection
PO Box 8911, 2811 Agriculture Drive
Madison, WI 53708-8911
Ph: (608) 246-4514
Fax: (608) 246-5804
Email: clease@cityofmadison.com

Brian Lemon
Industry Canada-Competition Bureau
400 St Mary Avenue, 4th Floor
Winnipeg, Manitoba R3C 4K5
Canada
Ph: (204) 983-8911
Fax: (204) 984-2658
Email: lemon.brian@cb-bc.gc.ca

NCWM 91st Annual Meeting
July 9 - 13, 2006 – Chicago, IL

Attendee List

Paul Lewis
Rice Lake Weighing Systems, Inc.
230 West Coleman Street, PO Box 272
Rice Lake, WI 54868-2404
Ph: (715) 234-3494 x5322
Fax: (715) 234-6967
Email: paulew@rlws.com

Richard Lewis
Georgia Department of Agriculture
Agriculture Bldg., 19 MLK Drive, Rm 321
Atlanta, GA 30334
Ph: (404) 656-3605
Fax: (404) 656-9648
Email: rlewis@agr.state.ga.us

Robert Lilley
San Luis Obispo County Weights & Measures
2156 Sierra Way, Suite A
San Luis Obispo, CA 93401
Ph: (805) 781-5924
Fax: (805) 781-1035
Email: rlilley@co.slo.ca.us

Todd Lucas
Ohio Department of Agriculture
8995 East Main Street, Building 5
Reynoldsburg, OH 43068
Ph: (614) 728-6290
Fax: (614) 728-6424
Email: lucas@mail.agri.state.oh.us

L. Edward Luthy
Brechbuhler Scales Inc
1424 Scale Street SW
Canton, OH 44706
Ph: (330) 453-2424
Fax: (330) 471-8909
Email: eluthy@bscales.com

Keith L. Mahan
Merced County Weights & Measures
2139 Wardrobe Avenue
Merced, CA 95340-6495
Ph: (209) 385-7431
Fax: (209) 725-3961
Email: kmahan@co.merced.ca.us

Thomas Malesh
Dept. of Consumer Services, Weights & Measures
1615 West Chicago Avenue
Chicago, IL 60622
Ph: (312) 746-4882
Fax:
Email:

Steven Malone
Nebraska Division of Weights & Measures
301 Centennial Mall South, Box 94757
Lincoln, NE 68509-4757
Ph: (402) 471-4292
Fax: (402) 471-2759
Email: smalone@agr.ne.gov

Judy Markoe
National Conference on Weights & Measures
15245 Shady Grove Road, Suite 130
Rockville, MD 20850
Ph: (240) 632-9454
Fax: (301) 990-9771
Email: jmarkoe@mgmtsol.com

Vernon Lee Massey
Shelby County Weights & Measures
157 Poplar Suite 402
Memphis, TN 38103
Ph: (901) 545-3920
Fax: (901) 545-3906
Email: vmassey@co.shelby.tn.us

Terence McBride
Memphis Weights & Measures
590 Washington St
Memphis, TN 38105
Ph: (901) 528-2905
Fax: (901) 528-2948
Email: terence.mcbride@memphistn.gov

James McGetrick
BP Products
Mail Code J-8, 150 W. Warrenville Road
Naperville, IL 60563
Ph: (630) 420-4579
Fax: (630) 420-4832
Email: mcgetrje@bp.com

Robert McGrath
Boston ISD Weights & Measures
1010 Massachusetts Ave
Boston, MA 02118-2606
Ph: (617) 961-3376
Fax: (617) 635-5383
Email: robert.mcrath.isd@ci.boston.ma.us

Colleen Merrill
Albertsons/Super Value
250 Parkcenter Blvd. #70410
Boise, ID 83726
Ph: (208) 395-5864
Fax:
Email: colleen.merrill@albertsons.com

Rachelle Miller
Wisconsin Dept. of Ag & Consumer Protection
PO Box 8911, 2811 Agriculture Drive
Madison, WI 53708-8911
Ph: (608) 224-4938
Fax: (608) 224-4939
Email: rachelle.miller@datcp.state.wi.us

Nigel G. Mills
Hobart Corporation
701 South Ridge Avenue
Troy, OH 45374-0001
Ph: (937) 332-3205
Fax: (937) 332-3007
Email: nigel.mills@hobartcorp.com

Charlie Mitchell
Total Petrochemicals, Inc.
P.O. Box 849
Port Arthur, TX 77641-0849
Ph: (409) 963-6885
Fax: (409) 962-3458
Email: charlie.mitchell@total.com

Robert Murnane
Seraphin Test Measure
PO Box 227 30 Indel Avenue
Rancocas, NJ 08073-0227
Ph: (609) 267-0922
Fax: (609) 261-2546
Email: rmurnane@pemfab.com

NCWM 91st Annual Meeting
July 9 - 13, 2006 – Chicago, IL
Attendee List

Mark Nickel
Wisconsin Dept. of Ag & Consumer Protection
517 South Madison Street
Waupun, WI 53963
Ph: (920) 324-8849
Fax: (608) 224-4939
Email: mark.nickel@datcp.state.wi.us

Neal J. Nover
WinWamSoftware
Atrium Executive Suites
3000 Atrium Way, Suite 2203
Mt. Laurel, NJ 08054-3910
Ph: (856) 273-6988
Fax: (856) 751-0559
Email: sales@winwam.com

Charlene Numrych
Liquid Controls LLC
105 Albrecht Drive
Lake Bluff, IL 60044
Ph: (847) 283-8330
Fax: (847) 295-1170
Email: cnumrych@idexcorp.com

O.R. "Pete" O'Bryan
Foster Farms
P.O. Box 457
Livingston, CA 95334-9900
Ph: (209) 398-6740
Fax: (209) 398-6742
Email: obryanp@fosterfarms.com

Don Onwiler
Nebraska Division of Weights & Measures
301 Centennial Mall South, Box 94757
Lincoln, NE 68509
Ph: (402) 471-4292
Fax: (402) 471-2759
Email: donwiler@agr.ne.gov

Henry Oppermann
Weights & Measures Consulting
3313 Prytania Street
New Orleans, LA 70115
Ph: (504) 218-5422
Fax: (504) 218-5422
Email: wmconsulting@cox.net

Vincent Orr
ConAgra Foods
Six ConAgra Drive, PDL-405
Omaha, NE 68102
Ph: (402) 595-6248
Fax: (402) 595-7660
Email: vince.orr@conagrafoods.com

Javier Ortiz
Dept. of Consumer Services, City of Chicago
1615 West Chicago Avenue
Chicago, IL 60622
Ph: (312) 746-8673
Fax:
Email: jortiz@cityofchicago.org

Stephen Pahl
Texas Department of Agriculture
1700 North Congress Avenue,
Stephen F. Austin Building, 11th Floor
Austin, TX 78701
Ph: (512) 463-7483
Fax: (512) 463-8225
Email: stephen.pahl@agr.state.tx.us

Beth W. Palys, CAE
National Conference on Weights & Measures
15245 Shady Grove Road, Suite 130
Rockville, MD 20850
Ph: (240) 632-9454
Fax: (301) 990-9771
Email: bpalys@mgmtsol.com

Johnny Parrish
Brodie Meter Co., LLC
19267 Highway 301 North
Statesboro, GA 30461
Ph: (912) 489-0203
Fax: (912) 489-0298
Email: johnny.parrish@brodiemeter.com

Steve Patoray
National Conference on Weights & Measures
15245 Shady Grove Road, Suite 130
Rockville, MD 20850
Ph: (240) 632-9454
Fax: (301) 990-9771
Email: spatoray@mgmtsol.com

Steve Pedersen
Iowa Weights & Measures Bureau
Iowa Dept. of Agriculture & Land Stewardship, 2230 S. Ankeny Blvd.
Ankeny, IA 50023-9093
Ph: (515) 725-1492
Fax: (515) 725-1459
Email: steve.pedersen@idals.state.ia.us

William Pierpont
Hawaii Measurement Standards
1851 Auiki Street
Honolulu, HI 96819-3100
Ph: (808) 832-0694
Fax: (808) 832-0683
Email: william.e.pierpont@hawaii.gov

Michael Pinagel
Michigan Department of Agriculture
940 Venture Lane
Williamston, MI 48895-2451
Ph: (517) 655-8202 ext 301
Fax: (517) 655-8303
Email: PinagelM@michigan.gov

Marvin G. Pound
Georgia Department of Agriculture
815 Milledeville Hwy
Devereux, GA 31087
Ph: (404) 656-3605
Fax: (404) 656-9648
Email: mpound@agr.state.ga.us

Gale Prince
Kroger Company
1014 Vine Street
Cincinnati, OH 45202-1100
Ph: (513) 762-4209
Fax: (513) 762-4372
Email: gale.prince@kroger.com

Tom Pugh
Arkansas Bureau of Standards
4608 West 61st Street
Little Rock, AR 72209
Ph: (501) 570-1159
Fax: (501) 562-7605
Email: tom.pugh@aspb.ar.gov

NCWM 91st Annual Meeting
July 9 - 13, 2006 – Chicago, IL

Attendee List

Julie Quinn
Minnesota Dept. of Commerce
2277 Highway 36
St. Paul, MN 55113
Ph: (651) 215-5842
Fax: (651) 639-4014
Email: julie.quinn@state.mn.us

Robert A. Reinfried
Scale Manufacturers Association
6724 Lone Oak Boulevard
Naples, FL 34109
Ph: (239) 514-3441
Fax: (239) 514-3470
Email: bob@scalemanufacturers.org

Bill Ripka
Thermo Electron
501 90th Ave NW
Minneapolis, MN 55433
Ph: (763) 783-2664
Fax: (763) 780-1537
Email: bill.ripka@thermo.com

Michael Sarachman
Kraft Foods Global Inc.
801 Waukegan Road, TC-03
Glenview, IL 60025
Ph: (847) 646-6180
Fax: (847) 646-4820
Email: msarachman@kraft.com

Jim Sexton
Rice Lake Weighing Systems, Inc.
230 West Coleman Street
Rice Lake, WI 54868
Ph: (715) 234-9171
Fax: (715) 234-6967
Email: jimsex@rlws.com

Terrance Shook
Lake County Weights & Measures
105 Main Street P.O. Box 490
Painesville, OH 44077-0490
Ph: (440) 350-2535
Fax: (440) 350-2667
Email: auditor@lakecountyohio.org

David Rajala
Veeder-Root Company
P.O. Box 1673
Altoona, PA 16603-1673
Ph: (814) 696-8125
Fax: (814) 695-7605
Email: drajala@veeder.com

Robert E. Reynolds
Downstream Alternatives Inc.
1657 Commerce Drive, Suite 20B
South Bend, IN 46628
Ph: (574) 250-2811
Fax:
Email: rreynolds-dai@earthlink.net

Kirk Robinson
Washington Department of Agriculture
PO Box 42560
Olympia, WA 98504-2560
Ph: (360) 902-1856
Fax: (360) 902-2086
Email: KRobinson@agr.wa.gov

Brett Saum
San Luis Obispo County Weights & Measures
2156 Sierra Way, Suite A
San Luis Obispo, CA 93401-4556
Ph: (805) 781-5922
Fax: (805) 781-1035
Email: BSaum@co.slo.ca.us

Janet Sheiner
PETCO
9125 Rehco Road
San Diego, CA 92121
Ph: (858) 453-7845
Fax: (858) 638-2247
Email: janets@petco.com

Stephanie Siedschlag
ConAgra Foods
6 ConAgra Drive, 6-405
Omaha, NE 68102
Ph: (402) 595-6088
Fax: (402) 517-4238
Email: stephanie.siedschlag@conagrafoods.com

Kenneth R. Ramsburg
Maryland Department of Agriculture
50 Harry S. Truman Parkway
Annapolis, MD 21401
Ph: (410) 841-5790
Fax: (410) 841-2765
Email: RamsbuKR@mda.state.md.us

Ralph A. Richter
NIST, Weights & Measures Division
100 Bureau Drive MS 2600
Gaithersburg, MD 20899-2600
Ph: (301) 975-3997
Fax: (301) 975-8091
Email: ralph.richter@nist.gov

Paula Rosenfeld
General Mills, Inc.
#1 General Mills Boulevard, MS W01D
Minneapolis, MN 55426
Ph: (763) 764-5527
Fax: (763) 764-2109
Email: paula.rosenfeld@genmills.com

Alex Schuettenberg
ConocoPhillips Petroleum
148 AL, Phillips Research Center
Bartlesville, OK 74004
Ph: (918) 661-3563
Fax: (918) 661-8060
Email: alex.schuettenberg@conocophillips.com

Agatha Shields
Franklin County Weights & Measures
373 South High Street, 21st Floor
Columbus, OH 43215-6310
Ph: (614) 462-7380
Fax: (614) 462-3111
Email: aashield@franklincountyohio.gov

Michael Sikula
New York Bureau of Weights & Measures
Building 7A State Campus
Albany, NY 12235
Ph: (518) 457-3452
Fax: (518) 457-2552
Email: mike.sikula@agmkt.state.ny.us

NCWM 91st Annual Meeting
July 9 - 13, 2006 – Chicago, IL

Attendee List

David Silvers
Alabama Department of Agriculture & Industry
1445 Federal Drive
Montgomery, AL 36107
Ph: (334) 240-7133
Fax: (334) 240-7133
Email: marlena.surles@agi.alabama.gov

Bruce Smith
Boston ISD Weights & Measures
1010 Massachusetts Ave
Boston, MA 02118-2606
Ph: (617) 635-5328
Fax: (617) 635-5383
Email:

Robert Stobb
Wisconsin Dept. of Ag & Consumer Protection
2242 Willow Way
Oshkosh, WI 54904-7771
Ph: (920) 237-2909
Fax: (920) 224-4939
Email: robert.stobb@datcp.state.wi.us

Lawrence Stump
Indiana Weights & Measures
2525 N. Shadeland Avenue, #03
Indianapolis, IN 46219-1791
Ph: (317) 356-7078
Fax: (317) 351-2877
Email: lstump@isdh.state.in.us

John Sullivan
Mississippi Dept. of Agriculture
12575 River Road
Natchez, MS 39120-8373
Ph: (601) 877-3822
Fax: (601) 877-3872
Email: johns1@mdac.state.ms.us

Brian Thompson
AssetSmart
2800 28th Street, Suite 109
Santa Monica, CA 90405
Ph: (310) 450-2566
Fax: (310) 450-1311
Email: brian.thompson@assetsmart.com

Joseph Silvestro
Weights & Measures
115 Bud Boulevard
Woodbury, NJ 08096
Ph: (856) 384-6857
Fax: (856) 384-6858
Email:

David Sorlie
Fort Wayne Weights & Measures
1903 St Mary's Avenue
Fort Wayne, IN 46808
Ph: (260) 427-5668
Fax: (260) 427-5789
Email: david.sorlie@ci.ft-wayne.in.us

Louis E. Straub
Fairbanks Scales, Inc.
3056 Irwin Drive SE
Southport, NC 28461
Ph: (910) 253-3250
Fax: (910) 253-3250
Email: strauble@yahoo.com

Richard Suiter
NIST, Weights & Measures Division
100 Bureau Drive MS 2600
Gaithersburg, MD 20899-2600
Ph: (301) 975-4406
Fax: (301) 975-8091
Email: richard.suiter@nist.gov

William Sveum
Kraft Foods Global, Inc.
910 Mayer Avenue
Madison, WI 53704
Ph: (608) 285-4280
Fax: (608) 285-6288
Email: wsveum@kraft.com

Michael Timmons
City of Medford
85 George P. Hassett Drive
Medford, MA 02155
Ph: (781) 393-2463
Fax: (781) 396-4217
Email: mwtimmons@medford.org

San Sim
Virtual Measurements & Control, LLC
3196 Coffey Lane, Suite 604
Santa Rosa, CA 95403
Ph: (707) 573-3111
Fax: (707) 573-3113
Email: san@virtualmc.com

Steven Steinborn
Hogan & Hartson
555 13th Street, NW
Washington, DC 20004
Ph: (202) 637-5969
Fax: (202) 637-5910
Email: sbsteinborn@hhlaw.com

Bill Strelioff
Norac Systems International, Inc.
803 46th Street E.
Saskatoon, Saskatewan 57K0X1
Canada
Ph: (515) 289-2906
Fax: (515) 289-0057
Email: bill@norac.ca

Rich Sulinski
AgriFuels
450 Dunbar Hill Road
Hamden, CT 06514
Ph: (203) 288-5872
Fax:
Email: richsulinski@agrifuels.com

Aves D. Thompson
Alaska Div of Measurement Standards/CVE
12050 Industry Way Bldg O, Ste. 6
Anchorage, AK 99515
Ph: (907) 341-3210
Fax: (907) 341-3220
Email: aves_thompson@dot.state.ak.us

James Truex
Ohio Department of Agriculture
8995 East Main Street
Reynoldsburg, OH 43068-3399
Ph: (614) 728-6290
Fax: (614) 728-6424
Email: truex@mail.agri.state.oh.us

NCWM 91st Annual Meeting
July 9 - 13, 2006 – Chicago, IL
Attendee List

Keith Tsujimoto
Safeway, Inc.
5918 Stoneridge Mall Road
Pleasanton, CA 94588-3229
Ph: (925) 467-2434
Fax: (925) 467-3126
Email: keith.tsujimoto@safeway.com

Pieter Van Breugel
NMI Certin B.V.
Hugo de Grootplein
Dordrecht, Dordrecht 3314 EG
The Netherlands
Ph: 0031-706-332300
Fax:
Email: pvanbreugel@nmi.nl

John Walsh
Framingham Weights & Measures
150 Concord Street
Framingham, MA 01702
Ph: (508) 626-9113
Fax: (508) 626-8991
Email: jbw@framinghamma.org

Steve Wildberger
Shimadzu Scientific Instruments
7102 Riverwood Drive
Columbia, MD 21046
Ph: (410) 381-1227
Fax: (410) 381-1222
Email: stwildberger@shimadzu.com

Cary Woodward
Hamilton County Weights & Measures
One Hamilton County Square
Noblesville, IN 46060
Ph: (317) 403-0639
Fax: (317) 776-8525
Email: ceewoody@msn.com

Steven Wrigley
Brodie Meter Co. LLC
19267 Highway 301, North
Statesboro, GA 30459
Ph: (912) 489-0270
Fax: (912) 489-0298
Email: steve.wrigley@brodiemeter.com

Pete Turner
Anniston Pump Shop, Inc., d/b/a APS Petroleum Equipment
2800 Hiway 431 N PO Box 1198
Anniston, AL 36202
Ph: (256) 820-2980
Fax: (256) 820-2981
Email: pete@apspetro.com

Manuel Villicana
Kern County Department of Agriculture
3708 Rainier Court
Bakersfield, CA 93312
Ph:
Fax:
Email: villican@co.kern.ca.us

Irene B. Warnlof
9705 Inaugural Way
Gaithersburg, MD 20886
Ph: (301) 926-8155
Fax:
Email:

Juana Williams
NIST, Weights & Measures Division
100 Bureau Drive MS 2600
Gaithersburg, MD 20899-2600
Ph: (301) 975-3989
Fax: (301) 975-8091
Email: juana.williams@nist.gov

Richard Wotthlie
Maryland Department of Agriculture
50 Harry S. Truman Parkway
Annapolis, MD 21401
Ph: (410) 841-5790
Fax: (410) 841-2765
Email: wotthlrw@mda.state.md.us

Russ Wyckoff
Oregon Department of Agriculture
635 Capitol Street, N.E.
Salem, OR 97301-2532
Ph: (503) 986-4767
Fax: (503) 986-4784
Email: rwyckoff@oda.state.or.us

Tim Tyson
Kansas Department of Agriculture/W&M Division
PO Box 19282/Forbes Field Building 282
Topeka, KS 66619-0282
Ph: (785) 862-2415
Fax: (785) 862-2460
Email: ttyson@kda.state.ks.us

Gilles Vinet
Measurement Canada
Standards Bldg #4, Tunney's Pasture, Holland Ave.
Ottawa, Ontario K1A0C9
Canada
Ph: (613) 952-0657
Fax: (613) 952-1736
Email: vinet.gilles@ic.gc.ca

Otto K. Warnlof
9705 Inaugural Way
Gaithersburg, MD 20886
Ph: (301) 926-8155
Fax: (301) 963-2871
Email: warnlof@aol.com

Robert Williams
Tennessee Department of Agriculture
PO Box 40627 Melrose Station
Nashville, TN 37204-0627
Ph: (615) 837-5109
Fax: (615) 837-5015
Email: robert.g.williams@state.tn.us

Michelle Wright
ConAgra Foods
6 ConAgra Drive
Omaha, NE 68102
Ph: (402) 595-7823
Fax: (402) 595-7660
Email: michelle.wright@conagrafoods.com

Jennifer Yezak
NASDA
1156 15th Street, N.W., Suite 1020
Washington, DC 20005
Ph: (202) 296-9680
Fax: (202) 296-9686
Email: jennifer@nasda.org

NCWM 91st Annual Meeting
July 9 - 13, 2006 – Chicago, IL

Attendee List

Kristin Young
Colorado Department of Agriculture
3125 Wyandot Street
Denver, CO 80211
Ph: (303) 477-4220
Fax: (303) 477-4248
Email: kristin.young@ag.state.co.us

NCWM 91ˢᵗ Annual Meeting
July 9 - 13, 2006 – Chicago, IL

Guest List

Dawn Beitzel	*Loretta McBride*
Terra Brown	*Dan Nichols*
Wendy Bukowski	*Pat Pedersen*
Kristen Cleary	*Sydney Pinagel*
Cynthia Cote	*Cindy Pugh*
Cindy Deitzler	*Elsie Pugh*
Karen Gill	*Jaclyn Pugh*
Anabel Hackett	*Cynthia Rajala*
Joan Hankel	*Peggy Saum*
Carolyn Hicks	*Jeremy Schmitz*
Carol Johnston	*Debbie Straub*
Colleen Keilty	*Carol Suiter*
Judy Kingsbury	*Jeremy Suiter*
Rose Marie Lammers	*Phyllis Thompson*
Susie Lilley	*Margaret Turner*
Judy Mahan	*Ellen Walsh*
Donnie Massey	*Lauren Young*

NIST Technical Publications

Periodical

Journal of Research of the National Institute of Standards and Technology—Reports NIST research and development in metrology and related fields of physical science, engineering, applied mathematics, statistics, biotechnology, and information technology. Papers cover a broad range of subjects, with major emphasis on measurement methodology and the basic technology underlying standardization. Also included from time to time are survey articles on topics closely related to the Institute's technical and scientific programs. Issued six times a year.

Nonperiodicals

Monographs—Major contributions to the technical literature on various subjects related to the Institute's scientific and technical activities.

Handbooks—Recommended codes of engineering and industrial practice (including safety codes) developed in cooperation with interested industries, professional organizations, and regulatory bodies.

Special Publications—Include proceedings of conferences sponsored by NIST, NIST annual reports, and other special publications appropriate to this grouping such as wall charts, pocket cards, and bibliographies.

National Standard Reference Data Series—Provides quantitative data on the physical and chemical properties of materials, compiled from the world's literature and critically evaluated. Developed under a worldwide program coordinated by NIST under the authority of the National Standard Data Act (Public Law 90-396). NOTE:The Journal of Physical and Chemical Reference Data (JPCRD) is published bimonthly for NIST by the American Institute of Physics (AIP). Subscription orders and renewals are available from AIP, P.O. Box 503284, St. Louis, MO63150-3284.

National Construction Safety Team Act Reports—This series comprises the reports of investigations carried out under Public Law 107-231, the technical cause(s) of the building failure investigated; any technical recommendations for changes to or the establishment of evacuation and emergency response procedures; any recommended specific improvements to building standards, codes, and practices; and recomendations for research and other appropriate actions to help prevent future building failures.

Building Science Series—Disseminates technical information developed at the Institute on building materials, components, systems, and whole structures. The series presents research results, test methods, and performance criteria related to the structural and environmental functions and the durability and safety characteristics of building elements and systems.

Technical Notes—Studies or reports which are complete in themselves but restrictive in their treatment of a subject. Analogous to monographs but not so comprehensive in scope or definitive in treatment of the subject area. Often serve as a vehicle for final reports of work performed at NIST under the sponsorship of other government agencies.

Voluntary Product Standards—Developed under procedures published by the Department of Commerce in Part 10, Title 15, of the Code of Federal Regulations. The standards establish nationally recognized requirements for products, and provide all concerned interests with a basis for common understanding of the characteristics of the products. NIST administers this program in support of the efforts of private-sector standardizing organizations.

Order the followingNIST publications—FIPS and NISTIRs—from the National Technical Information Service, Springfield, VA22161.

Federal Information Processing Standards Publications (FIPS PUB)—Publications in this series collectively constitute the Federal Information Processing Standards Register. The Register serves as the official source of information in the Federal Government regarding standards issued by NIST pursuant to the Federal Property and Administrative Services Act of 1949 as amended, Public Law 89-306 (79 Stat. 1127), and as implemented by Executive Order 11717 (38 FR 12315, dated May 11, 1973) and Part 6 of Title 15 CFR (Code of Federal Regulations).

NIST Interagency or Internal Reports (NISTIR)—The series includes interim or final reports on work performed by NIST for outside sponsors (both government and nongovernment). In general, initial distribution is handled by the sponsor; public distribution is handled by sales through the National Technical Information Service, Springfield, VA22161, in hard copy, electronic media, or microfiche form. NISTIR's may also report results of NIST projects of transitory or limited interest, including those that will be published subsequently in more comprehensive form.

www.ingramcontent.com/pod-product-compliance
Lightning Source LLC
Chambersburg PA
CBHW081720170526
45167CB00009B/3642